PELICAN BOOKS

LANGUAGE AND SOCIAL CONTEXT

Pier Paolo Giglioli is Reader in Sociology at the
University of Milan.

Language and Social Context

Selected Readings

Edited by Pier Paolo Giglioli

Penguin Books

Penguin Books Ltd, Harmondsworth, Middlesex, England
Viking Penguin Inc., 40 West 23rd Street, New York, New York 10010, U.S.A.
Penguin Books Australia Ltd, Ringwood, Victoria, Australia
Penguin Books Canada Limited, 2801 John Street, Markham, Ontario, Canada L3R 1B4
Penguin Books (N.Z.) Ltd, 182–190 Wairau Road, Auckland 10, New Zealand

First published 1972
Reprinted 1973, 1975, 1976, 1977, 1979, 1980
Reprinted with revised 'Further Reading' Section 1982
Reprinted 1983, 1985, 1986

This selection copyright © Pier Paolo Giglioli, 1972
Introduction and notes copyright © Pier Paolo Giglioli, 1972
All rights reserved

Set, printed and bound in Great Britain by
Cox & Wyman Ltd, Reading
Set in Monotype Times

Contents

Introduction

Since the beginning of this century, sociology and linguistics have grown in mutual isolation: the sociology of language has long been a rather underdeveloped area of sociology; similarly, linguistics has generally chosen to disregard the analysis of the social aspects of language. This reciprocal indifference has probably depended upon two somewhat paradoxical reasons. The first consists in the very early sociological recognition of the essential role of language in society. Just because they viewed language as a necessary prerequisite of every human group, sociologists thought that it was of no consequence in differentiating social behaviour and therefore neglected its study. The second reason is implicit in Saussure's seminal distinction between *langue* and *parole*[1] (rephrased, from time to time, as the distinction between language and speech, code and message, competence and performance). While this distinction seemed at first to draw linguistics and sociology together, actually, unwittingly or not, it produced the contrary result. For, if *langue* is defined as a set of grammatical rules existing in the mind of everyone, it becomes unnecessary to bother with the study of actual speech in social interaction. It appears much more fruitful to analyse the homogeneous, abstract and invariant rules of *langue* on the basis of the linguistic intuitions of a few informants, or, for that matter, of the linguist himself.

In the last few years, however, the gulf between the two disciplines has begun to narrow. Some linguists have become concerned with socially conditioned linguistic phenomena, and some social scientists have become more aware of the social nature of

1. 'Langue' (language) and 'parole' (speech). The notion of *langue* refers to a totality of grammatical rules shared by all the members of a linguistic community, whereas *parole* refers to actual utterances of individual speakers. Speaking does, of course, follow rules of grammar, but also reflects the personal choices of language users; the grammatical system, on the other hand, is the social part of language and 'has potential existence in each mind, or, more specifically, in the minds of a group of individuals' (see Saussure (1916) posthumously composed from lecture notes).

language. The term sociolinguistics refers to this mutual convergence. Its most significant feature is its stress on *parole*, on the speech act in all its social dimensions. In contrast to Saussure's views, sociolinguistics has shown that speech is not the haphazard result of mere individual choices, the manifestation of a person's psychological states, but that it is remarkably patterned. And, while attempts to establish direct relationships between grammatical rules and social structures have generally failed, systematic variations of speech behaviour have been shown to reflect the underlying constraints of a system of social relations. This is often evident at first view: no one uses the same speech style at home and at public ceremonies, in talking to a boyhood friend or to a high religious dignitary. However, to find an order in subtle phonological variations in the same speech community or in bilingual shifting from one language to another in the context of the same conversation is much more difficult; in these cases, regular patterns of concomitant variations at the social and linguistic levels are brought to light only through a painstaking analysis of speech and of the social situation in which speech unfolds.

The recent interest in the social patterning of language use is not limited to sociology and linguistics only, but is shared by several other disciplines – anthropology, political science, philosophy and even psychiatry. This interdisciplinary approach makes the substantive boundaries of sociolinguistics somewhat imprecise. However, from an analytical point of view it is possible to discern two quite distinct research directions.

The first may be considered as a part of general linguistics. It consists in the study of the influence of social factors (e.g., the social stratification of the speech community) on language structures and historical evolution. The label 'sociolinguistics', as opposed to 'linguistics', is useful to characterize these studies because they are at variance with currently leading linguistic theory. The latter, following Saussure's suggestions, postulates the existence of completely homogeneous speech communities each using a uniform linguistic code, primarily for referential functions. On the basis of this assumption, the aim of theoretical linguistics is the elaboration of context-free linguistic rules accounting for that part of linguistic behaviour which is uniform and homogeneous. Therefore language variations are considered as theoretically insignificant deviations from the norm. Recently, this approach has been vigorously challenged by some dialectologically and anthropologically trained linguists (e.g. Labov, 1970; Hymes, 1964). Though not denying the heuristic value of Saussure's distinction, they claim that in order to solve some essential theoretical problems – most notably, but not only, those of linguistic change – one must go back to the analysis of actual speech in concrete social groups and reintegrate the social context of the speech act in linguistic descriptions. An increasing number of scholars are now working in this area and making important contributions to linguistic theory. This volume, however, will not deal, except in passing (see Labov's and Gumperz' papers in Part Four), with the strictly linguistic aspect of sociolinguistics.

The second research direction is illustrated by the works of those social scientists who have pointed out the importance of linguistic data for a better understanding and explanation of certain social phenomena. The frame of reference of these studies is quite different from the linguistic one outlined above. What they are trying to elucidate are not linguistic, but, broadly speaking, sociological problems; their conceptual apparatus and research methods are the traditional ones of the social sciences; their results are codified in terms of sociological theories.

The analysis of the social role of language has been primarily carried out by anthropology and sociology; their contributions, however, have been unequal. In part for exigencies of field work, but also because language is such an integral part of culture, anthropologists have long been interested in the linguistic behaviour of the populations they study. Major anthropologists like Boas, Kroeber and Sapir have frequently engaged in linguistic analyses; indeed, in the case of Sapir, his linguistic production has been so outstanding that he is rightly viewed as a central figure in American linguistics. Yet, unlike linguists, anthropologists have never considered language in isolation from social life but have insisted on its interdependence with cultural and social structures. In this sense, their technical linguistic analyses are means to an end, data from which it is possible to make inferences about larger anthropological issues. Hence, under the somewhat vague label 'language and culture', anthropologists study topics such as the relations between world views, grammatical categories and semantic fields, the influence of speech on socialization and personal relationships, and the interaction of linguistic and social communities. Such a stress on the psychological, cultural and social aspects of language has led linguistic anthropology to point out two important phenomena: the different functional role of language in different communities and the use of multiple linguistic codes within the same community. As Hymes has aptly remarked, 'language is not everywhere equivalent in communicative role and social value; speaking may carry different functional loads in the communicative economy of different societies'; and, 'no normal person, and no normal community is limited in repertoire to a single variety of code, to an unchanging monotony which would preclude the possibility of indicating respect, insolence, mock-seriousness, humor, role-distance, etc. by switching from one code variety to another' (Hymes, 1967, pp. 9–10). Consequently, the relation between languages and social groups cannot be taken for granted, but is a problem which must be ethnographically investigated.

Like other anthropological areas, linguistic anthropology has of late been influenced by a number of studies which, under the names of 'ethno-semantics' and 'cognitive anthropology', have strongly insisted on the importance of formalized ethnographic descriptions, conceived of as adequate and replicable accounts of concrete social events within specific cultures. When this methodological approach is applied to speech, it directs attention to what has been called the 'ethnography of speaking', that is, the comparative analysis of speech events, of their elements and of the functions fulfilled by speech in particular settings. This area of research, which is treated in Hymes' paper in Part One, has become an important part of modern sociolinguistics.

In comparison with the long and flourishing tradition of linguistic anthropology, sociological contributions to sociolinguistics are fewer and more recent. The early insights of Mead and of the Durkheimenian school about the nature of language have been developed by other disciplines, namely social psychology and anthropology; and the current concern of many sociologists with sociolinguistics does not go beyond a vague acquaintance with the Whorfian hypothesis. I have already mentioned the main reason for this, that sociologists have considered language as an omnipresent and invariant feature of every society, thereby failing to see its causal influence on social action. However, this sociological neglect of language seems finally to have come to an end. In the first place, the extension of comparative research to bi- and pluri-lingual societies has exposed sociologists to the social determinants and, in particular, the social consequences of language varieties. Once they have become aware of these phenomena, it is easier for them to realize that even in predominantly monoglot Western societies there exist regional, social class and stylistic variations of language behaviour which have important, and sometimes dramatic, social effects. A clear example is the widespread scholastic failure of lower class children, in which linguistic causes play a major role (see Part Three of this volume). At a more analytical level, the causal influence of language behaviour has been revealed by the first sociolinguistic inquiries into theoretical problems such as group formation, the relationship between social and cultural systems and small group interaction. Finally, from a very general point of view, the renewed sociological interest in language is linked to several theoretical approaches – phenomenology, hermeneutics, symbolic interactionism – which, despite their differences, all stress the crucial role of symbolism in social life.[2]

As of now the sociological study of language seems to proceed along two lines. On the one hand, it is centred both synchronically and diachronically on the question 'Who speaks what language to whom and on what occasion?' The substantive themes explored by scholars working within this framework are those of linguistic minorities, of bilingualism, of language conflicts, and of language planning and standardization. On the other hand, sociology is concerned not so much with language as a substantive sub-field, but with the theoretical contributions that the analysis of speech can offer to other sociological areas, for example face-to-face interaction, socialization, sociology of knowledge and social change.

In characterizing the linguistic and the socio-anthropological approaches to sociolinguistics, I have perhaps over-stressed their

2. For a recent reader on these new theoretical directions see Dreitzel (1970).

analytical differences. As a correction to this, it should be kept in mind that linguists, sociologists and anthropologists have worked up to now in close collaboration. For, in order to identify language and speech variations, social scientists often need the help of the linguist; similarly, linguists need the sociologist to conceptualize those social factors which influence linguistic phenomena. As a result of this interaction descriptive categories necessary for handling sociolinguistic data have been elaborated and are now increasingly used by all those working in the field, independently from their disciplinary origins. Moreover, there are some areas (e.g., the analysis of conversations and of communicative competence) which not only utilize contributions from linguistics, anthropology and sociology, but try to unify and integrate them in an attempt at theory building.

The selection of Readings offered in this book is not meant to cover all the current directions in sociolinguistic work. My first guiding consideration has been to design a volume for a sociological audience. Therefore I have excluded purely linguistic works as well as those which treat topics usually well covered in readers in anthropological linguistics (for example, language and cognition). At the same time, I have not bothered about the disciplinary affiliations of the authors as long as they treat themes of sociological interest. Thus I have included papers by anthropologists, sociologists, linguists, political scientists and philosophers.

Part One deals with general approaches to the field and provides a necessary frame of reference for the following papers. The rest of the book is concerned with three sociological areas which can, I think, be fruitfully studied from a sociolinguistic point of view: the analysis of face-to-face interaction, the relationship between social and cultural structures, and the study of social change and social conflict.

Under the title Speech and Situated Action, Part Two is especially concerned with the analysis of conversations and tries to bring together philosophic, ethnographic and ethnomethodological works. In the last few years, conversational analysis has been deeply influenced by ethnomethodology, and it may be useful to spell out the latter's implications for sociolinguistics.

Ethnomethodologists suggest that, in contrast to Durkheim's dictum (or to certain positivistic interpretations of it), social reality is not a 'fact', but an ongoing accomplishment, the often precarious result of the routine activities and tacit understandings of social actors. In this perspective speech acquires a particular importance. It is essentially through speech that men communicate with their fellow men; yet speech becomes understandable only in connection with social interaction. This embeddedness of speech in interactive processes makes social meaning 'reflexive' or 'indexical'. In other words, in natural conversations sentences are almost always incomplete or ambiguous. Language provides a variety of different labels to refer to an object or an action; moreover, the social meaning of a term shifts with the situation. Nonetheless, the identification of the 'right' term in a semantic field of 'correct' ones, or the expansion of incomplete or polysemic utterances is, as Schegloff's paper shows, rarely problematic for the conversationalists, for they can rely on their common stock of knowledge. The object of ethnomethodology consists in the analysis of the structure of such knowledge, in the study of the 'ethno-methods', the interpretative procedures by which social actors make sense of speech and orient themselves in the social world. This approach merges in several respects with the ethnography of communicative events and with the philosophical analysis of speech acts: the former provides the comparative material necessary for building a theory of 'interactional universals' for the analysis of conversations; the second offers the conceptual precision and clarification which are needed at the beginning of empirical work on conversational data.

Part Three deals with a theoretical issue which lies at the heart of sociological and anthropological thought: the problem of the relationship between symbolic and social structures. While classic sociological theory maintains the primacy of society as a causal force shaping not only the value system of a society, but also its conceptual tools (Durkheim and Mauss, 1903), some linguistically oriented anthropologists have tended to attenuate and sometimes to reverse this hypothesis. Indeed, in its strong formulation, the thesis of linguistic relativity advanced by Whorf asserts that it is the structure of language which determines ways of thought and cultural patterns, thereby influencing social structures as well.

Modern sociolinguists, especially Basil Bernstein, have tried to synthesize the two opposite hypotheses, providing a fresh approach to this problem. Here, again, the distinction between language and speech is vital. The type of social relations does not directly influence linguistic codes, but exerts certain constraints on speech; in its turn, the type of speech used reinforces the selective perception of the speaker, shaping his apprehension of social reality. Thus, in the process of socialization, the child learns, together with sociolinguistic uses and overt or implicit attitudes toward language, the requirements of a certain social structure.

The papers included in Part Four continue to explore the ways in which society determines regular patterns of choice from the options offered by verbal repertoires. In contrast to the micro-sociological approach of Part Two, here society refers to larger social structures. The sociolinguistic options range from minute phonological features to linguistic codes in the case of diglossia. Part Four is more linguistically oriented than the others, but can easily be grasped by sociologists without special linguistic training.

Part Five is centred on the relation between language, social change and social conflict. It provides two approaches to the problem of change and conflict, one based on a broad evolutionary perspective that is becoming fashionable again in some quarters of sociology, the other focused on the more convulsive changes which have taken and continue to take place in con-comitance with the process of nation building. The first approach is illustrated with reference to literacy. While discussions on the origin of speech are inevitably speculative, literacy is an historical fact and a search for its pre-conditions, correlates and implications might well shed a new and richer light on the classic typological dichotomies of *Gemeinschaft* and *Gesellschaft*, of mechanical and organic solidarity. The second approach deals with the linguistic problems of modernizing countries as well as with the persistent struggles along linguistic lines in well established Western nations. The point at issue concerns the factors which transform language differences into political and social conflicts.

Although the papers in this volume are arranged in terms of

substantive issues, there are certain conceptual themes which cross-cut this arrangement and may help the reader to peruse the book in a more analytical way.

One of these themes is that of linguistic repertoire, elaborated by John Gumperz in contrast to the concept of linguistic code. As noted above, sociolinguists do not find the notion of a homogeneous code too useful for their purposes. If one deals with actual speech instead of with *langue*, one is obliged to recognize the existence of a plurality of codes or code varieties in the same linguistic community. The concept of linguistic repertoire tries to cope with this phenomenon by referring to 'the totality of linguistic forms regularly employed in the course of socially significant interaction', to 'all the accepted ways of formulating messages' (Gumperz, 1964, pp. 137–8). The notion of repertoire is developed in Gumperz' article on the speech community and, to a lesser extent, in Fishman's paper, but it is implicit in many of the others which point out the range of linguistic varieties among which the speaker selects his utterances in a rule-governed way (see Ferguson's paper on diglossia, Bernstein's notion of elaborated and restricted codes, Brown and Gilman's study of pronominal choices, and Schegloff's paper on the formulation of locations).

Another important theme is that of communicative competence, a concept formulated as an extension of Chomsky's notion of linguistic competence. By competence Chomsky means the speaker-hearer's implicit knowledge of his language, contrasting it with performance, the actual use of language in concrete situations. Hence competence does not deal with speech but with the ability of the speaker to produce, out of a finite set of rules, an infinite number of grammatical sentences. However, it has been suggested that a person endowed with mere linguistic competence would be a sort of cultural monster. He would know the grammatical rules of his language, but he would not know when to speak, when to be silent, which sociolinguistic options to select from a repertoire on what occasion, and so on. In an effort to deal with these problems, Hymes has elaborated the concept of communicative competence which refers to the psychological, cultural and social rules which discipline the use of speech in social settings (Hymes, forthcoming). The notion of communicative competence runs through several of the present papers, most notably Bernstein's analysis of speech socialization, Frake's study of conversational strategies among the Subanun, and Basso's ethnographic account of silence in Western Apache culture.

The concept of communicative competence implies that of sociolinguistic rules. Although all the papers in this volume (with the exception of the two in Part Five) explore rules of sociolinguistic selection, the formulation of these rules is not yet wholly satisfactory. Only Labov's paper and some recent work on pronominal choices, not reprinted here, have achieved a degree of formalization and rigour comparable to that which is usual in linguistic theory. No doubt this depends on the fact that sociolinguistic rules are far more difficult to formulate than linguistic ones, since they must take into account the complexity of social situations, but it is probably due also to a certain misunderstanding of the nature of sociolinguistic rules. The distinction in Searle's paper between constitutive and regulative rules and that in Labov's paper between variant and invariable rules are important attempts at clarification in this area.

A last conceptual theme common to many papers is that of 'social meaning'. Selection among referentially equivalent linguistic forms (be they two languages, two varieties within a language, or lexical choices within a variety) carries primarily, if not exclusively, social information. Sociolinguistic choices may inform the hearer about the speaker's social and regional origin as well as about the nature of the social situation at hand, about shifts in the topic of the conversation and so forth. However, social meaning transmitted through style switching or other sociolinguistic devices is effective only when the participants share common cultural norms and common background knowledge about the particular situation in which they are engaged. The recognition of this fact has brought some scholars to maintain that meaning is always embedded in social interaction. While there is some truth in this view, as we have seen in regard to conversations, it seems more productive to consider the indexicality of meaning as a matter of degree ranging from meanings totally free from a given context to meanings which are completely context bound. The question of different orders of meaning is taken up in Bernstein's discussion of restricted and elaborated codes and in Goody and Watt's typological contrast between literate and pre-literate societies.

All the papers in this volume are fairly recent and reflect, I hope, the development of the field in the past decade. This concentration on recent material has entailed the exclusion of the 'founding fathers' of sociolinguistics: Durkheim, Mead, Meillet, Sapir, etc. While I would have liked to have had space enough to include all of them, I think that my choice is justified by the strong continuity between the concerns of these early authors and those of the writers selected for this volume. If, after reading these modern contributions, the student would like to go back to the insights of the 'classics', he will find some bibliographic indications at the end of the book.

Bologna November 1970

References

DREITZEL, H. P. (ed.) (1970), *Recent Sociology No 2: Patterns of Communicative Behaviour*, Macmillan.

DURKHEIM, E. and MAUSS, M.(1903), 'De quelques formes primitives de classification', Année Sociologique, vol. 7.

GUMPERZ, J. (1964), 'Linguistic and social interaction in two communities', *Amer. Anthrop.*, vol. 66, no. 6, part 2.

HYMES, D. (1964), 'Directions in (ethno) linguistic theory', *Amer. Anthrop.*, vol. 66. no. 3, part 2, pp, 6–56.

HYMES, D. (1967), 'Models of the interaction of language and social setting', *J. soc. Issues*, vol. 23, no. 2.

HYMES, D. (forthcoming), *On Communicative Competence*, University of Pennsylvania Press.

LABOV, W. (1970), 'The study of language in its social context', *Studium Generale*, vol. 23, fasc. 1, p. 23. This article is partially reprinted in Part Four of this volume.

SAUSSURE, F. de (1916), *Course in General Linguistics*, translated by W. Baskin (1966), McGraw-Hill.

Part One Approaches to Sociolinguistics

An integrated body of substantive sociolinguistic theory does not yet exist. Theoretical approaches are still engaged in the work of conceptual clarification, that is, in the identification of certain crucial variables more than in the specification of the values that such variables take under given conditions. The two selections of Part One illustrate the anthropological and sociological approaches to sociolinguistics. Hymes' paper outlines some of the major characteristics of the anthropological approach and provides a preliminary framework for the analysis of a basic unit of sociolinguistics – the communicative event. Fishman describes the domain of the sociology of language, identifying three different subfields: (1) descriptive sociology of language, addressed to the study of the general patterns of language use in a speech community; (2) dynamic sociology of language, concerned with the patterns and causes of change in the organization of language use; and (3) applied sociology of language, interested in a wide number of topics which range from language teaching to political and social modernization.

1 D. Hymes

Toward Ethnographies of Communication:
The Analysis of Communicative Events[1]

Excerpts from D. Hymes, 'Introduction: toward ethnographies of
communication', *American Anthropologist*, vol. 66, 1964, no. 6, part 2,
pp. 12–25.

The present papers[2] report concepts, methods, and kinds of
studies now at hand. They cannot attempt a systematic exposition
of the ethnography of communication, or of the theory it may
help build. Too little systematic work has been done for such an
exposition to be possible. Some over-all sketch is needed, however, as an indication of relations among various lines of work
that does not otherwise emerge, and of some of the specific content a systematic theory would comprise. In the sketch that

1. To Susan Ervin-Tripp, John Gumperz, Michael Halliday, Sydney
Lamb, Sheldon Sacks, and Dan Slobin, I am indebted for warm discussions
of language and its social study; to Bob Scholte and Erving Goffman, for
pointed argument as to the notion of communication; to Harold Conklin,
Charles Frake, Ward Goodenough, Floyd Lounsbury, and William C.
Sturtevant, for discussion through several years of the nature of ethnography.
To all much thanks and no blame.

2. This article was originally written as an introduction to a special issue
of the *American Anthropologist* (vol. 66, 1964, no. 6, part 2) dedicated to the
ethnography of communication and edited by J. Gumperz and D. Hymes.
The papers to which Hymes refers are the following: E. M. Albert, '"Rhetoric", "logic", and "poetics" in Burundi: culture patterning of speech behavior'; B. Bernstein, 'Elaborated and restricted codes: their social origins
and some consequences'; E. O. Arewa and A. Dundes, 'Proverbs and the
ethnography of speaking folklore'; S. Ervin-Tripp, 'An analysis of the
interaction of language, topic and listener'; C. A. Ferguson, 'Baby talk in
six languages'; J. L. Fischer, 'Words for self and others in some Japanese
families'; C. O. Frake, 'How to ask for a drink in Subanun' (reprinted in
this volume, pp. 87–94); E. Goffman, 'The neglected situation' (reprinted in
this volume, pp. 61–66); J. J. Gumperz, 'Linguistic and social interaction
in two communities'; E. T. Hall, 'Adumbration as a feature of intercultural
communication'; W. Labov, 'Phonological correlates of social stratification'; Y. Malkiel, 'Some diachronic implications of fluid speech communities' [*Ed.*]

follows I emphasize the needs and content of an ethnographic approach, and relations among anthropological interests. There are four aspects to be sketched, concerned, respectively, with (1) the components of communicative events, (2) the relations among components, (3) the capacity and state of components, and (4) the activity of the system so constituted. It is with respect to the third and fourth aspects that two topics prominently associated with the topic of communication, communication theory (in the sense of information theory), and cybernetics, find a place.

The components of communicative events

The starting point is the ethnographic analysis of the communicative habits of a community in their totality, determining what count as communicative events, and as their components, and conceiving no communicative behavior as independent of the set framed by some setting or implicit question. The communicative event thus is central. (In terms of language proper, the statement means that the linguistic code is displaced by the speech act as focus of attention.)

Some frame of reference is needed for consideration of the several kinds of components co-present in a communicative event. The logic or other superiority of one classification over another is not at issue. What is at issue is the provision of a useful guide in terms of which relevant features can be discerned – a provisional phonetics, as it were, not an *a priori* phonemics, of the communicative event.

For what has to be inventoried and related in an ethnographic account, a somewhat elaborated version of factors identified in communications theory, and adapted to linguistics by Roman Jakobson (1953; 1960), can serve. Briefly put, (1,2) the various kinds of participants in communicative events – senders and receivers, addressors and addressees, interpreters and spokesmen, and the like; (3) the various available channels, and their modes of use, speaking, writing, printing, drumming, blowing, whistling, singing, face and body motion as visually perceived, smelling, tasting and tactile sensation; (4) the various codes shared by various participants, linguistic, paralinguistic, kinesic, musical and other; (5) the settings (including other communication) in which communication is permitted, enjoined, encouraged, abridged; (6) the forms of messages, and their genres, ranging verbally from single-morpheme sentences to the patterns and diacritics of sonnets, sermons, salesmen's pitches and any other organized routines and styles; (7) the topics and comments that a message may be about; (8) the events themselves, their kinds and characters as wholes – all these must be identified in an adequate ethnographic way.

Ethnography here is conceived in reference to the various efforts of Conklin, Frake, Goodenough, Metzger, Romney, and others to advance the techniques of ethnographic work and to conceptualize its goal, such that the structural analysis of cultural behavior generally is viewed as the development of theories adequate to concrete cases, just as the structural analysis of behavior as manifestation of a linguistic code is viewed. One way to phrase the underlying outlook is as a question of validity. Just as analysis of phonological capabilities must determine what set of phonological features is to be taken as relevant to identification and distinction of phonological sound on the part of the possessors of the capabilities in question, so analysis of cultural capabilities generally must determine what sets of features are to be taken as relevant to identification and contrast of cultural behavior on the part of the participants in same. (Sapir's 'Sound patterns in language' (1925), seen as implying a general statement about the cultural aspect of behavior, remains classic and crucial to the development of anthropological thought in this regard, although it has taken a generation for its ethnographic import to become salient.) Another way to phrase the underlying outlook is as a question of the common element in the situation of ethnographer and person-in-the-culture. Each must formulate from finite experience theories adequate to predict and judge as appropriate or inappropriate what is in principle an infinite amount of cultural behavior. (Judgments of grammaticality are a special case.)

Mere observation, however, systematic and repeated, can obviously never suffice to meet such high standards of objectivity and validity. As Sapir once observed regarding a rule of avoidance among the Wishram Chinook:

Incidentally there is a lesson here for the theoretical ethnologist. If the avoidance of man and woman here were known only objectively it would present a situation resembling that, say, in Melanesia. One might suppose then the explanation to be that women were set apart from the man's social fabric because of the low esteem in which they were held, or that men avoided them because of their periodic impure state. Either guess would be a shot far wide of the mark. The moral is that it is as necessary to discover what the native sentiment is as well as to record the behavior.[3]

The point is essentially the same as that of 'Sound patterns of language', from which stems the current distinction of 'etic' and 'emic'. An 'emic' account is one in terms of features relevant in the behavior in question; an etic account, however useful as a preliminary grid and input to an emic (structural) account, and as a framework for comparing different emic accounts, lacks the emic account's validity. The point is an old one in anthropology, only made more trenchant by the clarity with which the point can be made in terms of the contrast between phonetics and phonemics. (See Pike, 1954 for coinage of the terms, and conscious development of the perspective from a linguistic basis beyond linguistics, under inspiration from Sapir.) Ethnographic objectivity is intersubjective objectivity, but in the first instance, the intersubjective objectivity in question is that of the participants in the culture. No amount of acoustic apparatus and sound spectography can crack the phonemic code of a language, and a phonemic analysis, based on the intersubjective objectivity in the behavior of those who share the code, is the necessary basis for other studies, experimental and otherwise (cf. Hockett 1955, pp. 210–11; Lisker, Cooper and Liberman, 1962). The same is true for the shared codes which constitute the mutual intelligibility of the rest of cultural behavior. The advantages of such an approach in providing a criterion against which to appraise participants' own explanations and conceptualizations of their behavior, their 'home-made models', should be obvious, as should the advantages in providing a basis for controlled comparison, study of diffusion, and any other generalizing or analysing approach that depends in the last analysis on the adequacy and precision of

3. Spier and Sapir (1930, p. 217, n. 97). The point and the language indicate that the comment is due particularly to Sapir. The Wishram avoidance is due to the severe punishment, even death, visited for constructive adultery, which offense may be attributed in some circumstances even for private conversation or physical contact.

ethnographic records of cultural behavior. (Ethnographic records, of course, may be of other things: censuses, for example.)

In a discussion of genealogical method, Conklin (1964, pp. 25–6), observing that all kinship data derive from ethnographic contexts, makes explicit his assumptions regarding the nature and purpose of ethnography (citing also Goodenough, 1956, and noting Frake, 1962b, 1964, and a previous article of his own (1962)). The statement applies to communicative data as well as to kinship data, and can be adopted here:

An adequate ethnography is here considered to include the culturally significant arrangement of productive statements about the relevant relationships obtaining among locally defined categories and contexts (of objects and events) within a given social matrix. These nonarbitrarily ordered statements should comprise, essentially, a cultural grammar (Goodenough, 1957a; Frake, 1962a). In such an ethnography, the emphasis is placed on the interpretation, evaluation, and selection of alternative statements about a particular set of cultural activities within a given range of social contexts. This in turn leads to the critical examination of intracultural relations and ethnotheoretical models (Conklin, 1955; Goodenough, ms.). Demonstrable intracultural validity for statements of covert and abstracted relationships should be based on prior analysis of particular and generalized occurrences in the ethnographic record (Lounsbury, 1955, pp. 163–4; 1956; cf. Morris, 1946). Criteria for evaluating the adequacy of ethnographic statements with reference to the cultural phenomena described, include: (1) productivity (in terms of appropriate anticipation if not actual prediction); (2) replicability or testability; and (3) economy. In actual field situations, recording activities, analytic operations, and evaluative procedures (in short, the application of ethnographic technique, method, and theory) can, and I think should, be combined. The improvement and constant adjustment of field recording is, in fact, dependent upon simultaneous analysis and evaluation.

Notice that strict conception of ethnography constrains the conception of communication that is admissable. Just as what counts as phonemic feature or religious act cannot be identified in advance, so with what counts as a communicative event. There are, of course, general criteria for phonemic and for communicative status; it is a question of the phenomena by which they are satisfied in a given case. If one examines the writings of anthropologists and linguists, one finds that general conceptions of communicative status vary, sometimes in ways at variance with the conception of ethnography adopted here.

The concept of message would seem to suffice as starting point for any conception, if one grants two kinds of things. The first is that the concept of message implies the sharing (real or imputed) of (1) a code or codes in terms of which the message is intelligible to (2) participants, minimally an addressor and addressee (who may be the same person), in (3) an event constituted by its transmission and characterized by (4) a channel or channels, (5) a setting or context, (6) a definite form or shape to the message, and (7) a topic and comment, i.e., that it says something about something – in other words, that the concept of message implies the array of components previously given. The second is that what can count as instances of messages, and as instances of the components of the event constituted by the transmission of a message, must be determined in the given case along the lines of the ethnographic approach just discussed and just characterized by Conklin.

If one accepts the latter point, then some anthropological conceptions of communication must be judged to exclude too much, or to include too much, or, occasionally, both. To take first the problem of excluding too much, one cannot *a priori* define the sound of approaching footsteps (Sapir, 1921, p. 3) or the setting of the sun (Hockett, 1958, p. 574) as not communicative. Their status is entirely a question of their construal by a receiver. In general, no phenomenon can be defined in advance as never to be counted as constituting a message. Consider a case related by Hallowell (1964, p. 64):

An informant told me that many years before he was sitting in a tent one afternoon during a storm, together with an old man and his wife. There was one clap of thunder after another. Suddenly the old man turned to his wife and asked, 'Did you hear what was said?' 'No,' she replied, 'I didn't catch it.' My informant, an acculturated Indian, told me he did not at first know what the old man and his wife referred to. It was, of course, the thunder. The old man thought that one of the Thunder Birds had said something to him. He was reacting to this sound in the same way as he would respond to a human being, whose words he did not understand. The casualness of the remark and even the trivial character of the anecdote demonstrate the psychological depth of the 'social relations' with other-than-human beings that becomes explicit in the behavior of the Ojibwa as a consequence of the cognitive 'set' induced by their culture.

There are manifold instances from cultures around the world, e.g., to take a recent report, the drinking, questioning and answering in which Amahuaca men are joined by the class of supernaturals known as *yoshi* associated interestingly enough with a specific form of chant and use of the vocal channel (vocal chords tightly constricted) (Carneiro, 1964, p. 8). Hallowell's account of the Ojibwa concept of person shows with particular depth the implications of cultural values and world view for occurrences of communicative behavior. As indication of the contribution a conscious ethnography of communication, focused on occurrences of activity such as speech, might make to such anthropological concerns as world view, let me cite one other Ojibwa instance and Hallowell's interpolated regret: having discussed the fact that stones are classified grammatically as animate in gender, and are conceived as potentially capable of animate behavior, especially in ceremonially-linked circumstances, Hallowell records (1964, p. 56):

A white trader, digging in his potato patch, unearthed a large stone similar to the one just referred to. He sent for John Duck, an Indian who was the leader of the *wábano*, a contemporary ceremony that is held in a structure something like that used for the Midewiwin (a major ceremony during which stones occasionally had animate properties such as movement and opening of a mouth). The trader called his attention to the stone, saying that it must belong to his pavilion. John Duck did not seem pleased at this. He bent down and spoke to the boulder in a low voice, inquiring whether it had ever been in his pavilion. According to John the stone replied in the negative.

It is obvious that John Duck spontaneously structured the situation in terms that are intelligible within the context of Ojibwa language and culture.... I regret that my field notes contain no information about the use of direct verbal address in the other cases mentioned (movement of stone, opening of a mouth). But it may well have taken place. In the anecdote describing John Duck's behavior, however, his use of speech as a mode of communication raises the animate status of the boulder to the level of social interaction common to human beings. Simply as a matter of observation we can say that the stone was treated *as if* it were a 'person', not a 'thing', without inferring that objects of this class are, for the Ojibwa, necessarily conceptualized as persons.

D. Hymes 27

The question of the boundaries of the speech community, and indeed, of how many speech communities within a community there are, becomes problematic from a strict ethnographic viewpoint. Ordinarily the question of the speech community of the Wishram Chinook would be discussed as a question as to whether or not the objective linguistic differences (few) between the Wishram village and that of the Wasco across the river, and perhaps those of others down the river, sufficed to constitute separate dialects, or only one. On the basis of Wishram culture, however, an ethnographic approach must recognize three speech communities within the Wishram village itself. One such community consisted of normal adults and children past babyhood; a second comprised babies, dogs, coyotes, and guardian spirits Dog and Coyote, and, possibly, old people possessing those guardian spirits; a third comprised those whose guardian spirit experience had granted them the power of being able to interpret the language of the spirits.[4]

If the strict ethnographic approach requires us to extend the concept of communication to the boundaries granted it by participants of a culture, it also makes it necessary to restrict it to those boundaries. To define communication as the triggering of a response (as Hockett (1958, p. 573) has done, and Kluckhohn (1961, p. 895) has accepted), is to make the term so nearly equivalent to behavior and interaction in general as to lose its specific value as a scientific and moral conception. There are many illustrations possible of actions that trigger response and are not taken as communicative by one or both participants. As an act clearly based on the triggering of response (in another or

4. With regard to the first and second communities, babyhood lasted 'until they could talk clearly' (Spier and Sapir 1930, p. 218) – in Wishram, of course. With regard to the second, 'Such guardian spirits could understand the language of babies. They maintain that a dog, a coyote, and an infant can understand each other, but the baby loses his language when he grows old enough to speak and understand the tongue of his parents' (p. 255). With regard to the third, the group may have been individuated into various dyadic relationships between particular persons and spirits, for the example is given as 'For instance, one who had gained the protection of Coyote could tell, on hearing a coyote's howl, what person was going to die' (p. 239). The matter would depend on information, probably now unobtainable, as to whether the language of the spirits was common to all of them.

oneself), sexual intercourse would be an ideal event to test this point; what part, less than all, of triggering of response is sent or received as communication? Again, it is desirable to treat the transmission or receipt of information as not the same as, but a more general category than, communication, the latter being treated as a more specific sphere, necessarily either participated in or constituted by persons (cf. Cherry, 1961, p. 247, note). The sound of footsteps or the setting of the sun may be taken as a source of information without being taken as a message (although in either case a receiver may interpret the event as a message).

From this standpoint, genes may transmit information, but the process is communicative only from the standpoint of, and as reported by, an observer and interpreter. For the human observer to report and treat the process experienced or inferred as a communicative one is of course a right not to be challenged, for, formally, it is the same right that the ethnographer accepts when acted upon by an Ojibwa, Wishram, or other participant in a culture. The formal feature is that the evidence for the communicative event is a report by one who did not participate in it as either addressor or addressee. Such reported events (E^n, or narrated events, in Roman Jakobson's symbolization (1957) for the constituents of speech events) are common in myth, for example, and are of course of considerable importance, as when the origin of the world is so described by the ancient Hebrews, or the origin of death explained by the Wishram in a narrative culminating (as is typical for their myths) in an announcement ordaining how that aspect of cultural life is to be and what people will say in its regard.

We deal here, in short, with the fact that the communicative event is the metaphor, or perspective, basic to rendering experience intelligible. It is likely to be employed at any turn, if with varying modes of imputation of reality (believed, supposed, entertained in jest, etc.). It is this fact that underlies the apparently central role of language in cultural life. Of codes available to human beings, language, as the one more than any other capable at once of being explicitly detailed and transcendent of single contexts, is the chief beneficiary under many circumstances of the primary centrality of communication. Under some circumstances, of course, it is not.

D. Hymes 29

In general, any and all of the components of a communicative event, and the occurrence of a message itself, can be imputed by one who adopts the standpoint of an addressor, addressee, or receiver as observer. One consequence is the point already made, that the ethnographic observer must do more than observe to prevent his own habits of imputation from interfering with recognition of where and what participants in another culture impute. Another consequence, since persons can impute either an addressor and intent or an addressee and attention, is to make heuristically useful for ethnographic purposes a characterization of a communicative event as one in which to the observer one at least of the participants is real. [...]

The discussion so far has been concerned with gross identification of events as such and of components individually. In point of fact, adequate determination usually will involve more than inventory of channels, setting, etc. The structures of relations among different events, and their components; the capabilities and states of the components; the activity of the system which is the event; all will be involved. Explication of genres of verbal art, once such have been identified (e.g., Ssukung Tu, 1963),[5] commonly involves appeal at least to relations among components, and often to their states and activity. Such questions comprise the other aspects of the frame of reference being sketched, and to these we now turn.

Relations among components

In one sense, the focus of the present approach is on communities organized as systems of communicative events. Such an object of study can be regarded as part of, but not identical with, an ethnography as a whole.[6] One way in which to indicate that

5. The classical writer Ssukung Tu discriminated twenty-four modes, translated as Grand Mode, Unemphatic, Ornate, Grave, Lofty, Polished, Refined, Vigorous, Exquisite, Spontaneous, Pregnant, Untrammeled, Evocative, Well-knit, Artless, Distinctive, Devious, Natural, Poignant, Vivid, Transcendent, Ethereal, Light-hearted, Flowing (Ssukung Tu, as translated (1963) with accompanying discussion by Wu Tiao-kung, 'Ssukung Tu's poetic criticism,' pp. 78–83).

6. Notice Conklin (1962, p. 199): 'An adequate ethnographic description of the culture (Goodenough, 1957a) of a particular society presupposes a detailed analysis of the communications system and of the culturally defined situations in which all relevant distinctions in that system occur.'

there is a system, either in the community or in the particular event, is to observe that there is not complete freedom of co-occurrence among components. Not all imaginably possible combinations of participants, channels, codes, topics, etc., can occur.

It is to the structure of relations among components that much of the surge of work in sociolinguistics is directed. The papers[7] by Ervin-Tripp and Gumperz are exemplary in this respect, and suggest the richness of the subject. Bernstein can be said to explore in depth the consequences of certain structures of relations, while Labov explores correlations, and patterns of change in the correlations, between speakers, hearers, settings, and features of the code, correlations and changes that can be of considerable consequence. All the papers exemplify such relations to some extent, including that by Ferguson, which is concerned primarily with a marginal part of the code component. (Notice that focus on relations among components more readily invites description and comparative analysis of the variety of such marginal systems than does focus on the code alone. Also, more generally, it leads into description and comparison of whatever may characterize such an event or relationship, e.g., talk to babies, whether or not special features characterize it from the standpoint of the code as such. It is equally important to know the characteristics of talk to babies in societies where 'baby talk' is eschewed. With regard to message-form, there is much to be discovered and described in the sequential patterning of speech as routines, specialized to certain relationships.)

Ervin-Tripp suggests that the structures of relations with respect to language will prove to be specific in some ways, to be more than illustration of more general sociological or psychological or cultural notions. The same is likely to prove true for each of the kinds of codes employed in a community. The heuristic assumption is that their separate maintenance implies some specific role for each which is not wholly duplicated by any other (including language). On the other hand, studies focused on the relations among components of communicative events are likely to discern patterns general to them, but partly independent of,

7. For the papers referred to in this paragraph see editor's note on p. 21 [*Ed*.]

and cutting across, the other departments of study into which the events might be cast ethnographically. Once looked for, areal styles, in the use of specific codes, and areal communicative styles generally, are likely to be found. Lomax (1959) has suggested such for musical performance, and Melville Jacobs has suggested such may be the case for the dramatic performances that enact myths.

It is especially important to notice that delineations of communities in these respects are crucial to understanding of the place of language in culture, and to understanding of the particular place of language in culture signalled by what is commonly called the Sapir-Whorf hypothesis. To assume that differences in language shape or interact with differences in world view is to assume that the functional role of language in relation to world view is everywhere the same. Indeed, anthropological thought quite generally has tended to assume identity or equivalence of function for language throughout the world (see discussion in Hymes, 1961; 1962).

When a particular code is considered but one component of communicative events, the studies of the structure of communicative events in a society will provide detailed evidence on the differential ways in which the code enters into communicative purposes and cultural life. The different ways and stages in which a language enters into enculturation, transmission of adult roles and skills, interaction with the supernatural, personal satisfactions, and the like will appear. Languages, like other cultural traits, will be found to vary in the degree and nature of their integration into the societies and cultures in which they occur. It will be possible to focus on the consequences of such differences for acculturation and adaptation of both languages and peoples. Such information has been brought to attention in studies of acculturation, bilingualism and standard languages. What is necessary is to realize that the functional relativity of languages is general, applying to monolingual situations too.

With particular regard to the Sapir-Whorf hypothesis, it is essential to notice that Whorf's sort of linguistic relativity is secondary, and dependent upon a primary sociolinguistic relativity, that of differential engagement of languages in social life. For example, description of a language may show that it expresses a certain cognitive style, perhaps implicit metaphysical assumptĬons, but what chance the language has to make an impress upon individuals and behavior will depend upon the degree and pattern of its admission into communicative events. The case is clear in bilingualism; we do not expect a Bengali using English as a fourth language for certain purposes of commerce to be influenced deeply in world view by its syntax. What is necessary is to realize that the monolingual situation is problematic as well. Peoples do not all everywhere use language to the same degree, in the same situations, or for the same things; some peoples focus upon language more than others. Such differences in the place of a language in the communicative system of a people cannot be assumed to be without influence on the depth of a language's influence on such things as world view.

More particularly, if a language is taken as a device for categorizing experience, it is not such a device in the abstract. There remains the question of what may be the set of events in which categorizing dependent upon the language occurs. (The set includes events in which a single person is using a language excogitatively.) Although anthropologists have sometimes talked of the use of language 'merely' as a tool of communication, and of the categorizing of experience as if it were a superior category, the role of a language as a device for categorizing experience and its role as an instrument of communication cannot be so separated, and indeed, the latter includes the former. This is the more true when a language, as is often the case, affords alternative ways of categorizing the same experience, so that the patterns of selection among such alternatives must be determined in actual contexts of use – as must also, indeed, the degree to which a language is being used as a full-fledged semantic instrument (as distinct from its use as an expressive, directive, etc., instrument) at all in a given case.

Such considerations broach the third aspect of our frame of reference.

Capacity and state of components

So far we have considered the identification of events and components, and the structures of relations among them. Now we must consider their capacities, or capabilities, and states. It is here that 'communication theory', in the sense in which the term is equivalent to 'information theory', enters, with its concern for the measurement of capacity. Although associated primarily with the capacity of channels and codes, the underlying notion extends equally to all components of a communicative event, and to the events of a system.

Questions of capability can be broached in terms of focus upon some one of the components of an event (or the event itself) in relation to all other components in turn. Some topics of long-standing anthropological interest find a place here. The relation of language to environment, both natural and social, in the sense of elaboration of a code's capacity, especially via vocabulary, to deal with snow, cattle, status, etc., as topics, is one. Another is the relationship between the capability of a code, and the capabilities of its users, in the sense of the Whorfian concern with habitual behavior and fashions of speaking. In both cases there must be reference from the start to the distribution in use of the portion of the code in question, both among communicative events and in relation to their other components. (The necessity of this has been argued for the Whorfian problem above; on cultural focus, elaboration of vocabulary, and folk-taxonomy of semantic domains, cf. the views on dependence on context of situation of Brown (1958, pp. 255–8), Frake (1961, pp. 121–2), Gluckman (1959), Meillet (1906) and Service (1960).

With regard to participants, differential competence and performance are salient concerns of Bernstein's[8] analysis of elaborated and restricted codes. Gumperz' concept of verbal repertoire also singles out a participant's capabilities in relation to the code component. Albert and Frake touch upon the subject with regard to special forms of usage. Code-switching, ability to translate, range of dialects or levels or socially advantageous routines at command, are familiar examples. John Roberts (MS) has undertaken ingenious studies of capacity with respect to communicative tasks. Often this level and the preceding one are but faces of the same coin, the formal structure of relations being grounded culturally in judgments (and facts) as to capability, and circumstances as to capability being dependent upon the structures of relations.

8. For references to Bernstein, Gumperz, Albert and Frake in this paragraph see editor's note on p. 21 [Ed.]

The ethnography of communication deals in an empirical and comparative way with many notions that underlie linguistic theory proper. This is particularly so when linguistic theory depends upon notions such as those of 'speech community', 'speech act', and 'fluent speaker'. How varied the capabilities of speakers can be in even a small and presumably homogeneous tribe is sketched incisively by Bloomfield (1927) in a paper that deserves to be classic for its showing that such variation, including possibilities of grammatical mistake, is universal. The range and kind of abilities speakers and hearers show is an area largely unexplored by ethnographers and linguists, but one of great import both to cultural and linguistic theory. (I have tried to draw some implications of a focus on the concept of speakers' abilities in another paper [Hymes, 1964].)[9]

9. The term 'capability' is used with conscious reference to Tylor's definition of culture (or civilization) as all those capabilities acquired by man in society (1873, p. 1). I subscribe to the view that what is distinctively cultural as an aspect of behavior or things is a question of capabilities acquired, or elicited, in social life, not a question of the extent to which the behavior or things themselves are socially shared. The point is like that made by Sapir (1916, p. 425) with regard to similarity due to diffusion, namely, that its difference from similarity due to independent retention of a common heritage is one of degree rather than of kind, since the currency of a culture element in a single community is already an instance of diffusion that has radiated out, at last analysis, from a single individual. Sapir's point converges with the focus of generative grammatical theory on the individual's ability to produce and interpret novel, yet acceptable, sentences. The frequency and spread of a trait is important, but secondary, so far as the criteria for its being a product of cultural behavior, as having a cultural aspect, are concerned. A sonnet, for example, is such a product, whether or not it survives the moment of completion. In the course of the conduct of much cultural behavior, including verbal behavior, it will not be known, or will be problematic to the participants, whether or not some of what occurs and is accepted as cultural, has in fact ever previously occurred. For many typical anthropological problems, it is essential to single out for study cultural behavior that is shared to the limits of a community, or as nearly so as possible. For other problems, a group, family, person, or the *ad hoc* productivity of adaptation to an event, will be the desired focus. To restrict the concept of the cultural to something shared to the limits of a community is an arbitrary limitation on understanding, both of human beings and of the cultural. The viewpoint sketched here has the same fulcrum as that of Sapir's 'Why Cultural Anthropology Needs the Psychiatrist' (1938), but Sapir's insights need not imply his virtual reduction of cultural behavior to psychiatric subject matter.

Capacity varies with event, and with the states in which participants, channels, etc., may be in the event, including the values and beliefs of participants, as properties of their states that help constitute events as communicative, and that determine other properties. Here Albert's paper[10] illustrates possibilities of approach. In part the question is one not of what a language does for and to participants, their personalities, culture, and the like, but of what participants, their personalities, and the like, do for and to a language.

Only by reference to the state of participants, moreover, does it seem possible to introduce in a natural way the various types of functions which communicative events may serve for them.

There has been a bias in American linguistics, and in American extensions of linguistic methodology, favoring a 'surface-level' approach that stresses identification and segmentation of overt material, and hesitates to venture far into inner structural relations and ascription of purpose. (The bias perhaps reflects the favoring of visual over acoustic space, the trust of the eye, not the ear, that Carpenter and McLuhan (1960, pp. 65–70) find characteristic of our society.) In Kenneth Burke's terms, there has been a tendency to treat language and its use as matters of 'motion' (as if of the purely physical world) rather than as matters of 'action' (as matters of the human, dramatistic world of symbolic agency and purpose). With all the difficulties that notions of purpose and function entail, there seems no way for the structural study of language and communication to engage its subject in social life in any adequate, useful way, except by taking this particular bull by the horns. The purposes, conscious and unconscious, the functions, intended and unintended, perceived and unperceived, of communicative events for their participants are here treated as questions of the states in which they engage in them, and of the norms by which they judge them. (Those aspects of purpose and function that have to do with feedback, exchange, response to violations of norms, and the like, are considered with the fourth aspect of the present frame of reference, that of the activity of the system.)

For ethnographic purposes, an initial 'etic grid' for delineating and 'notating' possible types of functions is needed, and it does

10. See editor's note on p. 21 [Ed.]

seem possible to provide one, by considering the possibilities of focus upon each component in turn in relation to each of the others. The grid so derived has proven adequate to accommodate the various schemes of functions, and of functional types of messages, which have come to my attention. Ethnographic work will of course test and probably enlarge and revise it, just as experience of additional languages has enlarged and revised phonetic charts. Literary, philosophical, and other schemes of functions, and of functional types of messages, are also useful as sources of insight and details. (It may prove desirable to undertake a comparative and historical analysis of such schemes, as 'home-made models' from our own culture. Among reviews, note Schaff, 1962, part 2, and Stern, 1931, ch. 2.)

It must be kept in mind that functions may prove specific to individuals and cultures, and that they require specific identification and labeling in any case, even when subsumable under broad types. The 'etic grid' serves only to help perceive kinds of functions that may be present, and possibly to facilitate comparison.

Focus on the addressor or sender in relation to other components entails such types of function as identification of the source, expression of attitude toward one or another component or toward the event as a whole, excogitation (thinking aloud), etc. Such functions may be of course intended, attributed, conscious, unconscious. *Focus on the addressee* or other receiver entails such types of function as identification of the destination, and the ways in which the message and event may be governed by anticipation of the attitude of the destination. Persuasion, appeal, rhetoric, and direction enter here, including as well the sense in which the characteristics of the addressee govern the other aspects of the event as a matter of protocol. Effects on receivers may be of course intended, attributed, conscious, unconscious, achieved, frustrated. *Focus on channels* in relation to other components entails such functions as have to do with maintenance of contact and control of noise, both physical and psychological in both cases. *Focus on codes* in relation to other components entails such functions as are involved in learning, analysis, devising of writing systems, checking on the identity of an element of the code use in conversation, and the like. *Focus on settings* in relation to other components entails all that is considered contextual, apart from the event itself, in that any and all components may be taken as defining the setting of the event, not just its location in time and space. Such context has two aspects, verbal and nonverbal from the standpoint of speech, kinesic and nonkinesic from the standpoint of body motion, and, generally, for any one code or modality, context constituted for a message by other messages within the same code or modality, as distinct from context constituted by all other facets of the event. *Focus on message-form* in relation to other components entails such functions as proof-reading, mimicry, aspects of emendation and editing, and poetic and stylistic concerns. *Focus on topic* in relation to other components entails functions having to do with reference (in the sense both of linguistic meaning proper and denotation) and content. *Focus on the event* itself entails whatever is comprised under metacommunicative types of function. If the message is taken as subsuming all, or all the immediately relevant, other components, then focus on the message as surrogate of the whole event may be taken as entailing metacommunicative functions ('the message "this is play"'; Russell's types, etc.; see Bateson, 1963 on the importance of this function).

Common broad types of functions associated with each type of focus can be variously labelled: expressive, directive, contact (phatic), metalinguistic, contextual, poetic (stylistic), referential, and metacommunicative are useful. The etic framework implied here can be handled with pencil and paper for visual purposes (and expanded also) by two devices, one of horizontal placement, one of vertical placement, of components relative to each other. In handling the five broad types of components of action used in his analysis (Scene, Act, Agent, Agency, Purpose), Burke devises various 'ratios'; thus, the relation of Scene to Act is the Scene-Act ratio, and can be represented as if a numerator over a denominator: Scene/Act (Burke, 1945). In explicating grammatical categories in terms of the components of speech events, Jakobson (1957) discriminates speech events (E^s) and narrated events (E^n), and participants in each (P^s, P^n), expressing relations with a diagonal; thus, the relation of the narrated event to the speech event (involved in verbal categories) is expressed E^n/E^s. Either device could be used to express all the possible combinations and permutations of focus upon the relation of one component of a communicative event to each of the others. Either device is useful in explicating other logical and empirical schemes of functions and functional types of messages in terms of a common denominator, a problem which is a converse in effect of the usual problem of componential analysis. (There one proceeds from etic grid to discover an emic system, here one is concerned to proceed from a possibly emic system to discover an etic grid.)

Most of the functions and components noted above have been discussed with examples of Jakobson (1960) and Hymes (1962).

Activity of the system

Information theory is one topic notably associated with communication; cybernetics is the other. Having taken information theory in its quantitative sense as pertaining to the third aspect of the present frame of reference, we take cybernetics as pertaining to the fourth. Studies concerned with the information theory aspect of ethnographic systems of communication are almost nonexistent, and the case is the same for studies concerned with the cybernetic aspect. One can think in both respects of work by John Roberts that should become far better known than it is (note his forthcoming book, *Four Southwestern Men*), and of a few celebrated and isolated examples in the work of Lévi-Strauss (1953) and Bateson (1949; 1958) where cybernetic notions are applied.[11] [. . .]

The activity of the system is the most general aspect of the four, and ultimately the one in terms of which it is necessary to view the rest. For particular purposes, of course, any one aspect, or part of one, can be segregated for analysis, and there is much to be done in the ethnographic and comparative study of every aspect and component. To take the channel component as an illustration, there are few if any ethnographic studies to compare with Herzog's multi-faceted account of the system of channels elaborated among the Jabo of Liberia, considering, as it does, the structure of the code in each, the relation of code and messages

11. Goodenough (1957b) introduces communication theory in the Shannon sense into his critical review of an anthropological book on communication (Keesing and Keesing, 1956) that does not itself make use of such theory.

in each to base messages in speech, native categories and conceptions, social correlates, and circumstances of use (Herzog, 1945). There is a fair variety of reports of specialized uses of the vocal channel, but the account of Mazateco whistle talk by Cowan (1948) again is almost unique in providing a technical linguistic base and ethnographic context that could support controlled comparison. We have noted that paralinguistic and kinesic investigations have but begun to be extended cross-culturally, and attention to the sociopsychological context of attitude toward use of a channel, or modality, such as voice and gesture, such as Devereux (1949; 1951) has shown in work with the Mohave, is far to seek. The two recent general comparative studies (May, 1956; Stern, 1957) look toward historical interpretation in terms of distribution and origins, but not toward controlled comparison of structures and functions, perhaps because the available data offers little encouragement. Stern's classification of speech surrogates, derived from notions of communication theory, needs clarification and extension to include writing systems, which are logically comprised by the categories. As for the structural and functional aspects of writing and literacy, empirical studies of the diversity of the patterns that occur are few, and as for contrastive studies of their absence, that of Bloomfield (1927) is the only one known to me. Interpretations of the determinism of particular channels, such as those of McLuhan (1962) and of Goody and Watt (1963), and interpretations of the determinism of media (channels) generally, such as are expressed in the orientation of Carpenter and McLuhan (1960) and McLuhan (1964), interesting as they are, seem oversimplified, where not simply wrong, in the light of what little ethnographic base we have. There is a tendency to take the value of a channel as given across cultures, but here, as with every aspect and component of communication, the value is problematic and requires investigation. (Consider for example the specialization of writing to courtship among young people by the Hanunóo, and to a borrowed religion among the Aleut; and the complex and diverse profiles with regard to the role of writing in society, and in individual communicative events, for traditional Chinese, Korean, and Japanese cultures, with regard both to the Chinese texts shared by all and to the materials specific to each.) To provide a better ethnographic basis for the understanding of the place of alternative channels and modalities in communication is indeed one of the greatest challenges to studies of the sort we seek to encourage. At the same time, such work, whether on channels or some other aspect and component, profits from taking into account the complete context of the activity of the system of communication of the community as a whole.

It is with this aspect that the ethnographic study of communication makes closest contact with the social, political, and moral concerns with communication, conceived as value and a determinant in society and in personal lives.

References

BATESON, G. (1949), 'Bali: the value system of a steady state', in M. Fortes (ed.), *Social structure: Studies presented to A. R. Radcliffe-Brown*, Oxford University Press.

BATESON, G. (1958), *Naven*, 2nd ed., Stanford University Press.

BATESON, G. (1963), 'Exchange of information about patterns of human behavior', in W. Fields and W. Abbot (eds.), *Information Storage and Neural Control*, C. Thomas, pp. 1–12.

BLOOMFIELD, L. (1927), 'Literate and illiterate speech', *American Speech*, vol. 2, pp. 432–439.

BROWN, R. (1958), *Words and Things*, Free Press of Glencoe.

BURKE, K. (1945), *A Grammar of Motives*, Prentice-Hall.

CARNEIRO, R. L. (1964), 'The Amahuaca and the spirit world', *Ethnology*, vol. 3.

CARPENTER, E. and MCLUHAN, M. (eds.) (1960), *Explorations in Communication: An Anthology*, Beacon Press.

CHERRY, E. C. (1961), *On Human Communication: A Review, a Survey and a Criticism*, Science Editions. Originally published 1957.

CONKLIN, H. C. (1955), 'Hanunóo color categories', *Southwestern J. Anthrop.*, vol. 11, pp. 339–44.

CONKLIN, H. C. (1962), 'Lexicographical treatment of folk taxonomies', in F. W. Householder and S. Saporta (eds.), *Problems of Lexicography*: supplement to *International Journal of American Linguistics*, part II, vol. 28, no. 2; *Publication 21 of the Indiana University Research Center in Anthropology, Folklore and Linguistics*, pp. 119–41.

CONKLIN, H. C. (1964), 'Ethnogenealogical method', in W. H. Goodenough (ed.), *Explorations in Cultural Anthropology*, McGraw-Hill, pp. 25–55.

COWAN, G. (1948), 'Mazateco whistle speech', *Language*, vol. 24, pp. 280–86.

DEVEREUX, G. (1949), 'Mohave voice and speech mannerisms', *Word*, vol. 5, pp. 268–72.

DEVEREUX, G. (1951), 'Mohave Indian verbal and motor profanity', in
G. Róheim (ed.), *Psychoanalysis and the Social Sciences*, vol. 3,
International Universities Press, pp. 99–127.

FRAKE, C. O. (1961), 'The diagnosis of disease among the Subanun of
Mindanao', *Amer. Anthrop.*, vol. 63, pp. 113–32.

FRAKE, C. O. (1962a), 'Cultural ecology and ethnography', *Amer.
Anthrop.*, vol. 64, pp. 53–9.

FRAKE, C. O. (1962b), 'The ethnographic study of cognitive systems', in
T. Gladwin and W. C. Sturtevant (eds.), *Anthropology and Human
Behavior*, Anthropological Society of Washington, pp. 72–85.

FRAKE, C. O. (1964), 'A structural description of Subanun "religious
behavior"', in W. H. Goodenough (ed.), *Explorations in Cultural
Anthropology*, McGraw-Hill.

GLUCKMAN, M. (1959), 'The technical vocabulary of Barotse
jurisprudence', *Amer. Anthrop.*, vol. 61, pp. 743–59.

GOODENOUGH, W. H. (1956), 'Residence rules', *Southwestern J.
Anthrop.*, vol. 12, pp. 22–37.

GOODENOUGH, W. H. (1957a), 'Cultural anthropology and linguistics',
in P. L. Garvin (ed.), *Report of the Seventh Annual Round Table Meeting
on Linguistics and Language Study*, Georgetown University Press,
pp. 167–73.

GOODENOUGH, W. H. (1957b), 'Review of Keesing and Keesing (1956)',
Language, vol. 3, pp. 424–9.

GOODENOUGH, W. H. (MS), 'Formal properties of status relationships',
Paper read at the annual meeting of the American Anthropological
Association, 16 November 1961, Philadelphia. Reprinted in a revised
version in M. Banton (ed.), *The Relevance of Models for Social
Anthropology*, Tavistock Publication and Praeger, 1965.

GOODY, J., and WATT, I. (1963), 'The consequences of literacy',
Comparative Studies in Society and History, vol. 5 (partially reprinted
in this volume pp. 311–57).

HALLOWELL, A. I. (1964), 'Ojibwa ontology, behavior and world view',
in S. Diamond (ed.), *Primitive Views of the World*, Columbia University
Press, pp. 49–82, [Selections from *Culture in History*, Columbia
University Press (1960)].

HERZOG, G. (1945), 'Drum-signaling in a West African tribe', *Word*,
vol. 1, pp. 217–38.

HOCKETT, C. F. (1955), 'A manual of phonology', Memoir 11 of the
International Journal of American Linguistics; Indiana University
Publications in Anthropology and Linguistics.

HOCKETT, C. F. (1958), *A course in modern linguistics*, Macmillan Co.

HYMES, D. (1961), 'Functions of speech: an evolutionary approach', in
F. C. Gruber (ed.), *Anthropology and Education*, University of
Pennsylvania Press, pp. 55–83.

HYMES, D. (1962), 'The ethnography of speaking', in T. Gladwin and
W. C. Sturtevant (eds.), *Anthropology and Human Behaviour*,
Anthropological Society of Washington, pp. 15–53.

HYMES, D. (1964), 'Directions in (ethno-)linguistic theory', *Amer. Anthrop.*, vol. 66, no. 3, part 2, pp. 6–56.

HYMES, D. (MS), 'Two types of linguistic relativity', Paper presented to conference on sociolinguistics, UCLA, 17 May 1964. Reprinted in W. Bright (ed.), *Sociolinguistics*, Mouton, 1966, pp. 114–67.

JAKOBSON, R. (1953), Chapter two, in *Results of the conference of anthropologists and linguists*, by C. Lévi-Strauss, R. Jakobson, C. F. Voegelin and T. A. Sebeok, Memoir 8 of *the International Journal of American Linguistics*; Indiana University Publications in Anthropology and Linguistics, pp. 11–21.

JAKOBSON, R. (1957), 'Shifters, verbal categories, and the Russian verb', Harvard University, Russian language project.

JAKOBSON, R. (1960), 'Concluding statement: linguistics and poetics', in T. A. Sebeok (ed.), *Style in Language*, M.I.T. Press and Wiley, pp. 350–73.

KEESING, F., and KEESING, M. M. (1956), *Elite communication in Samoa*, Stanford University Press.

KLUCKHOHN, C. (1961), 'Notes on some anthropological aspects of communication', *Amer. Anthrop.*, vol. 63, pp. 895–910.

LÉVI-STRAUSS, C. (1953), 'Social structure', in A. L. Kroeber *et al.* (eds.), *Anthropology Today*, University of Chicago Press.

LISKER, L., COOPER, F. S., and LIBERMAN, A. M. (1962), 'The uses of experiment in language description', *Word*, vol. 18, pp. 82–106.

LOMAX, A. (1959), 'Folk-song style', *Amer. Anthrop.*, vol. 61, pp. 927–54.

LOUNSBURY, F G. (1955), 'The varieties of meaning', in R. H. Weinstein (ed.), *Report of the Sixth Annual Round Table Meeting on Linguistics and Language Teaching*, Georgetown University Press, pp. 158–64.

LOUNSBURY, F. G. (1956), 'A semantic analysis of the Pawnee kinship usage', *Language*, vol. 32, pp. 158–94.

MAY, L. C. (1956), 'A survey of glossolalia and related phenomena in non-Christian religions', *Amer. Anthrop.*, vol. 58, pp. 75–96.

McLUHAN, M. (1962), *The Gutenberg Galaxy: The Making of Typographic Man*, Routledge and Kegan Paul.

McLUHAN, M. (1964), *Understanding Media: The Extensions of Man*, McGraw-Hill.

MEILLET, A. (1906), 'Comment les mots changent de sens', *L'Année Sociologique*, reprinted in *Linguistique historique et linguistique générale*, vol. 1, pp. 230–71.

MORRIS, C. W. (1946), *Signs, Language and Behavior*, Prentice-Hall.

PIKE, K. L. (1954), 'Language in relation to a unified theory of the structure of human behavior', part 1, preliminary edn., Glendale, Summer Institute of Linguistics.

ROBERTS, J. M. (MS), 'Four Southwestern men'.

SAPIR, E. (1916), 'Time perspective in aboriginal American culture: a study in method', Canada, Department of Mines, Geological Survey, Memoir 90; Anthropological Series, No. 13, Ottawa, Government Printing Bureau. Reprinted in D. G. Mandelbaum (ed.), *Selected Writings of Edward Sapir*, University of California Press, 1949.

SAPIR, E. (1921), *Language*, Harcourt, Brace.

SAPIR, E. (1925), 'Sound patterns in language', *Language*, vol. 1, pp. 37–51. Reprinted in D. G. Mendelbaum (ed.), *Selected Writings of Edward Sapir*, University of California Press, 1949.

SAPIR, E. (1938), 'Why cultural anthropology needs the psychiatrist', *Psychiatry*, vol. 1, pp. 7–12. Reprinted in D. G. Mendelbaum (ed.), *Selected Writings of Edward Sapir*, University of California Press, 1949.

SCHAFF, A. (1962), *Introduction to Semantics*, Pergamon Press.

SERVICE, E. R. (1960), 'Kinship terminology and evolution', *Amer. Anthrop.*, vol. 62, pp. 747–63.

SPIER, L., and SAPIR, E. (1930), 'Wishram ethnography', University of Washington Publications in anthropology, vol. 3, no. 3, pp. 151–300.

SSUKUNG TU (1963), 'The twenty-four modes of poetry', *Chinese Literature*, vol. 7, Foreign Language Press, Peking.

STERN, G. (1931), *Meaning and Change of Meaning*, Elanders boktruckei aktiebolag, Göteborg.

STERN, T. (1957), 'Drum and whistle languages: an analysis of speech surrogates', *Amer. Anthrop.*, vol. 59, pp. 487–506.

TYLOR, E. B. (1871), *Primitive culture*, 2nd edn, John Murray, 1873.

2 J. A. Fishman

The Sociology of Language

Revised and enlarged version of a lecture prepared for the Voice of
America Forum Lecture Series, George A. Miller, Rockefeller
University, Coordinator; reprinted in G. A. Miller (ed.), *Psychology and
Communication*, Basic Books, in press.

Man is constantly using language – spoken language, written
language, printed language – and man is constantly linked to
others via shared norms of behavior. The sociology of language
examines the interaction between these two aspects of human
behavior: use of language and the social organization of behavior. Briefly put, the sociology of language focuses upon the
entire gamut of topics related to the social organization of language behavior, including not only language usage per se but also
language attitudes, overt behavior toward language and toward
language users.

The latter concern of the sociology of language – overt behavior toward language and toward language users – is also a concern shared by political and educational leaders in many parts
of the world and is an aspect of sociolinguistics that frequently
makes the headlines. Many French-Canadian university students
oppose the continuation of public education in English in the
Province of Quebec. Many Flemings in Belgium protest vocifer-
ously against anything less than full equality – at the very least –
for Dutch in the Brussels area. Some Welsh nationalists daub
out English signs along the highways in Wales and many Irish
revivalists seek stronger governmental support for the restoration
of Irish than that made available during half a century of Irish
independence. Jews throughout the world protest the Soviet
government's extermination of Yiddish writers and the forced
closing of Yiddish schools, theatres and publications.

Swahili, Filipino, Indonesian, Malay and the various pro-
vincial languages of India are all being consciously expanded in
vocabulary, standardized in spelling and grammar so that they

can increasingly function as the exclusive languages of government and of higher culture and technology. The successful revival and modernization of Hebrew has encouraged other smaller language communities – the Catalans, the Provençals, the Frisians, the Bretons – to strive to save *their* ethnic mother tongues (or their traditional cultural tongues) from oblivion. New and revised writing systems are being accepted – and, at times, rejected – in many parts of the world by communities that hitherto had little interest in literacy in general or in literacy in their mother tongues in particular.

Such examples of consciously organized behavior toward language and toward users of particular languages can be listed almost endlessly. The list becomes truly endless if we include examples from earlier periods of history, such as the displacement of Latin as the language of religion, culture and government in Western Christendom and the conscious cultivation of once lowly vernaculars – first in Western Europe and then subsequently in Central, Southern and Eastern Europe, and finally in Africa and Asia as well – as *independent* languages, as languages suitable for *all* higher purposes, and as languages of state-building and *state-deserving* nationalities. All of these examples too feed into the broad data pool of modern sociology of language, providing it with historical breadth and depth in addition to its ongoing interest in current language issues throughout the world.

However, the sociology of language reaches far beyond interest in case studies and in catalogs of language conflict and language planning in the public arena. The ultimate quest of the sociology of language is pursued diligently in many universities and is very far from dealing directly with headlines or news reports. One part of this quest is concerned with describing the generally accepted social organization of language usage within speech community (or within speech-and-writing communities, to be more exact). This part of the sociology of language – descriptive sociology of language – seeks to provide an answer to the question 'who speaks (or writes) what language (or what language variety) to whom and when and to what end?' (Fishman, in press a). Descriptive sociolinguistics tries to disclose the language usage norms – i.e., the generally accepted and implemented social patterns of language use and of behavior toward language – for particular larger or smaller social networks and communities. Another part of sociolinguistics – dynamic sociology of language – seeks to provide an answer to the question 'what accounts for differential changes in the social organization of language use and behavior toward language?' Dynamic sociology of language tries to explain why and how the social organization of language use and behavior toward language have become selectively different in the *same* social networks or communities on two different occasions. Dynamic sociology of language also seeks to explain why and how two once similar social networks or communities have arrived at a quite different social organization of language use and behavior toward language.

Descriptive sociolinguistics

Let us look first at descriptive sociology of language, since it is the basic task of the discipline per se. Unless we can attain reliable and insightful description of any *existing* patterns of social organization in language use and behavior toward language it will obviously be impossible to contribute very much that is sound toward the explanation of why or how this pattern changes or remains stable. One of the basic insights of descriptive sociology of language is that members of social networks and communities do not always display either the same language usage or the same behavior toward language. Perhaps a few examples will help illustrate this crucial point.

Government functionaries in Brussels who are of Flemish origin do not always speak Dutch *to each other*, even when they all know Dutch *very* well and *equally* well. Not only are there occasions when they speak French *to each other* instead of Dutch, but there are some occasions when they speak standard Dutch and others when they use one or another regional variety of Dutch with each other. Indeed, some of them also use different varieties of French with each other as well, one variety being particularly loaded with governmental officialese, another corresponding to the non-technical conversational French of highly educated and refined circles in Belgium, and still another being not only a 'more colloquial French' but the colloquial French of those who are Flemings. All in all, these several varieties of Dutch and of French constitute the *linguistic repertoire* of certain social networks in Brussels. The task of descriptive sociology of language is to describe the general or normative patterns of language use within a speech network or speech community so as to show the *systematic nature* of the alternations between one variety and another among individuals who *share* a repertoire of varieties (Fishman, 1970; Fishman, Cooper, Ma, *et al.*, in press).

However, not only multilingual speech networks or communities utilize a repertoire of language varieties. In monolingual speech communities the linguistic repertoire of particular social networks may consist of several social class varieties, or of social class and regional varieties, or, even, of social class, regional and occupational varieties *of the same language*. Thus, monolingual native born New Yorkers speak differently to each other on different occasions – and these differences can be pinpointed phonologically (i.e. in the way words are pronounced), lexically (i.e. in the very words that are used) and grammatically (i.e. in the systematic relationship between words). The same young man who sometimes says 'I sure hope yuz guys 'll shut the lights before leavin'' also is quite likely to say, or at least to write, 'Kindly extinguish all illumination prior to vacating the premises'. It's all a question of *when* to say the one and *when* the other, when interacting with individuals who could equally well understand both but who would consider use of the one when the other is called for as a serious *faux pas*.

Situational shifting

The description of societal patterns of language variety use – a variety being *either* a different language *or* a different social 'dialect', *or* a different occupational 'dialect' *or* a different regional 'dialect' – whenever any two varieties are present in the linguistic repertoire of a social network – commonly utilizes the concept of *situation*. A situation is defined by the co-occurrence of two (or more) interlocutors related to each other in a particular way, communicating about a particular topic, in a particular setting. Thus, a social network or community may define a beerparty between university people as a quite different situation than a lecture involving *the same people*. The topics of talk in the two situations are likely to be different; their locales and times are likely to be different; and the relationships or roles of the interlocutors vis-à-vis each other are likely to be different. Any *one* of these differences may be sufficient for the situations to be defined as *sufficiently* different by the members of the university community to require that a different language variety be utilized in each case.

Members of social networks sharing a linguistic repertoire must (and do) know when to shift from one variety to another. One category of such shifts is that known as situational shifts. A shift in situation *may* require a shift in language variety. A shift in language variety *may* signal a shift in the relationship between co-members of a social network, or a shift in the topic and purpose of their interaction, or a shift in the privacy or locale of their interaction (Blom and Gumperz, 1968).

The careful reader will note that I have written '*may* require' and '*may* signal'. Does this mean that a shift in situation does not always and invariably require a shift in language variety or that a change in language variety does not always and invariably signal a change in situation? Yes, precisely. At times, members of the same speech network or community go from one situation to another without changing from one variety to another. Thus, interaction with one's friends and with one's younger siblings – two seemingly different role relations that may well transpire in generally different settings and involve at least somewhat different topics – may still be acceptably conducted in the same variety. Thus, what is or is not a different situation with respect to language variety use is a matter of the internal social organization of particular speech networks or communities. Native members of such networks or communities slowly and unconsciously acquire *sociolinguistic communicative competence* with respect to appropriate language usage. They are not necessarily aware of the norms that guide their sociolinguistic behavior. Newcomers to such networks or communities – including sociolinguistic researchers – must discover these norms more rapidly, more painfully and, therefore, more consciously (Hymes, 1967).

One thing is clear: there are classes of occasions recognized by each speech network or community such that several seemingly different situations are classed as being of the same kind. No speech network has a linguistic repertoire which is as differentiated as the complete list of apparently different role relations, topics and locales in which its members are involved. Just *where the boundaries come* that do differentiate between the *class of situations* generally requiring one variety and another class of situations generally requiring another variety must be empirically determined by the investigator, and constitutes one of the major tasks of descriptive sociolinguistics. Such classes of situations are referred to as *domains*. The derivation of domains and of domain appropriate usage from the data of numerous discrete situations and the variety shifting or non-shifting which they reveal, is a task of descriptive sociology of language – descriptive macro-sociology of language to be exact – which proceeds via participant observation, survey methods, experimental designs and depth interviews (Fishman, 1971).

Metaphorical switching

The fact that co-members of the same speech networks or speech communities also change from one variety to another without signaling any change in situation is also indicative of the categorizing in which native members so frequently and effortlessly engage. When variety switching is fleeting and non-reciprocal it is commonly *metaphorical* in nature. This means that it is utilized for purposes of emphasis or contrast, rather than as an indication of situational discontinuity. A switch to Cockney where Received Pronounciation (and grammar) is called for may well elicit a brief raising of eyebrows or a pause in the conversation – until it is clear from the speaker's demeanor and from the fact that he has reverted to *RP* that no change in situation was intended. However, such metaphorical switching can be risky. Someone might feel that Cockney for the situation at hand is in poor taste. Metaphorical switching is a luxury that can be afforded only by those that comfortably share not only the same *set* of situational norms but also *the same view as to their inviolability*. Since most of us are members of several speech networks, each with somewhat different sociolinguistic norms, the chances that situational shifting and metaphorical switching will be misunderstood and conflicted – particularly where the norms pertaining to variety selection have few or insufficiently powerful guardians – are obviously great (Blom and Gumperz, 1968; Kimple, Cooper and Fishman, 1969).

A speech community maintains its sociolinguistic pattern as long as the functional differentiation of the varieties in its linguistic repertoire is systematically and widely maintained. As long as each variety is associated with a separate class of situations there is good reason and established means for retaining them all, each in its place, notwithstanding the modicum of metaphorical switching that may occur. However, two or more varieties with the same societal function become difficult to maintain and, in the end, one must either displace the other or a new functional differentiation must be arrived at between them. Let us look quickly at how such changes in linguistic repertoire or in functional allocation occur.

Dynamic sociology of language: the bases of repertoire change

At the very same time that a linguistic repertoire with its particular societal functional allocation of varieties exists in a particular speech community, certain of these same or very similar varieties may be found in other or neighboring speech communities in association with other functions. If the members of these speech communities are brought into greater interaction with each other, or if their relative power to influence or control one another changes sufficiently, then the societal functional allocation of linguistic repertoire of one or another or both communities is likely to undergo change. Thus, most immigrants to the United States have experienced sufficient interaction with English-speaking Americans, particularly in the work domain and in the education domain to learn English. This has also long been true for French Canadians in large industrial centers such as Montreal. Yet, how differently these two processes of linguistic repertoire change have worked out. In the United States the immigrants largely lost their mother tongues within one, two, or at most, three generations. In Montreal each new French Canadian generation starts off monolingual in French and then acquires English later in life without, however, handing on this second language to the next generation as its initial language. How can we best describe and account for this difference in outcome between two populations each of which was *forced* to acquire English for its educational and economic improvement? The difference seems to be related to the ability of one population to maintain a certain societal functional differentiation within its linguistic repertoire while the other was unable to do so.

Unstable bilingualism

American immigrants needed English both as a lingua franca because they came from so many different speech communities and as a passport to social and economic advancement. Because of the severe dislocation of their 'old-country' rural or small town *ways* (as a result of rapid exposure to American urban, industrial contexts) it quickly became impossible for them to maintain the original home and family patterns *upon which their only chance for domain separation depended.* Those whose English was better, progressed more rapidly on the American scene and became models *within* the immigrant home and *within* the immigrant organization and neighborhood. Thus, the home and immigrant life itself became domains of English – particularly under the onslaught of the American school and the Americanizing and amalgamating efforts of American churches. As a result, children of immigrants soon became bilingual in the family and immigrant contexts themselves. Since English was the only language of value outside of the home and immigrant organization only the latter might have been capable of preserving the non-English mother-tongue if they had been able to maintain themselves as separate, self-contained domains.

This, the immigrant speech networks could do only in those few cases where immigrants of a single background clearly predominated (as they had for a long time in the case of German- and Scandinavian-language islands in the Mid-West) or where their social mobility via English was sharply restricted (as in the case of Spanish speakers in the Southwest). Almost everywhere else, economic advancement and the dislocation of traditional home, neighborhood and organizational practices went hand in hand. There was no domain in which the non-English ethnic language alone was required for 'membership' and as a result, there was no domain in which it was retained. The non-English ethnic languages continued somewhat longer to serve fleeting metaphorical purposes but there were soon no situational shifts in which they were required. As a result, children who had become bilingual in the very bosom of the family and the immigrant neighborhood became increasingly monolingual English speakers as they passed to and through their English-speaking schools, their English-speaking careers and their English-speaking neighborhoods. Such individuals raised their own children in English (Haugen, 1953; Fishman *et al.*, 1966).

Stable bilingualism

In Montreal the situation was and still is much different. French speakers were initially exposed to English instruction and to English job success only slowly over a long period of time. Their elementary schools long remained entirely French (as did their churches) and even their secondary schools (in which English instruction *was* offered to those rather few who were fortunate enough to attend) were under French (and under Church) auspices. The result was that the monolingual French-speaking child remained such as long as his life was restricted to home, neighborhood and church. He became increasingly bilingual as he passed through more advanced levels of the school and work domains, but he then reverted to increasing French monolingualism if his school and work careers were kept at lower levels or when he passed beyond their reach. As a result, the domains of English and the domains of French were kept functionally quite separate. Not only did the English domains reach proportionally fewer French Canadians and not only did they reach them more superficially, but, chronologically, the early and late domains of the speech community's networks were basically French-speaking (except for metaphorical purposes), thus assuring that the next generation would be monolingual French-speaking as well (Lieberson, 1965).

However, something new has recently been added to the Montreal picture. French-Canadian education expanded to the point that it produced more well-qualified or highly qualified individuals than could be assimilated into the various English-managed industrial, commercial and cultural enterprises which traditionally reserved most of their leading positions for English Canadians. As a result, French-speaking elites have increasingly claimed and formed their own enterprises in these domains. For them English has become increasingly superfluous in view of its lack of domain separation and situational need. In addition, of course, it has become symbolic of their not being masters in their own home, and, as such, is opposed both for general symbolic as well as for specifically functional reasons (Lieberson, 1970; Hughes, 1971).

These two sociolinguistic patterns, the American immigrant and the French-Canadian nationalist, have been repeated many times in the past century. The Russification of Soviet minorities – particularly the smaller ones – whether they be immigrants to large urban centers in other regions or inundated by Russian and various other immigrants into their own regions (Lewis, in press), has followed the same path as that of the Anglification of immigrants to the United States, the Hispanization of indigenous populations moving to urban centers throughout Latin America, or the Wolofization of diverse Senegalese populations in Dakar. Similarly, the 'indigenization' of the domains of education, industry and government (which has previously 'belonged' to English, so to speak), that has increasingly typified French-Canada, is not at all unlike the growing displacement of English in Puerto Rico, Tanzania, India, Malaysia and the Philippines (Epstein, 1970; Das Gupta, 1970; Ramos *et al.*, 1967; Whiteley, 1969).

The last four instances – Tanzania, India, Malaysia and the Philippines – also exemplify the constantly recurring need to *develop* newly promoted indigenous national languages, so that they can be effectively and uniformly utilized in the new domains and situations that they have won or are winning for themselves. How this process of language planning is conducted, who accepts and who rejects the manufactured terminologies, orthographies and grammars, whether their differential acceptance can be influenced by differing approaches to the implementation of language planning and language policy, these too are parts of the sociology of language – applied sociology of language to be sure – a topic in itself and one which deserves a few words before this review is brought to a close.

Applied sociology of language

The sociology of language has applied significance for all of the topics normally considered within the field of applied linguistics: native language teaching, second language teaching, translation, the creation and revision of writing systems, language policy decisions, and language planning as a whole. In connection with each of these topics successful 'application' depends not only on competent linguistic analysis of the languages being taught, used or developed but also (and, perhaps, even primarily) upon the social circumstances surrounding all applied efforts in connection with these languages. Similarly all branches of applied sociology stand to benefit from the sociology of language, since all of them (sociology of education, sociology of medicine, sociology of planning, industrial sociology, etc.) deal with group boundaries, role networks, role repertoires, role compartmentalization, social situations, institutional domains, etc. The confluence between applied linguistics and applied sociology is most dramatically illustrated in the context of social and national modernization, a context in which the applied sociology of language has been most actively pursued (Fishman, Ferguson, Das Gupta, 1968). Let us look at some examples.

The creation and revision of writing systems

The progress of social and national modernization depends to a large extent upon sufficiently widespread as well as sufficiently advanced literacy. However, such literacy is often impossible because writing systems as such have not yet been devised for the languages spoken natively in various larger and smaller speech communities throughout the world. However, devising a simple and technically exact system of representing spoken sounds via written symbols is not at all a *sufficient* step for the acceptance of this system by its intended users.

To begin with there must be some felt need for reading and writing, some actual or implied gain as a result of the acquisition of literacy and, not infrequently, an absence of major status loss to those who have hitherto been the status and power elites of the society (Garvin, 1959).

Furthermore, the purely visual aspect of writing systems is also a factor in their acceptance or rejection.

Many speech communities have insisted on indigenous writing systems unlike those of other written languages, in order to stress their separateness from their neighbors and their independence from 'big brothers' at a greater geographic distance. Others, on the other hand, have demonstrated positive modelling (rather than anti-modelling), or have had such modelling foisted upon them. It is hardly accidental that the new writing systems of many North American Indian groups 'look like English', that those of Latin American Indians 'look like Spanish', that those of Siberian peoples 'look like Russian', etc. The determining factors of such modelling and anti-modelling are all social and political rather than merely linguistic and pedagogical (Fishman, Cooper, Ma, *et al.*, in press).

Even more complicated, socially, than the creation of new writing systems is the revision of old ones. Attempts to simplify spelling or writing systems per se have been singularly ineffective in modern times although an inordinate amount of time and effort has gone into such attempts (Smalley, 1964). While the writing systems for Polish, Czech and Roumanian were changed from Cyrillic to Roman alphabets, during the nineteenth century, and while the Soviets have changed the writing systems of many Asian nationalities (sometimes more than once within a decade or two), others have experienced far greater difficulty, even under similar authoritarian conditions. Communist Chinese plans to phoneticize the writing of Mandarin seem to have been postponed for the indefinite future and Soviet efforts to 'declericalize' Yiddish spelling by abandoning the four 'end of word' letters of the traditional Hebrew alphabet have also been abandoned.

In more widely participatory decision-making settings spelling reform has proved to be, if anything, even more difficult to execute. Thus, while many developing nations of an earlier period were able to push through spelling reforms before literacy became much more than an elitist preoccupation (e.g. nineteenth-century Germany, post-Revolutionary USSR) neither Israel nor Indonesia nor Pakistan nor India nor any other developing nation of today has been able to push through the spelling or writing reforms that would make literacy more accessible to all its citizens. Nevertheless, Norway has been able to revise the spelling of both of its standard national languages in modern times, albeit in an atmosphere of considerable conflict (Haugen, 1966).

Language planning

As the above discussion reveals, it is exceedingly difficult to come to conclusions of applied significance when entire countries or national entities are taken as the unit of analysis, particularly when these units are at vastly different stages of social, economic and political development. As a result, the applied sociology of language has tended more and more toward the in-depth study of localized cases of language planning. Focusing increasingly upon differential reactions to centrally authorized and controlled language innovations (whether these be orthographic or lexical, on the one hand, or the functional reallocation of codes within a speech-and-writing community, on the other hand), such studies do not speak of success or failure as a nation-wide phenomenon but rather, of differential rates of acceptance or rejection (cognitively, affectively and/or overtly) in various population segments.

As a result of recent studies it is becoming increasingly possible for language planning agencies (e.g., for those seeking to foster the use of recently established national languages for purposes of higher education, government or technology) to pinpoint the particular programs, projects or products that are successful with particular target populations and those that are not. It is becoming increasingly clear that the study of role relationships, role networks, role compartmentalization and role access in speech communities and speech networks is a very *practical* matter indeed.

For only such study can demonstrate where language planning per se must leave off and where wider social planning (including the expansion of opportunity as well as of participation in decision making and decision evaluation) must begin (Rubin and Jernudd, in press). This is the stage at which the applied sociology of language now finds itself.

References

BLOM, J. P. and GUMPERZ, J. (1968) 'Fattori sociali determinanti del comportamento verbale', in P. P. Giglioli (ed.), *Sociolinguistica*, special issue of the *Rassegna Italiana di Sociologia*, vol. 9, no. 2, pp. 301–328 (to appear in English as 'Social Meaning in Linguistic Structures', in J. Gumperz and D. Hymes (eds.), *Directions in Sociolinguistics*, Holt-Rinehart-Winston, in press).

DAS GUPTA, J. (1970), *Language Conflict and National Development*, University of California Press.

EPSTEIN, ERWIN H. (ed.) (1970), *Politics and Education in Puerto Rico; A Documentary Survey of the Language Issue*, Methuen; Scarecrow.

FISHMAN, J. A. *et al*. (1966), *Language Loyalty in the United States*, Mouton.

FISHMAN, J. A., FERGUSON, C. A. and DAS GUPTA, J. (eds.) (1968), *Language Problems of Developing Nations*, Wiley.

FISHMAN, J. A. (1970), *Sociolinguistics: A Brief Introduction*, Rowley, Newbury House.

FISHMAN, J. A. (1971), 'The sociology of language: an interdisciplinary social science approach to sociolinguistics', in J. A. Fishman (ed.), *Advances in the Sociology of Language*, Mouton.

FISHMAN, J. A. (in press, a), 'The link between macro- and micro-sociology in the study of who speaks what to whom and when', in J. Gumperz and D. Hymes (eds.), *Directions in Sociolinguistics*, Holt-Rinehart-Winston.

FISHMAN, J. A. (in press, b), 'The uses of sociolinguistics', *Proceedings of the Second International Congress of Applied Linguistics*, Cambridge University Press.

FISHMAN, J. A., COOPER, R. L., MA, R. *et al*. (in press), *Bilingualism in the Barrio*, Language Sciences, Indiana University Press.

GARVIN, P. (1959), 'The standard language problem: concepts and methods', *Anthrop. Linguistics*, no. 2, pp. 28–31.

HAUGEN, E. (1953), *The Norwegian Language in America*, University of Pennsylvania Press, 2 vols.

HAUGEN, E. (1966), *Language Planning and Language Conflict; The Case of Modern Norwegian*, Harvard University Press.

HUGHES, E. (1971), 'The linguistic division of labor in Montreal', *Monograph Series on Languages and Linguistics*, Georgetown University Press; also in J. A. Fishman (ed.), *Advances in the Sociology of Language*, Mouton.

HYMES, D. (1967), 'Models of the interaction of language and social setting', *J. Soc. Issues*, vol. 23, no. 2, pp. 8–28.

KIMPLE JR, J., COOPER, R. L. and FISHMAN, J. A. (1969), 'Language switching in the interpretation of conversations, *Lingua*, vol. 23, pp. 127–34.

LEWIS, G. (in press), 'Language maintenance and language shift in the Soviet Union', *Inter. Migration Rev*.

LIEBERSON, S. (1965), 'Bilingualism in Montreal: a demographic analysis', *Amer. J. Sociol.*, vol. 71, pp. 10–25; also in J. A. Fishman (ed.), *Advances in the Sociology of Language*, Mouton.

LIEBERSON, S. (1970), *Language and Ethnic Relations in Canada*, Wiley.

RAMOS, M. *et al*. (1967), *The Determination and Implementation of Language Policy*, Alemar-Phonnix.

RUBIN, J. and JERNUDD, B. (eds.) (in press), *Can Language be Planned?* East West Center Press, Honolulu.

SMALLEY, W. A. (1964), *Orthography Studies: Articles on New Writing Systems*, United Bible Societies.

WHITELEY, W. (1969), *Swahili; The Rise of a National Language*, Methuen.

Part Two **Speech and Situated Action**

Erving Goffman's work (1961; 1963) has made us familiar with the fact that social situations have a structure of their own, different from and sometimes opposite to the characteristics of larger social structures. Since speech occurs in social situations, it is important to see in what ways the underlying structures of situations determine the organization of talk. Goffman's paper succinctly states the problems explored in this section; the other articles may be viewed as extensions of his remarks. Basso shows that not only how, but also when to speak is culturally and situationally determined. He finds that in Western Apache culture silence is associated with ambiguity in role expectations, but he treats the concept of role not as a given feature of social structure, but rather as an attribute which is re-defined by the particular context in which social interaction unfolds.

Conversations are patterned both syntagmatically and paradigmatically. Syntagmatic patterning refers to the sequential organization of conversation, to the fact that utterances are connected in a meaningful way; paradigmatic patterning refers to the speaker's selection from a range of permissible alternates. Frake studies the syntagmatic rules of conversations in drinking encounters, a highly relevant social event among the Subanun (another contribution to the analysis of the syntagmatic aspect of conversations is Labov's paper in Part Four). Schegloff explores the social determinants of the selection from a paradigmatic field, the formulation of locations.

The speech act, a central unit of conversation, is studied in Searle's paper. This article is set somewhat apart from the others in that it consists in a conceptual rather than in an empirical analysis of speech. Such philosophical efforts at conceptualization provide 'etic grids' useful as starting points for empirical research which can, in turn, refine and test them.

References

GOFFMAN, E. (1961), *Encounters*, Bobbs-Merrill.
GOFFMAN, E. (1963), *Behavior in Public Places*, Free Press.

3 E. Goffman

The Neglected Situation

E. Goffman, 'The Neglected Situation', *American Anthropologist*, vol. 66, 1964, no. 6, part 2, pp. 133–6.

It hardly seems possible to name a social variable that doesn't show up and have its little systematic effect upon speech behavior: age, sex, class, caste, country of origin, generation, region, schooling; cultural cognitive assumptions; bilingualism, and so forth. Each year new social determinants of speech behavior are reported. (It should be said that each year new psychological variables are also tied in with speech.)

Alongside this correlational drive to bring in ever new social attributes as determinants of speech behavior, there has been another drive, just as active, to add to the range of properties discoverable in speech behavior itself, these additions having varied relations to the now classic phonetic, phonemic, morphemic and syntactical structuring of language. It is thus that new semantic, expressive, paralinguistic and kinesic features of behavior involving speech have been isolated, providing us with a new bagful of indicators to do something correlational with.

I'm sure these two currents of analysis – the correlational and the indicative – could churn on forever (and probably will), a case of scholarly coexistence. However, a possible source of trouble might be pointed out. At certain points these two modes of analysis seem to get unpleasantly close together, forcing us to examine the land that separates them – and this in turn may lead us to feel that something important has been neglected.

Take the second-mentioned current of analysis first – the uncovering of new properties or indicators in speech behavior. That aspect of a discourse that can be clearly transferred through writing to paper has been long dealt with; it is the greasy parts of speech that are now increasingly considered. A wagging tongue (at certain levels of analysis) proves to be only one part of a complex human act whose meaning must also be sought in the movement of the eyebrows and hand. However, once we are willing to consider these gestural, nonwritable behaviors associated with speaking, two grave embarrassments face us. First, while the substratum of a gesture derives from the maker's body, the form of the gesture can be intimately determined by the microecological orbit in which the speaker finds himself. To describe the gesture, let alone uncover its meaning, we might then have to introduce the human and material setting in which the gesture is made. For example, there must be a sense in which the loudness of a statement can only be assessed by knowing first how distant the speaker is from his recipient. The individual gestures with the immediate environment, not only with his body, and so we must introduce this environment in some systematic way. Secondly, the gestures the individual employs as part of speaking are much like the ones he employs when he wants to make it perfectly clear that he certainly isn't going to be drawn into a conversation at this juncture. At certain levels of analysis, then, the study of behavior while speaking and the study of behavior of those who are present to each other but not engaged in talk cannot be analytically separated. The study of one teasingly draws us into the study of the other. Persons like Ray Birdwhistell and Edward Hall have built a bridge from speaking to social conduct, and once you cross the bridge, you become too busy to turn back.

Turn now from the study of newly uncovered properties or indicators in speech to the first-mentioned study of newly uncovered social correlates of speech. Here we will find even greater embarrassment. For increasingly there is work on a particularly subversive type of social correlate of speech that is called 'situational'. Is the speaker talking to same or opposite sex, subordinate or superordinate, one listener or many, someone right there or on the phone; is he reading a script or talking spontaneously; is the occasion formal or informal, routine or emergency? Note that it is not the attributes of social structure that are here considered, such as age and sex, but rather the value placed on these attributes as they are acknowledged in the situation current and at hand.

And so we have the following problem: a student interested in the properties of speech may find himself having to look at the physical setting in which the speaker performs his gestures, simply because you cannot describe a gesture fully without reference to the extra-bodily environment in which it occurs. And someone interested in the linguistic correlates of social structure may find that he must attend to the social occasion when someone of given social attributes makes his appearance before others. Both kinds of student must therefore look at what we vaguely call the social situation. And that is what has been neglected.

At present the idea of the social situation is handled in the most happy-go-lucky way. For example, if one is dealing with the language of respect, then social situations become occasions when persons of relevant status relationships are present before each other, and a typology of social situations is drawn directly and simply from chi-squaredom: high-low, low-high and equals. And the same could be said for other attributes of the social structure. An implication is that social situations do not have properties and a structure of their own, but merely mark, as it were, the geometric intersection of actors making talk and actors bearing particular social attributes.

I do not think this opportunistic approach to social situations is always valid. Your social situation is not your country cousin. It can be argued that social situations, at least in our society, constitute a reality *sui generis* as He used to say, and therefore need and warrant analysis in their own right, much like that accorded other basic forms of social organization. And it can be further argued that this sphere of activity is of special importance for those interested in the ethnography of speaking, for where but in social situations does speaking go on?

So let us face what we have been offhand about: social situations. I would define a social situation as an environment of mutual monitoring possibilities, anywhere within which an individual will find himself accessible to the naked senses of all others who are 'present', and similarly find them accessible to him. According to this definition, a social situation arises whenever two or more individuals find themselves in one another's immediate presence, and it lasts until the next-to-last person leaves. Those in a given situation may be referred to aggregatively as a *gathering*, however divided, or mute and distant, or only momentarily present, the participants in the gathering appear to be. Cultural rules establish how individuals are to conduct themselves by virtue of being in a gathering, and these rules for commingling, when adhered to, socially organize the behavior of those in the situation.[1]

Although participation in a gathering always entails constraint and organization, there are special social arrangements of all or some of those present which entail additional and greater structuring of conduct. For it is possible for two or more persons in a social situation to jointly ratify one another as authorized co-sustainers of a single, albeit moving, focus of visual and cognitive attention. These ventures in joint orientation might be called *encounters* or face engagements. A preferential mutual openness to all manner of communication is involved. A physical coming together is typically also involved, an ecological huddle wherein participants orient to one another and away from those who are present in the situation but not officially in the encounter. There are clear rules for the initiation and termination of encounters, the entrance and departure of particular participants, the demands that an encounter can make upon its sustainers, and the decorum of space and sound it must observe relative to excluded participants in the situation. A given social gathering of course may contain no encounter, merely unengaged participants bound by unfocused interaction; it may contain one encounter which itself contains all the persons in the situation – a favored arrangement for sexual interaction; it may contain an accessible encounter, one that must proceed in the presence of unengaged participants or other encounters.

Card games, ball-room couplings, surgical teams in operation and fist fights provide examples of encounters; all illustrate the social organization of shared current orientation, and all involve an organized interplay of acts of some kind. I want to suggest that when speaking occurs it does so within this kind of social arrangement; of course what is organized therein is not plays or steps or procedures or blows, but turns at talking. Note then that

1. I have attempted to present this argument in detail in *Behavior in Public Places*, Free Press, 1963.

the natural home of speech is one in which speech is not always present.

I am suggesting that the act of speaking must always be referred to the state of talk that is sustained through the particular turn at talking, and that this state of talk involves a circle of others ratified as coparticipants. (Such a phenomenon as talking to oneself, or talking to unratified recipients as in the case of collusive communication, or telephone talk, must first be seen as a departure from the norm, else its structure and significance will be lost.) Talk is socially organized, not merely in terms of who speaks to whom in what language, but as a little system of mutually ratified and ritually governed face-to-face action, a social encounter. Once a state of talk has been ratified, cues must be available for requesting the floor and giving it up, for informing the speaker as to the stability of the focus of attention he is receiving. Intimate collaboration must be sustained to ensure that one turn at talking neither overlaps the previous one too much, nor wants for inoffensive conversational supply, for someone's turn must always and exclusively be in progress. If persons are present in the social situation but not ratified as participants in the encounter, then sound level and physical spacing will have to be managed to show respect for these accessible others while not showing suspicion of them.

Utterances do of course submit to linguistic constraints (as do meanings), but at each moment they must do a further job, and it is this job that keeps talk participants busy. Utterances must be presented with an overlay of functional gestures – gestures which prop up states of talk, police them, and keep these little systems of activity going. Sounds are used in this gestural work because sounds, in spoken encounters, happen to be handy; but everything else at hand is systematically used too. Thus many of the properties of talk will have to be seen as alternatives to, or functional equivalents of, extra-linguistic acts, as when, for example, a participant signals his imminent departure from a conversational encounter by changing his posture, or redirecting his perceivable attention, or altering the intonation contour of his last statement.

At one level of analysis, then, the study of writable statements and the study of speaking are different things. At one level of analysis the study of turns at talking and things said during one's turn are part of the study of face-to-face interaction. Face-to-face interaction has its own regulations; it has its own processes and its own structure, and these don't seem to be intrinsically linguistic in character, however often expressed through a linguistic medium.

4 K. H. Basso

'To Give Up on Words':
Silence in Western Apache Culture[1]

A version of this paper appeared in the *Southwestern Journal of Anthropology*, Autumn 1970.

It is not the case that a man who is silent says nothing.
Anonymous

Anyone who has read about American Indians has probably run across statements which impute to them a strong predilection for keeping silent or, as one writer has put it, '. . . a fierce reluctance to speak except when absolutely necessary'. In the popular literature, where this characterization is particularly widespread, it is commonly portrayed as the outgrowth of such dubious causes as 'instinctive dignity', 'an impoverished language' or, perhaps worst of all, the Indians' 'lack of personal warmth'. Although statements of this sort are plainly erroneous and dangerously misleading, it is noteworthy that professional anthropologists have made few attempts to correct them. Traditionally, ethnographers and linguists have paid little attention to cultural interpretations given to silence nor, equally important, the types of social contexts in which it regularly occurs.

1. At different times during the period extending from 1964–9 the research on which this paper is based was supported by USPHS Grant M H-12691-01, a grant from the American Philosophical Society, and funds from the Doris Duke Oral History Project at the Arizona State Museum. I am pleased to acknowledge this support. I would also like to express my gratitude to the following scholars for commenting upon an earlier draft: Y. R. Chao, Harold C. Conklin, Roy G. D'Andrade, Charles O. Frake, Paul Friedrich, John Gumperz, Kenneth Hale, Harry Hoijer, Dell Hymes, Stanley Newman, David M. Schneider, Joel Sherzer and Paul Turner. Although the final version gained much from their criticisms and suggestions, responsibility for its present form and content rests solely with the author. A preliminary version of this paper was presented to the Annual Meeting of the American Anthropological Association in New Orleans, Louisiana, November 1969.

This study investigates certain aspects of silence in the culture of the Western Apache of east-central Arizona. After considering some of the theoretical issues involved, I will briefly describe a number of situations – recurrent in Western Apache society – in which one or more of the participants typically refrain from speech for lengthy periods of time.[2] This is accompanied by a discussion of how such acts of silence are interpreted and the reasons they are encouraged and deemed appropriate. I conclude by advancing an hypothesis that accounts for why the Western Apache refrain from speaking when they do and suggest that, with proper testing, this hypothesis may be shown to have relevance to silence behavior in other cultures.

A basic finding of sociolinguistics is that, although both language and language usage are structured, it is the latter which responds most sensitively to extra-linguistic influences (Hymes, 1962, 1964; Ervin-Tripp, 1964, 1967; Gumperz, 1964; Slobin, 1967). Accordingly, a number of recent studies have addressed themselves to the problem of how factors in the social environment of speech events delimit the range and condition the selection of message forms (cf. Brown and Gilman, 1960; Conklin, 1959; Ervin-Tripp, 1964, 1967; Frake, 1964; Friedrich, 1966; Gumperz, 1961, 1964; Martin, 1964). These studies may be viewed as taking the now familiar position that verbal communication is fundamentally a decision-making process in which, initially, a speaker, having elected to speak, selects from among a repertoire of available codes that which is most appropriately suited to the situation at hand. Once a code has been selected, the speaker chooses a suitable channel of transmission and then, finally, from a set of referentially equivalent expressions within the code. The intelligibility of the expression he chooses will, of course, be subject to grammatical constraints. But its acceptability will not. Rules for the selection of linguistic alternates operate on features

2. The situations described in this paper are not the only ones in which the Western Apache refrain from speech. There is a second set – not considered here because my data are incomplete – in which silence appears to occur as a gesture of respect, usually to persons in positions of authority. A third set, very poorly understood, involves ritual specialists, who claim they must keep silent at certain points during the preparation of ceremonial paraphernalia.

of the social environment and are commensurate with rules governing the conduct of face-to-face interaction. As such, they are properly conceptualized as lying outside the structure of language itself.

It follows from this that for a stranger to communicate appropriately with the members of an unfamiliar society it is not enough that he learn to formulate messages intelligibly. Something else is needed: a knowledge of what kinds of codes, channels and expressions to use, in what kinds of situations, to what kinds of people – as Hymes (1964) has termed it, an 'ethnography of communication'.

There is considerable evidence to suggest that extra-linguistic factors influence not only the use of speech but its actual occurrence as well. In our own culture, for example, remarks such as 'Don't you know when to keep quiet?', 'Don't talk until you're introduced' and 'Remember now, no talking in church' all point to the fact that one's decision to speak may be directly contingent upon the character of his surroundings. Few of us would maintain that 'silence is golden' or 'a virtue' for all people at all times. But we feel that it is for some people some times, and we encourage children on the road to cultural competence to act accordingly.

Although the form of silence is always the same, the function of a specific act of silence – that is, its interpretation by and effect upon other people – will vary according to the social context in which it occurs. For example, if I choose to keep silent in the chambers of a Justice of the Supreme Court my action is likely to be interpreted as a sign of politeness or respect. On the other hand, if I refrain from speaking to an established friend or colleague I am apt to be accused of rudeness or harboring a grudge. In one instance, my behavior is judged by others to be 'correct' or 'fitting'; in the other it is criticized as being 'out of line'.

The point, I think, is fairly obvious. For a stranger entering an alien society, a knowledge of when *not* to speak may be as basic to the production of culturally acceptable behavior as a knowledge of what to say. It stands to reason, then, that an adequate ethnography of communication should not confine itself exclusively to the analysis of choice within verbal repertoires. It should also, as Hymes (1962, 1964) has suggested, specify those conditions under which the members of the society regularly decide to refrain from verbal behavior altogether.

The research on which this paper is based was conducted over a period of sixteen months (1964–69) in the Western Apache settlement of Cibecue, which is located near the center of the Fort Apache Indian Reservation in east-central Arizona. Cibecue's 800 residents participate in an unstable economy that combines subsistence agriculture, cattle-raising, sporadic wage-earning, and Government subsidies in the form of welfare checks and social security benefits. Unemployment is a serious problem and sub-standard living conditions are widespread.

Although Reservation life has precipitated far-reaching changes in the composition and geographical distribution of Western Apache social groups, consanguineal kinship – real and imputed – remains the single most powerful force in the establishment and regulation of interpersonal relationships (Kaut, 1957; Basso, 1970). The focus of domestic activity is the individual 'camp', or *gowáá*. This term labels both the occupants and the location of a single dwelling or, as is more apt to be the case, several dwellings built within a few feet of each other. The majority of *gowáá* in Cibecue are occupied by nuclear families. The next largest residential unit is the *gotáá* ('camp cluster'): a group of spatially localized *gowáá*, each of which has at least one adult member who is related by ties of matrilineal kinship to persons living in all the others. An intricate system of exogamous clans serves to extend kinship relationships beyond the *gowáá* and *gotáá* and facilitates concerted action in projects – most notably the presentation of ceremonials – requiring large amounts of manpower. Despite the presence in Cibecue of a variety of Anglo missionaries and a dwindling number of medicine men, diagnostic and curing rituals, as well as the girls' puberty ceremonial, continue to be performed with regularity (Basso, 1966, 1970). Witchcraft persists in un-diluted form (Basso, 1969).

Of the many broad categories of events, or scenes, that comprise the daily round of Western Apache life, I shall deal here only with those that are co-terminous with what Goffman (1961, 1964) has called *focused gatherings* or *encounters*. The concept *situation*, in keeping with established usage, will refer inclusively to the location of such a gathering, its physical setting, its point in time, the standing behavior patterns that accompany it, and the social attributes of the persons involved (Hymes, 1962, 1964; Ervin-Tripp, 1964, 1967).

In what follows, however, I will be mainly concerned with the roles and statuses of participants. This is because the critical factor in the Apache's decision to speak or keep silent seems always to be the nature of his relationships to other people. To be sure, other features of the situation are significant, but apparently only to the extent that they influence the perception of status and role.[3] What this implies, of course, is that roles and statuses are not fixed attributes. Although they may be depicted as such in a static model (and often with good reason), they are appraised and acted upon in particular social contexts and, as a result, subject to re-definition and variation.[4] With this in mind, let us now turn our attention to the Western Apache and the types of situations in which, as one of my informants put it, '... it is right to give up on words.'

1. 'Meeting strangers' (*nda dòhwáá 'iltsééda*). The term *nda* labels categories at two levels of contrast. At the most general level, it designates any person – Apache or non-Apache – who, prior to an initial meeting, has never been seen and therefore cannot be identified. In addition, the term is used to refer to Apaches who, though previously seen and known by some external criteria such as clan affiliation or personal name, have

3. Recent work in the sociology of interaction, most notably by Goffman (1963) and Garfinkel (1967), has led to the suggestion that social relationships are everywhere the major determinants of verbal behavior. In this case, as Gumperz (1967) makes clear, it becomes methodologically unsound to treat the various components of communicative events as independent variables. Gumperz (1967) has presented a hierarchical model, sensitive to dependency, in which components are seen as stages in the communication process. Each stage serves as the input for the next. The basic stage, i.e., the initial input, is 'social identities or statuses.' For further details see Slobin (1967, pp. 131–4).

4. I would like to stress that the emphasis placed on social relations is fully in keeping with how the Western Apache interpret their own behavior. When my informants were asked to explain why they or someone else was silent on a particular occasion, they invariably did so in terms of *who* was present at the time.

never been engaged in face-to-face interaction. The latter category, which is more restricted than the first, typically includes individuals who live on the adjacent San Carlos Reservation, in Fort Apache settlements geographically removed from Cibecue, and those who fall into the category *kii dòhandáágo* ('non-kinsmen'). In all cases, 'strangers' are separated by social distance. And in all cases it is considered appropriate, when encountering them for the first time, to refrain from speaking.

The type of situation described as 'meeting strangers' (*nda dòhwáá 'iltsééda*) can take place in any number of different physical settings. However, it occurs most frequently in the context of events such as fairs and rodeos which, owing to the large number of people in attendance, offer unusual opportunities for chance encounters. In large gatherings, the lack of verbal communication between 'strangers' is apt to go unnoticed, but in smaller groups it becomes quite conspicuous. The following incident, involving two 'strangers' who found themselves part of a four man round-up crew, serves as a good example. My informant, who was also a member of the crew, recalled:

One time, I was with A, B and X down at Gleason Flat working cattle. That man, X, was from East Fork (a community nearly forty miles from Cibecue) where B's wife was from. But he didn't know A, never knew him before, I guess. First day, I worked with X. At night, when we camped, we talked with B, but X and A didn't say anything to each other. Same way, second day. Same way, third. Then, at night on fourth day, we were sitting by the fire. Still, X and A didn't talk. Then A said: 'Well, I know there is a stranger to me here, but I've been watching him and I know he is alright.' After that, X and A talked a lot.... Those two men didn't know each other, so they took it easy at first.

As this incident suggests, the Western Apache do not feel compelled to 'introduce' persons who are unknown to each other. Eventually it is assumed, 'strangers' will begin to speak. However, this is a decision that is properly left up to the individuals involved and no attempt is made to hasten it. Outside help in the form of 'introductions' or other verbal routines is viewed as presumptuous and unnecessary.

'Strangers' who are quick to launch into conversation are frequently eyed with undisguised suspicion. A typical reaction to such individuals is that they 'want something', that is, their willingness to violate convention is attributed to some urgent need which is likely to result in requests for money, labor or transportation. Another common reaction to talkative 'strangers' is that they are drunk.

If the stranger is an Anglo, it is usually assumed that he 'wants to teach us something' (i.e., give orders or instructions) or that he 'wants to make friends in a hurry'. The latter response is especially revealing, since Western Apaches are extremely reluctant to be hurried into friendships – with Anglos or each other. Their verbal reticence with 'strangers' is directly related to the conviction that the establishment of social relationships is a serious matter that calls for caution, careful judgement and plenty of time.

2. 'Courting' (*líígoláá*). During the initial stages of courtship, young men and women go without speaking for conspicuous lengths of time. 'Courting' may occur in a wide variety of settings – practically anywhere, in fact – and at virtually any time of the day or night, but it is most readily observable at large public gatherings such as ceremonials, wakes and rodeos. At these events, 'sweethearts' (*zééde*) may stand or sit (sometimes holding hands) for as long as an hour without exchanging a word. I am told by adult informants that the young people's reluctance to speak may become even more pronounced in situations where they find themselves alone.

Apaches who have just begun to court attribute their silence to 'intense shyness' (*'isté'*) and a feeling of acute 'self-consciousness' (*dàyéézi'*) which, they claim, stems from their lack of familiarity with one another. More specifically, they complain of 'not knowing what to do' in each other's presence and of the fear that whatever they say – no matter how well thought out in advance – will sound 'dumb' or 'stupid'.[5]

5. Among the Western Apache, rules of exogamy discourage courtship between members of the same clan (*kii àlhánigo*) and so-called 'related' clans (*kii*), with the result that 'sweethearts' are almost always 'non-matrilineal kinsmen' (*dòh-wàkíída*). Compared to 'matrilineal kinsmen' (*kii*), such individuals have fewer opportunities during childhood to establish close personal relationships and thus, when courtship begins, have relatively little knowledge of each other. It is not surprising, therefore, that their behavior is similar to that accorded 'strangers'.

One informant, a youth seventeen years old, commented as follows:

It's hard to talk with your sweetheart at first. She doesn't know you and won't know what to say. It's the same way towards her. You don't know how to talk yet ... so you get very bashful. That makes it sometimes so you don't say anything. So you just go around together and don't talk. At first, it's better that way. Then, after a while, when you know each other, you aren't shy anymore and can talk good.

The Western Apache draw an equation between the ease and frequency with which a young couple talks and how well they know each other. Thus, it is expected that after several months of steady companionship 'sweethearts' will start to have lengthy conversations. Earlier in their relationship, however, protracted discussions may be openly discouraged. This is especially true for girls, who are informed by their mothers and older sisters that silence in courtship is a sign of modesty and that an eagerness to speak betrays previous experience with men. In extreme cases, they add, it may be interpreted as a willingness to engage in sexual relations. Said one woman, aged 32:

This way I have talked to my daughter. 'Take it easy when boys come around this camp and want you to go somewhere with them. When they talk to you, just listen at first. Maybe you won't know what to say. So don't talk about just anything. If you talk with those boys right away, then they will know you know all about them. They will think you've been with many boys before and they will start talking about that.

3. 'Children, coming home' (*čəɡə́še nakáii*). The Western Apache lexeme *iltá' ìnatsáá* ('reunion') is used to describe encounters between an individual who has returned home after a long absence and his relatives and friends. The most common type of 'reunion', called *čəɡə́še nakáii* ('children, coming home'), involves boarding school students and their parents. This type of 'reunion' occurs in late May or early in June, and its setting is usually a trading post or school, where parents congregate to await the arrival of buses bringing the children home. As the latter disembark and locate their parents in the crowd, one anticipates a flurry of verbal greetings. Typically, however, there are very few or none at all. Indeed, it is not unusual for parents and child to go without speaking for as long as fifteen minutes.

When the silence is broken, it is almost always the child who breaks it. His parents listen attentively to everything he says, but speak hardly at all themselves. This pattern persists even after the family has reached the privacy of its camp, and two or three days may pass before the child's parents seek to engage him in sustained conversation.

According to my informants, the silence of Western Apache parents at (and after) 'reunions' with their children is ultimately predicted on the possibility that the latter have been adversely affected by their experiences away from home. Uppermost is the fear that, as a result of protracted exposure to Anglo attitudes and values, the children have come to view their parents as ignorant, old-fashioned and no longer deserving of respect. One of my most thoughtful and articulate informants commented on the problem as follows:

You just can't tell about those children after they've been with Whitemen for a long time. They get their minds turned around sometimes ... they forget where they come from and get ashamed when they come home because their parents and relatives are poor. They forget how to act with these Apaches and get mad easy. They walk around all night and get into fights. They don't stay at home.

At school, some of them learn to want to be Whitemen, so they come back and try to act that way. But we are still Apaches! So we don't know them anymore, and it is like we never knew them. It is hard to talk to them when they are like that.

Apache parents openly admit that, initially, children who have been away to school seem distant and unfamiliar. They have grown older, of course, and their physical appearance may have changed. But more fundamental is the concern that they have acquired new ideas and expectations which will alter their behavior in unpredictable ways. No matter how pressing this concern may be, however, it is considered inappropriate to directly interrogate a child after his arrival home. Instead, parents anticipate that within a short time he will begin to divulge information about himself that will enable them to determine in what ways, if any, his views and attitudes have changed. This, the Apache say, is why children do practically all the talking in the hours following a 'reunion' and their parents remain unusually silent.

Said one man, the father of two children who had recently returned from boarding school in Utah:

Yes, it's right that we didn't talk much to them when they came back, my wife and me. They were away for a long time and we didn't know how they would like it, being home. So we waited. Right away, they started to tell stories about what they did. Pretty soon we could tell they liked it, being back. That made us feel good. So it was easy to talk to them again. It was like they were before they went away.

4. 'Getting cussed out' (*šílditéé*). This lexeme is used to describe any situation in which one individual, angered and enraged, shouts insults and criticisms at another. Although the object of such invective is in most cases the person or persons who provoked it, this is not always the case because an Apache who is truly beside himself with rage is likely to vent his feelings on anyone he sees or who happens to be within range of his voice. Consequently, 'getting cussed out' may involve large numbers of people who are totally innocent of the charges being hurled against them. But whether they are innocent or not, their response to the situation is the same. They refrain from speech.

Like the types of situations we have discussed thus far, 'getting cussed out' can occur in a wide variety of physical settings: at ceremonial dance-grounds and trading posts, inside and outside wickiups and houses, on food-gathering expeditions and shopping trips – in short, wherever and whenever individuals lose control of their tempers and lash out verbally at persons nearby.

Although 'getting cussed out' is basically free of setting-imposed restrictions, the Western Apache fear it most at gatherings where alcohol is being consumed. My informants observed that especially at 'drinking parties' (*dá' idláá*), where there is much rough joking and ostensibly mock criticism, it is easy for well-intentioned remarks to be misconstrued as insults. Provoked in this way, persons who are intoxicated may become hostile and launch into explosive tirades, often with no warning at all.

The silence of Apaches who are 'getting cussed out' is consistently explained in reference to the belief that individuals who are 'enraged' (*haškéé*) are also irrational or 'crazy' (*bíné' idíí*). In this condition, it is said, they 'forget who they are' and become oblivious to what they say or do. Concomitantly, they lose all concern for the consequences of their actions on other people. In a word, they are dangerous. Said one informant:

When people get mad they get crazy. Then they start yelling and saying bad things. Some say they are going to kill somebody for what he has done. Some keep it up that way for a long time, maybe walk from camp to camp, real angry, yelling, crazy like that. They keep it up for a long time, some do.

People like that don't know what they are saying, so you can't tell about them. When you see someone like that, just walk away. If he yells at you, let him say whatever he wants to. Let him say anything. Maybe he doesn't mean it. But he doesn't know that. He will be crazy and he could try to kill you.

Another Apache said:

When someone gets mad at you and starts yelling, then just don't do anything to make him get worse. Don't try to quiet him down because he won't know why you're doing it. If you try to do that, he may just get worse and try to hurt you.

As the last of these statements implies, the Western Apache operate on the assumption that enraged persons – because they are temporarily 'crazy' – are difficult to reason with. Indeed, there is a widely held belief that attempts at mollification will serve to intensify anger, thus increasing the chances of physical violence. The appropriate strategy when 'getting cussed out' is to do nothing, to avoid any action that will attract attention to oneself. Since speaking accomplishes just the opposite, the use of silence is strongly advised.

5. 'Being with people who are sad' (*nde dòbílgòzóóda bigáá*). Although the Western Apache phrase that labels this situation has no precise equivalent in English, it refers quite specifically to gatherings in which an individual finds himself in the company of someone whose spouse or kinsman has recently died. Distinct from wakes and burials, which follow immediately after a death, 'being with people who are sad' is most likely to occur several weeks later. At this time, close relatives of the deceased emerge from a period of intense mourning (during which they rarely venture beyond the limits of their camps) and start to resume their normal activities within the community. To persons anxious to convey their sympathies, this is interpreted as a sign that

visitors will be welcomed and, if possible, provided with food and drink. To those less solicitous, it means that unplanned encounters with the bereaved must be anticipated and prepared for.

'Being with people who are sad' can occur on a foot-path, in a camp, at church or in a trading post, but whatever the setting – and regardless of whether it is the result of a planned visit or an accidental meeting – the situation is marked by a minimum of speech. Queried about this, my informants volunteered three types of explanations. The first is that persons 'who are sad' are so burdened with 'intense grief' (*dólgozóóda*) that speaking requires of them an unusual amount of physical effort. It is courteous and considerate, therefore, not to attempt to engage them in conversation.

A second native explanation is that in situations of this sort verbal communication is basically unnecessary. Everyone is familiar with what has happened, and talking about it – even in the interests of conveying solace and sympathy – would only reinforce and augment the sadness felt by those who were close to the deceased. Again, for reasons of courtesy, this is something to be avoided.

The third explanation is rooted in the belief that 'intense grief', like intense rage, produces changes in the personality of the individual who experiences it. As evidence for this, the Western Apache cite numerous instances in which the emotional strain of dealing with death coupled with an overwhelming sense of irrevocable personal loss, has caused persons who were formerly mild and even-tempered to become abusive, hostile, and physically violent.

That old woman, X, who lives across (Cibecue Creek), one time her first husband died. After that she cried all the time, for a long time. Then, I guess she got mean because everyone said she drank a lot and got into fights. Even with her close relatives, she did like that for a long time. She was too sad for her husband. That's what made her like that; it made her lose her mind.

My father was like that when his wife died. He just stayed home all the time and wouldn't go anywhere. He didn't talk to any of his relatives or children. He just said: 'I'm hungry. Cook for me.' That's all. He stayed that way for a long time. His mind was not with us. He was still with his wife.

My uncle died in 1941. His wife sure went crazy right away after that. Two days after they buried the body, we went over there and stayed with those people who had been left alone. My aunt got mad at us. She said: 'Why do you come over here? You can't bring my husband back. I can take care of myself and those others in my camp, so why don't you go home.' She sure was mad that time, too sad for someone who died. She didn't know what she was saying because in about one week she came to our camp and said: 'My relatives, I'm alright now. When you came to help me I had too much sadness and my mind was no good. I said bad words to you. But now I am alright and I know what I am doing.'

As these statements indicate, the Western Apache assume that a person suffering from 'intense grief' is likely to be disturbed and unstable. Even though he may appear outwardly composed, they say, there is always the possibility that he is emotionally upset and therefore unusually prone to volatile outbursts. Apaches acknowledge that such an individual might welcome conversation in the context of 'being with people who are sad' but, on the other hand, they fear it might prove incendiary. Under these conditions, which resemble those in situation number 4, it is considered both expedient and appropriate to keep silent.

6. 'Being with someone for whom they sing' (*nde bìdádìstááha bigáá*). The last type of situation to be described is restricted to a small number of physical locations and is more directly influenced by temporal factors than any of the situations we have discussed so far. 'Being with someone for whom they sing' takes place only in the context of 'curing ceremonials' (*gòjitál; èdotál*). These events begin early at night and come to a close shortly before dawn the following day. In the late fall and throughout the winter, curing ceremonials are held inside the patient's wickiup or house. In the spring and summer, they are located outside, at some open place near the patient's camp or at specially designated dance-grounds where group rituals of all kinds are regularly performed.

Prior to the start of a curing ceremonial, all persons in attendance may feel free to talk with the patient; indeed, because he is so much a focus of concern it is expected that friends and relatives will seek him out to offer encouragement and support. Conversation breaks off, however, when the patient is informed that the ceremonial is about to begin, and it ceases entirely when the presiding medicine man commences to chant. From this point on – until the completion of the final chant next morning – it is inappropriate for anyone except the medicine man (and, if he has them, his aides) to speak to the patient.[6]

In order to appreciate the explanation Apaches give for this prescription, we must briefly discuss the concept of 'supernatural power' (*diyi'*,) and describe some of the effects it is believed to have on persons at whom it is directed. Elsewhere (Basso, 1969, p. 30) I have defined 'power' as follows:

The term *diyi'* refers to one or all of a set of abstract and invisible forces which are said to derive from certain classes of animals, plants, minerals, meteorological phenomena, and mythological figures within the Western Apache universe. Any of the various powers may be acquired by man and, if properly handled, used for a variety of purposes.

A 'power' that has been antagonized by disrespectful behavior towards its source may retaliate by causing the offender to become sick. 'Power-caused illnesses' (*kásití diyi'bil*) are properly treated with curing ceremonials in which one or more medicine men, using chants and various items of ritual paraphernalia, attempt to neutralize the sickness-causing 'power' with 'powers' of their own.

Roughly two-thirds of my informants assert that a medicine man's 'power' actually enters the body of the patient; others maintain that it simply closes in and envelops him. In any case, all agree that the patient is brought into intimate contact with a potent supernatural force which elevates him to a condition labeled *gòdiyó'* ('sacred'; 'holy').

The term *gòdiyó'* may also be translated as 'potentially harmful' and, in this sense, is regularly used to describe classes of objects (including all sources of 'power') that are surrounded with taboos. In keeping with the semantics of *gòdiyó'*, the Western Apache explain that, besides making patients 'holy', 'power' makes them 'potentially harmful'. And it is this transformation, they explain, that is basically responsible for the cessation of verbal communication during curing ceremonials.

6. I have witnessed over seventy-five curing ceremonials since 1961 and have seen this rule violated only six times. On four occasions, drunks were at fault. In the other two cases, the patient fell asleep and had to be awakened.

Said one informant:

When they start singing for someone like that, he sort of goes away with what the medicine man is working with (i.e. a power). Sometimes people they sing for don't know you, even after it (the curing ceremonial) is over. They get 'holy' and you shouldn't try to talk to them when they are like that . . . it's best to leave them alone.

Another informant commented along similar lines:

When they sing for someone, what happens is like this: that man for whom they sing doesn't know why he is sick or which way to go. So the medicine man has to show him and work on him. That is when he gets 'holy' and that makes him go off somewhere in his mind, so you should stay away from him.

Because Apaches undergoing ceremonial treatment are perceived as having been changed by 'power' into something different from their normal selves, they are regarded with caution and apprehension. Their newly acquired status places them in close proximity to the supernatural and, as such, carries with it a very real element of danger and uncertainty. These conditions combine to make 'being with someone for whom they sing' a situation in which speech is considered disrespectful and, if not exactly harmful, at least potentially hazardous.

Although the types of situations described below differ from one another in obvious ways, I will argue in what follows that the underlying determinants of silence are in each case basically the same. Specifically, I will attempt to defend the hypothesis that keeping silent in Western Apache culture is associated with social situations in which participants perceive their relationships *vis à vis* one another to be ambiguous and/or unpredictable.

Let us begin with the observation that, in all the situations we have described, *silence is defined as appropriate with respect to a specific individual or individuals*. In other words, the use of speech is not directly curtailed by the setting of a situation, nor by the physical activities that accompany it, but rather by the perceived social and psychological attributes of at least one focal participant.

It may also be observed that, in each type of situation, *the status of the focal participant is marked by ambiguity* – either because he is unfamiliar to other participants in the situation or because, owing to some recent event, a status he formerly held has been changed or is in a process of transition.

Thus, in situation number 1, persons who earlier considered themselves 'strangers' move towards something else, perhaps 'friend' (*šídikéé*), perhaps 'enemy' (*šikédndíí*). In situation number 2, young people who have had relatively limited exposure to one another attempt to adjust to the new and intimate status of 'sweetheart'. These two situations are similar in that the focal participants have little or no prior knowledge of each other. Their social identities are not as yet clearly defined and their expectations, lacking the foundation of previous experience, are poorly developed.

Situation number 3 is somewhat different. Although the participants – parents and their children – are well known to each other, their relationship has been seriously interrupted by the latter's prolonged absence from home. This, combined with the possibility that recent experiences at school have altered the children's attitudes, introduces a definite element of unfamiliarity and doubt. Situation number 3 is not characterized by the absence of role expectations but by the participants' perception that those already in existence may be outmoded and in need of revision.

Status ambiguity is present in situation number 4 because a focal participant is enraged and, as a result, considered 'crazy'. Until he returns to a more rational condition, others in the situation simply have no way of telling how he will behave. Situation number 5 is similar in that the personality of a focal participant is seen to have undergone a marked shift which makes his actions more difficult to anticipate. In both situations, the status of focal participants is uncertain because of real or imagined changes in their psychological makeup.

In situation number 6, a focal participant is ritually transformed from an essentially neutral state to one which is contextually defined as 'potentially harmful'. Ambiguity and apprehension accompany this transition and, as in situation numbers 4 and 5, established patterns of interaction must be waived until the focal participant reverts to a less threatening condition.

This discussion points up a third feature characteristic of all situations: *the ambiguous status of focal participants is accom-*

panied either by the absence or suspension of established role expectations. In every instance, as we have seen, non-focal participants (i.e. those who refrain from speech) are either uncertain of how the focal participant will behave towards them or, conversely, how they should behave towards him. Stated in the simplest way possible, their roles become blurred with the result that established expectations – if they exist – lose their relevance as guidelines for social action and must be temporarily discarded or abruptly modified.

We are now in a position to expand upon our initial hypothesis and make it more explicit.

1. In Western Apache culture, the absence of verbal communication is associated with social situations in which the status of focal participants is ambiguous.

2. Under these conditions, fixed role expectations lose their applicability and the illusion of predicability in social interaction is lost.

3. To sum up and reiterate: keeping silent among the Western Apache is a response to uncertainty and unpredicability in social relations.

The question remains to what extent the foregoing hypothesis helps to account for silence behavior in other cultures. Unfortunately, it is impossible at the present time to provide anything approaching a conclusive answer. Standard ethnographies contain very little information about the circumstances under which verbal communication is discouraged, and it is only within the past few years that problems of this sort have engaged the attention of socio-linguists. The result is that adequate cross-cultural data are almost completely lacking.

As a first step towards the elimination of this deficiency, an attempt is now being made to investigate the occurrence and interpretation of silence in other Indian societies of the American Southwest. Our findings at this early stage, though neither fully representative nor sufficiently detailed, suggest that the types of social contexts in which Western Apaches refrain from speech are closely paralleled by those in which the members of several other Arizona tribes – most notably the Navajo and Papago – exhibit similar behavior.[7] If this impression is confirmed by further research, it will lend obvious cross-cultural support to the hypothesis advanced above. But regardless of the final outcome, the situational determinants of silence seem eminently deserving of further study. For as we become better informed about the types of contextual variables that mitigate against the use of verbal codes, we should also learn more about those variables that encourage and promote them.

7. By way of illustration, I quote below from portions of a preliminary report prepared by Priscilla Mowrer (1970), herself a Navajo, who inquired into the situational features of Navajo silence behavior in the vicinity of Tuba City on the Navajo Reservation in east-central Arizona.

(a) *Silence and Courting:* Navajo youngsters of the opposite sex just getting to know one another say nothing, except to sit close together and maybe hold hands. . . . In public, they may try not to let on that they are interested in each other, but in private it is another matter. If the girl is at a gathering where the boy is also present, she may go off by herself. Falling in step, the boy will generally follow. They may just walk around or find someplace to sit down. But, at first, they will not say anything to each other.

(b) *Silence and Long Absent Relatives:* When a male or female relative returns home after being gone for six months or more, he (or she) is first greeted with a handshake. If the returnee is male, the female greeter may embrace him and cry – the male, meanwhile, will remain dry-eyed and silent.

(c) *Silence and Anger:* The Navajo tend to remain silent when being shouted at by a drunk or angered individual because that particular individual is considered temporarily insane. To speak to such an individual, the Navajo believe, just tends to make the situation worse. . . . People remain silent because they believe that the individual is not himself, that he may have been witched, and is not responsible for the change in his behavior.

(d) *Silent Mourning:* Navajos speak very little when mourning the death of a relative. . . . The Navajo mourn and cry together in pairs. Men will embrace one another and cry together. Women, on the other hand, will hold one another's hand and cry together.

(e) *Silence and the Ceremonial Patient:* The Navajo consider it wrong to talk to a person being sung over. The only people who talk to the patient are the medicine man and a female relative (or male relative if the patient is male) who is in charge of food preparation. The only time the patient speaks openly is when the medicine man asks her (or him) to pray along with him.

References

BASSO, K. H. (1966), 'The gift of changing woman', *Bulletin of the Bureau of American Ethnology*, no. 196, Smithsonian Institution.
BASSO, H. (1969), 'Western Apache witchcraft', *Anthropological Papers of the University of Arizona*, no. 15.

BASSO, H. (1970), 'The Cibecue Apache', in G. and L. Spindler (eds.),
   Case Studies in Cultural Anthropology, Holt, Rinehart and Winston.
BROWN, R. W. and GILMAN, A. (1960), 'The pronouns of power and
   solidarity', in T. Sebeck (ed.), *Style in Language*, MIT Press,
   (reprinted in this volume, pp. 252–82.)
CONKLIN, H. C. (1959), 'Linguistic play in its cultural context',
   Language, vol. 35, 631–36.
ERVIN-TRIPP, S. (1964), 'An analysis of the interaction of language,
   topic and listener', in J. Gumperz and D. Hymes (eds.), *The
   Ethnography of Communication*, *Amer. Anthrop.*, vol. 66, no. 6, part 2,
   pp. 86–102.
ERVIN-TRIPP, S. (1967), 'Sociolinguistics', Working Paper no. 3,
   Language-Behavior Research Laboratory, University of California,
   Berkeley.
FRAKE, C. O. (1964), 'How to ask for a drink in Subanun', in J. Gumperz
   and D. Hymes (eds.), *The Ethnography of Communication*, *Amer.
   Anthrop.*, vol. 66, no. 6, part 2, pp. 127–32 (reprinted in this volume
   pp. 87–94).
FRIEDRICH, P. (1966), 'Structural implications of Russian pronominal
   usage', in W. Bright (ed.), *Sociolinguistics*, Mouton.
GARFINKEL, H. (1967), *Studies in Ethnomethodology*, Prentice-Hall.
GOFFMAN, E. (1961), *Encounters: Two Studies in the Sociology of
   Interaction*, Bobbs-Merril.
GOFFMAN, E. (1963), *Behavior in Public Places*, Free Press.
GOFFMAN, E. (1964), 'The Neglected Situation', in J. Gumperz and
   D. Hymes (eds.), *The Ethnography of Communication*, *Amer. Anthrop.*
   vol. 66, pp. 133–6 (reprinted in this volume pp. 61–6).
GUMPERZ, J. (1961), 'Speech variation and the study of Indian
   civilization', *Amer. Anthrop.*, vol. 63, pp. 976–88.
GUMPERZ, J. (1964), 'Linguistic and social interaction in two
   communities', in J. Gumperz and D. Hymes (eds.), *The Ethnography of
   Communication*, *Amer. Anthrop.*, vol. 66, no. 6, part 2, pp. 137–53.
GUMPERZ, J. (1967), 'The social setting of linguistic behavior', in
   D. I. Slobin (ed.), *A Field Manual for Cross-cultural Study of the
   Acquisition of Communicative Competence* (second draft), University of
   California Press.
HYMES, D. (1962), 'The ethnography of speaking', in T. Gladwin and
   W. C. Sturtevant (eds.), *Anthropology and Human Behavior*, The
   Anthropological Society of Washington.
HYMES, D. (1964), *Introduction: Toward Ethnographies of Communication*,
   J. Gumperz and D. Hymes (eds.), *Amer. Anthrop.*, vol. 66, no. 6, part 2,
   pp. 1–34 (Partially reprinted in this volume, pp. 21–44).
KAUT, C. R. (1957), 'The western Apache clan system: its origins and
   development', *University of New Mexico Publications in Anthropology*,
   no. 9, Albuquerque.
MARTIN, S. (1964), 'Speech levels in Japan and Korea', in D. Hymes
   (ed.), *Language in Culture and Society*, Harper and Row.

MOWRER, P. (1970), 'Notes on Navajo silence behavior', unpublished manuscript, University of Arizona.

NEWMAN, S. (1955), 'Vocabulary levels: Zuni sacred and slang', *Southwestern J. of Anthrop.*, vol. 11, pp. 345–54.

SLOBIN, D. I. (ed.) (1967), *A Field Manual for Cross-cultural Study of the Acquisition of Communicative Competence* (second draft), University of California Press.

5 C. O. Frake

How to Ask for a Drink in Subanun[1]

C. O. Frake, 'How to ask for a drink in Subanun',
American Anthropologist, vol. 66, 1964, no. 6, part 2, pp. 127–32.

Ward Goodenough (1957) has proposed that a description of a culture – an ethnography – should properly specify what it is that a stranger to a society would have to know in order appropriately to perform any role in any scene staged by the society. If an ethnographer of Subanun culture were to take this notion seriously, one of the most crucial sets of instructions to provide would be that specifying how to ask for a drink. Anyone who cannot perform this operation successfully will be automatically excluded from the stage upon which some of the most dramatic scenes of Subanun life are performed.

To ask appropriately for a drink among the Subanun it is not enough to know how to construct a grammatical utterance in Subanun translatable in English as a request for a drink. Rendering such an utterance might elicit praise for one's fluency in Subanun, but it probably would not get one a drink. To speak appropriately it is not enough to speak grammatically or even sensibly (in fact some speech settings may require the uttering of nonsense as is the case with the semantic-reversal type of speech play common in the Philippines. See Conklin, 1959). Our stranger requires more than a grammar and a lexicon; he needs what Hymes (1962) has called an ethnography of speaking: a specification of what kinds of things to say in what message forms to

1. The Subanun are pagan swidden agriculturists occupying the mountainous interior of Zamboanga Peninsula on the island of Mindanao in the Philippines. This paper refers to the Eastern Subanun of Zamboanga del Norte Province. Descriptions of Subanun social structure, festive activities, and some aspects of *gasi* manufacture are given in Frake 1960, 1963, 1964a, and 1964b. The ethnographic methodology of this paper is that described in Frake 1964b. Single quotation marks enclose English substitutes for (but not translations of) Subanun expressions.

what kinds of people in what kinds of situations. Of course an ethnography of speaking cannot provide rules specifying exactly what message to select in a given situation. If messages were perfectly predictable from a knowledge of the culture, there would be little point in saying anything. But when a person selects a message, he does so from a set of appropriate alternatives. The task of an ethnographer of speaking is to specify what the appropriate alternatives are in a given situation and what the consequences are of selecting one alternative over another.

Drinking defined. Of the various substances which the Subanun consider 'drinkable', we are here concerned only with a subset called *gasi*, a rice-yeast fermented beverage made of a rice, manioc, maize, and/or Job's tears mash. *Gasi*, glossed in this paper as 'beer', contrasts in linguistic labelling, drinking technique, and social context with all other Subanun beverages (*tebaq* 'toddy', *sebug* 'wine', *binu*, 'liquor', *sabaw* 'juice-broth', *tubig* 'water').

The context of drinking. Focused social gatherings (Goffman, 1961) among the Subanun fall into two sharply contrasted sets: festive gatherings or 'festivities' and nonfestive or informal gatherings (Frake, 1964b). The diagnostic feature of a festivity is the consumption of a festive meal as a necessary incident in the encounter. A 'meal' among the Subanun necessarily comprises a serving of a cooked starchy-staple food, the 'main dish', and ordinarily also includes a 'side dish' of vegetables, fish, or meat. A festive meal, or 'feast', is a meal with a meat side dish. A 'festivity' comprises all socially relevant events occurring between the arrival and dispersal of participants in a feast. Apart from a feast, the necessary features of a festivity are (1) an occasioning event, (2) multi-family participation, and (3) beer. The drinking of beer, unlike the consumption of any other beverage, occurs only during a festivity and must occur as part of any festivity. It occupies a crucial position as a focus of formal social gatherings.

Drinking technique. 'Beer', uniquely among Subanun drinks, is drunk with bamboo straws inserted to the bottom of a Chinese jar containing the fermented mash. Just prior to drinking, the jar is filled to the rim with water. Except in certain types of game drinking, one person drinks at a time, after which another person replenishes the water from an agreed-upon 'measure'. As one sucks on the straw, the water disappears down through the mash where it picks up a surprising amount of alcohol and an indescribable taste. After initial rounds of tasting, drinking etiquette requires one to gauge his consumption so that when a full measure of water is added, the water level rises exactly even with the jar rim.

The drinking encounter. Each beer jar provided for a festivity becomes the focus of a gathering of persons who take turns drinking. A *turn* is a single period of continuous drinking by one person. Each change of drinkers marks a new turn. A circuit of turns through the gathering is a *round*. As drinking progresses, rounds change in character with regard to the number and length of constituent turns and to variations in drinking techniques. Differences in these features among successive sets of rounds mark three distinct stages of the drinking encounter: tasting, competitive drinking and game drinking (table 1).

The first round is devoted to *tasting*, each person taking a brief turn with little regard to formal measurement of consumption. Successive turns become longer and the number of turns per round fewer, thus cutting out some of the participants in the encounter. These individuals go to other jars if available or withdraw from drinking during this stage of *competitive drinking*. Measurement is an important aspect of competitive rounds, participants keeping a mental record of each other's consumption. Within a round, successive drinkers must equal the consumption of the drinker who initiated the round. In later rounds, as the brew becomes weaker, the measure tends to be raised. Continued competitive drinking may assume an altered character signaled by accompanying music, dancing, and singing. The scope of the gathering may enlarge and turns become shorter. Special types of drinking games occur: 'chugalug' (*saŋgayuq*) and dual-drinking by opposite-sexed partners under the cover of a blanket. These rounds form a stage of *game drinking*.

Drinking talk. The Subanun expression for drinking talk, *taluq bwat dig beksuk* 'talk from the straw', suggests an image of the drinking straw as a channel not only of the drink but also of

Table 1 Subanun Drinking Talk

Encounter stages	Discourse stages	Focus of speech acts	Function
1. Tasting	1. Invitation – permission	Role expression	Assignment of role distances and authority relations to participants
2. Competitive drinking	2. Jar talk	Role expression and context definition	Allocation of encounter resources (turns at drinking and talking)
	3. Discussion 3.1. Gossip 3.2. Deliberation	Topic	Exchange of information; disputation, arbitration; deciding issues on basis of cogent argument
3. Game drinking	4. Display of verbal art	Stylistic	Establishment of euphoria. Deciding issues on basis of skill in use of special styles of discourse (singing, verse)

Segments of a drinking encounter:
1. A turn (continuous drinking by one person)
2. A round (a set of related turns)
3. Encounter stage (a set of related rounds)

Segments of drinking talk:
1. An utterance (continuous speech by one person)
2. An exchange (a set of related utterances)
3. Discourse stage (a set of related exchanges)

drinking talk. The two activities, drinking and talking, are closely interrelated in that how one talks bears on how much one drinks and the converse is, quite obviously, also true. Except for 'religious offerings', which must precede drinking, whatever business is to be transacted during a festivity occurs during drinking encounters. Consequently drinking talk is a major medium of interfamily communication. Especially for an adult male, one's role in the society at large, insofar as it is subject to manipulation, depends to a considerable extent on one's verbal performance during drinking encounters.

Subanun society contains no absolute, society-wide status

positions or offices which automatically entitle their holder to deference from and authority over others. The closest approximation to such a formal office is the status of religious specialist or 'medium' who is deferred to in religious matters but who has no special voice in affairs outside his domain (Frake, 1964b). Assumption of decision-making roles in legal, economic, and ecological domains depends not on acquisition of an office but on continuing demonstration of one's ability to make decisions within the context of social encounters. This ability in turn depends on the amount of deference one can evoke from other participants in the encounter. Although relevant, no external status attributes of sex, age or wealth are sufficient to guarantee such deference; it must be elicited through one's skill in the use of speech. Apart from age, sex and reputation from performances in previous encounters, the most salient external attributes brought to an encounter by a participant are his relational roles based on kinship, neighborhood and friendship with specific other participants. Because of consanguineal endogamy and residential mobility, the relationship ties between an ego and any given alter are likely to be multiple and complex, giving wide latitude for manipulation of roles within particular encounters. Moreover, most kinship roles permit a range of interpretation depending upon other features of the relationship such as friendship and residential proximity.

The strategy of drinking talk is to manipulate the assignment of role relations among participants so that, within the limits of one's external status attributes, one can maximize his share of encounter resources (drink and talk), thereby having an opportunity to assume an esteem-attracting and authority-wielding role. Variations in the kinds of messages sent during periods devoted to different aspects of this strategic plan mark four distinct *discourse stages* within the drinking talk of the encounter: invitation-permission, jar talk, discussion, and display of verbal art (table 1). The constituents of a discourse stage are *exchanges:* sets of utterances with a common topic focus. (Boundaries of exchanges in American speech are often marked by such expressions as 'Not to change the subject, but . . .' or 'By the way, that reminds me . . .'.) The constituents of exchanges are *utterances:* stretches of continuous speech by one person.

1. *Invitation-Permission.* The Subanun designate the discourse of the initial tasting round as 'asking permission'. The provider of the jar initiates the tasting round by inviting someone to drink, thereby signaling that this person is the one to whom he and those closest to him in the encounter owe the greatest initial deference on the basis of external status attributes. The invited drinker squats before the jar and asks permission to drink of the other participants. He has two variables to manipulate: the order in which he addresses the other participants and the terms of address he employs. Apart from the latter variable, message form remains relatively constant: *naa, A, sep pa u* 'Well, *A*, I will be drinking.' (*A* represents a term of address.) Role relations with persons who are not lineal consanguineal or lineal affinal kin (Mo, F, Ch, Sp, SpPr, ChSp, ChSpPr) permit a variety of forms of address each with different implications for social distance with respect to ego (Frake, 1960). The drinker's final opportunity to express role relations comes when he finishes tasting and invites another (ordinarily the person who invited him) to drink.

2. *Jar talk.* As competitive drinking begins, asking permission is reduced in scope and importance, and there is an increase in messages sent during drinking itself. The topic focus of these exchanges is the drink being consumed. The drinker responds to queries about the taste and strength of the beer, explanations are advanced for its virtues and defects, and the performance of drinkers is evaluated. During this stage the topic of messages is predictable. The informative aspect of the messages is the quantity and quality of verbal responses a drinker can elicit. This information signals the amount of drinking and talking time the gathering will allot him. Those who receive little encouragement drop out, and the encounter is reduced generally to less than half-a-dozen persons, who can thereby intensify their interaction with each other and with the beer straw.

3. *Discussion.* As the size and role-structure of the gathering becomes defined, discourse changes in topic to removed referents, usually beginning with relatively trivial gossip, proceeding to more important subjects of current interest, and, finally, in many cases arriving at litigation. Since there are no juro-political offices in Subanun society, a legal case is not only a contest

between litigants, but also one between persons attempting to assume a role of legal authority by settling the case. Success in effecting legal decisions depends on achieving a commanding role in the encounter and on debating effectively from that position. Since there are no sanctions of force legally applicable to back up a decision, the payment of a fine in compliance with a decision is final testimony to the prowess in verbal combat of the person who made the decision.

4. Display of verbal art. If drinking continues long enough, the focus of messages shifts from their topics to play with message forms themselves, following stylized patterns of song and verse composition. Songs and verses are composed on the spot to carry on discussions in an operetta-like setting. Even unsettled litigation may be continued in this manner, the basis for decision being shifted from cogent argument to verbal artistry. The most prestigious kinds of drinking songs require the mastery of an esoteric vocabulary by means of which each line is repeated with a semantically equivalent but formally different line. Game drinking is a frequent accompaniment to these displays of verbal art. Together they help assure that the festivity will end with good feelings among all participants, a goal which is explicitly stated by the Subanun. Participants who have displayed marked hostility toward each other during the course of drinking talk may be singled out for special ritual treatment designed to restore good feelings.

The Subanun drinking encounter thus provides a structured setting within which one's social relationships beyond his everyday associates can be extended, defined, and manipulated through the use of speech. The cultural patterning of drinking talk lays out an ordered scheme of role play through the use of terms of address, through discussion and argument, and through display of verbal art. The most skilled in 'talking from the straw' are the *de facto* leaders of the society. In instructing our stranger to Subanun society how to ask for a drink, we have at the same time instructed him how to get ahead socially.

References

CONKLIN, H. C. (1959), 'Linguistic play in its cultural setting', *Language*, vol. 35, pp. 631–36.

C. O. Frake 93

FRAKE, C. O. (1960), 'The Eastern Subanun of Mindanao', in G. P. Murdock (ed.), *Social Structure in Southeast Asia*, Viking Publications in Anthropology, vol. 29, pp. 51–64.

FRAKE, C. O. (1963), 'Litigation in Lipay: a study in Subanun law', *The Proceedings of the Ninth Pacific Science Congress*, 1957, vol. 3, Bangkok.

FRAKE, C. O. (1964a), 'Notes on queries in ethnography', *Amer. Anthrop.*, vol. 66, no. 3, part 2, pp. 132–45.

FRAKE, C. O. (1964b), 'A structural description of Subanun "religious behavior"', in W. G. Goodenough (ed.), *Explorations in Cultural Anthropology: Essays in Honor of George Peter Murdock*, McGraw-Hill.

GOFFMAN, E. (1961), *Encounters: Two Studies in the Sociology of Interaction*, Bobbs-Merrill.

GOODENOUGH, W. G. (1957), 'Cultural anthropology and linguistics', in P. L. Garvin (ed.), *Report of the Seventh Annual Round Table Meeting on Linguistics and Language Study*, Georgetown University Monograph Series on Language and Linguistics, vol. 9, pp. 167–73.

HYMES, D. H. (1962), 'The ethnography of speaking', in T. Gladwin and W. C. Sturtevant (eds.), *Anthropology and Human Behavior*, Anthropological Society of Washington, pp. 15–53.

6 E. A. Schegloff

Notes on a Conversational Practice: Formulating Place[1]

Excerpts from E. A. Schegloff, 'Notes on a Conversational Practice:
Formulating Place', in D. Sudnow (ed.), *Studies in Social Interaction*,
Free Press, 1971.

Selection of location formulations

It has been argued (Sacks, 1967 and forthcoming, b) that a
central observation about 'topic talk' (the argument is made
initially about stories, more generally about 'talk on a topic', and
perhaps holds more generally still) is 'co-selection of features for
topic'. By this is intended: if one looks to the places in conversation where an object (including persons) or activity is identified
(or as I shall call it, 'formulated'), then one can notice that there
is a set of alternative formulations for each such object or activity,
all the formulations being, in some sense, correct (i.e., each
allowing under some circumstance 'retrieval' of the same refer-
rent). Furthermore, that the selections made at each spot are
'fitted' to each other, or 'go together'. Rather than saying 'they
fit the topic', or are 'appropriate to the topic', it may be

1. The research on which this discussion is based was supported by the
Advanced Research Projects Agency, Department of Defense, through the
Air Force Office of Scientific Research under Contract Numbers F-44620-
68-0040 and AF 49 (638)-1761. An earlier version of some parts of the paper
was presented in a public lecture at the University of California, Berkeley,
under the auspices of the Program on Language, Society and the Child in
July, 1968. Both on that occasion and subsequently, I have discussed these
matters with Harvey Sacks to my great profit. I have tried in various places
to specify my indebtedness to him, but there are many others where I might
have done so. While responsibility for the outcome is mine alone, I must
thank Alan Blum for fruitful discussion in the early stages of this paper, and
Erving Goffman and William Labov for critical reading and suggestions.

Symbols used in the transcriptions are explained at the end of the bibliography. Each citation of transcript is followed by a code giving its source. A
description of the bodies of material from which the data are drawn may
also be found at the end of the bibliography. Place names are occasionally
changed to protect anonymity.

preferable to say that in their co-selection, they, at least in part, 'constitute' the topic.

If this is the case, then it would clearly seem foolhardy to try to excerpt from its conversational surroundings some particular formulation, and examine how it was selected out of the set of terms which are, by a correspondence test of truth, equally 'correct'. The selection would seem understandable only as part of the co-selection of the variety of terms occurring in the conversational segment. Nevertheless, at the current stage of investigation, it may be advantageous to undertake just such an examination for certain kinds of collections of terms from which one is selected for use at some point in a conversation.

One such area is that of formulations of members. Because selection of identification of persons is a central resource for invoking common sense knowledge organized by reference to the collections of membership categories (Sacks, 1969, and n.d.), because it is nearly omnipresent in conversation, and because its unexamined co-optation into social science literature can be seen (for some social sciences) as a source of fundamental ambiguity, it appears useful to have considered the problem of the selection of formulations or identification terms for members in temporary isolation from topical context, where it might be analyzed best as part of a co-selection of terms for that conversational fragment. The yield is such as we find in Sacks' papers in this area (see 'Search for help', and forthcoming book).

Although the warrant is considerably weaker, I propose to sketch some considerations relevant to the selection of formulations for another domain – locations. While in that domain also, and perhaps especially, the selection of a formulation or term must ultimately be analyzed in the context of co-selection of many terms, each from a collection of terms of which it is a member, I hope to derive some gains from some reflections on location formulation selection divorced from conversational context. As I am proceeding here in explicit divorce from conversational context, I shall occasionally take a liberty not otherwise to be condoned, of relying at various points on data easily enough recalled to have happened but not recorded and out of conversational context, or invented for the occasion.[2]

2. A central reason for frowning on invented data is that while it can be

When speakers in a conversation make reference to a place, they use some term or formulation of it. This has taken work. I want here to show that this is so; to begin to investigate the character of that work, and its implications; and to suggest one way in which what we can learn about formulating locations can be of help in understanding seeemingly quite unrelated conversational practices.

The problem

The 'problem'[3] of locational formulation is this: for any location to which reference is made, there is a set of terms each of which, by a correspondence test, is a correct way to refer to it. On any actual occasion of use, however, not any member of the set is 'right'. How is it that on particular occasions of use some term from the set is selected, and other terms are rejected?

Were I now to formulate where my notes are, it would be correct to say that they are: right in front of me, next to the telephone, on the desk, in my office, in the office, in Room 213, in Lewisohn Hall, on campus, at school, at Columbia, in Morningside Heights, on the upper West Side, in Manhattan, in New York City, in New York State, in the Northeast, on the Eastern Seaboard, in the United States, etc. Each of these terms could in some sense be correct (if that is where my notes were), were its relevance provided for. On some occasion of use, for some co-conversationalists, under some conditions, in some conversational context, each of these terms (and undoubtedly many others) could, not only 'correctly', but also 'rightly', relevantly, appropriately, be used to formulate that place, while the others would not be used appropriately (or, if used, would be heard as possibly formulating some location, but in addition doing some other activity, such as 'name-dropping', being arrogant, silly, etc.). I seek to direct attention to the sorts of considerations that enter

---

easily invented, it is invented only from the point at which it is relevant to the point being made, thereby eliminating a central resource members use in hearing it, i.e., its placement at some 'here' in a conversation, after X, in short by eliminating its conversational context.

3. By 'problem' I intend not that speakers will have pondered the matter, but that what they say is to be seen by analysts, both professional and lay (i.e. hearers), as a solution, as the outcome of work.

into the selection of a particular formulation, considerations which are part of the work a speaker does in using a particular locational formulation, and the work a hearer does in analyzing its use.

Before turning to those considerations, however, it would be well to discriminate this problem from a related one. Aside from there being a range of place terms available to formulate a location, we should note that place terms can be used to formulate objects other than place. To choose but a few examples, terms which are place terms can be used to formulate occupation:

A: You uh wha 'dijuh do, fer a living?
B: Ehm, I work inna driving school.   1
(BC, B, 20)

They can be used to formulate 'stage of life':

A: When did this happen?
B: When I was in Junior High School.   2
(GTS II, 23)

They can be used to formulate activities:

*4A: What's Jim doing?
B: Oh, he's at the ballpark.

Where a place term is used to formulate something other than location, the first question may be not how that term was selected out of the set of terms that are correct for that place, but rather how a place term came to be used to do a non-place formulation. Such analyses cannot be undertaken here, but it can be noted that in 2 there follows an introduction into the story being told of persons formulated as 'principal', 'teacher', etc., and that in 1, although A understands from B's answer that he is a driving teacher (as the ensuing data makes clear) it later turns out that he is a messenger boy.[5]

The analysis of how a place term was used to do non-locational

4. *Indicates invented data; here the answer could indicate either work or leisure activities, depending on 'Jim's' occupation.

5. On choosing that way of identifying oneself which maximizes status, see Moerman (1967).

Suttles (1968) reports for the slum he studied that with the exception of five occupations, persons answer inquiries about their occupations by reporting the place where they work or the industry, rather than their job title, pp. 46, 100.

formulation may have as its outcome the consequence that of the various terms that are correct for that place, only the one used was responsive to the problem that led to the choice of a location term in the first place (for example, street address would not have set the stage for a cast of characters formulated as school personnel, as in 2, nor would it have allowed inferences about occupation, as in 1). Under those circumstances, the considerations relevant to using *some* place term, may without reference to other considerations select *which* place term. In such cases the central problem is not 'which of alternative place terms would be chosen', but rather 'which of alternative ways of formulating X (stage of life, occupation, current activity, etc.)' one of which is a place term. Here, then, although location formulations are involved, the problem of the selection of location formulations is not the primary one. (The reverse case occurs when non-place terms are used to formulate a location as in: 'A: Is Terry there? B: No, he's teaching a class.' While such cases will not be given much attention here, it is clear that they expand greatly the size of the set from which selection is made in choosing a locational formulation.)

There is a third form, in which place terms are indeed used to formulate location, but where some terms may do other things in addition. For example, 'Good to be back home' may differ from 'Good to be back in Chicago' in that the former is also an account, saying why 'it's good', by reference to the kind of tie there is between members and 'home', it being where one 'belongs'. Or to take another example, to report one's return from 'The Catskills' (rather than Peekskill), from 'The Cape' (rather than Buzzards Bay), Zermatt (rather than Europe) can indicate simultaneously that it is a vacation one is returning from, and the sense of expectable answers to questions such as 'who else was there?'. However, here we are dealing with terms which are properly seen as selected by reference to the problem outlined above, and show attention to the selection for topic of which we spoke earlier. They, therefore, properly fall within the domain we are investigating, and we shall have more to say below about the term 'home', as well as those classes of terms which are 'classes-for-a-topic' (as the class of 'vacation place terms' just used). We turn now to several orders of considerations

I shall argue are relevant to the selection of a location formulation and its hearing.

Location analysis

A first sort of consideration relevant to the selection of a location formulation is a location analysis. By that I mean to suggest that the selection of a location formulation requires of a speaker (and will exhibit for a hearer) an analysis of his own location and the location of his co-conversationalist(s), and of the objects whose location is being formulated (if that object is not one of the co-conversationalists). One important dimension of such an analysis is whether, for some formulation, the objects of the analysis are co-present or not. For many conversational activities or topics, a formulation under which the co-conversationalists are co-present will be rejected. For example, the following segment is from a collection of calls to the police department of a mid-western city. Throughout this collection of conversations, there is a great deal of inquiring and reporting of the location of various parties, events, directions, etc. Throughout, the name of the city, 'Centurb', does not occur, never being the answer or part of the answer to questions like 'Where are you?', 'What is the address?', 'Where is this?', 'Where did this happen?'. In this particular call, two police dispatchers are on the line with a lady who has reported a gas leak in her home. The conversation alternates between the precautions she should take (these points are omitted here) and finding where help should be sent:

D: Radio, Jones.
C: Uh, this is Mrs Lodge calling from one twenty one Sierra Drive/
D: One twenty one Sierra/
C: Yes.
. . .
D2: Ma'am/where's Sierra located?
C: It's on the corner of Sierra and uh-hh Smith Drive.
D2: Sierra and Smith/
C: Yes ...   3
D2: Uh where is this Sierra and Smith located? We gotta know about this.

c: One twenty one Sierra Drive. It's right on the corner.
D2: Right on the corner of Si- uh of what. Sierra/and Smith.
Where is Smith?
c: Sierra Drive. Sierra and Smith.

. . .

D2: I wanna know where Smith is located.
c: Well, it's uh right off Flint Ridge.
D2: Off Flint Ridge.
c: Yeah.
D2: Where're you at ma'am, are you in the County/
c: Uhm uh I'm in Exurb uhm
D2: (Alright)
c: Oh!!! Right near the A and P Shopping Center.
Across – the creek.
D2: Alright, calm down now, you're – you're in Exurb/
c: Yes uh.
D2: Alright, we'll get somebody out there then tuh one twenty
one Sierra.
(CPD, 22–23)

In this segment, the failure to report as part of the formulation of
place the city's name is heard as being produced by a finding of
co-presence for that formulation.[6] This is indeed the case in the
other calls in the corpus. The failure to formulate the city leads
then to hearing that the caller is in the city (co-present in it with
the police, and thus not using it in her formulation), and to a
search for her street on the city map. The formulation of place is
not adequate (i.e. no further asking) until this is called into
question and corrected. The usual adequate formulation names
some formulation for which the object being located and the
conversationalists are not co-present.

A has offered B, both in Pacifictown, a nursing job.

B: And where is it?
A: Out in Edgertown, on Strawson Road.   4
(SBL, 1, 10, 2)

6. A curious appearance of this: if your tobacconist uses 'remaindered'
matches you may find yourself with one which advertises 'Al's Liquor Shop,
122 Main St', and wonder where it is.

In some conversational contexts, for some conversational activities, finding a formulation for which the conversationalists are co-present may lead not to its rejection but to its selection. For example, in being 'brought up to date' on the doings and whereabouts of old friends and upon learning of their wide dispersal, one might get, in New York, the exchange: 'A: And where's Jim? B: Oh, *he's* in New York.' Without speculating on the relevance for such an exchange of its placement in a series of locational formulations and its contrastive use in the series, or the relevance of such a discussion as prefiguring the possibility of reunions and their feasibility, it may nonetheless be noted that a finding of co-presence or non-co-presence is relevant, and requires as a consideration in the selection of a locational formulation a locational analysis by the speaker of the respective placement of the parties. And, hearers take account of the use of that procedure to see how the formulation employed was arrived at (so that while it is the case that if Jim is in New York he is in the East, a report that he was in the East would be heard by A as reporting that he was not in New York).

Much of the preceding discussion relies on a notion of a 'commonsense geography' which many North Americans (at least) share. It is presumed by the interactants in their conversation with one another, and by me in reporting on their interactions and in inventing others for illustrative purposes. Because the terms in which locational analyses are conducted are supplied, at least in part (I say 'in part' because some such analysis will be done in much more micro-ecological terms, e.g., 'this room, that room'), by this shared ('everyman's') geography, it is to the point to remark on it briefly.

A considerable number of the terms suggested above as possible formulations for 'where my notes are' seem to fall into a sort of concentric organization, each earlier term of the list being included in a later term. A similar relation holds between 'the city' and 'county' in 3. The same kind of structure seems to be relied upon in an inference such as:

A: Where did she train?
B: Uh I think in Oregon.
A: Oh. Mm mmm.   5

B: Now, I'm not sure, Fran, but I think in Oregon, 'cause she's *from* Portland.
(SBL/ 1, 12, 25)

It is possible that the search for a term for which the conversationalist and/or referent are or are not co-present is organized for some set of terms in a fashion ordered by such a concentric or hierarchic organization of terms.

What such a commonsense geography is, and how it is organized (hierarchically or in some other manner); whether there is a single layman's geography or alternative geographies from which a selection is made on particular occasion of use – these are empirical questions, and not ones to be settled by consulting geography books. Such geographies are a cultural fact to be discovered[7] and perhaps subjected to a sort of 'componential analysis' of place terms,[8] but have no necessary further consequences for the analysis with which we are concerned here. That there are such geographies in use, that some of them have a hierarchical organization, and that which one will be used may turn on current and recent respective locations of the parties, can be seen in the following:

A, who has recently returned to the country, has called B.

B: How *are* you?
A: I'm fine. How're you?
B: Fine. Back from the wilds of Peru.
A: Yeah.
.... [*invitation talk*]   6
B: I – oh I can't wai'tuh *see* you.
A: Mmmhhehh heh!
B: That's really neat [*1·0 second pause*]. Didje get tuh travel in South America a lot?
(TAC, 2, 5)

For Americans, it appears, one goes 'to South America' not 'Peru', just as one goes to 'Europe', not 'France'. If one says one went to France, one is asked 'Where else?' rather than

7. See, for one attempt in this direction, Lynch (1960).
8. On componential analysis, see, e.g., Conklin (1955), Frake (1961), Goodenough (1956) and Lounsbury (1956).

'Where in France did you visit?' Persons who went 'just to France' may have to account for it (e.g. via what they had to do, better and worse ways of travelling, etc.). And the same seems to hold for South America and countries in it; not 'where in Peru' but 'where else in South America'. For Americans, the units parallel to the United States seem to be not France or Peru, but Europe and South America. On the other hand, when people 'return' from any of these places, they return to 'America'. In giving the context for 6 above, I quite naïvely and automatically wrote 'returned to the country'. Typically one who is said to have 'returned to California' is heard to have returned from some other state.

These materials would seem to display elements of a common sense geography. They seem to display also a kind of hierarchic or concentric organization of units, which can be further appreciated by seeing that what is asked is 'Didje get tuh travel in South America?' while 'Did you get to Spain?' would be strange, though clearly for some classes Spain and Peru would be co-class members. That persons may have more than one such geography and select among them according to a locational analysis is suggested by the possibility that for Americans spending a year or two in England, the response to 'I was in France' may well be 'Where in France?' Similarly, for speakers in New York, a response to the report 'I went to Philadelphia' of 'Did you get to Boston?' might be strange, but for West Coast inhabitants it might not be.

These few notes on common sense geography may be helpful tools in trying to see how the remarks that have been developed on the relevance of locational analysis to the selection of a locational formulation may shed light on somewhat unrelated problems as a by-product. There are two such 'throw-offs' to be suggested here.

The first has to do with one kind of circumstance in which a member makes what another might call an 'overgeneralization'. The datum involved is the following. An American returned from a stay of several years in another country writes a letter to a friend, a native of the country from which the writer has returned. At the beginning of the third paragraph, he writes in connection with race relations: 'Things here in the States are much worse than the press would have you believe.' Having spent all his time since his return in New York City, persons might say that is an overgeneralization; he does not know what is going on in the rest of the country, he knows about New York. And there are lay theories to account for such overgeneralization: people do not think precisely; they are careless with language. Such views treat the utterance as if the speaker is, in the first part of the utterance, bounding the domain for which his assertion is true. One can then find that there is insufficient evidence to warrant the assertion for that domain. But we can take another view, and ask: how is such an utterance assembled? It has parts; are all its parts produced in the same way? Instead of seeing the utterance as the defective or inadequate product of one procedure (e.g., a quasi-scientific one), can we see it as the proper outcome of some other? We can, perhaps, propose that different sets of considerations are relevant to producing the various parts of the utterance, and that the part 'here in — ' may be produced, in part, by reference to such considerations of locational analysis as have been sketched above. In filling in some place formulation in such a phrase, the selection of a term will be guided by the respective locations of the parties (and not necessarily by a specification of the domain for which the assertion is proposed to hold). We noted above that with respect to other countries, persons return to 'the United States'. The 'here' on which a recent returnee reports to his friend still abroad may then get as its formulation 'the States'. If persons use some such considerations to select a location formulation, while other parts of their utterance are produced by reference to other considerations, we can see one way in which statements which may come to be seen as 'overgeneralizations' are generated.

The second 'throw-off' has to do with the use and understandability of what could be called 'locational pro-terms', most predominantly, terms such as 'here' or 'there'. These terms are prototypical members of a class logicians have called 'indexical expressions',[9] terms whose referent varies with the context of its use. For terms like these, it would appear that for the retrieval of their referent to be possible, they should be used only after

9. Garfinkel and Sacks (1969) review the terms and discussions by philosophers, logicians, and linguists. Their paper is relevant to several themes in the present discussion.

some referent is named. On the occasion of their appearance, one could then search to find the term to which they refer. However, in some instances, these pro-terms are used as first references, without prior place names, and without causing difficulty. Utterances such as 'How are things there?' or 'Things here are going well' do not elicit responses such as 'How are things where?' or 'What do you mean "here"?' One way in which a 'solution' of these pro-terms would be possible would be to look to the locational formulation that some location analysis by the speaker would yield as relevant, and hear that as the intended use of the pro-term.

Similarly, relational terms such as 'downstairs', 'in front', 'across the street', etc. although they can be combined with place terms, are also used alone. When so used, they are purely formal and may be applied (for terms like 'in front') to any structure, or (for terms like 'downstairs' or 'across the street') to any structure with certain properties (e.g., multi-leveled, or on a street). Agreements to 'meet downstairs' or to 'wait in front', in so far as they yield successful meetings, would seem to have involved the parties in finding the objects, never explicitly formulated, to which these relational terms were to be applied. And, a locational analysis would seem to be involved in the adequacy of such usages, both in the making of arrangements (e.g., to meet) and in the recounting of tales, as in:

A: En' I couldn' remember what I did with it, so I said to Joan, 'Go ahead uh an' I'll run *back*.' An' I ran back and when I came down, uh, I uh – they said 'you've missed all the 7 ex*cite*ment' . . .
(Trio, 7)

or (for terms like 'back', as in 'going back') to any circumstances in which a 'history of recent movement' is available.

Similarly, the term 'home' has a shifting referent; it is not used only for the house one normally occupies, but stands as an alternative term to a range of others. One can be 'glad to be home' when one gets back to the United States, to New York State, New York City, the neighborhood, the house, etc. (With flights to the moon, a Soviet Astronaut may soon announce the Russian equivalent of 'it's good to be home' upon splashing down in the Indian Ocean.) A locational analysis allows one to see how 'home' is being used, i.e., in contrast to what kind of location formulation, and not necessarily to assume that all who express pleasure at being 'home' when landing at Kennedy Airport live in the International Arrivals Building.

Membership analysis

A second order of considerations in the selection of a locational formulation, which may be called 'membership analysis', has to do with the categories of members of the society of which the hearer(s) in the first instance, but also the speaker, are members; that is, there are relationships between the identifications made (by the parties) of the parties to the conversation on the one hand ('membership categorizations', as in Sacks, 1969), and the selection and hearing of locational formulation, on the other. Consider for example that members who are asked for directions or information may see that the inquiry was directed to them because the inquirer identified them in a particular way and saw their membership in some category as grounds for seeking the information from them. In such circumstances, if the membership identification the inquirer used as the warrant for the inquiry is incorrect, the request for information may be met not by an answer or plea of ignorance, but a denial or correction of the identification on which the inquiry was based. Something such as this is going on, it appears, when persons answer inquiries on the street with 'I'm a stranger here myself'; or when shoppers, mistaken as sales personnel in department stores, answer inquiries about the whereabouts of 'better dresses' not with 'I don't know', but with 'I don't work here'. That the kind of place formulation involved in the inquiry is related to the membership categories is suggested by the likelihood that the question 'what floor is this?' asked of the same persons, may be answered.

Seen from the point of view of an inquirer in such situations, the kind of formulation they have of the location about which they seek information may be used to decide on a search procedure for finding to which member of a population of possible answerers the inquiry should be directed. One New Yorker, for example, trying to find 'Fillmore East' (a center for rock music) and knowing only its name, reports 'looking for the hippiest looking person on the street' to ask for directions. Perhaps, armed with the alternative formulation '105 Second Avenue', the possibly helpful population would have not been so restricted. Similarly, someone looking for 'Kent Hall' at Columbia University, a place which does not have a street address as an alternative formulation, may feel that they might need a person 'from Columbia' to recognize their goal and help in finding it. I was, for example, stopped by such a person after getting off the bus at the University and asked 'Are you going to Columbia?' 'Yes.' 'Can you tell me where Kent Hall is?' (Of course, the initial question not only establishes my membership in a class whose members can be expected to be able to deal with 'Kent Hall', it prepares me to recognize the name 'Kent Hall' for the kind of thing it will be the name of, i.e. a Columbia thing.)

Furthermore, the use of certain formulations of a location will allow an interlocutor to hear that the speaker is for some membership class 'a stranger', and that that identification is relevant in formulating a response. Examples here are difficult, because that some formulation marks its user as a stranger will (and this is what is at issue) be recognizable to non-strangers, and for any example chosen some readers will not be non-strangers. Nonetheless: one who asks in New York City how to get to the 'Long Island Train Terminal' (instead of 'Penn Station' or 'Pennsylvania Station') will thereby be recognizable to New Yorkers (a class of members) as a non-New Yorker, a stranger (a non-class member). And although this is merely one membership identification of many that are correct for such a person (he being perhaps also a male, white, a father, a soldier, etc.), it is one which has relevance to the response, providing a sense of the sorts of locational formulations that can be used. (Where directions are asked for a place whose formulation does not allow a determination of the asker's status in this respect, it may be inquired into as a preliminary to answering. For example, if one is asked for the 'Brooklyn Museum', the return may be 'Do you know Brooklyn?' On the answer turns (1) which of alternative sets of directions will be given and/or (2) how the places the directions make reference to will be formulated. Will they, for example, refer to 'where Ebbetts Field used to be'.)

Similarly, persons are marked as strangers when they call to check on the safety of relatives in Burbank upon hearing there are riots 'in Los Angeles' Watts section'. The often-noted deluge of phone calls into areas of natural disaster and civil disturbance in contrast to the relatively little calling out to give reassurance (Fritz and Mathewson, 1957) appears to be related to the need of mass media to formulate the location of the events in terms recognizable to strangers, while their location is formulated locally in native terms. For Bostonians, both their relatives and the riots are in Los Angeles; for the relatives, the riots are in Watts, whereas they live in Burbank.

These remarks are intended to illustrate a variety of ways in which the relationship between members' categorizations of one another and selection or hearing of locational formulations manifests itself. To begin to spell out the features on which the linkage is based we must touch at least briefly on several more general issues.

It appears to be the case that persons (in this society, at least) in using names and in asking for them, claim their recognizability (an important variant omitted here is asking for a name to provide for its future recognizability). Persons introducing themselves use different 'frames' in their introductions when claiming the recognizability of their name and when no such claim is made. On the telephone, for example, the frame 'my name is____' makes no claim to recognizability, while the frame 'this is____' does (Schegloff, 1967, ch. 2). Where the claim to recognizability is warranted, but failure of recognition is anticipated, the 'claim' form is used with assistance supplied for the recognition (e.g., 'Professor Van Druten, this is Sally Bowes. I was in your course on German History.') When asking a name where the grounds for expecting its recognizability may not be apparent, grounds are given. Thus, in the classic ploy, 'What did you say your name was again?', recognizability is based on a claim that the name has been already given. To cite actual data:

B has been talking about people she is having to lunch.
A: Who didju say it was? I think you *told* me.   8
(SBL, 2, 1, 8, 5)

This is far from the only grounds that may be offered. For example:

A, who is visiting the city, has spoken of visiting a friend in Van Nuys.

B: Wh-what is yer friend's name, cuz my *son* lives in Van Nuys.
A: Glazer.   9
B: Mmhmm no. And uh, if she uh ...
A: She lives on Mariposa,
   [*1.6 second pause*]
B: No, I don' even know that street.
A: Mm no.
(D A, 3)

Similarly, when a name has been asked for, the request can be rejected on the grounds of no expectable recognizability.

B: Who is that?
A: Uh she's uh not known here. She lives out in South town. 10
B: Mm.
A: She's uhm – hum, just moved here about a year ago.
(S B L, 1, 10, 8)

For our concerns here, place names and personal names may be considered as of a piece, the issue of recognizability holding for both. 'Name-dropping', for example, can be done with place names as well as with personal names, and depends for its operation on the recognizability of the name.

To speak of the 'recognizability of the name' is insufficiently precise here. What is central is more than hearing once again a sequence of morphemes that have been heard before. What we mean by 'recognizability' is that the hearer can perform operations on the name – categorize it, find as a member of which class it is being used, bring knowledge to bear on it, detect which of its attributes are relevant in context, etc. It is the ability to do such operations on a name that allow such responses as:

*A: Who did you go with?
 B: Mary.
 A: Oh, it was a family affair.

*A: I had lunch with Jones.
 B: When's his book coming out?

*A: I saw Bundy.
 B: Any chance of getting money?

Names themselves are on the whole neutral with respect to the categories of which their bearers are members. Whereas in English, personal names may indicate sex, ethnicity, and sometimes social class, they are otherwise mute. Recognition involves, then, the ability to bring knowledge to bear on them, to categorize, see the relevant significance, to see 'in what capacity' the name is used.

In this respect, too, place names are like personal names.

A: And he said that some teacher, who's coming uhm from I believe he might have said Brooklyn, some place in the east.   **11**

(SBL, 1, 1, 12, 21)

Here the particular place that had been mentioned is not clearly remembered, but the outcome of some operation (some analysis of the place that was mentioned) is. This sort of finding has wider import; however, our interest here is only in showing that: on hearing, such operations, classifications, in short, 'analyses' are done, their outcome may be retained while the particular is not, and that what is meant here by 'recognizability' is 'analyzability' in this sense. Thus, names are to be used only when expectably recognizable, where that means 'analyzable'. When prospective users are not sure that some name will be recognizable in this sense, they may ask that about the name before using it.

A: Well tell me, do you – does the name Charles Weidman mean anything to you?
B: Well, I should say so.   **12**
(SBL, 2, 2, 4, 11)

*A: D'ya know where the Triboro Bridge is?
 B: Yeah.
 A: Well make a right there ...

And, if it is not recognizable, they may supply the relevant attributes.
*A: Do you know George Smith?
 B: No.
 A: Well, he's an artist, and he says ...

Members treat the recognizability of particular names as variably distributed. For some name, recognition can be expected of the members of some membership categories. And not only recognition, but adequate recognition, i.e. not only can it be expected that they can perform some operations or analyses, but the ones that yield the adequate-for-the-occasion outcome, the relevant recognition. Which categories of member can be expected to recognize a name turns on the kind of name. For place names, one relevant category is territorially based. Persons in a place, or in proximity to it, may be expected to be able to recognize place names in it, or near it, and they may offer current or former proximity, or territorially based category membership, as evidence, warrant, or account for their recognitions.

D: ... They're setting up emergency at uh uh the cattle barn. Y'know where that is?   **13**
C: Yeah. I live on 38th about 10 blocks east.
(IPD., 371)

And a show of knowledge about a place may prompt an inquiry, 'Oh, have you been there?' Knowledge of places is, in that sense, locally organized.[10] Although the structure of knowledge about a 'sort of place' may be general and formal, everyone organizing knowledge in the same categories and on the same dimensions, the particulars which are so organized are assumed to vary with territorially-based memberships. Thus, most persons live similarly, in a place, in an environment of places, in a house, in a neighborhood, in a 'part of town' – which can be similarly talked of (and it is an important fact that some do not). Their place, and

10. Although the unit to which 'local organization' applies may be quite large. Thus, for example, the 'common sense geography' to which we referred earlier involves some knowledge about places never visited, but expectably known by competent members. Whereas asking of one returned from Peru whether he travelled to Colombia does not necessarily exhibit the asker's intimate familiarity with those places, remarking to someone who reports living on West Fourth Street, 'Oh, you're in the Village', can be seen to exhibit a knowledge based on personal experience. Which sorts of places are known generally, in the manner of a common sense geography, and which are known 'locally' in the sense intended in the text, is a matter for empirical investigation. I am indebted here to Diana Cook.

For one ethnographic report on the variation of naming and knowledge of an area by proximity to it, cf. Suttles (1968, pp. 24–5).

its environment of places, have characteristics, character, a population composition, etc. These categories are filled by persons with their particular situations, *their* house, *their* street, *their* neighborhood, *their* part of town, *their* city, *their* state, etc., on which they are knowledgeable and can speak, while others can respond accordingly. The sharing of particulars at one or another of these levels is perhaps one sense of membership in a 'same community'. It is by reference to the adequate recognizability of detail, including place names, that one is in this sense a member, and those who do not share such recognition are 'strangers'.

In this way, the 'right' selection and adequate recognition of place formulations can be seen to be one basis for demonstrations of, claims to, failings in, decisions about, etc., the competent membership of either speaker or hearer. Where 'trouble' occurs, it can be seen either that the speaker's analysis was incorrect, or that the analysis was correct but the hearer is not a fully competent instance of the class of which he is (relevantly for the place term employed) a member. The occurrence of 'trouble' can be most clearly recognized when the use of a place formulation produces a question or second question about the location of the initial place formulation as in **3** above or:

*A: I just came back from Irzuapa.
 B: Where's that?

*A: Where are you?
 B: Sloan Street.
 A: Where's that?

In the first case, perhaps B can see the incorrect analysis A made of him to come up with that term as a claimedly adequate one, and can perhaps use that incorrect analysis himself to see what sort of person A must be to have produced it. Alternatively, A can see B as a deficient version of some class in which B claims membership, for members of which 'Irzuapa' ought to be an adequately recognizable place formulation. Insofar as friendships, reputations, marriages, collaborations, etc. may turn on someone's competent membership in some class of members (e.g., 'swinger', 'anthropologist', 'good Jewish girl', 'Africanist', etc.), each occasion of the use of a place formulation selected because of its presumed recognizability to a member of such a class is part of a never ending potential test in which persons can be shown to be inadequate members of the class, and thereby inadequate candidates for the activity. Alternatively, each place term a person uses can be inspected to see if it is the term such a person, a member of a certain class of members, should use. The stream of conversation is thus full of places getting mentioned off-hand in some formulation, and requiring recognition. And much can turn on their being recognized and on their being 'rightly' selected (where 'right', as compared to 'correct' may mean 'not subject to further question, and not giving cause for a re-analysis of the membership of the user'). Aside from inferences about the membership and competence of the parties, trouble over a place formulation can lead to reparative work in the conversation to show that although the place formulation used was not recognized, the speaker's membership analysis used to choose that term was correct, and the hearer is not a defective member, but rather some particular account is available to explain the 'momentary non-recognition'. Thus:

B: I played bridge today, and I – I was in the home – an awfully nice party down on El Ravina – El Ravina.
A: Yeah.
   [*Talk regarding bad cards*] . . .
A: This was a – This was a party, where *is* El Ravina.
B: Well, I'll tell you sum'n, the way I went, I went onto Pacific Boulevard, and I went up past El S – uh Prairie. *You* know,
A: Oh.
B: Rest Home. And then I turned to the left, and it's the very first street.
A: Oh! Of course. I know where it is,
B: Uh huh.
A: I know.
B: Uh huh.
A: [*Clears throat*]
B: And it's a very nice little street,
A: Uh.   **14**
B: Close to the ocean.

A: I was getting it – mixed up with uh there's something like that out in uh *Litt*le Falls.

B: Well, that could be,

A: A-and uh like

B: Mm hmm.

A: Maybe it's just Ravina, not El Ravina.

B: Mm hmm

A: Out in Little Falls.

B: Mm hmm.

A: That's awfully –

B: Well this is E-l, r-a, v-i-n-a.

A: Yeah, *I* know where it is.

B: Uh huh. Yah – yeah, it's very easy to find. I was – I just got to the – got to the // first (   ),

A: It's the main one, to go down to,

B: Yeah.

A: Mm // hm.

B: Uh huh. And then when I was going to – you know, out, there I was facing the wrong way, so I thought, etc.

(SBL, 1, 12, 15–16)

A, having failed initially to recognize the name, eventually comes to say the speaker was not wrong to have used it; the membership analysis which might have produced this formulation was correct; it ought to have been recognized, and there is a reason why it was not.

Two further remarks are relevant on this point. First the account given for the non-recognition is curious, i.e. 'I was getting it – mixed up with uh there's something like that out in uh *Litt*le Falls.' For why should the location of El Ravina have been a thing to ask for if she recognized it as being in Little Falls? They can turn out to be 'mixed up' only *after* she gets a formulation of El Ravina from B. Before that, she heard it as 'in Little Falls', i.e. that's where it is. Why then ask where it is? And how can a 'mix-up' which is possible only after the clarification that there are two different places involved account for the failure to recognize the name when it is first used? Perhaps it would have been strange to A that B would go to a party at 'Little Falls', given some analysis of the 'kind of place' that is and the 'kind of person' B is. This lack of fit produced the failure of recognition. (On fit between places and persons, see next section) Second, throughout the segment A asserts several times her recognition of the place. But the discussion of where it is does not end until she demonstrates the recognition. We can note that transformations from one formulation to another can not only show a preferred formulation (as will be suggested below), but can demonstrate that the transformer has recognized and understood, by showing he can analyze the first formulation and find a correct transformation. Thus, for time formulations:

B: How long y'gonna be here?
A: *Uh* / not too long. Uh, just til uh Monday.   **15**
B: Til – oh (yeh mean) like a week f'm t'morrow.
A: Yeah.
(D A, 1)

So when A begins a transformation of El Ravina, exhibiting the product of an analysis, 'It's the main one, to go down to', she demonstrates the recognition that B had a 'right' to expect and relied on in employing the place name initially.

Of the variety and range of locational formulations from which a speaker selects, a significant number are place names (e.g., of parts of town, city, neighborhood, street, business, building, etc.). If the use of a locational formulation which is a place name requires, as a condition of use, its expectable recognizability; if recognizability involves the hearer's ability to categorize, bring knowledge to bear, analyze; if the hearer's ability to do so is seen to turn on his membership in some category of member; then selection of such a term will require a membership analysis by the speaker of the hearer. The analysis is to determine the availability to the hearer of that competence on which the speaker must rely if he is to use some locational formulation adequately, i.e. understandably, without further elaboration, with no further question. It is in the light of such considerations that the illustrative materials at the beginning of this section are to be understood, and the relevance of a membership analysis, in addition to the locational analysis discussed earlier, to the selection of place formulations is to be appreciated.

Topic or activity analysis

A third order of consideration which seems to be involved is an orientation to 'topic' or to the activity being accomplished in an utterance; in short, a 'topic analysis' or 'activity analysis' is also relevant to the selection and hearing of a place formulation. This is suggested by the discussion above of the requirements of a hearer that he perform operations on names – categorize, analyze, etc. – to find the relevant respects in which they are used. Perhaps the central focus of relevance in this connection is the topic that is being built up or talked to, the activities being enacted in the utterance. In order to begin to get at this orientation to topic in the selection of place formulations, it will be useful first to consider whether the collection of formulations from which a selection is made is homogeneous and undifferentiated, or whether it is structured, and has sub-sets, or 'sorts of formulations'. I shall propose several 'sorts of formulations' and propose that such sub-collection structures of terms are a resource in the sensitivity to topic of the selection of place formulations.

One sort of formulation I shall call G for geographical, and note it without discussion. Such formulations as street address (2903 Main Street) and latitude-longitude specifications are of this sort.

Another sort of term can be abbreviated as R_m, for 'relation to members'. Such forms as 'John's place', 'Al's house', 'Dr Brown's office', are among those intended. Also terms such as 'home', 'the office', 'the supermarket', 'the store' are of this sort, the first two (and ones like them) being formulated by their relationship to the speaker or hearer; the latter two, on some occasions of use, being heard as 'the X to which we both know we go' (though in other conversational contexts they may be used as members of a class of places, a sort of place).

Of the R_m terms, ones of the form 'the X' where it is used as 'my X' or 'your X', where the member by relation to whom the place is formulated is said 'to have an X' (e.g., home, house, office, etc.) have special uses and properties. First, for most persons, there are relatively few terms which can be used this way. 'Home' and 'office' (or some such work place equivalent) may exhaust the list for most persons. For those who have others, the character of the activity they are seen to do in using them may depend on whether their interlocutors knew they had such additional places.

K: Oh I – I never saw it before, cause I was on the *ranch* when it first came *out*. And it was so funny.   16
R: Oh, do you own a ranch too?
(GTS I, 13)

Note that the usage 'the ranch' is recognized as K's ranch, K's 'having' a ranch. And that can be seen, by those who did not know it before, as boasting, showing off, etc. Here, then, we have one way in which doing a correct membership analysis in picking a locational formulation can have consequences. 'The ranch' can be used with persons who know you have one, while the talk continues to be focused on the movie that is under discussion. Alternatively, with those who do not know it, 'away' would allow the same outcome. But here, 'the ranch' becomes the focus of the conversation, and the 'movie' topic is deflected.

These special R_m terms, 'the X' type R_m terms, and especially the term 'home', have the special character not only of 'belonging to' the member in relation to whom they are formulated, but, as we noted earlier, such a place is for a member 'where he belongs'. One way of showing how this expresses itself in member's practices is to consider the use of terms like 'out' or 'not here'.

Were someone to inquire at my home, by phone or in person, for 'John Smith', there is a sense in which it would be true to say he was 'out' or 'not here'. A search of the premises would reveal no one with that name. But, that is not what would be said. What persons say in such circumstances is something like 'You have the wrong number (address).' Being 'out', or 'not here', or 'not here right now', is what people are with respect to a limited class of places, formulated typically as R_m places (where the m or member can be their name) especially of 'the X' type, which might be called 'base places' for them, places in which it is warranted to search for them without an account for looking for them *there*. It is for such places that when they are not there, they are 'not here' or 'out'. And if a place stops having that relation to a member, others will normally be told upon inquiry 'He doesn't work (live) here any more'. In one case I know, someone was trying to reach an editor at 'his office' for three weeks. Told each time that 'Mr Smith is out', he called back again. Only after some time did he learn that Smith had left his position, whereupon, of course, the caller discontinued his efforts.

The status of such places under R_m formulations as places where one belongs, whose presence there is not accountable, can be seen in another way. When a place is formulated by an R_m term, and especially as 'X's home', persons calling on the telephone who fail to recognize the voice that answers as belonging to one by relation to whom the place can be formulated often ask 'Who is this?' There are two kinds of answers to this challenge. One is 'Who's *this*?' or 'Whom do you want?' (which children are often taught to ask, before answering); the other is some kind of self-identification by the answerer. It appears that in choosing between these kinds of answers, an analysis by the answerer of his relation to the place he is in is relevant. If he is a person by relation to whom the place can be formulated, if he 'belongs' there, if his presence is not accountable, he will counter-challenge 'Who's *this*?' If not, some self-identification will be returned and in many cases such a self-identification will be chosen as will also provide an account of the answerer's presence; e.g., 'This is Mr X's nephew' or 'The babysitter', the latter showing not only why the answerer is there, but why she is answering the phone.

One further point before returning to R_m formulations in general. It was noted above that for most persons there is a restricted number of places of 'the X' type. There are, however, resources for greatly expanding the set of terms that can be used to formulate such places. There is a set of terms mentioned earlier and discussed further below, which are relationship terms such as 'near', 'with', 'in front of', etc. When combined with some object, these terms generate a large set of terms which can stand as transformed formulations of an R_m term.

B: Uh if you'd care to come over and visit a little while this morning, I'll give you a cup of *co*ffee.   17

A: Hehh! Well, that's awfully sweet of you, I don't think I can make it this morning, hh uhm I'm running an ad in the paper and – and uh I have to stay near the phone.
(SBL, 1, 10, 14)

'Near the phone' seems here to be a place formulation chosen 'for topic' to go with 'running an ad.'. Clearly, selecting a term 'for topic', given the resources of the collection of relational terms, can generate an extended collection of formulations which are transformations of 'home' (e.g., 'with the children', 'in front of the stove', 'working out back', 'at my desk', 'at the typewriter', etc.). I call them 'transformations' for two reasons, neither to be supported by data here. First, if someone were to call B in **17** and ask where A was, the answer would probably not be 'near the phone' (and might not be understandable if it were), but 'at home'. The basic formulation is 'home'; 'near the phone' is a topically-sensitive transformation; when removed from topical context, it is not a relevant transformation. Second, A, in selecting a place formulation, does not select from among '120 Main Street' (or whatever her address may be), 'home', and 'near the phone' to refer only to the sorts of formulations so far introduced into this discussion. It appears more likely, though there is no evidence, that she selects first between a G and R_m term, and having selected the latter, then modifies it for topic, or transforms it.

Why should she, however, have chosen an R_m term over a G term? Is there a preference rule for this choice? In general, it appears the rule is: use an R_m term if you can. The qualifier 'if you can' refers largely to the earlier finding that names should be used only where expectably recognizable. The consequence here is that one should use an R_m term if one can formulate the place by relationship to a member the hearer(s) can be expected to recognize. So we find R_m forms used because the other knows the m, where that involves introducing a second or third formulation:

B: Euhhmm uh they live uh right at – They live on Oleander Street, and that's a street beyond Terrace Lane.
A: Yeah.   **18**
B: Where Sarah lives.

A: Yeah.
(SBL 1, 12, 9)

And where an R_m formulation is not used, it may be understood that it is because the other does not know the member involved, as in:

B: I played bridge today, and I – I was in the home – and awfully nice party down on El Ravina – (*1.0*) – El Ravina   **19**
(SBL 1, 12, 15)

And where a G term has been used to a hearer who knows the place by an R_m formulation, he may transform it:

*A: Meet you in front of one fifty three seventeenth avenue.
B: Oh, at Bill White's house?
A: Yeah, I didn't know you knew Bill.

On the whole, then, the preference rule appears to be: use an R_m formulation if you can. Clearly, this makes the choice of an R_m formulation turn on the outcome of a membership analysis, requiring an analysis of who knows whom, who are strangers, whether persons are members of such pair-relationships as would allow use of an R_m term. And since R_m terms are preferred, such a membership analysis may be required as a first procedure, if only to reject an R_m formulation and select another. The character of R_m terms and the preference rule thus suggests that a membership analysis has been done not only when an R_m term has been used, but when one has not but was possible.

Another expansion of the collection from which selection of a locational formulation is made can be seen to occur when we recognize that members may formulate members as being not 'in' or 'at' a place, but 'between' places. Persons 'on their way home', for example, may select that formulation in place of 'in the station', 'at 125th Street', 'in the train', 'in the third car', etc. A person dressed in a swimsuit in his car, may have a gas station attendant ask him 'going to the beach?' Someone who will 'return your call' wants to know if 'you're in your office' and the answer may be 'I'm on my way home'. So, another set of formulations is provided by the possibility of being 'on the way to___, ' 'on way from___ ', etc.

Similarly, there are places formulated so that their main character is not only, or not so much, where they are as where they are 'on the way to', 'between', i.e. where they are in relation to something else. Such formulations we will call R*l*, or relation to landmark, where by 'landmark' is not intended public buildings or monuments, but any object recognizable from description (here using 'recognizable' not in the earlier sense of 'analyzable', but as 'capable of being seen as the place mentioned or described'). 'Three doors from the corner', 'three blocks after the traffic signal', 'the last street before the shopping center', 'behind Macy's', 'to the left of the billboard', 'next to the school building', 'two houses down from Jack's place', are examples. Such terms are compounds of certain relationship terms and recognizable objects or place formulations of other sorts (being in this way like the transformation formulations for R*m* places discussed earlier, e.g., 'near the phone'). In such cases, whether or not the second part of the compound can be formulated as a place in its own right, it may also be formulated for what we may call its 'relational' or 'transitional' properties, as a point of reference. Conversely, a place that could be formulated in its own right may be formulated by using some other place as a point of reference. And if there are many such places which can be used for their transition value and be used as points of reference, then the size of the set of possible formulations from which selection is to be made is enormously increased. (For example, a place which can be formulated in its own right as Penn Station can then become 'under Madison Square Garden', '*n* blocks south of Macy's', 'across the street from Hotel Q', etc.).

Landmarks, in the sense being used here, have as probably their most prominent use, their inclusion in directions,[11] where they are used specifically as in-between places. Directions formulate getting from point A to point F by moving from A to B, B to C, C to D . . . to F, where B, C, D, E, are used for their transition value. Any place can be so formulated for some places as 'between them' for some class of members (for whom they would be recognizable; hence, again, the relevance of membership analysis).

Some places in the society may have almost solely transition
11. On direction giving, see Psathas and Kozloff (1968).

value, and others will, for certain categories of members, have largely transition value. The phenomenon of seeing people 'waiting' seems to rest on seeing them located in a transitional place, being thereby not in a place, but on the way to some other place. Places which have high transitional value may thereby accrue great economic value, certain businesses seeking to be located precisely at places which are treated by members as transition places for many points of origin and many destinations. They are places, then, where people can meet, in some independence of where they may later be going. That members of this society could produce Schelling's results (1963) in which an absolute majority of persons told to meet someone in New York could agree on where to do it with no further information (e.g., where they were going to go after meeting, where the other was coming from, etc.), suggests their familiarity with the notion of a place in-between places, even where these are unknown, i.e. a place with absolute transition value, or maximum transition value (and further, that they saw such a place as relevant to their task, and that an absolute majority could independently arrive at the same one). It is this feature which is central to the kind of formulation of location we are calling R_l.

Another sort of formulation is of what might be called 'course of action places', i.e. places which are identifiable places only by virtue of what goes on there and are so formulated (e.g., 'where they leave the garbage'). In the history of the Western world, of course, that is how many places were made (e.g., where battle X was fought, etc., the latest being the spot, otherwise unidentifiable, where Kennedy was killed. The 'otherwise unidentifiable' routinely leads to some mark of identification being put there, whether monument or city).

Finally, a prominent sort of location formulation is place name, be it street, city, section, store or whatever. Names, we argued before, are used when analysable, and so we should note that the indefinitely large collection of place names is organized into a variety of sub-collections, whose recovery is the work of analysis. The very terms just used to suggest kinds of place names are themselves names of sub-collections or categories. Each place name may be a member of many sub-collections (for example, 'Bloomingdale's' as a store, a department store, a 'better' department store, an East Side store, a store on 59th Street, etc.. for each of which it is grouped with different co-class members) But even groups of names as a group may together be members of alternative collections ('Bloomingdale's', 'Macy's', 'Gimbels' all being department stores, Manhattan stores, etc.). As a limiting case we should note those classes whose co-members are grouped together for a single attribute, and hence may be a class for a single (or limited range of) topic, as in the case used earlier of vacation places, or even more specifically skiing places: perhaps for no other topic would Aspen, Zermatt and Stowe be used and heard as co-class members.

Having suggested that locational formulations fall into types and collections, we can return to the concern with 'orientation to topic' or 'topic analysis' which occasioned this discussion.

The relevance of the organization of place formulations into collections is that, where one has collections, one has the possibility of attending in the selection of formulations, to the collections of which they are members. One can, for example, use a consistency rule in selecting a set of formulations to be used (see Sacks, 1969), selecting formulations which are members of a same collection (or, otherwise put, using the collection membership of the first formulation used to locate the collection from which subsequent terms are chosen). For place formulations one can select terms that will allow selection of other terms by use of a consistency rule, and which will allow a hearer to observe that a consistent (i.e. from some same collection) set of formulations has been employed.

For example, the relationship terms discussed earlier have a collection usage, independent of the place terms with which they are combined. So 'in front of____', 'in back of____', 'to the right of____', etc., can be seen, when used serially, to be drawn from a collection of such terms. And the place formulations to which this collection can be applied can have collection usages. We have already noted that place names can be analyzed as members of alternative collections. Here we can note that R_m terms are also capable of such organization, either by reference to the collection of places for some member (e.g., 'He could be at home, at the office or on the ranch'), or by reference to the places formulated by reference to members who are members of a single collection (e.g., 'Should we play at Bob's place, or Arthur's, or Bill's?' for a 'bridge circle'). Finally, the members of the collection of relational terms can be combined with a single place term ('in front of X', 'across the street from X', etc.), thus formulating a set of places, each of which could be formulated in a variety of ways (even within the constraints of a location and membership analysis), by their respective relations to a single point of reference. In such a circumstance (but not only in such a circumstance) it would appear not only that the terms were being chosen for consistency, but that they had consistency for a focus. Thus in the following data, all the place terms (which I have bracketed) appear to be formulated by reference to 'Shepherd's'.

JEANNETTE: Hello.
ESTELLE: Jeannette.
JEANNETTE: Yeah.
ESTELLE: Well, I just thought I'd – re – better report to you what's happen' at [Shepherd's] today /
JEANNETTE: What'n the world's happened // ed.
ESTELLE: D'you have the day off /
JEANNETTE: Yeah.
ESTELLE: Well I – v – got outta my car at five thirty I drove aroun' an' at first I had t'go by [the front a' the store,]
JEANNETTE: Eyeah /   20
ESTELLE: An' there was two / p'leece cars [across the street], andeh-colored lady wan'tuh go in [the main entrance] [there where the silver is] an' all the // [(gifts an' things),]
JEANNETTE: Yeah.
ESTELLE: And they, wouldn' let'er go [in], an' he hadda gun / He was holding a gun / in 'is hand, a great big long gun /
JEANNETTE: Yeh.
ESTELLE: An'nen [over on the other side], I mean [to the *right* of there], [where the – em*ploy*ees come out], there was a whole – oh musta been tenuh eight'r ten employees stanning there, because there musta been a – It seem like they had every entrance barred. I don' know what was go // ing *on*.
JEANNETTE: Oh, my *God*.
(Trio, 1–2)

And in another conversation a few minutes later:

JEANNETTE: Maybe it was uh somebody from maybe – They wuh – was it [from the bank] / maybe there was a bank / holdup an' they were just you know – p – pre*pared* the – maybe there were – yiknow sometimes the – hh they – rob 21 the bank, an' then they go [through Shepherd's] 'r something like that.
ESTELLE: Where's the *bank*?
JEANNETTE: [Right on the corner]
(Trio, 14–15)

That the terms are selected by reference to Shepherd's is the outcome of work. The police cars 'across the street' from Shepherd's were also 'in front of' some other store, but the former formulation is selected; the 'bank' is on the corner of some two intersecting streets (e.g. 'on the corner of Main and Spring'), but is here formulated as 'right on the corner', i.e. of Shepherd's block. Formulation selection *can* be done to focus *off* some object. For example:

B: Now for instance wu – she use to b*o*rrow from me. She borrowed twice, from me once.
A: Uh huh.   22
B: An', oh I was setting in 'er house, 'n Cal Major came 'n de*live*red something, and she w – said she didn't have the *change*. Would I loan 'er the money to *pay* 'im . . .
(SBL, 1, 1, 11, 1)

Here 'what was delivered' is focused away from by being formulated as 'something'. So 'focusing off' can be done conversationally. In the data of 20 and 21, 'Shepherd's' can, then, be focused *off* or focused *on*. The choice of formulations has done some work in focusing on it. And that focus is a focus on topic or oriented to topic, or partly constitutive of what the topic is. This, then, is an elaboration of one element of what we spoke of at the beginning of this paper (pp. 95–96) as 'co-selection of features (or descriptors) for topic', namely, selection of place formulations for topic.

As place formulations can have a collection membership and a consistency usage, so can membership identifications (see

Sacks, 1969), i.e. one can use a membership term that allows a subsequent one to be selected for its consistency with the first. Is there any relationship between consistent selections of membership identifications on the one hand, and consistent selections of location formulations on the other? Can there be, in other words, not only 'within type' consistency, but 'cross-type consistency'? We cannot pursue such an inquiry here. It is part of the much larger question: what types of descriptors can be massed for consistency considerations (as between types and not only within them) so as to show that each term was not picked randomly, without reference to topic, but was picked for (or to constitute) that topic for which the cross-type consistency is relevant. And, how is such co-selection done (e.g., is the selection for topic done within each type separately, or for one type initially, with subsequent types coordinated to the first, etc.)? The data already introduced can offer at least a suggestion in this respect.

There are a number of collections of membership identification terms available for formulating the persons referred to in the story under discussion in the conversations from which 20 and 21 are taken. Consistent identifications would have been made by, e.g., the terms 'men' and 'women'. But although consistent among themselves, these member identifications would have stood in no relevant relation to the selection of place terms focused on 'Shepherd's'. On the other hand, the collection whose terms include 'employees', 'customers', etc., would be relevant to that focus, to the type of place 'Shepherd's' is. It seems that this is the collection of membership terms used. At the end of 20, 'employees' is used to formulate the persons 'stanning there' (persons who 'could have been' formulated by sex, age, race, etc.). As for the term near the beginning of 20 'andeh-colored lady', it can be shown that it is used here as a description of a 'kind of customer' where 'customer' is not said.

That such 'unspoken' primary categorizations are done can be seen in the use made of the identification 'a blond'. Although it appears that this term identifies as its primary category 'color hair' or 'type of member with blond hair', the term is used to specify a sub-class of female. 'Female' is then the primary categorization, though unstated. Unstated primary categorizations, then, are possible. That 'colored lady' is used here as a secondary sub-classification within a primary 'customer' (or 'non-employee') is suggested by the following data from 'Jeannette's' call to a fellow employee at Shepherd's to find out 'what happened' which occurred between the conversations from which **20** and **21** are respectively excerpted. Passing on what was reported to her, she says:

JEANNETTE: Well, she said that there was some *wo*man that – the – they they were whh – had held up in the front there, thet they were pointing the *gun* at, 'n everything. A c-negro woman.
PENELOPE: NO::: *No.*
JEANNETTE: What.
PENELOPE: Dat was one of the emPLOYees.
JEANNETTE: Oh.   **23**
PENELOPE: He ran up to 'er an' she jus' ran up to 'im an' sez 'What's happ'n what's 'app'n'' W'l the kids were all laffing abou//t it,
JEANNETTE: Oh/ heh heh heh heh // heh heh
PENELOPE: An' she wuh – That was somebody thet worked in the *sto//re*
(Trio, 10)

It appears, then, that there can be links of consistency or relevance between types of descriptions, e.g., for personnel and for place; that one gets an adaptation to 'Shepherd's', that given the type of place 'Shepherd's' is there are constraints on the kind of identification that will be made of personnel, and that selection of each kind of term can be produced with an orientation to topic. Aside from location and membership analysis, then, 'topic analysis' seems to be relevant to the selection of a locational formulation. It is relevant to a speaker in building or assembling 'a topic', and relevant to a hearer in analyzing what is being talked to, what the focus is; indeed, as a hearer must analyze place formulations that are used to find their relevance, place formulations can be used to focus his analysis; their co-selection with other descriptors creates the relevance that he finds in his analysis. It may be in the light of this co-selection that we should appreciate that the use of 'Junior High School' to answer 'When did this happen' in **2** above is followed by the introduction into the story of characters formulated as 'principal' and 'teacher', and the answer 'I work in a driving school' to the question 'Wha' dijuh do for a living' in 1 occurs in the middle of a conversation which began:

B: I like tuh ask you something.
A: Shoot.
B: Y'know _I_ 'ad my licen'suspendid fuh six munts.   **24**
A: Uh huh.
B: Y'know for a reaz'n which, I rathuh not mensh'n tuh you, in othuh words – a serious reaz'n, en I like tuh know if I w'd talk to my senator, or – somebuddy, could _they_ help me get it back.
(BC, B, 20)

It may be that co-selection for topic is relevant not only for selection of _a_ place term given the relevance of _some_ place term; it may also be relevant to the selection of a place term to formulate a non-place descriptor.

   I have urged that in the selection and adequate hearing of a locational formulation, at least three orders of consideration are relevant – a location analysis, a membership analysis and a topic analysis – and I have tried to sketch the dimensions of the selection problem, and the kinds of work subsumed under the analyses that are involved [...]

Concluding remarks

I have argued that for any 'place', there is a set of terms or formulations which are 'correct'. On any occasion of employing a term for that 'place', much less than the full set is 'right' or adequate (i.e. not producing questions, or further questions, requiring reformulations).[12] It happens, on the whole, that speakers select 'right' or adequate formulations, and do preliminary work if it is required in order to do so. The selection of a

12. Although we have omitted consideration of the following point earlier, it is important to note it here. 'Right' formulations need _not_ be drawn from the set of 'correct' formulations; it is not a set-sub-set relationship. When one office worker says to another at the end of a coffee break, 'Well, back to the salt mines', the rightness of the formulation is not precluded by the 'incorrectness' of the term as a description of his work place. This is a direct parallel for place formulations to what Sacks calls 'intentional mis-identification' for membership identification.

'right' term, and the hearing of a term as adequate, appears to involve sensitivity to the respective locations of the participants and referent (which can change over the course of the interaction); to the membership composition of the interaction, and the knowledge of the world seen by members to be organized by membership categories (where the composition can change over the course of the interaction); and to the topic or activity being done in the conversation at that point in its course, and which is, at least in part, constituted as 'that topic' or 'that activity' by the formulations selected to realize it.

If this is so, then it seems to follow that on each occasion in conversation on which a formulation of location is used, attention is exhibited to the particulars of the occasion. In selecting a 'right' formulation, attention is exhibited to 'where-we-know-we-are', to 'who-we-know-we-are', to 'what-we-are-doing-at-this-point-in-the-conversation'. A 'right' formulation exhibits, in the very fact of its production, that it is some 'this conversation, at this place, with these members, at this point in its course' which has been analyzed to select that term; it exhibits, in the very fact of its production, that it is some particular 'this situation' which is producing it.[13]

13. This point is reminiscent of a classic concern of the sociology of knowledge. It has been part of the program of one approach in the sociology of knowledge that accounts, descriptions, theories, etc. are to be examined most importantly not with respect to the objects with which they seek to come to terms, but with respect to the circumstances of the producers of the account, or its audience. To understand how some account comes to be offered, an investigator should look not to the objects being addressed; they will not explain the production of the account. It is to the circumstances of its production (its environing class structure, Zeitgeist, psychic states, cultural values, professional ambience, etc. in traditional studies) that one must look to understand its occurrence. I have argued here that formulations of location are used by reference to, and hence exhibit or 'reflect,' the situational or contextual features of their production. That a formulation is 'correct' is, in this context, the least interesting of its features, for it would be equally true of a range of other formulations. Not any 'correct' formulation will do. 'Right' formulations are 'right' in part by exhibiting the particulars of the situation of their use. These notes may then be read as bearing not only on issues in the study of conversational interaction, but also (if the two are separable) as an essay in the sociology of common sense knowledge. See Garfinkel (1967), and, especially, Garfinkel and Sacks (1969).

It is one lesson of these materials that formulation of locations accomplish and exhibit the particularities of an interaction, and they do this through general, formal structures. (By the last phrase I mean to note that the problem of selecting a term from a collection of terms, or of selecting a collection from a set of collections, is a general, formal procedure, although its outcomes can be particular to the circumstances in which the operation is done. The contrast might be where particularities of situation would be exhibited by unique markers for a situation or class of situations.) We can now look to see for what other domains this lesson is relevant. Are there kinds of conversational practices which cannot do this? Are there many others designed for that kind of use, which permit conversation to operate within very tight constraints, while each one can be at each point a matter for analysis as the outcome of a general practice and part of a general structure?

As for the former question, it appears that the most general sequencing structures of conversation for which we have descriptions hold across such variations as place formulations reflect (Sacks, 1967, and forthcoming, a). As for the second question, it seems to invite a detailed, empirical examination of the gloss 'context'.

These notes may be read as pertinent to some ways 'contextual variation' affects interaction. It is being proposed that the much invoked 'dependence on context' must be investigated by showing that, and how, *participants* analyze context and use the product of their analysis in producing their interaction. To say that *interaction* is context-sensitive is to say that *interactants* are context-sensitive, and for what and how that is so is an empirical matter which can be researched in detail (cf. Hymes, 1967). One dimension has to do with the ways in which interactants particularize their contributions so as to exhibit attention to the 'this-one-here-and-now-for-us-at-this-point-in-it' character of the interaction. I have tried to suggest that place formulations particularize at least for location, composition (at least with respect to those membership categories relevant to the selection of place formulation) and place in conversation (topic, activity). It is now in order to see what range of conversational practices are subject to similar usage, what kinds of organization they have, whether or not they are fitted to one another, etc.

That others await description seems clear. One need only note that selection of age terms for members (see Sacks, 1969), and the selection of collections of age terms from which to select a term, seems to exhibit attention to particularities, especially of membership (although other categories of member seem to be involved than in the case of place-formulation-selection). Thus, terms like 'older man' or 'young woman' can not be divorced from the age composition of participants in the conversation in which they occur, as 'he's forty-five' may on occasion be. So the alternative collection of age terms – the one being the set of terms of the form 'n years old', the other the set of terms including 'young, old, younger, older, middle-aged, not so old, . . .' – may have different potential for exhibiting attention to particularities of membership composition, and may be selected accordingly. If a term is chosen from the latter collection, it may then be used to exhibit attention to the specific membership composition of an interaction.

More directly parallel to discussion of place formulation are temporal formulations. Although this is certainly not the place to develop an analysis, a few observations may suggest that temporal formulations may particularize in their domain in a manner congruent with location formulation. Note that an event may be formulated as occurring at '2:06; about 2; in the afternoon; Monday afternoon; Monday; the third week in January; January; 23 January; 23 January 1964; 23 January 1964 AD'; providing a seeming calendrical parallel to what were called G terms above. Or an event can be formulated as 'before we met', 'after the baby was born', 'a month after your grandfather died', etc., forms which appear to be for temporal formulations similar to R_m terms in place formulations. Formulations such 'as the day after the Kennedy assassination', 'a week before the election', 'the day of the storm', etc. are for various membership groups located by 'reference to landmark', here 'landmark' dates. There seem to be preferred temporal formulations and transformations to them (as is the case with place formulations), as in the following data:

A: You know when the next meeting of the curriculum committee is?

B: Friday morning, at 10:00
A: Tomorrow.
B: Right.

in which B's choice of formulation is found not 'right' in not exhibiting a grasp of the 'when' of the conversation in relation to the object being talked of.

In short, there is reason to believe that a search for other conversational practices which exhibit attention to the particularities of the interaction in which they occur will find others; some perhaps with a structure similar to that discussed here in connection with place formulations, others perhaps quite different. As more such practices are subjected to analyses, we may be able more fully to document empirically an argument which can be suggested only tentatively from this discussion, concerning the 'efficiency' of language as a resource in interaction. Various investigators have claimed that language is overbuilt for the kind of use it ordinarily gets (see e.g., Sapir, 1921, p. 13; Weinreich, 1966, p. 147); that it would be more efficient to have a single term for each referent, and each term refer to but a single referent, and not have synonyms; that there is much redundancy built into human communication because of the defectiveness of language or of humans as senders and receivers of messages, and redundancy allows messages to get through anyhow (Cherry, 1957, p. 117). If one takes conversational interaction among a society's members as one's domain (rather than characteristics of communication channels or linguistic structures exempted from daily use), then the major interest may rather be in the way alternative available formulations of objects allow the exploitation of members' analytic skills to accomplish a fundamental feature of everyday, organized social life. For it is through such resources that the production of a world of particular specific scenes through a set of general formal practices is accomplished and exhibited.

References

CHERRY, C. (1957), *On Human Communication*, M.I.T. Press.
CONKLIN, H. (1955), 'Hanunoo color categories', *Southwestern Journal of Anthropology*, vol. 11, no. 4, pp. 339–43.
FRAKE, C. O. (1961), 'The diagnosis of disease among the Subanun of Mindanao', *American Anthropologist*, vol. 62, no. 1, pp. 113–32.

FRITZ, C. E. and MATHEWSON, J. H. (1957), *Convergence Behavior in Disasters: A Problem in Social Control*, National Academy of Science, National Research Council, Washington.

GARFINKEL, H. (1967), *Studies in Ethnomethodology*, Prentice-Hall.

GARFINKEL, H. and SACKS, H. (1969), 'On formal structures of practical actions', in J. C. McKinney and E. Tiryakian (eds.), *Theoretical Sociology: Perspectives and Developments*, Appleton-Century-Crofts, forthcoming.

GOODENOUGH, W. (1956), 'Componential analysis and the study of meaning', *Language*, vol. 32, pp. 195–216.

HYMES, D. (1967), 'Models of the interaction of language and social setting', *Journal of Social Issues*, vol. 33, no. 2, pp. 8–28.

LOUNSBURY, F. (1956), 'A semantic analysis of the Pawnee kinship usage', *Language*, vol. 32, pp. 158–94.

LYNCH, K. (1960), *The Image of the City*, M.I.T. Press.

MOERMAN, M. (1967), 'Being Lue: uses and abuses of ethnic identification' American Ethnological Society, Proceedings of 1967 Spring Meetings.

PSATHAS, G. and KOZLOFF, M. (1968), 'The structure of directions: an analysis of an everyday activity', mimeo.

SACKS, H. (n.d.), 'On a device basic to social interaction', mimeo.

SACKS, H. (1967), Transcribed Lectures, mimeo.

SACKS, H. (1969), 'The search for help', in D. Sudnow (ed.), *Studies in Social Interaction*, Free Press, in press.

SACKS, H. (forthcoming, a), *The Organization of Conversation*, Prentice-Hall.

SACKS, H. (forthcoming, b), 'The Baby Cried,' in H. Garfinkel and H. Sacks (eds.), *Contributions to Ethnomethodology*, Indiana University Press.

SAPIR, E. (1921), *Language*, Harcourt, Brace & Co.

SCHEGLOFF, E. A. (1967), 'The first five seconds: the order of conversational openings', Ph.D. dissertation, Department of Sociology, University of California, Berkeley.

SCHELLING, T. (1963), *The Strategy of Conflict*, Oxford University Press.

SUTTLES, G. D. (1968), *The Social Order of the Slum: Ethnicity and Territory in the Inner City*, University of Chicago Press.

WEINREICH, U. (1966), 'On the semantic structure of language,' in Joseph Greenberg (ed.), *Universals of Language*, 2nd edn, M.I.T. Press.

Data sources

BC   Telephone conversations on a radio 'talk show'.

GTS   Group psychotherapy sessions with teenagers.

CPD   Calls to the emergency desk of the police department of a midwestern city.

SBL   Phone conversations in a western city.

Trio   A series of three phone conversations, A to B, B to C,
        B to A.
DA   Phone conversation.
IPD   Phone calls to midwestern police department in immediate
        aftermath of a disaster.
TAC   Phone conversations among young adults in a western
        city.
*   indicates invented data.

Symbols used in transcripts

/	indicates upward intonation
//	indicates point at which following line interrupts
(n.o)	indicates pause of n.o seconds
[[	indicates simultaneous utterances when bridging two lines
( )	indicates something said but not transcribable
(word)	indicates probably what said, but not clear
but	indicates accent
em*PLOY*ee	indicates heavy accent
: : :	indicates stretching of sound immediately preceding, in proportion to number of colons inserted
becau–	indicates broken word

7 J. Searle

What Is a Speech Act?

J. Searle, 'What is a speech act?', in M. Black (ed.), *Philosophy in America*, Allen & Unwin and Cornell University Press, 1965, pp. 221–39

Introduction

In a typical speech situation involving a speaker, a hearer, and an utterance by the speaker, there are many kinds of acts associated with the speaker's utterance. The speaker will characteristically have moved his jaw and tongue and made noises. In addition, he will characteristically have performed some acts within the class which includes informing or irritating or boring his hearers; he will further characteristically have performed acts within the class which includes referring to Kennedy or Khrushchev or the North Pole; and he will also have performed acts within the class which includes making statements, asking questions, issuing commands, giving reports, greeting, and warning. The members of this last class are what Austin (1962) called illocutionary acts and it is with this class that I shall be concerned in this paper, so the paper might have been called 'What is an Illocutionary Act?' I do not attempt to define the expression 'illocutionary act', although if my analysis of a particular illocutionary act succeeds it may provide the basis for a definition. Some of the English verbs and verb phrases associated with illocutionary acts are: state, assert, describe, warn, remark, comment, command, order, request, criticize, apologize, censure, approve, welcome, promise, express approval and express regret. Austin claimed that there were over a thousand such expressions in English.

By way of introduction, perhaps I can say why I think it is of interest and importance in the philosophy of language to study speech acts, or, as they are sometimes called, language acts or linguistic acts. I think it is essential to any specimen of linguistic communication that it involve a linguistic act. It is not, as has generally been supposed, the symbol or word or sentence, or even the token of the symbol or word or sentence, which is the unit of linguistic communication, but rather it is the *production* of the token in the performance of the speech act that constitutes the basic unit of linguistic communication. To put this point more precisely, the production of the sentence token under certain conditions is the illocutionary act, and the illocutionary act is the minimal unit of linguistic communication.

I do not know how to *prove* that linguistic communication essentially involves acts but I can think of arguments with which one might attempt to convince someone who was skeptical. One argument would be to call the skeptic's attention to the fact that when he takes a noise or a mark on paper to be an instance of linguistic communication, as a message, one of the things that is involved in his so taking that noise or mark is that he should regard it as having been produced by a being with certain intentions. He cannot just regard it as a natural phenomenon, like a stone, a waterfall, or a tree. In order to regard it as an instance of linguistic communication one must suppose that its production is what I am calling a speech act. It is a logical presupposition, for example, of current attempts to decipher the Mayan hieroglyphs that we at least hypothesize that the marks we see on the stones were produced by beings more or less like ourselves and produced with certain kinds of intentions. If we were certain the marks were a consequence of, say, water erosion, then the question of deciphering them or even calling them hieroglyphs could not arise. To construe them under the category of linguistic communication necessarily involves construing their production as speech acts.

To perform illocutionary acts is to engage in a rule-governed form of behavior. I shall argue that such things as asking questions or making statements are rule-governed in ways quite similar to those in which getting a base hit in baseball or moving a knight in chess are rule-governed forms of acts. I intend therefore to explicate the notion of an illocutionary act by stating a set of necessary and sufficient conditions for the performance of a particular kind of illocutionary act, and extracting from it a set of semantical rules for the use of the expression (or syntactic device) which marks the utterance as an illocutionary act of that kind. If I am successful in stating the conditions and the corresponding rules for even one kind of illocutionary act, that will provide us with a pattern for analyzing other kinds of acts and consequently for explicating the notion in general. But in order to set the stage for actually stating conditions and extracting rules for performing an illocutionary act I have to discuss three other preliminary notions: *rules*, *propositions* and *meaning*. I shall confine my discussion of these notions to those aspects which are essential to my main purposes in this paper, but, even so, what I wish to say concerning each of these notions, if it were to be at all complete, would require a paper for each; however, sometimes it may be worth sacrificing thoroughness for the sake of scope and I shall therefore be very brief.

Rules

In recent years there has been in the philosophy of language considerable discussion involving the notion of rules for the use of expressions. Some philosophers have even said that knowing the meaning of a word is simply a matter of knowing the rules for its use or employment. One disquieting feature of such discussions is that no philosopher, to my knowledge at least, has ever given anything like an adequate formulation of the rules for the use of even one expression. If meaning is a matter of rules of use, surely we ought to be able to state the rules for the use of expressions in a way which would explicate the meaning of those expressions. Certain other philosophers, dismayed perhaps by the failure of their colleagues to produce any rules, have denied the fashionable view that meaning is a matter of rules and have asserted that there are no semantical rules of the proposed kind at all. I am inclined to think that this skepticism is premature and stems from a failure to distinguish different sorts of rules, in a way which I shall now attempt to explain.

I distinguish between two sorts of rules: some regulate antecedently existing forms of behavior; for example, the rules of etiquette regulate interpersonal relationships, but these relationships exist independently of the rules of etiquette. Some rules on the other hand do not merely regulate but create or define new forms of behavior. The rules of football, for example, do not merely regulate the game of football but as it were create the possibility of or define that activity. The activity of playing football is constituted by acting in accordance with these rules; football has no existence apart from these rules. I call the latter kind of rules constitutive rules and the former kind regulative rules. Regulative rules regulate a pre-existing activity, an activity whose existence is logically independent of the existence of the rules. Constitutive rules constitute (and also regulate) an activity the existence of which is logically dependent on the rules.[1]

Regulative rules characteristically take the form of or can be paraphrased as imperatives, e.g. 'When cutting food hold the knife in the right hand', or 'Officers are to wear ties at dinner'. Some constitutive rules take quite a different form, e.g. a checkmate is made if the king is attacked in such a way that no move will leave it unattacked; a touchdown is scored when a player crosses the opponents' goal line in possession of the ball while a play is in progress. If our paradigms of rules are imperative regulative rules, such non-imperative constitutive rules are likely to strike us as extremely curious and hardly even as rules at all. Notice that they are almost tautological in character, for what the 'rule' seems to offer is a partial definition of 'checkmate' or 'touchdown'. But, of course, this quasi-tautological character is a necessary consequence of their being constitutive rules: the rules concerning touchdowns must define the notion of 'touchdown' in the same way that the rules concerning football define 'football'. That, for example, a touchdown can be scored in such and such ways and counts six points can appear sometimes as a rule, sometimes as an analytic truth; and that it can be construed as a tautology is a clue to the fact that the rule in question is a constitutive one. Regulative rules generally have the form 'Do X' or 'If Y do X'. Some members of the set of constitutive rules have this form but some also have the form 'X counts as Y'.[2]

The failure to perceive this is of some importance in philosophy. Thus, e.g., some philosophers ask 'How can a promise create an obligation?' A similar question would be 'How can a touchdown create six points?' And as they stand both questions can only be answered by stating a rule of the form 'X counts as Y'.

I am inclined to think that both the failure of some philosophers to state rules for the use of expressions and the skepticism of other

1. This distinction occurs in Rawls (1955), and Searle (1964).
2. The formulation 'X counts as Y' was originally suggested to me by Max Black.

philosophers concerning the existence of any such rules stem at least in part from a failure to recognize the distinctions between constitutive and regulative rules. The model or paradigm of a rule which most philosophers have is that of a regulative rule, and if one looks in semantics for purely regulative rules one is not likely to find anything interesting from the point of view of logical analysis. There are no doubt social rules of the form 'One ought not to utter obscenities at formal gatherings', but that hardly seems a rule of the sort that is crucial in explicating the semantics of a language. The hypothesis that lies behind the present paper is that the semantics of a language can be regarded as a series of systems of constitutive rules and that illocutionary acts are acts performed in accordance with these sets of constitutive rules. One of the aims of this paper is to formulate a set of constitutive rules for a certain kind of speech act. And if what I have said concerning constitutive rules is correct, we should not be surprised if not all these rules take the form of imperative rules. Indeed we shall see that the rules fall into several different categories, none of which is quite like the rules of etiquette. The effort to state the rules for an illocutionary act can also be regarded as a kind of test of the hypothesis that there are constitutive rules underlying speech acts. If we are unable to give any satisfactory rule formulations, our failure could be construed as partially disconfirming evidence against the hypothesis.

Propositions

Different illocutionary acts often have features in common with each other. Consider utterances of the following sentences:

1 Will John leave the room?
2 John will leave the room.
3 John, leave the room!
4 Would that John left the room.
5 If John will leave the room, I will leave also.

Utterances of each of these on a given occasion would characteristically be performances of different illocutionary acts. The first would, characteristically, be a question, the second an assertion about the future, that is, a prediction, the third a request or order, the fourth an expression of a wish and the fifth a hypothetical expression of intention. Yet in the performance of each the speaker would characteristically perform some subsidiary acts which are common to all five illocutionary acts. In the utterance of each the speaker *refers* to a particular person John and *predicates* the act of leaving the room of that person. In no case is that all he does, but in every case it is a part of what he does. I shall say, therefore, that in each of these cases, although the illocutionary acts are different, at least some of the non-illocutionary acts of reference and predication are the same.

The reference to some person John and predication of the same thing of him in each of these illocutionary acts inclines me to say that there is a common *content* in each of them. Something expressible by the clause 'that John will leave the room' seems to be a common feature of all. We could, with not too much distortion, write each of these sentences in a way which would isolate this common feature: 'I assert that John will leave the room', 'I ask whether John will leave the room', etc.

For lack of a better word I propose to call this common content a proposition, and I shall describe this feature of these illocutionary acts by saying that in the utterance of each of (1)–(5) the speaker expresses the proposition that John will leave the room. Notice that I do not say that the sentence expresses the proposition; I do not know how sentences could perform acts of that kind. But I shall say that in the utterance of the sentence the speaker expresses a proposition. Notice also that I am distinguishing between a proposition and an assertion or statement of that proposition. The proposition that John will leave the room is expressed in the utterance of all of (1)–(5) but only in (2) is that proposition asserted. An assertion is an illocutionary act, but a proposition is not an act at all, although the act of expressing a proposition is a part of performing certain illocutionary acts.

I might summarize this by saying that I am distinguishing between the illocutionary act and the propositional content of an illocutionary act. Of course, not all illocutionary acts have a propositional content, for example, an utterance of 'Hurrah!' or 'Ouch!' does not. In one version or another this distinction is an old one and has been marked in different ways by authors as diverse as Frege, Sheffer, Lewis, Reichenbach and Hare, to mention only a few.

From a semantical point of view we can distinguish between the propositional indicator in the sentence and the indicator of illocutionary force. That is, for a large class of sentences used to perform illocutionary acts, we can say for the purpose of our analysis that the sentence has two (not necessarily separate) parts, the proposition indicating element and the function indicating device.[3] The function indicating device shows how the proposition is to be taken, or, to put it in another way, what illocutionary force the utterance is to have, that is, what illocutionary act the speaker is performing in the utterance of the sentence. Function indicating devices in English include word order, stress, intonation contour, punctuation, the mood of the verb, and finally a set of so-called performative verbs: I may indicate the kind of illocutionary act I am performing by beginning the sentence with 'I apologize', 'I warn', 'I state', etc. Often in actual speech situations the context will make it clear what the illocutionary force of the utterance is, without its being necessary to invoke the appropriate function indicating device.

If this semantical distinction is of any real importance, it seems likely that it should have some syntactical analogue, and certain recent developments in transformational grammar tend to support the view that it does. In the underlying phrase marker of a sentence there is a distinction between those elements which correspond to the function indicating device and those which correspond to the propositional content.

The distinction between the function indicating device and the proposition indicating device will prove very useful to us in giving an analysis of an illocutionary act. Since the same proposition can be common to all sorts of illocutionary acts, we can separate our analysis of the proposition from our analysis of kinds of illocutionary acts. I think there are rules for expressing propositions, rules for such things as reference and predication, but those rules can be discussed independently of the rules for function indicating. In this paper I shall not attempt to discuss propositional rules but shall concentrate on rules for using certain kinds of function indicating devices.

3. In the sentence 'I promise that I will come' the function indicating device and the propositional element are separate. In the sentence 'I promise to come', which means the same as the first and is derived from it by certain transformations, the two elements are not separate.

Meaning

Speech acts are characteristically performed in the utterance of sounds or the making of marks. What is the difference between *just* uttering sounds or making marks and performing a speech act? One difference is that the sounds or marks one makes in the performance of a speech act are characteristically said to *have meaning*, and a second related difference is that one is characteristically said to *mean something* by those sounds or marks. Characteristically when one speaks one means something by what one says, and what one says, the string of morphemes that one emits, is characteristically said to have a meaning. Here, incidentally, is another point at which our analogy between performing speech acts and playing games breaks down. The pieces in a game like chess are not characteristically said to have a meaning, and furthermore when one makes a move one is not characteristically said to mean anything by that move.

But what is it for one to mean something by what one says, and what is it for something to have a meaning? To answer the first of these questions I propose to borrow and revise some ideas of Paul Grice. In an article entitled 'Meaning', Grice (1957) gives the following analysis of one sense of the notion of 'meaning'. To say that *A* meant something by *x* is to say that '*A* intended the utterance of *x* to produce some effect in an audience by means of the recognition of this intention'. This seems to me a useful start on an analysis of meaning, first because it shows the close relationship between the notion of meaning and the notion of intention, and secondly because it captures something which is, I think, essential to speaking a language: in speaking a language I attempt to communicate things to my hearer by means of getting him to recognize my intention to communicate just those things. For example, characteristically, when I make an assertion, I attempt to communicate to and convince my hearer of the truth of a certain proposition; and the means I employ to do this are to utter certain sounds, which utterance I intend to produce in him the desired effect by means of his recognition of my intention to produce just that effect. I shall illustrate this with an example. I might on the one hand attempt to get you to believe that I am French by speaking French all the time, dressing in the French manner, showing wild enthusiasm for de Gaulle, and cultivating French acquaintances. But I might on the other hand attempt to get you to believe that I am French by simply telling you that I am French. Now, what is the difference between these two ways of my attempting to get you to believe that I am French? One crucial difference is that in the second case I attempt to get you to believe that I am French by getting you to recognize that it is my purported intention to get you to believe just that. That is one of the things involved in telling you that I am French. But of course if I try to get you to believe that I am French by putting on the act I described, then your recognition of my intention to produce in you the belief that I am French is not the means I am employing. Indeed in this case you would, I think, become rather suspicious if you recognized my intention.

However valuable this analysis of meaning is, it seems to me to be in certain respects defective. First of all, it fails to distinguish the different kinds of effects – perlocutionary versus illocutionary – that one may intend to produce in one's hearers, and it further fails to show the way in which these different kinds of effects are related to the notion of meaning. A second defect is that it fails to account for the extent to which meaning is a matter of rules or conventions. That is, this account of meaning does not show the connection between one's meaning something by what one says and what that which one says actually means in the language. In order to illustrate this point I now wish to present a counter-example to this analysis of meaning. The point of the counter-example will be to illustrate the connection between what a speaker means and what the words he utters mean.

Suppose that I am an American soldier in the Second World War and that I am captured by Italian troops. And suppose also that I wish to get these troops to believe that I am a German officer in order to get them to release me. What I would like to do is to tell them in German or Italian that I am a German officer. But let us suppose I don't know enough German or Italian to do that. So I, as it were, attempt to put on a show of telling them that I am a German officer by reciting those few bits of German that I know, trusting that they don't know enough German to see through my plan. Let us suppose I know only one line of German, which I remember from a poem I had to memorize in a high school German course. Therefore I, a captured American, address my Italian captors with the following sentence: 'Kennst du das Land, wo die Zitronen blühen?' Now, let us describe the situation in Gricean terms. I intend to produce a certain effect in them, namely, the effect of believing that I am a German officer; and I intend to produce this effect by means of their recognition of my intention. I intend that they should think that I am trying to tell them that I am a German officer. But does it follow from this account that when I say 'Kennst du das Land ...' etc., what I mean is, 'I am a German officer'? Not only does it not follow, but in this case it seems plainly false that when I utter the German sentence what I mean is 'I am a German officer', or even 'Ich bin ein deutscher Offizier', because what the words mean is, 'Knowest thou the land where the lemon trees bloom?' Of course, I want my captors to be deceived into thinking that what I mean is 'I am a German officer', but part of what is involved in the deception is getting them to think that that is what the words which I utter mean in German. At one point in the *Philosophical Investigations* Wittgenstein (1953) says 'Say "it's cold here" and mean "it's warm here" '. The reason we are unable to do this is that what we can mean is a function of what we are saying. Meaning is more than a matter of intention, it is also a matter of convention.

Grice's account can be amended to deal with counter-examples of this kind. We have here a case where I am trying to produce a certain effect by means of the recognition of my intention to produce that effect, but the device I use to produce this effect is one which is conventionally, by the rules governing the use of that device, used as a means of producing quite different illocutionary effects. We must therefore reformulate the Gricean account of meaning in such a way as to make it clear that one's meaning something when one says something is more than just contingently related to what the sentence means in the language one is speaking. In our analysis of illocutionary acts, we must capture both the intentional and the conventional aspects and especially the relationship between them. In the performance of an illocutionary act the speaker intends to produce a certain effect by means of getting the hearer to recognize his intention to produce that effect, and furthermore, if he is using words literally, he intends this recognition to be achieved in virtue of the fact that the rules for using the expressions he utters associate the expressions with the production of that effect. It is this *combination* of elements which we shall need to express in our analysis of the illocutionary act.

How to promise

I shall now attempt to give an analysis of the illocutionary act of promising. In order to do this I shall ask what conditions are necessary and sufficient for the act of promising to have been performed in the utterance of a given sentence. I shall attempt to answer this question by stating these conditions as a set of propositions such that the conjunction of the members of the set entails the proposition that a speaker made a promise, and the proposition that the speaker made a promise entails this conjunction. Thus each condition will be a necessary condition for the performance of the act of promising, and taken collectively the set of conditions will be a sufficient condition for the act to have been performed.

If we get such a set of conditions we can extract from them a set of rules for the use of the function indicating device. The method here is analogous to discovering the rules of chess by asking oneself what are the necessary and sufficient conditions under which one can be said to have correctly moved a knight or castled or checkmated a player, etc. We are in the position of someone who has learned to play chess without ever having the rules formulated and who wants such a formulation. We learned how to play the game of illocutionary acts, but in general it was done without an explicit formulation of the rules, and the first step in getting such a formulation is to set out the conditions for the performance of a particular illocutionary act. Our inquiry will therefore serve a double philosophical purpose. By stating a set of conditions for the performance of a particular illocutionary act we shall have offered a partial explication of that notion and shall also have paved the way for the second step, the formulation of the rules.

I find the statement of the conditions very difficult to do, and I am not entirely satisfied with the list I am about to present. One reason for the difficulty is that the notion of a promise, like most notions in ordinary language, does not have absolutely strict rules. There are all sorts of odd, deviant, and borderline promises; and counter-examples, more or less bizarre, can be produced against my analysis. I am inclined to think we shall not be able to get a set of knock down necessary and sufficient conditions that will exactly mirror the ordinary use of the word 'promise'. I am confining my discussion, therefore, to the centre of the concept of promising and ignoring the fringe, borderline, and partially defective cases. I also confine my discussion to full-blown explicit promises and ignore promises made by elliptical turns of phrase, hints, metaphors, etc.

Another difficulty arises from my desire to state the conditions without certain forms of circularity. I want to give a list of conditions for the performance of a certain illocutionary act, which do not themselves mention the performance of any illocutionary acts. I need to satisfy this condition in order to offer an explication of the notion of an illocutionary act in general, otherwise I should simply be showing the relation between different illocutionary acts. However, although there will be no reference to illocutionary *acts*, certain illocutionary *concepts* will appear in the analysans as well as in the analysandum; and I think this form of circularity is unavoidable because of the nature of constitutive rules.

In the presentation of the conditions I shall first consider the case of a sincere promise and then show how to modify the conditions to allow for insincere promises. As our inquiry is semantical rather than syntactical, I shall simply assume the existence of grammatically well-formed sentences.

Given that a speaker S utters a sentence T in the presence of a hearer H, then, in the utterance of T, S sincerely (and nondefectively) promises that p to H if and only if:

1 *Normal input and output conditions obtain*

I use the terms 'input' and 'output' to cover the large and indefinite range of conditions under which any kind of serious linguistic communication is possible. 'Output' covers the conditions for intelligible speaking and 'input' covers the conditions for understanding. Together they include such things as that the speaker and hearer both know how to speak the language; both are conscious of what they are doing; the speaker is not acting under duress or threats; they have no physical impediments to communication, such as deafness, aphasia or laryngitis; they are not acting in a play or telling jokes, etc.

2 *S expresses that p in the utterance of T*

This condition isolates the propositional content from the rest of the speech act and enables us to concentrate on the peculiarities of promising in the rest of the analysis.

3 *In expressing that p, S predicates a future act A of S*

In the case of promising the function indicating device is an expression whose scope includes certain features of the proposition. In a promise an act must be predicated of the speaker and it cannot be a past act. I cannot promise to have done something, and I cannot promise that someone else will do something. (Although I can promise to see that he will do it.) The notion of an act, as I am construing it for present purposes, includes refraining from acts, performing series of acts, and may also include states and conditions: I may promise not to do something, I may promise to do something repeatedly, and I may promise to be or remain in a certain state or condition. I call conditions (2) and (3) the *propositional content conditions*.

4 *H would prefer S's doing A to his not doing A, and S believes H would prefer his doing A to his not doing A*

One crucial distinction between promises on the one hand and threats on the other is that a promise is a pledge to do something for you, not to you, but a threat is a pledge to do something to you, not for you. A promise is defective if the thing promised is something the promisee does not want done; and it is further defective if the promisor does not believe the promisee wants it done, since a non-defective promise must be intended as a promise and not as a threat or warning. I think both halves of this double condition are necessary in order to avoid fairly obvious counter-examples.

One can, however, think of apparent counter-examples to this condition as stated. Suppose I say to a lazy student 'If you don't hand in your paper on time I promise you I will give you a failing grade in the course'. Is this utterance a promise? I am inclined to think not; we would more naturally describe it as a warning or possibly even a threat. But why then is it possible to use the locution 'I promise' in such a case? I think we use it here because 'I promise' and 'I hereby promise' are among the strongest function indicating devices for *commitment* provided by the English language. For that reason we often use these expressions in the performance of speech acts which are not strictly speaking promises but in which we wish to emphasize our commitment. To illustrate this, consider another apparent counter-example to the analysis along different lines. Sometimes, more commonly I think in the United States than in England, one hears people say 'I promise' when making an emphatic assertion. Suppose, for example, I accuse you of having stolen the money. I say, 'You stole that money, didn't you?' You reply 'No, I didn't, I promise you I didn't'. Did you make a promise in this case? I find it very unnatural to describe your utterance as a promise. This utterance would be more aptly described as an emphatic denial, and we can explain the occurrence of the function indicating device 'I promise' as derivative from genuine promises and serving here as an expression adding emphasis to your denial.

In general the point stated in condition (4) is that if a purported promise is to be non-defective the thing promised must be something the hearer wants done, or considers to be in his interest, or would prefer being done to not being done, etc.; and the speaker must be aware of or believe or know, etc. that this is the case. I think a more elegant and exact formulation of this condition would require the introduction of technical terminology.

5 *It is not obvious to both S and H that S will do A in the normal course of events*

This condition is an instance of a general condition on many different kinds of illocutionary acts to the effect that the act must have a point. For example, if I make a request to someone to do something which it is obvious that he is already doing or is about to do, then my request is pointless and to that extent defective. In an actual speech situation, listeners, knowing the rules for performing illocutionary acts, will assume that this condition is satisfied. Suppose, for example, that in the course of a public speech I say to a member of my audience 'Look here, Smith, pay attention to what I am saying'. In order to make sense of this utterance the audience will have to assume that Smith has not been paying attention or at any rate that it is not obvious that he has been paying attention, that the question of his paying attention has arisen in some way; because a condition for making a request is that it is not obvious that the hearer is doing or about to do the thing requested.

Similarly with promises. It is out of order for me to promise to do something that it is obvious I am going to do anyhow. If I do seem to be making such a promise, the only way my audience can make sense of my utterance is to assume that I believe that it is not obvious that I am going to do the thing promised. A happily married man who promises his wife he will not desert her in the next week is likely to provide more anxiety than comfort.

Parenthetically I think this condition is an instance of the sort of phenomenon stated in Zipf's law. I think there is operating in our language, as in most forms of human behavior, a principle of least effort, in this case a principle of maximum illocutionary ends with minimum phonetic effort; and I think condition (5) is an instance of it.

I call conditions such as (4) and (5) *preparatory conditions*. They are *sine quibus non* of happy promising, but they do not yet state the essential feature.

6 *S intends to do A*

The most important distinction between sincere and insincere promises is that in the case of the sincere promise the speaker intends to do the act promised, in the case of the insincere promise he does not intend to do the act. Also in sincere promises the speaker believes it is possible for him to do the act (or to refrain from doing it), but I think the proposition that he intends to do it entails that he thinks it is possible to do (or refrain from doing) it, so I am not stating that as an extra condition. I call this condition the *sincerity condition*.

7 *S intends that the utterance of T will place him under an obligation to do A*

The essential feature of a promise is that it is the undertaking of an obligation to perform a certain act. I think that this condition distinguishes promises (and other members of the same family such as vows) from other kinds of speech acts. Notice that in the statement of the condition we only specify the speaker's intention;

further conditions will make clear how that intention is realized. It is clear, however, that having this intention is a necessary condition of making a promise; for if a speaker can demonstrate that he did not have this intention in a given utterance, he can prove that the utterance was not a promise. We know, for example, that Mr Pickwick did not promise to marry the woman because we know he did not have the appropriate intention.

I call this the *essential condition*.

8 *S intends that the utterance of T will produce in H a belief that conditions (6) and (7) obtain by means of the recognition of the intention to produce that belief, and he intends this recognition to be achieved by means of the recognition of the sentence as one conventionally used to produce such beliefs*

This captures our amended Gricean analysis of what it is for the speaker to mean to make a promise. The speaker intends to produce a certain illocutionary effect by means of getting the hearer to recognize his intention to produce that effect, and he also intends this recognition to be achieved in virtue of the fact that the lexical and syntactical character of the item he utters conventionally associates it with producing that effect.

Strictly speaking this condition could be formulated as part of condition (1), but it is of enough philosophical interest to be worth stating separately. I find it troublesome for the following reason. If my original objection to Grice is really valid, then surely, one might say, all these iterated intentions are superfluous; all that is necessary is that the speaker should seriously utter a sentence. The production of all these effects is simply a consequence of the hearer's knowledge of what the sentence means, which in turn is a consequence of his knowledge of the language, which is assumed by the speaker at the outset. I think the correct reply to this objection is that condition (8) explicates what it is for the speaker to 'seriously' utter the sentence, i.e. to utter it and mean it, but I am not completely confident about either the force of the objection or of the reply.

9 *The semantical rules of the dialect spoken by S and H are such that T is correctly and sincerely uttered if and only if conditions (1)–(8) obtain*

This condition is intended to make clear that the sentence uttered is one which by the semantical rules of the language is used to make a promise. Taken together with condition (8), it eliminates counter-examples like the captured soldier example considered earlier. Exactly what the formulation of the rules is, we shall soon see.

So far we have considered only the case of a sincere promise. But insincere promises are promises nonetheless, and we now need to show how to modify the conditions to allow for them. In making an insincere promise the speaker does not have all the intentions and beliefs he has when making a sincere promise. However, he purports to have them. Indeed it is because he purports to have intentions and beliefs which he does not have that we describe his act as insincere. So to allow for insincere promises we need only to revise our conditions to state that the speaker takes responsibility for having the beliefs and intentions rather than stating that he actually has them. A clue that the speaker does take such responsibility is the fact that he could not say without absurdity, e.g. 'I promise to do A but I do not intend to do A'. To say 'I promise to do A' is to take responsibility for intending to do A, and this condition holds whether the utterance was sincere or insincere. To allow for the possibility of an insincere promise then we have only to revise condition (6) so that it states not that the speaker intends to do A, but that he takes responsibility for intending to do A, and to avoid the charge of circularity I shall phrase this as follows:

6* *S intends that the utterance of T will make him responsible for intending to do A*

Thus amended (and with 'sincerely' dropped from our analysandum and from condition (9), our analysis is neutral on the question whether the promise was sincere or insincere.

Rules for the use of the function indicating device

Our next task is to extract from our set of conditions a set of rules for the use of the function indicating device. Obviously not all of our conditions are equally relevant to this task. Condition (1) and conditions of the forms (8) and (9) apply generally to all kinds of normal illocutionary acts and are not peculiar to promising. Rules for the function indicating device for promising are to be found corresponding to conditions (2)–(7).

The semantical rules for the use of any function indicating device *P* for promising are:

Rule 1. *P* is to be uttered only in the context of a sentence (or larger stretch of discourse) the utterance of which predicates some future act *A* of the speaker *S*.
I call this the *propositional content rule*. It is derived from the propositional content conditions (2) and (3).

Rule 2. *P* is to be uttered only if the hearer *H* would prefer *S*'s doing *A* to his not doing *A*, and *S* believes *H* would prefer *S*'s doing *A* to his not doing *A*.

Rule 3. *P* is to be uttered only if it is not obvious to both *S* and *H* that *S* will do *A* in the normal course of events.
I call rules (2) and (3) *preparatory rules*. They are derived from the preparatory conditions (4) and (5).

Rule 4. *P* is to be uttered only if *S* intends to do *A*.
I call this the *sincerity rule*. It is derived from the sincerity condition (6).

Rule 5. The utterance of *P* counts as the undertaking of an obligation to do *A*.
I call this the *essential rule*.

These rules are ordered: Rules 2–5 apply only if Rule 1 is satisfied, and Rule 5 applies only if Rules 2 and 3 are satisfied as well.

Notice that whereas rules 1–4 take the form of quasi-imperatives, i.e. they are of the form: utter *P* only if *x*, rule 5 is of the form: the utterance of *P* counts as *Y*. Thus rule 5 is of the kind peculiar to systems of constitutive rules which I discussed above.

Notice also that the rather tiresome analogy with games is holding up remarkably well. If we ask ourselves under what conditions a player could be said to move a knight correctly, we would find preparatory conditions, such as that it must be his turn to move, as well as the essential condition stating the actual positions the knight can move to. I think that there is even a sincerity rule for competitive games, the rule that each side tries to win. I suggest that the team which 'throws' the game is behaving in a way closely analogous to the speaker who lies or makes false promises. Of course, there usually are no propositional content rules for games, because games do not, by and large, represent states of affairs.

If this analysis is of any general interest beyond the case of promising then it would seem that these distinctions should carry over into other types of speech act, and I think a little reflection will show that they do. Consider, e.g., giving an order. The preparatory conditions include that the speaker should be in a position of authority over the hearer, the sincerity condition is that the speaker wants the ordered act done, and the essential condition has to do with the fact that the utterance is an attempt to get the hearer to do it. For assertions, the preparatory conditions include the fact that the hearer must have some basis for supposing the asserted proposition is true, the sincerity condition is that he must believe it to be true, and the essential condition has to do with the fact that the utterance is an attempt to inform the hearer and convince him of its truth. Greetings are a much simpler kind of speech act, but even here some of the distinctions apply. In the utterance of 'Hello' there is no propositional content and no sincerity condition. The preparatory condition is that the speaker must have just encountered the hearer, and the essential rule is that the utterance indicates courteous recognition of the hearer.

A proposal for further research then is to carry out a similar analysis of other types of speech acts. Not only would this give us an analysis of concepts interesting in themselves, but the comparison of different analyses would deepen our understanding of the whole subject and incidentally provide a basis for a more serious taxonomy than any of the usual facile categories such as evaluative versus descriptive, or cognitive versus emotive.

References

AUSTIN, J. L. (1962), *How To Do Things With Words*, Oxford University Press.

GRICE, P. (1957), 'Meaning', *Philosophical Review*.

RAWLS, J. (1955), 'Two concepts of rules', *Philosophical Review*.

SEARLE, J. R. (1964), 'How to derive "ought" from "is"', *Philosophical Review*.

WITTGENSTEIN, L. (1953), *Philosophical Investigations*, Oxford University Press, para. 510.

Part Three
Language, Socialization and Subcultures

It is through the writings of Basil Bernstein that many social
scientists have become aware of the scientific potential of
sociolinguistics. Indeed, Bernstein's work shows an exciting
solution to the problems of the connection between cultural and
social orders and of the ways in which culture is internalized.

Yet their very popularity has often deformed Bernstein's
arguments; unwittingly, he has been made to say that lower class
children are linguistically 'deprived' and that this deprivation
is responsible for their scholastic failures. In fact, Bernstein's
views are much more complex than that. First, he does not
share current theories on 'compensatory education' and
maintains that it is the organization of schools, not the language
of children, which must be changed (Bernstein, 1970). Second, he
carefully distinguishes between dialects (linguistic codes) and
language usages (sociolinguistic or speech codes): as he says, a
linguistic code 'is capable of generating any number of speech
codes, and there is no reason for believing that any one language
code is better than another in this respect' (see below, p. 161).
Third, he considers 'restricted' and 'elaborated' speech codes as
the product of two systems of social relationships, which cross-cut
lines of social stratification; thus, the fact that in Great Britain
restricted codes are often used by working class families is less a
theoretical postulate than an empirical finding which might not
occur in other countries. In the article reprinted, here, Bernstein
further elaborates his picture of the relation between speech
codes and social class by introducing the concept of speech
variant, which deals with the contextual aspect of conversations,
and of positional or person-centred family types.

Labov's paper is a vigorous attack against the theories of

linguistic deprivation held by some educational psychologists. He argues that (1) there is no connection whatsoever between non-standard English dialects and lack of ability in concept formation or other cognitive failures, and that (2) in the current American educational situation verbal deprivation theories can easily become self-fulfilling prophecies further hindering the scholastic achievement of children of ethnically different backgrounds.

Reference

BERNSTEIN, B. (1970), 'Education cannot compensate for society', *New Society*, no. 387, February 1970.

8 B. Bernstein

Social Class, Language and Socialization[1]

B. Bernstein, from Class, Codes and Control vol. 1: *Theoretical Studies Towards a Sociology of Language*, Routledge & Kegan Paul, 1970.

Introduction

It may be helpful to make explicit the theoretical origins of the thesis I have been developing over the past decade. Although, initially, the thesis appeared to be concerned with the problem of educability, this problem was imbedded in and was stimulated by the wider question of the relationships between symbolic orders and social structure. The basic theoretical question, which dictated the approach to the initially narrow but important empirical problem, was concerned with the fundamental structure and changes in the structure of cultural transmission. Indeed, any detailed examination of what superficially may seem to be a string of somewhat repetitive papers, I think would show three things.

1. The gradual emergence of the dominance of the major theoretical problem from the local, empirical problem of the social antecedents of the educability of different groups of children.

2. Attempts to develop both the generality of the thesis and to develop increasing specificity at the contextual level.

3. Entailed in (2) were attempts to clarify both the logical and empirical status of the basic organizing concept, code. Unfortunately, until recently these attempts were more readily seen in the

1. This work was supported by grants from the Department of Education and Science, the Ford Foundation and the Nuffield Foundation, to whom grateful acknowledgement is made. I would also like to take the opportunity of acknowledging my debt to Professor Courtney Cazden, Dr Mary Douglas, Professor John Gumperz, Professor Dell Hymes, and in particular to Professor Michael Halliday. I am also grateful for the constant constructive criticism I have received from members of the Sociological Research Unit, University of London Institute of Education.

planning and *analysis* of the empirical research than available as formal statements.

Looking back with hindsight, I think I would have created less misunderstanding if I had written about sociolinguistic codes rather than linguistic codes. Through using only the latter concept it gave the impression that I was reifying syntax and at the cost of semantics. Or at worse, suggesting that there was a one to one relation between meaning and a given syntax. Also, by defining the codes in a context free fashion, I robbed myself of properly understanding, at a theoretical level, their significance. *I should point out that nearly all the empirical planning was directed to trying to find out the code realizations in different contexts.*

The concept of socio-linguistic code points to the social structuring of meanings *and* to their diverse but *related* contextual linguistic realizations. A careful reading of the papers always shows the emphasis given to the form of the social relationship, that is the structuring of relevant meanings. Indeed, role is defined as a complex coding activity controlling the creation and organization of specific meanings and the conditions for their transmission and reception. The general sociolinguistic thesis attempts to explore how symbolic systems are both realizations and regulators of the structure of social relationships. The particular symbolic system is that of speech *not* language.

It is pertinent, at this point, to make explicit earlier work in the social sciences which formed the implicit starting point of the thesis. It will then be seen, I hope, that the thesis is an integration of different streams of thought. The major starting points are Durkheim and Marx, and a small number of other thinkers have been drawn into the basic matrix. I shall very briefly, and so selectively, outline this matrix and some of the problems to which it gave rise.

Durkheim's work is a truly magnificent insight into the relationships between symbolic orders, social relationships and the structuring of experience. In a sense, if Marx turned Hegel on his head, then Durkheim attempted to turn Kant on his head. For in *Primitive Classification* and in *The Elementary Forms of the Religious Life*, Durkheim attempted to derive the basic categories of thought from the structuring of the social relation. It is beside the point as to his success. He raised the whole question of the relation between the classifications and frames of the symbolic order *and* the structuring of experience. In his study of different forms of social integration he pointed to the implicit, condensed, symbolic structure of mechanical solidarity and the more explicit and differentiated symbolic structures of organic solidarity. Cassirer, the early cultural anthropologists, and in particular Sapir (I was not aware of Von Humboldt until much later) sensitized me to the cultural properties of speech. Whorf, particularly where he refers to the fashions of speaking, frames of consistency, alerted me to the selective effect of the culture (acting through its patterning of social relationships) upon the *patterning* of grammar *together* with the pattern's semantic and thus cognitive significance. Whorf more than anyone, I think, opened up, at least for me, the question of the deep structure of linguistically regulated communication.

In all the above work I found two difficulties. If we grant the fundamental linkage of symbolic systems, social structure and the shaping of experience it is still unclear *how* such shaping takes place. The *processes* underlying the social structuring of experience are not explicit. The second difficulty is in dealing with the question of change of symbolic systems. Mead is of central importance in the solution of the first difficulty, the HOW. Mead outlined in general terms the relationships between role, reflexiveness and speech and in so doing provided the basis of the solution to the HOW. It is still the case that the Meadian solution does not allow us to deal with the problem of change. For the concept, which enables role to be related to a higher order concept, 'the generalized other' is, itself, not subject to systematic enquiry. Even if 'the generalized other' is placed within a Durkheimian framework, we are still left with the problem of change. Indeed, in Mead change is introduced only at the cost of the re-emergence of a traditional Western dichotomy in the concepts of the 'I' and the 'me'. The 'I' is both the indeterminate response to the 'me' and yet at the same time shapes it. The Meadian 'I' points to the voluntarism in the affairs of men, the fundamental creativity of man, made possible by speech; a little before Chomsky.

Thus Meadian thought helps to solve the puzzle of the *how*

but it does not help with the question of change in the structuring of experience; although both Mead implicitly and Durkheim explicitly pointed to the conditions which bring about pathological structuring of experience.

One major theory of the development of and change in symbolic structures is, of course, that of Marx. Although Marx is less concerned with the internal structure and the process of transmission of symbolic systems he does give us a key to their institutionalization and change. The key is given in terms of the social significance of society's productive system and the power relationships to which the productive system gives rise. Further, access to, control over, orientation of and *change* in critical symbolic systems, according to the theory, is governed by these power relationships as these are embodied in the class structure. It is not only capital, in the strict economic sense, which is subject to appropriation, manipulation and exploitation, but also *cultural* capital in the form of the symbolic systems through which man can extend and change the boundaries of his experience.

I am not putting forward a matrix of thought necessary for the study of the basic structure and change in the structure of cultural transmission, *only* the specific matrix which underlies my own approach. Essentially and briefly I have used Durkheim and Marx at the macro level and Mead at the micro level, to realize a sociolinguistic thesis which could meet with a range of work in anthropology, linguistics, sociology and psychology.

Linguistic codes and speech codes

I want first of all to make clear what I am not concerned with. Chomsky (1965) neatly severs the study of the rule system of language from the study of the social rules which determine their contextual use. He does this by making a distinction between competence and performance. Competence refers to the child's tacit understanding of the rule system, performance relates to the essentially social use to which the rule system is put. Competence refers to man abstracted from contextual constraints. Performance refers to man in the grip of the contextual constraints which determine his speech acts. Competence refers to the Ideal, performance refers to the Fall. In this sense Chomsky's notion of competence is Platonic. Competence has its source in the very biology of man. There is no difference between men in terms of their access to the linguistic rule system. Here Chomsky, like many other linguists before him, announces the communality of man, all men have equal access to the creative act which is language. On the other hand, performance is under the control of the social – performances are culturally specific acts, they refer to the choices which are made in specific speech encounters. Thus from one point of view, Chomsky indicates the tragedy of man, the potentiality of competence and the degeneration of performance.

Clearly, much is to be gained in rigour and explanatory power through the severing of the relationship between the formal properties of the grammar and the meanings which are realized in its use. But if we are to study speech, *la parole*, we are inevitably involved in a study of a rather different rule system, we are involved in a study of rules, formal and informal, which regulate the options we take up in various contexts in which we find ourselves. This second rule system is the cultural system. This raises immediately the question of the relationship between the linguistic rule system and the cultural system. Clearly, specific linguistic rule systems are part of the cultural system, but it has been argued that the linguistic rule systems in various ways shape the cultural system. This very briefly is the view of those who hold a narrow form of the linguistic relativity hypothesis. I do not intend this evening to get involved in that particular quagmire. Instead, I shall take the view that the code which the linguist invents to explain the formal properties of the grammar is capable of generating any number of speech codes, and there is no reason for believing that any one language code is better than another in this respect. On this argument, language is a set of rules to which all speech codes must comply, but which speech codes are realized is a function of the culture acting through social relationships in specific contexts. Different speech forms or codes symbolize the form of the social relationship, regulate the nature of the speech encounters, and create for the speakers different orders of relevance and relation. The experience of the speakers is then transformed by what is made significant or relevant by the speech form. This is a sociological argument because the speech form is taken as a consequence of the form of the social relation or put more generally, is a quality of a social structure. Let me qualify this immediately. Because the speech form is initially a function of a given social arrangement, it does not mean that the speech form does not in turn modify or even change that social structure which initially evolved the speech form. This formulation, indeed, invites the question – under what conditions does a given speech form free itself sufficiently from its embodiment in the social structure so that the system of meanings it realizes point to alternative realities, alternative arrangements in the affairs of men. Here we become concerned immediately with the antecedents and consequences of the boundary maintaining principles of a culture or subculture. I am here suggesting a relationship between forms of boundary maintenance at the cultural level and forms of speech.

Social class, orders of meaning and speech codes

I am required to consider the relationship between language and socialization. It should be clear from these opening remarks that I am not concerned with language, but with speech, and concerned more specifically with the contextual constraints upon speech. Now what about socialization? I shall take the term to refer to the process whereby a child acquires a specific cultural identity, *and* to his responses to such an identity. Socialization refers to the process whereby the biological is transformed into a specific cultural being. It follows from this that the process of socialization is a complex process of control, whereby a particular moral, cognitive and affective awareness is evoked in the child and given a specific form and content. Socialization sensitizes the child to various orderings of society as these are made substantive in the various roles he is expected to play. In a sense then socialization is a process for making people safe. The process acts selectively on the possibilities of man by creating through time a sense of the inevitability of a given social arrangement, and through limiting the areas of permitted change. The basic agencies of socialization in contemporary societies are the family, the peer group, school and work. It is through these agencies, and in particular through their relationship to each other, that the various orderings of society are made manifest.

Now it is quite clear that given this view of socialization it is necessary to limit the discussion. I shall limit our discussion to socialization within the family, but it should be obvious that the focusing and filtering of the child's experience within the family in a large measure is a microcosm of the macroscopic orderings of society. Our question now becomes what are the sociological factors which affect linguistic performances within the family critical to the process of socialization?

Without a shadow of doubt the most formative influence upon the procedures of socialization, from a sociological viewpoint, is social class. The class structure influences work and educational roles and brings families into a special relationship with each other and deeply penetrates the structure of life experiences within the family. The class system has deeply marked the distribution of knowledge within society. It has given differential access to the sense that the world is permeable. It has sealed off communities from each other and has ranked these communities on a scale of invidious worth. We have three components, knowledge, possibility, invidious insulation. It would be a little naïve to believe that differences in knowledge, differences in the sense of the possible, combined with invidious insulation, rooted in differential *material* well-being would not affect the forms of control and innovation in the socializing procedures of different social classes. I shall go on to argue that the deep structure of communication itself is affected, but not in any final or irrevocable way.

As an approach to my argument, let me glance at the social distribution of knowledge. We can see that the class system has affected the distribution of knowledge. Historically and now, only a tiny percentage of the population has been socialized into knowledge at the level of the meta-languages of control and innovation, whereas the mass of the population has been socialized into knowledge at the level of context-tied operations.

A tiny percentage of the population has been given access to the principles of intellectual change whereas the rest have been denied such access. This suggests that we might be able to distinguish between two orders of meaning. One we could call universalistic, the other particularistic. Universalistic meanings are those in which principles and operations are made linguistically explicit whereas particularistic orders of meaning are meanings in which principles and operation are relatively linguistically implicit. If orders of meaning are universalistic, then the meanings are less tied to a given context. The meta-languages of public forms of thought as these apply to objects and persons realize meanings of a universalistic type. Where meanings have this characteristic then individuals have access to the grounds of their experience and can change the grounds. Where orders of meaning are particularistic, where principles are linguistically implicit, then such meanings are less context independent and *more* context bound. That is tied to a local relationship and to a local social structure. Where the meaning system is particularistic, much of the meaning is embedded in the context and may be restricted to those who share a similar contextual history. Where meanings are universalistic, they are in principle available to all because the principles and operations have been made explicit and so public.

I shall argue that forms of socialization orient the child towards speech codes which control access to relatively context-tied or relatively context-independent meanings. Thus I shall argue that elaborated codes orient their users towards universalistic meanings, whereas restricted codes orient, sensitize, their users to particularistic meanings: that the linguistic-realization of the two orders are different, and so are the social relationships which realize them. Elaborated codes are less tied to a given or local structure and thus contain the potentiality of change in principles. In the case of elaborated codes the speech is freed from its evoking social structure and takes on an autonomy. A university is a place organized around talk. Restricted codes are more tied to a local social structure and have a reduced potential for change in principles. Where codes are elaborated, the socialized has more access to the grounds of his own socialization, and so can enter into a reflexive relationship to the social order he has taken over. Where codes are restricted, the socialized has less access to the grounds of his socialization, and thus reflexiveness may be limited in range. One of the effects of the class system is to limit access to elaborated codes.

I shall go on to suggest that restricted codes have their basis in condensed symbols whereas elaborated codes have their basis in articulated symbols. That restricted codes draw upon metaphor whereas elaborated codes draw upon rationality. That these codes constrain the contextual use of language in critical socializing contexts and in this way regulate the orders of relevance and relation which the socialized takes over. From this point of view, change in habitual speech codes involves changes in the means by which object and person relationships are realized.

Types of social context, social roles and speech variants

I want first to start with the notions of elaborated and restricted speech variants. A variant can be considered as the contextual constraints upon grammatical-lexical choices.

Sapir, Malinowski, Firth, Vygotsky and Luria have all pointed out from different points of view that the closer the identifications of speakers the greater the range of shared interests and the more probable that the speech will take a specific form. The range of syntactic alternatives is likely to be reduced and the lexis to be drawn from a narrow range. Thus, the form of these social relations is acting selectively on the meanings to be verbally realized. In these relationships the intent of the other person can be taken for granted as the speech is played out against a back-drop of common assumptions, common history, common interests. As a result, there is less need to raise meanings to the level of explicitness or elaboration. There is a reduced need to make explicit through syntactic choices the logical structure of the communication. Further, if the speaker wishes to individualize his communication, he is likely to do this by varying the expressive associates of the speech. Under these conditions, the speech is likely to have a strong metaphoric element. In these situations the speaker may be more concerned with how something is said, when it is said and silence takes on a variety of meanings. Often in these encounters, the speech cannot be understood apart from the context and the context cannot be read by those who do not share the history of the relationships. Thus the form of the social relationship acts selectively in the meanings to be verbalized, which in turn affect the syntactic and lexical choices. The unspoken assumptions underlying the relationship are not available to those who are outside the relationship. For these are limited, and restricted to the speakers. The symbolic form of the communication is condensed yet the specific cultural history of the relationship is alive in its form. We can say that the roles of the speakers are communalized roles. Thus, we can make a relationship between restricted social relationships based upon communalized roles and the verbal realization of their meaning. In the language of the earlier part of this talk, restricted social relationships based upon communalized roles evoke particularistic, that is, context tied meanings, realized through a restricted speech variant.

Imagine a husband and wife have just come out of the cinema, and are talking about the film: 'What do you think?' 'It had a lot to say'. ''Yes, I thought so too – let's go to the Millers, there may be something going on there'. They arrive at the Millers, who ask about the film. An hour is spent in the complex, moral, political, aesthetic subtleties of the film and its place in the contemporary scene. Here we have an elaborated variant, the meanings now have to be made public to others who have not seen the film. The speech shows careful editing, at both the grammatical and lexical levels; it is no longer context tied. The meanings are explicit, elaborated and individualized. Whilst expressive channels are clearly relevant, the burden of meaning inheres predominantly in the verbal channel. The experience of the listeners cannot be taken for granted. Thus each member of the group is on his own as he offers his interpretation. Elaborated variants of this kind involve the speakers in particular role relationships, and *if you cannot manage the role, you can't produce the appropriate speech*. For as the speaker proceeds to individualize his meanings, he is differentiated from others like a figure from its ground.

The roles receive less support from each other. There is a measure of isolation. *Difference* lies at the basis of the social relationship, and is made verbally active, whereas in the other context it is *consensus*. The insides of the speaker have become psychologically active through the verbal aspect of the communication. Various defensive strategies may be used to decrease potential vulnerability of self and to increase the vulnerability of others. The verbal aspect of the communication becomes a vehicle for the transmission of individuated symbols. The 'I' stands over the 'We'. Meanings which are discreet to the speaker must be offered so that they are intelligible to the listener. Communalized roles have given way to individualized roles, condensed symbols to articulated symbols. Elaborated speech variants of this type realize universalistic meanings in the sense that they are less context-tied. Thus individualized roles are realized through elaborated speech variants which involve complex editing at the grammatical and lexical levels and which point to universalistic meanings.

Let me give another example. Consider the two following stories which Peter Hawkins, Assistant Research Officer in the Sociological Research Unit, University of London Institute of Education, constructed as a result of his analysis of the speech of middle-class and working-class five-year-old children. The children were given a series of four pictures which told a story and they were invited to tell the story. The first picture showed some boys playing football, in the second the ball goes through the window of a house, the third shows a woman looking out of the window and a man making an ominous gesture, and in the fourth the children are moving away.

Here are the two stories:

1. Three boys are playing football and one boy kicks the ball   and it goes through the window   the ball breaks the window   and the boys are looking at it   and a man comes out and shouts at them   because they've broken the window   so they run away   and then that lady looks out of her window   and she tells the boys off.

2. They're playing football   and he kicks it and it goes through there   it breaks the window and they're looking at it   and he comes out   and shouts at them   because they've broken it   so they run away   and then she looks out   and she tells them off.

With the first story the reader does not have to have the four pictures which were used as the basis for the story, whereas in the case of the second story the reader would require the initial pictures in order to make sense of the story. The first story is free of the context which generated it, whereas the second story is much more closely tied to its context. As a result the meanings of the second story are implicit, whereas the meanings of the first story are explicit. It is not that the working-class children do not have in their passive vocabulary the vocabulary used by the middle-class children. Nor is it the case that the children differ in their tacit understanding of the linguistic rule system. Rather, what we have here are differences in the use of language arising out of a specific context. One child makes explicit the meanings which he is realizing through language for the person he is telling the story to, whereas the second child does not to the same extent. The first child takes very little for granted, whereas the second child takes a great deal for granted. Thus for the first child the task was seen as a context in which his meanings were required to be made explicit, whereas the task for the second child was not seen as a task which required such explication of meaning. It would not be difficult to imagine a context where the first child would produce speech rather like the second. What we are dealing with here are differences between the children in the way they realize in language use apparently the same context. We could say that the speech of the first child generated universalistic meanings in the sense that the meanings are freed from the context and so understandable by all. Whereas the speech of the second child generated particularistic meanings, in the sense that the meanings are closely tied to the context and would be only fully understood by others if they had access to the context which originally generated the speech.

It is again important to stress that the second child has access to a more differentiated noun phrase, but there is a restriction on its *use*. Geoffrey Turner, Linguist in the Sociological Research Unit, shows that working-class, five-year-old children, in the same contexts examined by Hawkins, use fewer linguistic expressions of uncertainty when compared with the middle-class children. This does not mean that working-class children do *not* have access to such expressions, but that the eliciting speech context did not provoke them. Telling a story from pictures, talking about scenes on cards, *formally framed* contexts, do not encourage working-class children to consider the possibilities of alternate meanings and so there is a reduction in the linguistic expressions of uncertainty. Again, working-class children have access to a wide range of syntactic choices which involve the use of logical operators, 'because', 'but', 'either', 'or', 'only'. The constraints exist on the conditions for their *use*. Formally framed contexts used for eliciting context independent universalistic meanings may evoke in the working-class child, relative to the middle-class child, restricted speech variants, because the working-class child has difficulty in managing the role relationships which such contexts require. This problem is further complicated when such contexts carry meanings very much removed from the child's cultural experience. In the same way we can show that there are constraints upon the middle-class child's use of language. Turner found that when middle-class children were asked to role play in the picture story series, a higher percentage of these children, when compared with working-class children, initially refused. When the middle-class children were asked 'What is the man saying?', or linguistically equivalent questions, a relatively higher percentage said 'I don't know'. When this question was followed by the hypothetical question 'What do you think the man might be saying?' they offered their interpretations. The working-class children role played without difficulty. It seems then that middle-class children at five need to have a very precise instruction to *hypothesize in that particular* context. This may be because they are more concerned here with getting their answers right or correct. When the children were invited to tell a story about some doll-like figures (a little boy, a little girl, a sailor and a dog) the working-class children's stories were freer, longer, more imaginative than the stories of the middle-class children. The latter children's stories were tighter, constrained within a strong narrative frame. It was as if these children were dominated by what they took to be the *form* of a narrative and the content was secondary. This is an example of the concern of the middle-class child with the structure of the contextual frame. It may be worthwhile to amplify this further. A number of studies have shown that when working-class black children are asked to associate to a series of words, their responses show considerable diversity, both from the meaning and form-class of the stimulus word. In the analysis offered in the text this may be because the children for the following reasons are less constrained. The form-class of the stimulus word may have reduced associative significance and so would less constrain the selection of potential words *or* phrases. With such a weakening of the grammatical frame a greater range of alternatives are possible candidates for selection. Further, the closely controlled middle-class linguistic socialization of the young child may point the child towards both the grammatical significance of the stimulus word and towards a tight logical ordering of semantic space. Middle-class children may well have access to deep interpretive rules which regulate their linguistic responses in certain formalized contexts. The consequences may limit their imagination through the tightness of the frame which these interpretive rules create. It may even be that with *five*-year-old children, the middle-class child will innovate *more* with the arrangements of objects (e.g. bricks) than in his linguistic usage. His linguistic usage is under close supervision by adults. He has more *autonomy* in his play.

To return to our previous discussion, we can say briefly that as we move from communalized to individualized roles, so speech takes on an increasingly reflexive function. The unique selves of others become palpable through speech and enter into our own self, the grounds of our experience are made verbally explicit; the security of the condensed symbol is gone. It has been replaced by rationality. There is a change in the basis of our vulnerability.

Social class, family types, language and socialization

So far, then, I have discussed certain types of speech variants and the code relationships which occasion them. I am now going to raise the generality of the discussion and focus upon the title of the paper. The socialization of the young in the family proceeds within a critical set of inter-related contexts. Analytically, we may distinguish four contexts.

1. The regulative context – these are authority relationships where the child is made aware of the rules of the moral order and their various backings.

2. The instructional context, where the child learns about the objective nature of objects and persons, and acquires skills of various kinds.

3. The imaginative or innovating contexts, where the child is encouraged to experiment and re-create his world on his own terms, and in his own way.

4. The interpersonal context, where the child is made aware of affective states – his own, and others.

I am suggesting that the critical orderings of a culture or sub-culture are made substantive – are made palpable – through the forms of its linguistic realizations of these four contexts – initially in the family and kin.

Now if the linguistic realization of these four contexts involves the predominant use of restricted speech variants, I shall postulate that the deep structure of the communication is a restricted code having its basis in communalized roles, realizing context bound meanings, i.e. particularistic meaning orders. Clearly the specific grammatical and lexical choices will vary from one context to another.

If the linguistic realization of these four contexts involves the predominant usage of elaborated speech variants, I shall postulate that the deep structure of the communication is an elaborated code having its basis in individualized roles realizing context free universalistic meanings.

In order to prevent misunderstanding an expansion of the text is here necessary. It is likely that where the code is restricted, the speech in the regulative context may well be limited to command and simple rule announcing statements. The latter statements are not context-dependent in the sense previously given for they announce general rules. We need to supplement the context independent (universalistic) and context dependent (particularistic) criteria with criteria which refer to the extent to which the speech in the regulative context varies in terms of its *contextual specificity*. If the speech is context-specific then the socializer cuts his meanings to the *specific* attributes/intentions of the socialized, the specific characteristics of the problem, the specific requirements of the context. Thus the general rule may be transmitted with degrees of *contextual specificity*. When this occurs the rule is individualized (fitted to the local circumstances) in the process of its transmission. Thus with code elaboration we should expect:

1. Some developed grounds for the rule
2. Some qualification of it in the light of the particular issue
3. Considerable *specificity* in terms of the socialized, the context and the issue.

This does *not* mean that there would be an *absence* of command statements. It is also likely that with code elaboration the socialized would be *given* opportunities (role options) to question.

Bernstein and Cook (1968) and Cook (1970) have developed a semantic coding grid which sets out with considerable delicacy a general category system which has been applied to a limited regulative context. Turner is attempting a linguistic realization of the same grid.

We can express the two sets of criteria diagrammatically. A limited application is given by Henderson (1970).

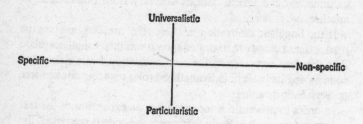

It may be necessary to utilize the two sets of criteria for *all* four socializing contexts. Bernstein (1967, published 1970) suggested that code realization would vary with context.

If we look at the linguistic realization of the regulative context in greater detail we may be able to clear up another source of possible misunderstanding. In this context it is very likely that syntactic markers of the logical distribution of meaning will be extensively used.

'If you do that, then . . .'
'Either you . . . or . . .'
'You can do that but if . . .'
'You do that and you'll pay for it'

Thus it is very likely that young children may well in the *regulative* context have access to a range of syntactic markers which express the logical/hypothetical irrespective of code restriction or elaboration. However, where the code is restricted it is expected that there will be reduced specificity in the sense outlined earlier. Further, the speech in the control situation is likely to be well-organized in the sense that the sentences come as wholes. The child responds to the total *frame*. However, I would suggest that the informal *instructional* contexts within the family may well be limited in range and frequency. Thus the child, of course, would have access to and so have *available*, the hypotheticals, conditionals, disjunctives, etc. but these might be rarely used in *instructional* contexts. In the same way, as we have suggested earlier, all children have access to linguistic expressions of uncertainty but they may differ in the context in which they receive and realize such expressions.

I must emphasize that because the code is restricted it does not mean that speakers at no time will not use elaborated speech var ants. Only that the use of such variants will be infrequent in the socialization of the child in his family.

Now, all children have access to restricted codes and their various systems of condensed meaning, because the roles the code pre-supposes are universal. But there may well be selective access to elaborated codes because there is selective access to the role system which evokes its use. Society is likely to evaluate differently the experiences realized through these two codes. I cannot here go into details, but the different focusing of experience through a restricted code creates a major problem of educability only where the school produces discontinuity between its symbolic orders and those of the child. Our schools are not made for these children; why should the children respond? To ask the child to switch to an elaborated code which presupposes different role relationships and systems of meaning without a sensitive understanding of the required contexts must create for the child a bewildering and potentially damaging experience.

So far, then, I have sketched out a relationship between speech codes and socialization through the organization of roles through which the culture is made psychologically active in persons. I have indicated that access to the roles and thus to the codes is broadly related to social class. However, it is clearly the case that social class groups today are by no means homogeneous groups. Further, the division between elaborated and restricted codes is too simple. Finally, I have not indicated in any detail how these codes are evoked by families, and how the family types may shape their focus.

What I shall do now is to introduce a distinction between family type and their communication structures. These family types can be found empirically within each social class, although any one type may be rather more modal at any given historical period.

I shall distinguish between families according to the strength of their boundary maintaining procedures. Let me first give some idea of what I mean by boundary maintaining procedures. I shall first look at boundary maintenance as it is revealed in the symbolic ordering of space. Consider the lavatory. In one house, the room is pristine, bare and sharp, containing only the necessities for which the room is dedicated. In another there is a picture on the wall, in the third there are books, in the fourth all surfaces are covered with curious postcards. We have a continuum from a room celebrating the purity of categories to one celebrating the mixture of categories, from strong to weak boundary maintenance. Consider the kitchen. In one kitchen, shoes may not be placed on the table, nor the child's chamber pot – all objects and utensils have an assigned place. In another kitchen the boundaries separating the different classes of objects are weak. The symbolic ordering of space can give us indications of the relative strength of boundary maintaining procedures. Let us now look at the relationship between family members. Where boundary procedures are strong, the differentiation of members and the authority structure is based upon clear-cut, unambiguous definitions of the status of the member of the family. The boundaries between the statuses are strong and the social identities of the members very much a function of their age, sex and age-relation status. As a short-hand, we can characterize the family as *positional*.

On the other hand, where boundary procedures are weak or flexible, the differentiation between members and the authority relationships are less on the basis of position, because here the status boundaries are blurred. Where boundary procedures are weak, the differentiation between members is based more upon *differences between persons*. In such families the relationships become more egocentric and the unique attributes of family members more and more are made substantive in the communication structure. We will call these *person-centred* families. Such families do not reduce but increase the substantive expression of ambiguity and ambivalence. In person-centred families, the role system would be continuously evoking, accommodating and assimilating the different interests, attributes of its members. In such families, unlike positional families, the members would be making their roles, rather than stepping into them. In a person-centred family, the child's developing self is differentiated by continuous adjustment to the verbally realized and elaborated intentions, qualifications and motives of others. The boundary between self and other is blurred. In positional families, the child takes over and responds to the formal pattern of obligation and privilege. It shculd be possible to see, without going into details, that the communication structures within these two types of family are somewhat differently focused. We might then expect that the reflexiveness induced by positional families is sensitized to the general attributes of persons, whereas the reflexiveness produced by person-centred families is more sensitive towards the particular aspects of persons. Think of the difference between Dartington Hall or Gordonstoun Public Schools in England, or the difference between West Point and a progressive school in the USA. Thus, in person-centred families, the insides of the members are made public through the communication structure, and thus more of the person has been invaded and subject to control. Speech in such families is a major media of control. In positional families of course, speech is relevant but it symbolizes the boundaries given by the formal structure of the relationships. So far as the child is concerned, in positional families he attains a strong sense of social identity at the cost of autonomy; in person-centred families, the child attains a strong sense of autonomy but his social identity may be weak. Such ambiguity in the sense of identity, the lack of boundary, may move such children towards a radically closed value system.

If we now place these family types in the framework of the previous discussion, we can see that although the code may be elaborated, it may be differently focused according to the family type. Thus, we can have an elaborate code focusing upon persons or an elaborated code in a positional family may focus more upon objects. We can expect the same with a restricted code. Normally, with code restriction we should expect a positional family, however, if it showed signs of person-centred, then we might expect the children to be in a situation of potential code switch.

Where the code is elaborated, and focused by a person-centred family, then these children may well develop acute identity problems, concerned with authenticity, of limiting responsibility – they may come to see language as phony, a system of counterfeit masking the absence of belief. They may move towards the restricted codes of the various peer group subcultures, or seek the condensed symbols of affective experience, or both.

One of the difficulties of this approach is to avoid implicit value judgements about the relative worth of speech systems and the cultures which they symbolize. Let it be said immediately that a restricted code gives access to a vast potential of meanings, of delicacy, subtlety and diversity of cultural forms, to a unique aesthetic whose basis in condensed symbols may influence the form of the imagining. Yet, in complex industrialized societies its differently focused experience may be disvalued, and humiliated within schools or seen, at best, to be irrelevant to the educational endeavour. For the schools are predicated upon elaborated code and its system of social relationships. Although an elaborated code does not entail any specific value system, the value system of the middle class penetrates the texture of the very learning context itself.

Elaborated codes give access to alternative realities yet they carry the potential of alienation of feeling from thought, of self from other, of private belief *from role obligation*.

Finally I should like to consider briefly the source of change of linguistic codes. The first major source of change I suggest is to be located in the division of labour. As the division of labour changes from simple to complex, then this changes the social and knowledge characteristics of occupational roles. In this process there is an extension of access, through education, to elaborated codes, but access is controlled by the class system. The focusing of the codes I have suggested is brought about by the boundary maintaining procedures within the family. However, we can generalize and say that the focusing of the codes is related to the boundary maintaining procedures as these affect the major socializing agencies, family, age group, education and work. We need, therefore, to consider together with the question of the degree and type of complexity of the division of labour the value orientations of society which it is hypothesized affect the boundary maintaining procedures. It is the case that we can have societies with a similar complexity in their division of labour but who differ in their boundary maintaining procedures.

I suggest then that it is important to make a distinction between societies in terms of their boundary maintaining procedures if we are to deal with this question of the focusing of codes. One possible way of examining the relative strength of boundary maintenance at a somewhat high level of abstraction is to consider the strength of the *constraints* upon the choice of values which legitimize authority/power relationships. Thus in societies where there is weak constraint upon such legitimizing values, that is, where there are a variety of formally permitted legitimizing values, we might expect a marked shift towards person type control. Whereas in societies with strong constraints upon legitimizing values, where there is a severe *restriction* upon the choice, we might expect a marked shift towards positional control.

I shall illustrate these relationships with reference to the family.

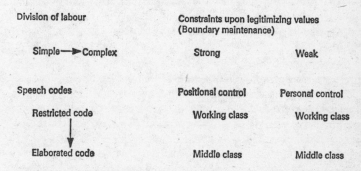

Division of labour	Constraints upon legitimizing values (Boundary maintenance)	
Simple ⟶ Complex	Strong	Weak
Speech codes	Positional control	Personal control
Restricted code	Working class	Working class
↓		
Elaborated code	Middle class	Middle class

Thus the division of labour influences the availability of elaborated codes; the class system affects their distribution; the focusing of codes can be related to the boundary maintaining procedures, i.e. the value system. I must point out that this is only a coarse interpretive framework.

Conclusion

I have tried to show how the class system acts upon the deep structure of communication in the process of socialization. I refined the crudity of the analysis by showing how speech codes may be differently focused through family types. Finally, it is conceivable that there are general aspects of the analysis which might provide a starting point for the consideration of symbolic orders other than languages. I must point out that there is more to socialization than the forms of its linguistic realization.

References

BERNSTEIN, B. and COOK, J. (1968), 'Coding grid for maternal control', available from Department of Sociology, University of London Institute of Education.

BERNSTEIN, B. (1970), 'Education cannot compensate for society', *New Society*, no. 387.

CHOMSKY, N. (1965), *Aspects of the Theory of Syntax*, M.I.T. Press.

COOK, J. (1970), 'An inquiry into patterns of communication and control between mothers and their children in different social classes', Ph.D. thesis, awaiting submission to the University of London.

HENDERSON, D. (1970), 'Contextual specificity, discretion and cognitive socialization, with special reference to language', *Sociology*, vol. 4, no. 3.

9 W. Labov

The Logic of Nonstandard English

Excerpts from W. Labov, 'The logic of nonstandard English'.
Georgetown Monographs on Language and Linguistics, vol. 22,
1969, pp. 1–22, 26–31.

In the past decade, a great deal of federally sponsored research has been devoted to the educational problems of children in ghetto schools. In order to account for the poor performance of children in these schools, educational psychologists have attempted to discover what kind of disadvantage or defect they are suffering from. The viewpoint which has been widely accepted, and used as the basis for large-scale intervention programs, is that the children show a cultural deficit as a result of an impoverished environment in their early years. Considerable attention has been given to language. In this area, the deficit theory appears as the concept of 'verbal deprivation': Negro children from the ghetto area receive little verbal stimulation, are said to hear very little well-formed language, and as a result are impoverished in their means of verbal expression: they cannot speak complete sentences, do not know the names of common objects, cannot form concepts or convey logical thoughts.

Unfortunately, these notions are based upon the work of educational psychologists who know very little about language and even less about Negro children. The concept of verbal deprivation has no basis in social reality: in fact, Negro children in the urban ghettos receive a great deal of verbal stimulation, hear more well-formed sentences than middle-class children, and participate fully in a highly verbal culture; they have the same basic vocabulary, possess the same capacity for conceptual learning, and use the same logic as anyone else who learns to speak and understand English.

The notion of 'verbal deprivation' is a part of the modern mythology of educational psychology, typical of the unfounded notions which tend to expand rapidly in our educational system.

In past decades linguists have been as guilty as others in promoting such intellectual fashions at the expense of both teachers and children. But the myth of verbal deprivation is particularly dangerous, because it diverts attention from real defects of our educational system to imaginary defects of the child; and as we shall see, it leads its sponsors inevitably to the hypothesis of the genetic inferiority of Negro children which it was originally designed to avoid.

The most useful service which linguists can perform today is to clear away the illusion of 'verbal deprivation' and provide a more adequate notion of the relations between standard and non-standard dialects. In the writings of many prominent educational psychologists, we find a very poor understanding of the nature of language. Children are treated as if they have no language of their own in the pre-school programs put forward by Bereiter and Engelmann (1966). The linguistic behavior of ghetto children in test situations is the principal evidence for their genetic inferiority in the view of Arthur Jensen (1969). In this paper, I will examine critically both of these approaches to the language and intelligence of the populations labelled 'verbally' and 'culturally deprived'.[1] I will attempt to explain how the myth of verbal deprivation has arisen, bringing to bear the methodological findings of sociolinguistic work, and some substantive facts about language which are known to all linguists. I will be particularly concerned with the relation between concept formation on the one hand, and dialect differences on the other, since it is in this area that the most dangerous misunderstandings are to be found.

Verbality

The general setting in which the deficit theory has arisen consists of a number of facts which are known to all of us: that Negro children in the central urban ghettos do badly on all school subjects, including arithmetic and reading. In reading, they average

1. I am indebted to Rosalind Weiner, of the Early Childhood Education group of Operation Headstart in New York City, and to Joan Baratz, of the Educational Development Corp., Washington D.C., for pointing out to me the scope and seriousness of the educational issues involved here, and the ways in which the cultural deprivation theory has affected federal intervention programs in recent years.

more than two years behind the national norm.[2] Furthermore, this lag is cumulative, so that they do worse comparatively in the fifth grade than in the first grade. Reports in the literature show that this bad performance is correlated most closely with socio-economic status. Segregated ethnic groups, however, seem to do worse than others: in particular, Indians, Mexican-Americans and Negro children. Our own work in New York City confirms the fact that most Negro children read very poorly; however, our studies in the speech community show that the situation is even worse than has been reported. If one separates the isolated and peripheral individuals from the members of the central peer groups, the peer group members show even worse reading records, and to all intents and purposes are not learning to read at all during the time they spend in school (Labov and Robins, 1969).

In speaking of children in the urban ghetto areas, the term 'lower-class' is frequently used as opposed to 'middle-class'. In the several sociolinguistic studies we have carried out, and in many parallel studies, it is useful to distinguish a 'lower-class' group from 'working-class'. Lower-class families are typically female-based or 'matri-focal', with no father present to provide steady economic support, whereas for the working-class there is typically an intact nuclear family with the father holding a semi-skilled or unskilled job. The educational problems of ghetto areas run across this important class distinction; there is no evidence, for example, that the father's presence or absence is

2. A report of average reading comprehension scores in New York City was published in the *New York Times* on 3 December 1968. The schools attended by most of the peer group members we have studied showed the following scores:

School	Grade	Reading score	National norm
J. H. S. 13	7	5·6	7·7
	9	7·6	9·7
J. H. S. 120	7	5·6	7·7
	9	7·0	9·7
I. S. 88	6	5·3	6·7
	8	7·2	8·7

The average is then more than two full years behind grade in the ninth grade.

closely correlated with educational achievement.[3] The peer groups we have studied in South Central Harlem, representing the basic vernacular culture, include members from both family types. The attack against 'cultural deprivation' in the ghetto is overtly directed at family structures typical of lower-class families, but the educational failure we have been discussing is characteristic of both working-class and lower-class children.

In the balance of this paper, I will therefore refer to children from urban ghetto areas, rather than 'lower-class' children: the population we are concerned with are those who participate fully in the vernacular culture of the street and who have been alienated from the school system.[4] We are obviously dealing with the effects of the caste system of American society – essentially a 'color marking' system. Everyone recognizes this. The question is, by what mechanism does the color bar prevent children from learning to read? One answer is the notion of 'cultural deprivation' put forward by Martin Deutsch and others: the Negro children are said to lack the favorable factors in their home environment which enable middle-class children to do well in school. (Deutsch *et al.*, 1967; Deutsch, Katz and Jensen, 1968). These factors involve the development of various cognitive skills through verbal interaction with adults, including the ability to reason abstractly, speak fluently, and focus upon long-range goals. In their publications, these psychologists also recognize broader social factors.[5] However, the deficit theory does not focus upon the

3. There are a number of studies reported recently which show no relation between school achievement and presence of a father in the nuclear family. Preliminary findings to this effect are cited from a study by Bernard Mackler of CUE in Thos. S. Langer and Stanley T. Michaels, *Life Stress and Mental Health* (New York: Free Press), Chapter 8. Jensen (1969) cites James Coleman's study *Equality of educational opportunity*, p. 506, and others to illustrate the same point.

4. The concept of 'nonstandard Negro English', and the vernacular culture in which it is embedded, is presented in detail in Labov, Cohen, Robins and Lewis (1968), sections 1. 2. 3 and 4. 1. See Volume II, section 4. 3, for the linguistic traits which distinguish speakers who participate fully in the NNE culture from marginal and isolated individuals.

5. For example, in Deutsch, Katz and Jensen (1968) there is a section on 'Social and Psychological Perspectives' which includes a chapter by Proshansky and Newton on 'The Nature and Meaning of Negro Self-Identity' and one by Rosenthal and Jacobson on 'Self-Fulfilling Prophecies in the Classroom'.

interaction of the Negro child with white society so much as on his failure to interact with his mother at home. In the literature we find very little direct observation of verbal interaction in the Negro home; most typically, the investigators ask the child if he has dinner with his parents, and if he engages in dinner-table conversation with them. He is also asked whether his family takes him on trips to museums and other cultural activities. This slender thread of evidence is used to explain and interpret the large body of tests carried out in the laboratory and in the school.

The most extreme view which proceeds from this orientation – and one that is now being widely accepted – is that lower-class Negro children have no language at all. The notion is first drawn from Basil Bernstein's writings that 'much of lower-class language consists of a kind of incidental "emotional" accompaniment to action here and now' (Jensen, 1968, p. 118). Bernstein's views are filtered through a strong bias against all forms of working class behavior, so that middle-class language is seen as superior in every respect – as 'more abstract, and necessarily somewhat more flexible, detailed and subtle'. One can proceed through a range of such views until one comes to the practical program of Carl Bereiter, Siegfried Engelmann and their associates (Bereiter et al., 1966; Bereiter and Engelmann, 1966). Bereiter's program for an academically oriented preschool is based upon their premise that Negro children must have a language with which they can learn, and their empirical finding that these children come to school without such a language. In his work with four-year-old Negro children from Urbana, Bereiter reports that their communication was by gestures, 'single words', and 'a series of badly-connected words or phrases', such as They mine and Me got juice. He reports that Negro children could not ask questions, that 'without exaggerating . . . these four-year-olds could make no statements of any kind'. Furthermore, when these children were asked 'Where is the book?', they did not know enough to look at the table where the book was lying in order to answer. Thus Bereiter concludes that the children's speech forms are nothing more than a series of emotional cries, and he decides to treat them 'as if the children had no language at all'. He identifies their speech with his interpretation of Bernstein's restricted code: 'the language of culturally deprived children . . . is not merely an underdeveloped version of standard English, but is a basically non-logical mode of expressive behavior' (Bereiter *et al.*, 1966, p. 113). The basic program of his preschool is to teach them a new language devised by Engelmann, which consists of a limited series of questions and answers such as *Where is the squirrel? The squirrel is in the tree.* The children will not be punished if they use their vernacular speech on the playground, but they will not be allowed to use it in the schoolroom. If they should answer the question *Where is the squirrel?* with the illogical vernacular form *In the tree* they will be reprehended by various means and made to say, *The squirrel is in the tree.*

Linguists and psycholinguists who have worked with Negro children are apt to dismiss this view of their language as utter nonsense. Yet there is no reason to reject Bereiter's observations as spurious: they were certainly not made up: on the contrary, they give us a very clear view of the behavior of student and teacher which can be duplicated in any classroom. In our own work outside of the adult-dominated environments of school and home,[6] we do not observe Negro children behaving like this, but on many occasions we have been asked to help analyze the results of research into verbal deprivation in such test situations.

Here, for example, is a complete interview with a Negro boy, one of hundreds carried out in a New York City school. The boy enters a room where there is a large, friendly white interviewer, who puts on the table in front of him a block or a fire engine, and says 'Tell me everything you can about this'. (The interviewer's further remarks are in parentheses.)

[*12 seconds of silence*]
(What would you say it looks like?)
[*8 seconds of silence*]
A space ship.
(Hmmmm.)

6. The research cited here was carried out in South Central Harlem and other ghetto areas in 1965–1968 to describe structural and functional differences between nonstandard Negro English and standard English of the classroom. It was supported by the Office of Education as Cooperative Research Projects 3091 and 3288. Detailed reports are given in Labov, Cohen and Robins (1965), Labov (1967) and Labov, Cohen, Robins and Lewis (1968).

[*13 seconds of silence*]
Like a je-et.
  [*12 seconds of silence*]
Like a plane.
  [*20 seconds of silence*]
(What color is it?)
Orange. [*2 seconds*] An' whi-ite. [*2 seconds*] An' green.
  [*6 seconds of silence*]
(An' what could you use it for?)
  [*8 seconds of silence*]
A je-et.
  [*6 seconds of silence*]
(If you had two of them, what would you do with them?)
  [*6 seconds of silence*]
Give one to some-body.
(Hmmm. Who do you think would like to have it?)
  [*10 seconds of silence*]
Cla-rence.
(Mm. Where do you think we could get another one of these?)
At the store.
(Oh ka-ay!)

We have here the same kind of defensive, monosyllabic behavior which is reported in Bereiter's work. What is the situation that produces it? The child is in an asymmetrical situation where anything he says can literally be held against him. He has learned a number of devices to *avoid* saying anything in this situation, and he works very hard to achieve this end. One may observe the intonation patterns of which Negro children often use when they

$$\begin{array}{c} 1 \quad {}^{3}\text{'o'} \quad 2\text{ know} \\ \text{a} \\ \hline 2 \quad \text{a space} \ {}^{2} \ \text{shi} \ \overline{\text{ip}}^{\,2} \end{array}$$

are asked a question to which the answer is obvious. The answer may be read as 'Will this satisfy you?'

If one takes this interview as a measure of the verbal capacity of the child, it must be as his capacity to defend himself in a hostile and threatening situation. But unfortunately, thousands of such interviews are used as evidence of the child's total verbal capacity, or more simply his 'verbality'; it is argued that this lack of verbality *explains* his poor performance in school. Operation Headstart and other intervention programs have largely been based upon the 'deficit theory' – the notions that such interviews give us a measure of the child's verbal capacity and that the verbal stimulation which he has been missing can be supplied in a preschool environment.

The verbal behavior which is shown by the child in the test situation quoted above is not the result of the ineptness of the interviewer. It is rather the result of regular sociolinguistic factors operating upon adult and child in this asymmetrical situation. In our work in urban ghetto areas, we have often encountered such behavior. Ordinarily we worked with boys 10–17 years old; and whenever we extended our approach downward to 8- or 9-year olds, we began to see the need for different techniques to explore the verbal capacity of the child. At one point we began a series of interviews with younger brothers of the 'Thunderbirds' in 1390 5th Avenue. Clarence Robins returned after an interview with 8-year-old Leon L., who showed the following minimal response to topics which arouse intense interest in other interviews with older boys.

CR: What if you saw somebody kickin' somebody else on the ground, or was using a stick, what would you do if you saw that?
LEON: Mmmm.
CR: If it was supposed to be a fair fight –
LEON: I don' know.
CR: You don' know? Would you do anything . . . huh? I can't hear you.
LEON: No.
CR: Did you ever see somebody got beat up real bad?
LEON: . . . Nope ? ? ?
CR: Well – uh – did you ever get into a fight with a guy?
LEON: Nope.
CR: That was bigger than you?
LEON: Nope.
CR: You never been in a fight?
LEON: Nope.
CR: Nobody ever pick on you?

LEON: Nope.

CR: Nobody ever hit you?

LEON: Nope.

CR: How come?

LEON: Ah 'on' know.

CR: Didn't you ever hit somebody?

LEON: Nope.

CR: [*incredulous*] You never hit nobody?

LEON: Mhm.

CR: Aww, ba -a-a-be, you ain't gonna tell me that.

It may be that Leon is here defending himself against accusations of wrong-doing, since Clarence knows that Leon has been in fights, that he has been taking pencils away from little boys, etc. But if we turn to a more neutral subject, we find the same pattern:

CR: You watch – you like to watch television? . . . Hey, Leon . . . you like to watch television? [*Leon nods*] What's your favorite program?

LEON: Uhhmmmm . . . I look at cartoons.

CR: Well, what's your favorite one? What's your favorite program?

LEON: Superman . . .

CR: Yeah? Did you see Superman – ah – yesterday, or day before yesterday: when's the last time you saw Superman?

LEON: Sa-aturday . . .

CR: You rem – you saw it Saturday? What was the story all about? You remember the story?

LEON: M-m.

CR: You don't remember the story of what – that you saw of Superman?

LEON: Nope.

CR: You don't remember what happened, huh?

LEON: Hm-m.

CR: I see – ah – what other stories do you like to watch on T.V.?

LEON: Mmmm ? ? ? ? . . . umm . . . [*glottalization*]

CR: Hmm? [*4 seconds*]

LEON: Hh?

CR: What's th'other stories that you like to watch?

LEON: ^{2}Mi - ighty ^{2}Mouse^2 . . .

CR: And what else?
LEON: Ummmm...ahm...

This nonverbal behavior occurs in a relatively *favorable* context for adult–child interaction; since the adult is a Negro man raised in Harlem, who knows this particular neighborhood and these boys very well. He is a skilled interviewer who has obtained a very high level of verbal response with techniques developed for a different age level, and he has an extraordinary advantage over most teachers or experimenters in these respects. But even his skills and personality are ineffective in breaking down the social constraints that prevail here.

When we reviewed the record of this interview with Leon, we decided to use it as a test of our own knowledge of the sociolinguistic factors which control speech. We made the following changes in the social situation: in the next interview with Leon, Clarence

1 brought along a supply of potato chips, changing the 'interview' into something more in the nature of a party;
2 brought along Leon's best friend, 8-year-old Gregory;
3 reduced the height imbalance (when Clarence got down on the floor of Leon's room, he dropped from 6 ft. 2 in. to 3 ft. 6 in.);
4 introduced taboo words and taboo topics, and proved to Leon's surprise that one can say anything into our microphone without any fear of retaliation.

The result of these changes is a striking difference in the volume and style of speech.

CR: Is there anybody who says *your momma drink pee?*
⎰LEON: [*rapidly and breathlessly*] Yee-ah!
⎱GREG: Yup!
LEON: And your father eat doo-doo for breakfas'!
CR: Ohhh!! [*laughs*]
LEON: And they say *your father – your father eat doo-doo for dinner*!
GREG: When they sound on me, I say *C. B. M.*
CR: What that mean?
⎰LEON: Congo booger-snatch! [*laughs*]
⎱GREG: Congo booger-snatcher! [*laughs*]
GREG: And sometimes I'll curse with *B. B.*

CR: What that?

GREG: Black boy! [*Leon – crunching on potato chips*] Oh that's a *M. B. B.*

CR: M. B. B. What's that?

GREG: 'Merican Black Boy!

CR: Ohh . . .

GREG: Anyway, 'Mericans is same like white people, right?

LEON: And they talk about Allah.

CR: Oh yeah?

GREG: Yeah.

CR: What they say about Allah?

{ LEON: Allah – Allah is God.

{ GREG: Allah –

CR: And what else?

LEON: I don' know the res'.

GREG: Allah i – Allah is God, Allah is the only God, Allah–

LEON: Allah is the *son* of God.

GREG: But can he make magic?

LEON: Nope.

GREG: I know who can make magic.

CR: Who can?

LEON: The God, the *real* one.

CR: Who can make magic?

GREG: The son of po' – [CR: Hm?] I'm sayin' the po'k chop God! He only a po'k chop God![7] [*Leon chuckles*]

The 'nonverbal' Leon is now competing actively for the floor; Gregory and Leon talk to each other as much as they do to the interviewer.

One can make a more direct comparison of the two interviews by examining the section on fighting. Leon persists in denying that he fights, but he can no longer use monosyllabic answers, and Gregory cuts through his façade in a way that Clarence Robins alone was unable to do.

7. The reference to the *pork chop God* condenses several concepts of black nationalism current in the Harlem community. A *pork chop* is a Negro who has not lost traditional subservient ideology of the South, who has no knowledge of himself in Muslim terms, and the *pork chop God* would be the traditional God of Southern Baptists. He and his followers may be pork chops, but he still holds the power in Leon and Gregory's world.

CR: Now, you said you had this fight, now, but I wanted you to tell me about the fight that you had.

LEON: I ain't had no fight.

⎧GREG: Yes, you did!　　　　　　　He said Barry,
⎩CR: You said you had one! you had a fight with Butchie,

⎧GREG:　　　　　　　An he say Garland . . . an' Michael.
⎩CR: an' Barry . . .

⎧LEON: I di'n'; you said that, Gregory!
⎩GREG:　　　You did.

⎧LEON: You know you said that!
⎩GREG:　　　　　　You said Garland, remember that?

⎧GREG: You said Garland!　　　Yes you did!
⎩CR:　　　　　　　You said Garland, that's right.

GREG: He said Mich – an' I say Michael.

⎧CR: Did you have a fight with Garland?
⎩LEON:　　　　　　　　　　　Uh-uh.

CR: You had one, and he beat you up, too!

GREG: Yes he did!

LEON: No, I di – I never had a fight with Butch! . . .

The same pattern can be seen on other local topics, where the interviewer brings neighborhood gossip to bear on Leon and Gregory acts as a witness.

CR: . . . Hey Gregory! I heard that around here . . . and I'm
　　　'on' tell you who said it, too . . .

LEON:　　　　　　　　　Who?

⎧CR: about you . . .
⎨LEON:　　　　Who?
⎩GREG:　　　　　　　I'd say it!

CR: They said that – they say that the only person you play with is David Gilbert.

⎧LEON: Yee-ah! yee-ah! yee-ah! . . .
⎩GREG:　　　　That's who you play with!

⎧LEON: I 'on' play with him no more!
⎩GREG:　　　　Yes you do!

LEON: I 'on' play with him no more!

GREG: But remember, about me and Robbie?

LEON: So that's not –

GREG: and you went to Petey and Gilbert's house, 'member? *Ah haaah!!*

LEON: So that's – so – but I would – I had came back out, an' I ain't go to his house no more . . .

The observer must now draw a very different conclusion about the verbal capacity of Leon. The monosyllabic speaker who had nothing to say about anything and cannot remember what he did yesterday has disappeared. Instead, we have two boys who have so much to say they keep interrupting each other, who seem to have no difficulty in using the English language to express themselves. And we in turn obtain the volume of speech and the rich array of grammatical devices which we need for analyzing the structure of nonstandard Negro English (NNE): negative concord [*I 'on' play with him no more*], the pluperfect [*had came back out*], negative perfect [*I ain't had*], the negative preterite [*I ain't go*], and so on.

One can now transfer this demonstration of the sociolinguistic control of speech to other test situations – including IQ and reading tests in school. It should be immediately apparent that none of the standard tests will come anywhere near measuring Leon's verbal capacity. On these tests he will show up as very much the monosyllabic, inept, ignorant, bumbling child of our first interview. The teacher has far less ability than Clarence Robins to elicit speech from this child; Clarence knows the community, the things that Leon has been doing, and the things that Leon would like to talk about. But the power relationships in a one-to-one confrontation between adult and child are too asymmetrical. This does not mean that some Negro children will not talk a great deal when alone with an adult, or that an adult cannot get close to any child. It means that the social situation is the most powerful determinant of verbal behavior and that an adult must enter into the right social relation with a child if he wants to find out what a child can do: this is just what many teachers cannot do.

The view of the Negro speech community which we obtain from our work in the ghetto areas is precisely the opposite from that reported by Deutsch, Engelmann and Bereiter. We see a child bathed in verbal stimulation from morning to night. We see many speech events which depend upon the competitive exhibition of verbal skills: sounding, singing, toasts, rifting, louding – a whole range of activities in which the individual gains status through his use of language.[8] We see the younger child trying to acquire these skills from older children – hanging around on the outskirts of the older peer groups, and imitating this behavior to the best of his ability. We see no connection between verbal skill at the speech events characteristic of the street culture and success in the schoolroom.

Verbosity

There are undoubtedly many verbal skills which children from ghetto areas must learn in order to do well in the school situation, and some of these are indeed characteristic of middle-class verbal behavior. Precision in spelling, practice in handling abstract symbols, the ability to state explicitly the meaning of words, and a richer knowledge of the Latinate vocabulary, may all be useful acquisitions. But is it true that *all* of the middle-class verbal habits are functional and desirable in the school situation? Before we impose middle-class verbal style upon children from other cultural groups, we should find out how much of this is useful for the main work of analyzing and generalizing, and how much is merely stylistic – or even dysfunctional. In high school and college middle-class children spontaneously complicate their syntax to the point that instructors despair of getting them to make their language simpler and clearer. In every learned journal one can find examples of jargon and empty elaboration – and complaints about it. Is the 'elaborated code' of Bernstein really so 'flexible, detailed and subtle' as some psychologists believe? (Jensen, 1968, p. 119) Isn't it also turgid, redundant, and empty? Is it not simply an elaborated *style*, rather than a superior code or system?[9]

Our work in the speech community makes it painfully obvious

8. For detailed accounts of these speech events, see Labov, Cohen, Robins and Lewis (1968, section 4.2).

9. The term *code* is central in Bernstein's description of the differences between working-class and middle-class styles of speech. The restrictions and elaborations of speech observed are labelled as 'codes' to indicate the principles governing selection from the range of possible English sentences. No rules or detailed description of the operation of such codes are provided as yet, so that this central concept remains to be specified.

that in many ways working-class speakers are more effective narrators, reasoners and debaters than many middle-class speakers who temporize, qualify, and lose their argument in a mass of irrelevant detail. Many academic writers try to rid themselves of that part of middle-class style that is empty pretension, and keep that part that is needed for precision. But the average middle-class speaker that we encounter makes no such effort; he is enmeshed in verbiage, the victim of sociolinguistic factors beyond his control.

I will not attempt to support this argument here with systematic quantitative evidence, although it is possible to develop measures which show how far middle-class speakers can wander from the point. I would like to contrast two speakers dealing with roughly the same topic – matters of belief. The first is Larry H., a 15-year-old core member of the Jets, being interviewed by John Lewis. Larry is one of the loudest and roughest members of the Jets, one who gives the least recognition to the conventional rules of politeness.[10] For most readers of this paper, first contact with Larry would produce some fairly negative reactions on both sides: it is probable that you would not *like* him any more than his teachers do. Larry causes trouble in and out of school; he was put back from the eleventh grade to the ninth, and has been threatened with further action by the school authorities.

JL: What happens to you after you die? Do you know?
LARRY: Yeah, I know.
JL: What?
LARRY: After they put you in the ground, your body turns into – ah – bones, an' shit.
JL: What happens to your spirit?
LARRY: Your spirit – soon as you die, your spirit leaves you.
JL: And where does the spirit go?
LARRY: Well, it all depends . . .
JL: On what?

10. A direct view of Larry's verbal style in a hostile encounter is given in Labov, Cohen, Robins and Lewis (1968), Vol. II, pp. 39–43. Gray's Oral Reading Test was being given to a group of Jets on the steps of a brownstone house in Harlem, and the landlord tried unsuccessfully to make the Jets move. Larry's verbal style in this encounter matches the reports he gives of himself in a number of narratives cited in section 4. 8.

LARRY: You know, like some people say if you're good an' shit,
your spirit goin' t'heaven . . . 'n' if you bad, your spirit goin' to
hell. Well, bullshit! Your spirit goin' to hell anyway, good or bad.
JL: Why?
LARRY: Why? I'll tell you why. 'Cause, you see, doesn' nobody
really know that it's a God, y'know, 'cause I mean I have
seen black gods, pink gods, white gods, all color gods,
and don't nobody know it's really a God. An' when they be
sayin' if you good, you goin' t'heaven, tha's bullshit, 'cause
you ain't goin' to no heaven, 'cause it ain't no heaven for
you to go to.

Larry is a paradigmatic speaker of nonstandard Negro English
(NNE) as opposed to standard English (SE). His grammar
shows a high concentration of such characteristic NNE forms as
negative inversion [*don't nobody know* . . .], negative concord
[*you ain't goin' to no heaven* . . .], invariant *be* [*when they be
sayin'* . . .], dummy *it* for SE *there* [*it ain't no heaven* . . .], optional
copula deletion [*if you're good* . . . *if you bad* . . .], and full forms of
auxiliaries [*I have seen* . . .]. The only SE influence in this passage
is the one case of *doesn't* instead of the invariant *don't* of NNE.
Larry also provides a paradigmatic example of the rhetorical style
of NNE: he can sum up a complex argument in a few words, and
the full force of his opinions comes through without qualification
or reservation. He is eminently quotable, and his interviews
give us many concise statements of the NNE point of view. One
can almost say that Larry *speaks* the NNE culture (see Labov,
Cohen, Robins and Lewis, 1968, vol. 2, pp. 38, 71–3, 291–2).

It is the logical form of this passage which is of particular
interest here. Larry presents a complex set of interdependent
propositions which can be explicated by setting out the SE
equivalents in linear order. The basic argument is to deny the
twin propositions

(A) If you are good,   (B) then your spirit will go to heaven.
(–A) If you are bad,   (C) then your spirit will go to hell.

Larry denies (B), and asserts that *if* (A) *or* (–A), *then* (C). His
argument may be outlined as follows:

(1) Everyone has a different idea of what God is like.

(2) Therefore nobody really knows that God exists.

(3) If there is a heaven, it was made by God.

(4) If God doesn't exist, he couldn't have made heaven.

(5) Therefore heaven does not exist.

(6) You can't go somewhere that doesn't exist.

(–B) Therefore you can't go to heaven.

(C) Therefore you are going to hell.

The argument is presented in the order: (C), because (2) because (1), therefore (2), therefore (–B) because (5) and (6). Part of the argument is implicit: the connection (2) therefore (–B) leaves unstated the connecting links (3) and (4), and in this interval Larry strengthens the propositions from the form (2) *Nobody knows if there is* ... to (5) *There is no* ... Otherwise, the case is presented explicitly as well as economically. The complex argument is summed up in Larry's last sentence, which shows formally the dependence of (–B) on (5) and (6):

An' when they be sayin' if you good, you goin' t'heaven,
[*The proposition, if* A, *then* B]
Tha's bullshit,
[*is absurd*]
'cause you ain't goin' to no heaven
[*because* –B]
'cause it ain't no heaven for you to go to.
[*because* (5) *and* (6)].

This hypothetical argument is not carried on at a high level of seriousness. It is a game played with ideas as counters, in which opponents use a wide variety of verbal devices to win. There is no personal commitment to any of these propositions, and no reluctance to strengthen one's argument by bending the rules of logic as in the (2–5) sequence. But if the opponent invokes the rules of logic, they hold. In John Lewis' interviews, he often makes this move, and the force of his argument is always acknowledged and countered within the rules of logic. In this case, he pointed out the fallacy that the argument (2–3–4–5–6) leads to (–C) as well as (–B), so it cannot be used to support Larry's assertion (C):

JL: Well, if there's no heaven, how could there be a hell?

LARRY: I mean – ye – eah. Well, let me tell you, it ain't no hell,
'cause this is hell right here, y'know!

JL: This is hell?

LARRY: Yeah, this is hell right here!

Larry's answer is quick, ingenious and decisive. The application
of the (3–4–5) argument to hell is denied, since hell is here, and
therefore conclusion (C) stands. These are not ready-made or
preconceived opinions, but new propositions devised to win the
logical argument in the game being played. The reader will note
the speed and precision of Larry's mental operations. He does
not wander, or insert meaningless verbiage. The only repetition is
(2), placed before and after (1) in his original statement. It is
often said that the nonstandard vernacular is not suited for dealing with abstract or hypothetical questions, but in fact speakers
from the NNE community take great delight in exercising their
wit and logic on the most improbable and problematical matters.
Despite the fact that Larry H. does not believe in God, and has
just denied all knowledge of him, John Lewis advances the following hypothetical question:

JL: . . . But, just say that there is a God, what color is he?
White or black?

LARRY: Well, if it is a God . . . I wouldn' know what color, I
couldn' say, – couldn' nobody say what color he is or
really *would* be.

JL: But now, jus' suppose there was a God –

LARRY: Unless'n they say . . .

JL: No, I was jus' sayin' jus' suppose there is a God, would he
be white or black?

LARRY: . . . He'd be white, man.

JL: Why?

LARRY: Why? I'll tell you why. 'Cause the average whitey out
here got everything, you dig? And the nigger ain't got
shit, y'know? Y'understan'? So – um – for – in order for
that to happen, you know it ain't no black God that's doin'
that bullshit.

No one can hear Larry's answer to this question without being
convinced that they are in the presence of a skilled speaker with
great 'verbal presence of mind', who can use the English lan-

guage expertly for many purposes. Larry's answer to John Lewis is again a complex argument. The formulation is not SE, but it is clear and effective even for those not familiar with the vernacular. The nearest SE equivalent might be: 'So you know that God isn't black, because if he was, he wouldn't have arranged things like that'.

The reader will have noted that this analysis is being carried out in standard English, and the inevitable challenge is: why not write in NNE, then, or in your own nonstandard dialect? The fundamental reason is, of course, one of firmly fixed social conventions. All communities agree that SE is the 'proper' medium for formal writing and public communication. Furthermore, it seems likely that SE has an advantage over NNE in explicit analysis of surface forms, which is what we are doing here. We will return to this opposition between explicitness and logical statement in sections 3 and 4.[11] First, however, it will be helpful to examine SE in its primary natural setting, as the medium for informal spoken communication of middle-class speakers.

Let us now turn to the second speaker, an upper-middle-class, college educated Negro man being interviewed by Clarence Robins in our survey of adults in Central Harlem.

CR: Do you know of anything that someone can do, to have someone who has passed on visit him in a dream?
CHARLES M: Well, I even heard my parents say that there is such a thing as something in dreams some things like that, and sometimes dreams do come true. I have personally never had a dream come true. I've never dreamt that somebody was dying and they actually died, (Mhm) or that I was going to have ten dollars the next day and somehow I got ten dollars in my pocket. (Mhm). I don't particularly believe in that, I don't think it's true. I do feel, though, that there is such a thing as – ah – witchcraft. I do feel that in certain cultures there is such a thing as witchcraft, or some sort of *science* of witchcraft; I don't think that it's just a matter of believing hard enough that there is such a thing as witchcraft. I do believe that there is such a thing that a person can put himself in a state of *mind* (Mhm), or

11. The third section is that under the heading 'Grammaticality'. The fourth section has not been reprinted in this volume [Ed.].

that – er – something could be given them to intoxicate them in a certain – to a certain frame of mind – that – that could actually be considered witchcraft.

Charles M. is obviously a 'good speaker' who strikes the listener as well-educated, intelligent and sincere. He is a likeable and attractive person – the kind of person that middle-class listeners rate very high on a scale of 'job suitability' and equally high as a potential friend.[12] His language is more moderate and tempered than Larry's; he makes every effort to qualify his opinions, and seems anxious to avoid any misstatements or over-statements. From these qualities emerge the primary characteristic of this passage – its *verbosity*. Words multiply, some modifying and qualifying, others repeating or padding the main argument. The first half of this extract is a response to the initial question on dreams, basically:

1 Some people say that dreams sometimes come true.
2 I have never had a dream come true.
3 Therefore I don't believe (1).

Some characteristic filler phrases appear here: *such a thing as, some things like that, particularly*. Two examples of dreams given after (2) are afterthoughts that might have been given after (1). Proposition (3) is stated twice for no obvious reason. Nevertheless, this much of Charles M.'s response is well-directed to the point of the question. He then volunteers a statement of his beliefs about witchcraft which shows the difficulty of middle-class speakers who (a) want to express a belief in something but (b) want to show themselves as judicious, rational and free from superstitions. The basic proposition can be stated simply in five words:

But I believe in witchcraft.

However, the idea is enlarged to exactly 100 words, and it is difficult to see what else is being said. In the following quotations, padding which can be removed without change in meaning is shown in brackets.

12. See Labov, Cohen, Robins and Lewis (1968), section 4.6, for a description of subjective reaction tests which utilize these evaluative dimensions.

1. 'I [do] feel, though, that there is [such a thing as] witchcraft.' *Feel* seems to be a euphemism for 'believe'.

2. '[I do feel that] in certain cultures [there is such a thing as witchcraft.]' This repetition seems designed only to introduce the word *culture*, which lets us know that the speaker knows about anthropology. Does *certain cultures* mean 'not in ours' or 'not in all'?

3. '[or some sort of *science* of witchcraft.]' This addition seems to have no clear meaning at all. What is a 'science' of witchcraft as opposed to just plain witchcraft?[13] The main function is to introduce the word 'science', though it seems to have no connection to what follows.

4. 'I don't think that it's just [a matter of] believing hard enough that [there is such a thing as] witchcraft.' The speaker argues that witchcraft is not merely a belief; there is more to it.

5. 'I [do] believe that [*there is such a thing that*] a person can put himself in a state of *mind* ... that [*could actually be considered*] witchcraft.' Is witchcraft as a state of mind different from the state of belief denied in (4)?

6. 'or that something could be given them to intoxicate them [to a certain frame of mind] ...' The third learned word, *intoxicate*, is introduced by this addition. The vacuity of this passage becomes more evident if we remove repetitions, fashionable words and stylistic decorations:

But I believe in witchcraft.
I don't think witchcraft is just a belief.
A person can put himself or be put in a state of mind that is witchcraft.

Without the extra verbiage and the O K words like *science, culture* and *intoxicate*, Charles M. appears as something less than a first-rate thinker. The initial impression of him as a good speaker is simply our long-conditioned reaction to middle-class verbosity: we know that people who use these stylistic devices are educated

13. Several middle-class readers of this passage have suggested that *science* here refers to some form of control as opposed to belief; the 'science of witchcraft' would then be a kind of engineering of mental states; other interpretations can of course be provided. The fact remains that no such subtleties of interpretation are needed to understand Larry's remarks.

people, and we are inclined to credit them with saying something intelligent. Our reactions are accurate in one sense: Charles M. is more educated than Larry. But is he more rational, more logical, or more intelligent? Is he any better at thinking out a problem to its solution? Does he deal more easily with abstractions? There is no reason to think so. Charles M. succeeds in letting us know that he is educated, but in the end we do not know what he is trying to say, and neither does he.

In the previous section I have attempted to explain the origin of the myth that lower-class Negro children are nonverbal. The examples just given may help to account for the corresponding myth that middle-class language is in itself better suited for dealing with abstract, logically complex and hypothetical questions. These examples are intended to have a certain negative force. They are not controlled experiments: on the contrary, this and the preceding section are designed to convince the reader that the controlled experiments that have been offered in evidence are misleading. The only thing that is 'controlled' is the superficial form of the stimulus: all children are asked 'What do you think of capital punishment?' or 'Tell me everything you can about this.' But the speaker's interpretation of these requests, and the action he believes is appropriate in response is completely uncontrolled. One can view these test stimuli as requests for information, commands for action, as threats of punishment, or as meaningless sequences of words. They are probably intended as something altogether different: as requests for display;[14] but in any case the experimenter is normally unaware of the problem of interpretation. The methods of educational psychologists like Deutsch, Jensen and Bereiter follow the pattern designed for animal experiments where motivation is controlled by such simple methods as withholding food until a certain weight reduction is reached. With human subjects, it is absurd to believe that an identical 'stimulus' is obtained by asking everyone the 'same question'. Since the crucial intervening variables of interpretation and motivation are uncontrolled, most of the literature on verbal deprivation tells us nothing about the capacities of children. They

14. The concept of a 'request for verbal display' is here drawn from Alan Blum's treatment of the therapeutic interview in *The Sociology of Mental Illness*, mimeographed (to appear in *For Thomas Szaz*).

are only the trappings of science: an approach which substitutes the formal procedures of the scientific method for the activity itself. With our present limited grasp of these problems, the best we can do to understand the verbal capacities of children is to study them within the cultural context in which they were developed.

It is not only the NNE vernacular which should be studied in this way, but also the language of middle-class children. The explicitness and precision which we hope to gain from copying middle-class forms are often the product of the test situation, and limited to it. For example, it was stated in the first part of this paper that working-class children hear more well-formed sentences than middle-class children. This statement may seem extraordinary in the light of the current belief of many linguists that most people do not speak in well-formed sentences, and that their actual speech production or 'performance' is ungrammatical.[15] But those who have worked with any body of natural speech know that this is not the case. Our own studies of the 'Grammaticality of Every-day Speech' show that the great majority of utterances in all contexts are complete sentences, and most of the rest can be reduced to grammatical form by a small set of 'editing rules'.[16] The proportions of grammatical sentences vary with class backgrounds and styles. The highest percentage of well-formed sentences are found in casual speech, and working-class speakers use more well-formed sentences than middle-class speakers. The widespread myth that most speech is ungrammatical is no doubt based upon tapes made at learned conferences, where we obtain the maximum number of irreducibly ungrammatical sequences.

It is true that technical and scientific books are written in a

15. In a number of presentations, Chomsky has asserted that the great majority of the sentences which a child hears are ungrammatical ('95 per cent'). In Chomsky 1965, p. 58), this notion is presented as one of the arguments in his gen. al statement of the 'nativist' position: 'A consideration of the character o. the grammar that is acquired, *the degenerate quality and narrowly limited extent of the available data* [my emphasis] the striking uniformity of the resulting grammars, and their independence of intelligence, motivation, and emotional state, over wide ranges of variation, leave little hope that much of the structure of the language can be learned ...'

16. The editing rules are presented in Labov (1966).

style which is markedly 'middle-class'. But unfortunately, we often fail to achieve the explicitness and precision which we look for in such writing; and the speech of many middle-class people departs maximally from this target. All too often, 'standard English' is represented by a style that is simultaneously over-particular and vague. The accumulating flow of words buries rather than strikes the target. It is this verbosity which is most easily taught and most easily learned, so that words take the place of thought, and nothing can be found behind them.

When Bernstein described his 'elaborated code' in general terms, it emerges as a subtle and sophisticated mode of planning utterances, achieving structural variety, taking the other person's knowledge into account, and so on. But when it comes to describing the actual difference between middle-class and working-class speakers, we are presented with a proliferation of 'I think', of the passive, of modals and auxiliaries, of the first person pronoun, of uncommon words; these are the bench marks of hemming and hawing, backing and filling, that are used by Charles M., devices which often obscure whatever positive contribution education can make to our use of language. When we have discovered how much middle-class style is a matter of fashion and how much actually helps us express our ideas clearly, we will have done ourselves a great service; we will then be in a position to say what standard grammatical rules must be taught to nonstandard speakers in the early grades.

Grammaticality

Let us now examine Bereiter's own data on the verbal behavior of the children he dealt with. The expressions *They mine* and *Me got juice* are cited as examples of a language which lacks the means for expressing logical relations – in this case characterized as 'a series of badly connected words'. (Bereiter, 1966, pp. 113 ff.) In the case of *They mine*, it is apparent that Bereiter confuses the notions of logic and explicitness. We know that there are many languages of the world which do not have a present copula, and which conjoin subject and predicate complement without a verb. Russian, Hungarian and Arabic may be foreign; but they are not by that same token illogical. In the case of nonstandard Negro English we are not dealing with even this superficial grammatical difference, but rather with a low-level rule which carries contraction one step farther to delete single consonants representing the verbs *is*, *have*, or *will* (Labov, Cohen, Robins and Lewis, 1968, sect. 3.4). We have yet to find any children who do not sometimes use the full forms of *is* and *will*, even though they may frequently delete it. Our recent studies with Negro children four to seven years old indicate that they use the full form of the copula *is* more often than pre-adolescents 10 to 12 years old, or the adolescents 14 to 17 years old.[17]

Furthermore, the deletion of the *is* or *are* in nonstandard Negro English is not the result of erratic or illogical behavior: it follows the same regular rules as standard English contraction. Wherever standard English can contract, Negro children use either the contracted form or (more commonly) the deleted zero form. Thus *They mine* corresponds to standard *They're mine*, not to the full form *They are mine*. On the other hand, no such deletion is possible in positions where standard English cannot contract: just as one cannot say *That's what they're* in standard English, *That's what they* is equally impossible in the vernacular we are considering. The internal constraints upon both of these rules show that we are dealing with a phonological process like contraction, sensitive to such phonetic conditions as whether or not the next word begins with a vowel or a consonant. The appropriate use of the deletion rule, like the contraction rule, requires a deep and intimate knowledge of English grammar and phonology. Such knowledge is not available for conscious inspection by native speakers: the rules we have recently worked out for standard contraction (Labov, Cohen, Robins and Lewis, 1968, sect. 3.4) have never appeared in any grammar, and are certainly not a part of the conscious knowledge of any standard English speakers. Nevertheless, the adult or child who uses these rules must have formed at some level of psychological organization clear concepts of 'tense marker', 'verb phrase', 'rule ordering', 'sentence embedding', 'pronoun', and many other grammatical categories which are essential parts of any logical system.

17. From work on the grammars and comprehension of Negro children four to eight years old being carried out by Professor Jane Torrey of Connecticut College in extension of the research cited above in Labov, Cohen, Robins and Lewis (1968).

Bereiter's reaction to the sentence *Me got juice* is even more puzzling. If Bereiter believes that *Me got juice* is not a logical expression, it can only be that he interprets the use of the objective pronoun *me* as representing a difference in logical relationship to the verb: that the child is in fact saying that *the juice got him* rather than *he got the juice*! If on the other hand the child means 'I got juice', then this sentence form shows only that he has not learned the formal rules for the use of the subjective form *I* and oblique form *me*. We have in fact encountered many children who do not have these formal rules in order at the ages of four, five, six or even eight.[18] It is extremely difficult to construct a minimal pair to show that the difference between *he* and *him*, or *she* and *her*, carries cognitive meaning. In almost every case, it is the context which tells us who is the agent and who is acted upon. We must then ask: what differences in cognitive, structural orientation are signalled by the fact that the child has not learned this formal rule? In the tests carried out by Jane Torrey it is evident that the children concerned do understand the difference in meaning between *she* and *her* when another person uses the forms; all that remains is that the children themselves do not use the two forms. Our knowledge of the cognitive correlates of grammatical differences is certainly in its infancy; for this is one of very many questions which we simply cannot answer. At the moment we do not know how to construct any kind of experiment which would lead to an answer; we do not even know what type of cognitive correlate we would be looking for.

Bereiter shows even more profound ignorance of the rules of discourse and of syntax when he rejects *In the tree* as an illogical, or badly-formed answer to *Where is the squirrel*? Such elliptical answers are of course used by everyone; they show the appropriate deletion of subject and main verb, leaving the locative which is questioned by *wh + there*. The reply *In the tree* demonstrates that the listener has been attentive to and apprehended the syntax of the speaker.[19] Whatever formal structure we wish to write for expressions such as *Yes* or *Home* or *In the tree*, it is obvious that they cannot be interpreted without knowing the

18. From the research of Jane Torrey cited in footnote 17.

19. The attention to the speaker's syntax required of the listener is analyzed in detail by Harvey Sacks in his unpublished 1968 lectures.

structure of the question which preceded them, and that they presuppose an understanding of the syntax of the question. Thus if you ask me 'Where is the squirrel?' it is necessary for me to understand the processes of *wh*-attachment, *wh*-attraction to the front of the sentence, and flip-flop of auxiliary and subject to produce this sentence from an underlying form which would otherwise have produced *The squirrel is there*. If the child had answered *The tree*, or *Squirrel the tree*, or *The in tree*, we would then assume that he did not understand the syntax of the full form, *The squirrel is in the tree*. Given the data that Bereiter presents, we cannot conclude that the child has no grammar, but only that the investigator does not understand the rules of grammar. It does not necessarily do any harm to use the full form *The squirrel is in the tree*, if one wants to make fully explicit the rules of grammar which the child has internalized. Much of logical analysis consists of making explicit just that kind of internalized rule. But it is hard to believe that any good can come from a program which begins with so many misconceptions about the input data. Bereiter and Engelmann believe that in teaching the child to say *The squirrel is in the tree* or *This is a box* and *This is not a box* they are teaching him an entirely new language, whereas in fact they are only teaching him to produce slightly different forms of the language he already has. [. . .]

What's wrong with being wrong?

If there is a failure of logic involved here, it is surely in the approach of the verbal deprivation theorists, rather than in the mental abilities of the children concerned. We can isolate six distinct steps in the reasoning which has led to programs such as those of Deutsch, Bereiter and Engelmann:

1. The lower-class child's verbal response to a formal and threatening situation is used to demonstrate his lack of verbal capacity, or verbal deficit.

2. This verbal deficit is declared to be a major cause of the lower-class child's poor performance in school.

3. Since middle-class children do better in school, middle-class speech habits are seen to be necessary for learning.

4. Class and ethnic differences in grammatical form are equated with differences in the capacity for logical analysis.

5. Teaching the child to mimic certain formal speech patterns used by middle-class teachers is seen as teaching him to think logically.

6. Children who learn these formal speech patterns are then said to be thinking logically and it is predicted that they will do much better in reading and arithmetic in the years to follow.

In the previous sections of this paper, I have tried to show that these propositions are wrong, concentrating on (1), (4), and (5). Proposition (3) is the primary logical fallacy which illicitly identifies a form of speech as the *cause* of middle-class achievement in school. Proposition (6) is the one which is most easily shown to be wrong in fact, as we will note below.

However, it is not too naïve to ask, 'What is wrong with being wrong?' There is no competing educational theory which is being dismantled by this program; and there does not seem to be any great harm in having children repeat *This is not a box* for twenty minutes a day. We have already conceded that NNE children need help in analysing language into its surface components, and in being more explicit. But there are serious and damaging consequences of the verbal deprivation theory which may be considered under two headings: (1) the theoretical bias, and (2) the consequences of failure.

(1). It is widely recognized that the teacher's attitude towards the child is an important factor in his success or failure. The work of Rosenthal on 'self-fulfilling prophecies' shows that the progress of children in the early grades can be dramatically affected by a single random labelling of certain children as 'intellectual bloomers' (Rosenthal and Jacobson, 1968). When the everyday language of Negro children is stigmatized as 'not a language at all' and 'not possessing the means for logical thought', the effect of such a labelling is repeated many times during each day of the school year. Every time that a child uses a form of NNE without the copula or with negative concord, he will be labelling himself for the teacher's benefit as 'illogical', as a 'nonceptual thinker'. Bereiter and Engelmann, Deutsch and Jensen are giving teachers a ready-made, theoretical basis for the prejudice they already feel against the lower-class Negro child and his language. When they hear him say *I don't want none* or *They mine*, they will be hearing through the bias provided by the verbal deprivation theory: not an English dialect different from theirs, but the primitive mentality of the savage mind.

But what if the teacher succeeds in training the child to use the new language consistently? The verbal deprivation theory holds that this will lead to a whole chain of successes in school, and that the child will be drawn away from the vernacular culture into the middle-class world. Undoubtedly this will happen with a few isolated individuals, just as it happens in every school system today, for a few children. But we are concerned not with the few but the many, and for the majority of Negro children the distance between them and the school is bound to widen under this approach.

Proponents of the deficit theory have a strange view of social organization outside of the classroom: they see the attraction of the peer group as a 'substitute' for success and gratification normally provided by the school. For example, Whiteman and Deutsch introduce their account of the deprivation hypothesis with an eye-witness account of a child who accidentally dropped his school notebook into a puddle of water and walked away without picking it up.

A policeman who had been standing nearby walked over to the puddle and stared at the notebook with some degree of disbelief (Whiteman and Deutsch, 1968, pp. 86-7).

The child's alienation from school is explained as the result of his coming to school without the 'verbal, conceptual, attentional and learning skills requisite to school success'. The authors see the child as 'suffering from feelings of inferiority because he is failing; ... he withdraws or becomes hostile, finding gratification elsewhere, such as in his peer group.'

To view the peer group as a mere substitute for school shows an extraordinary lack of knowledge of adolescent culture. In our studies in South Central Harlem we have seen the reverse situation: the children who are rejected by the peer group are quite likely to succeed in school. In middle-class suburban areas, many children do fail in school because of their personal deficiencies; in ghetto areas, it is the healthy, vigorous popular child with normal intelligence who cannot read and fails all along the line. It is not necessary to document here the influence of the peer group upon the behavior of youth in our society; but we may note that somewhere between the time that children first learn to talk and puberty, their language is restructured to fit the rules used by their peer group. From a linguistic viewpoint, the peer group is certainly a more powerful influence than the family (Gans, 1962). Less directly, the pressures of peer group activity are also felt within the school. Many children, particularly those who are not doing well in school, show a sudden sharp down turn in the fourth and fifth grades, and children in the ghetto schools are no exception. It is at the same age, at nine or ten years old, that the influence of the vernacular peer group becomes predominant.[20] Instead of dealing with isolated individuals, the school is then dealing with children who are integrated into groups of their own, with rewards and value systems which oppose those of the school. Those who know the sociolinguistic situation cannot doubt that reaction against the Bereiter–Engelmann approach in later years will be even more violent on the part of the students involved, and that the rejection of the school system will be even more categorical.

The essential fallacy of the verbal deprivation theory lies in tracing the educational failure of the child to his personal deficiencies. At present, these deficiencies are said to be caused by his home environment. It is traditional to explain a child's failure in school by his inadequacy; but when failure reaches such massive proportions, it seems to us necessary to look at the social and cultural obstacles to learning, and the inability of the school to adjust to the social situation. Operation Headstart is designed to repair the child, rather than the school; to the extent that it is based upon this inverted logic, it is bound to fail.

(2). The second area in which the verbal deprivation theory is doing serious harm to our educational system is in the consequences of this failure, and the reaction to it. If Operation Headstart fails,

20. For the relationship between age and membership in peer groups, see Wilmott (1966).

the interpretations which we receive will be from the same educational psychologists who designed this program. The fault will be found not in the data, the theory, nor in the methods used, but rather in the children who have failed to respond to the opportunities offered to them. When Negro children fail to show the significant advance which the deprivation theory predicts, it will be further proof of the profound gulf which separates their mental processes from those of civilized, middle-class mankind.

A sense of the 'failure' of Operation Headstart is already in the air. Some prominent figures in the program are reacting to this situation by saying that intervention did not take place early enough. Bettye M. Caldwell notes that:

... the research literature of the last decade dealing with social-class differences has made abundantly clear that all parents are not qualified to provide even the basic essentials of physical and psychological care to their children (Caldwell, 1967, p. 16).

The deficit theory now begins to focus on the 'long-standing patterns of parental deficit' which fill the literature. 'There is, perhaps unfortunately,' writes Caldwell, 'no literacy test for motherhood.' Failing such eugenic measures, she has proposed 'educationally oriented day care for culturally deprived children between six months and three years of age'. The children are returned home each evening to 'maintain primary emotional relationships with their own families', but during the day they are removed to 'hopefully prevent the deceleration in rate of development which seems to occur in many deprived children around the age of two to three years' (Caldwell, 1967, p. 17).

There are others who feel that even the best of the intervention programs, such as those of Bereiter and Engelmann, will not help the Negro child no matter when they are applied – that we are faced once again with the 'inevitable hypothesis' of the genetic inferiority of the Negro people. Many readers of this paper are undoubtedly familiar with the paper of Arthur Jensen in the *Harvard Educational Review* (1969) which received early and widespread publicity. Jensen begins with the following quotation from the United States Commission on Civil Rights as evidence of the failure of compensatory education.

The fact remains, however, that none of the programs appear to have raised significantly the achievement of participating pupils, as a group, within the period evaluated by the Commission (p. 138).

Jensen believes that the verbal deprivation theorists with whom he had been associated – Deutsch, Whiteman, Katz, Bereiter – have been given every opportunity to prove their case – and have failed. This opinion is part of the argument which leads him to the overall conclusion that 'the preponderance of the evidence is . . . less consistent with a strictly environmental hypothesis than with the genetic hypothesis'; that racism, or the belief in the genetic inferiority of Negroes, is a correct view in the light of the present evidence.

Jensen argues that the middle-class white population is differentiated from the working-class white and Negro population in the ability for 'cognitive or conceptual learning', which Jensen calls Level II intelligence as against mere 'associative learning' or Level I intelligence:

certain neural structures must also be available for Level II abilities to develop, and these are conceived of as being different from the neural structures underlying Level I. The genetic factors involved in each of these types of ability are presumed to have become differentially distributed in the population as a function of social class, since Level II has been most important for scholastic performance under the traditional methods of instruction.

Thus Jensen found that one group of middle-class children were helped by their concept-forming ability to recall twenty familiar objects that could be classified into four categories: animals, furniture, clothing, or foods. Lower-class Negro children did just as well as middle-class children with a miscellaneous set, but showed no improvement with objects that could be so categorized.

The research of the educational psychologists cited here is presented in formal and objective style, and is widely received as impartial scientific evidence. Jensen's paper has already been reported by Joseph Alsop and William F. Buckley Jr. as 'massive, apparently authoritative . . .' (N.Y. Post 3/20/69) It is not my intention to examine these materials in detail; but it is important to realize that we are dealing with special pleading by those who have a strong personal commitment. Jensen is concerned with class differences in cognitive style and verbal learning. His earlier papers incorporated the cultural deprivation theory which he now rejects as a basic explanation.[21] He classifies the Negro children who fail in school as 'slow-learners' and 'mentally-retarded', and urged that we find out how much their retardation is due to environmental factors and how much is due to 'more basic biological factors.' (Jensen 1968, p. 167). His conviction that the problem must be located in the child leads him to accept and reprint some truly extraordinary data. To support the genetic hypothesis he cites the following table of Heber for the racial distribution of mental retardation.

Table 1
Estimated Prevalence of Children with IQs below 75

SES	White	Negro
1	0·5	3·1
2	0·8	14·5
3	2·1	22·8
4	3·1	37·8
5	7·8	42·9

This report, that almost half of lower-class Negro children are mentally retarded, could be accepted only by someone who has no knowledge of the children or the community. If he had wished to, Jensen could easily have checked this against the records of any school in any urban ghetto area. Taking I Q tests at their face value, there is no correspondence between these figures and the communities we know. For example, among 75 boys we worked with in Central Harlem who would fall into Heber's S E S 4 or 5, there were only three with I Qs below 75: one spoke very little English, one could barely see, and the third was emotionally

21. In Deutsch, Katz and Jensen (1968), Jensen expounds the verbal deprivation theory in considerable detail. For example: 'During this "labeling" period ... some very important social-class differences may exert their effects on verbal learning. Lower-class parents engage in relatively little of this naming or "labeling" play with their children ... That words are discrete labels for things seems to be better known by the middle-class child entering first grade than by the lower-class child. Much of this knowledge is gained in the parent-child interaction, as when the parent looks at a picture book with the child ...' (p. 119).

disturbed. When the second was retested, he scored 91, and the third retested at 87.[22] There are of course hundreds of realistic reports available to Jensen: he simply selected one which would strengthen his case for the genetic inferiority of Negro children, and deliberately deleted the information that this was a study of an area selected in advance because of its high incidence of mental retardation.[23]

The frequent use of tables and statistics by educational psychologists serves to give outside readers the impression that this field is a science, and that the opinions of the authors should be given the same attention and respect that we give to the conclusions of physicists or chemists. But careful examination of the input data will often show that there is no direct relationship between the conclusions and the evidence (in Jensen's case, between IQ Tests in a specially selected district of Milwaukee and intelligence of lower-class Negro children). Furthermore, the operations performed upon the data frequently carry us very far from the common-sense experience which is our only safeguard against conclusions heavily weighted by the author's theory. As another example, we may take some of the evidence presented by Whiteman and Deutsch for the cultural deprivation hypothesis. The core of Martin Deutsch's environmental explanation of low school performance is the Deprivation Index – a numerical scale based on six dichotomized variables. One variable is 'The educational aspirational level of the parent for the child'. Most people would agree that a parent who did not care if a child finished high school would be a disadvantageous factor in the child's educational career. In dichotomizing this variable Deutsch was faced with the fact that the educational aspiration of Negro parents is in fact very high – higher than for the white population, as he shows

22. Heber's studies of 88 Negro mothers in Milwaukee are cited frequently throughout Jensen (1969). The estimates in this table are not given in relation to a particular Milwaukee sample, but for the general population. Heber's study was specifically designed to cover an area of Milwaukee which was known to contain a large concentration of retarded children, Negro and white, and he has stated that his findings were 'grossly misinterpreted' by Jensen (*Milwaukee Sentinel*, 11 June 1969).

23. The IQ scores given here are from group rather than individual tests and must therefore not be weighted heavily: the scores are from the Pintner–Cunningham test, usually given in the first grade in New York City schools in the 1950s.

in other papers.[24] In order to fit this data into Deprivation Index, he therefore set the cutting point for the deprived group as 'college or less'. (Whiteman and Deutsch, 1968, p. 100). Thus if a Negro child's father says that he wants his son to go all the way through college, the child will fall into the 'deprived' class on this variable. In order to receive the two points given to the 'less deprived' on the index, it would be necessary for the child's parent to insist on graduate school or medical school! This decision is never discussed by the authors: it simply stands as a *fait accompli* in the tables. Readers of this literature who are not committed to one point of view would be wise to look as carefully as possible at the original data which lie behind each statement, and check the conclusions against their own knowledge of the people and community being described.

No one can doubt that the inadequacy of Operation Headstart and of the verbal deprivation hypothesis has now become a crucial issue in our society.[25] The controversy which is beginning over

24. Table 15.1 in Deutsch *et al.* (1967, p. 312, section C), shows that some degree of college training was desired by 96, 97 and 100 per cent of Negro parents in Class levels I, II and III respectively. The corresponding figures for whites were 79, 95 and 97 per cent. In an earlier version of this paper, this discussion could be interpreted as implying that Whiteman and Deutsch used data in the same way as Jensen to rate the Negro group as low as possible. As they point out [personal communication], the inclusion of this item in the Deprivation Index had the opposite effect, and it could easily have been omitted if that had been their intention. They also argue that they had sound statistical grounds for dichotomizing as they did. The criticism which I intended to make is that there is something drastically wrong with operations which produce definitions of deprivation such as the one cited here. It should of course be noted that Whiteman and Deutsch have strongly opposed Jensen's genetic hypothesis and vigorously criticized his logic and data.

25. The negative report of the Westinghouse Learning Corporation and Ohio University on Operation Headstart was published in the *New York Times* (on 13 April 1969). This evidence for the failure of the program was widely publicized and it seems likely that the report's discouraging conclusions 'will be used by conservative Congressmen as a weapon against any kind of expenditure for disadvantaged' children, especially Negroes. The two hypotheses mentioned to account for this failure is that the impact of Headstart is lost through poor teaching later on, and more recently, that poor children have been so badly damaged in infancy by their lower-class environment that Headstart cannot make much difference. The third 'inevitable' hypothesis of Jensen is not reported here.

Jensen's article will undoubtedly take as given that programs such as Bereiter and Engelmann's have tested and measured the verbal capacity of the ghetto child. The cultural sociolinguistic obstacles to this intervention program are not considered; and the argument proceeds upon the data provided by the large, friendly interviewers that we have seen at work in the extracts given above. [. . .]

That educational psychology should be strongly influenced by a theory so false to the facts of language is unfortunate; but that children should be the victims of this ignorance is intolerable. It may seem that the fallacies of the verbal deprivation theory are so obvious that they are hardly worth exposing; I have tried to show that it is an important job for us to undertake. If linguists can contribute some of their available knowledge and energy towards this end, we will have done a great deal to justify the support that society has given to basic research in our field.

References

BEREITER, C. et al. (1966), 'An academically oriented pre-school for culturally deprived children', in F. M. Hechinger (ed.), Pre-School Education Today, Doubleday, pp. 105–37.

BEREITER, C. and ENGELMANN, S. (1966), Teaching Disadvantaged Children in the Pre-School, Prentice-Hall.

CALDWELL, B. M. (1967), 'What is the optional learning environment for the young child?', Amer. J. Orthopsychiatry, vol. 37, no. 1, pp. 8–21.

CHOMSKY, N. (1965), Aspects of the Theory of Syntax, M.I.T. Press.

DEUTSCH, M. et al. (1967), The Disadvantaged Child, Basic Books.

DEUTSCH, M., KATZ, I., and JENSEN, A. R. (eds.) (1968), Social Class, Race and Psychological Development, Holt.

GANS, H. (1962), 'The peer group society', in The Urban Villagers, Free Press.

JENSEN, A. (1968), 'Social class and verbal learning', in Deutsch, Katz and Jensen, Social Class, Race and Psychological Development, Holt.

JENSEN, A. (1969), 'How much can we boost IQ and scholastic achievement?' Harvard Educational Review, vol. 39, no. 1.

LABOV, W. (1966), 'On the grammaticality of everyday speech', Paper given at the annual meeting of the Linguistic Society of America, New York City, December.

LABOV, W. (1967), 'Some sources of reading problems for Negro speakers of non-standard English', in A. Frazier (ed.), New Directions in Elementary English, National Council of Teachers of English, pp. 140–67. Reprinted in Joan C. Baratz and R. W. Shuy (eds.), Teaching

Black Children to Read, Washington D.C., Center for Applied Linguistics, pp. 29–67.

LABOV, W., COHEN, P., and ROBINS, C. (1965), *A Preliminary Study of the Structure of English Used by Negro and Puerto Rican Speakers in New York City*. Final Report, Cooperative Research Project no. 3091, Office of Education, Washington D.C.

LABOV, W., COHEN, P., ROBINS, C. and LEWIS, J. (1968), *A Study of the Non-Standard English of Negro and Puerto Rican Speakers in New York City*, Final Report, Cooperative Research Project no. 3288, Office of Education, Washington, D.C., vols. 1 and 2.

LABOV, W., and ROBINS, C., (1969), 'A note on the relation of reading failure to peer-group status in urban ghettos', *The Teachers' College Record*, vol. 70, no. 5.

ROSENTHAL, R., and JACOBSON, L. (1968), 'Self-fulfilling prophecies in the classroom: teachers' expectations as unintended determinants of pupils' intellectual competence', in Deutsch, Katz and Jensen, *Social Class, Race and Psychological Development*, Holt.

WHITEMAN, M., and DEUTSCH, M. (1968), 'Social disadvantage as related to intellective and language development', in Deutsch, Katz and Jensen, *Social Class, Race and Psychological Development*, Holt.

WILMOTT, P. (1966), *Adolescent Boys of East London*, Routledge and Kegan Paul.

Part Four Language and Social Structures

Linguists and laymen alike know very well that social factors such as sex, age, locality, social stratification, etc. affect and differentiate linguistic behaviour. But, while the man in the street continually uses this knowledge in his everyday life, linguists have somewhat neglected this field of inquiry preferring to concentrate on the analysis of context-free, invariant linguistic structures. Yet, as the four papers in this section show, the study of the co-variation of social factors and speech is by no means trivial and can tell us much about the nature of language and society.

In the first paper, John Gumperz reviews early dialectological studies and discusses the most relevant concepts which characterize the sociolinguistic approach. The other three papers illustrate the analysis of linguistic varieties at three different levels. Ferguson studies the social functions of 'high' and 'low' language varieties in several speech communities; after describing the features of diglossia, he contrasts it with the more familiar situation of a standard language coexisting with regional dialects and examines the conditions under which diglossia arises and the language situation into which it can develop. Brown and Gilman study the semantic dimensions underlying pronominal choices in French, German and Italian; their seminal contribution has been followed by an outpouring of papers which explore the rules of pronominal usage in many different languages and cultures and refine the two dimensions (power and solidarity) discussed by Brown and Gilman. Labov tackles the problem of language variety at the phonological level; his paper is quite remarkable because he shows how to deal at the same time both with large-scale social structural features (e.g. stratification) and with the context of the situation (e.g. formal versus informal). Labov also illustrates the existence of two types of sociolinguistic rules (variable and invariant).

All the papers collected in this section are important for sociological purposes because, once co-variations between speech and sociological variables are established, speech variations may be used as sensitive and unobtrusive indicators in social research.

10 J. Gumperz

The Speech Community

J. Gumperz, 'The Speech Community', in *International Encyclopedia of the Social Sciences*, Macmillan, 1968, pp. 381–6.

Although not all communication is linguistic, language is by far the most powerful and versatile medium of communication; all known human groups possess language. Unlike other sign systems the verbal system can, through the minute refinement of its grammatical and semantic structure, be made to refer to a wide variety of objects and concepts. At the same time, verbal interaction is a social process in which utterances are selected in accordance with socially recognized norms and expectations. It follows that linguistic phenomena are analyzable both within the context of language itself and within the broader context of social behavior. In the formal analysis of language the object of attention is a particular body of linguistic data abstracted from the settings in which it occurs and studied primarily from the point of view of its referential function. In analyzing linguistic phenomena within a socially defined universe, however, the study is of language usage as it reflects more general behavior norms. This universe is the speech community: any human aggregate characterized by regular and frequent interaction by means of a shared body of verbal signs and set off from similar aggregates by significant differences in language usage.

Most groups of any permanence, be they small bands bounded by face-to-face contact, modern nations divisible into smaller subregions, or even occupational associations or neighborhood gangs, may be treated as speech communities, provided they show linguistic peculiarities that warrant special study. The verbal behavior of such groups always constitutes a system. It must be based on finite sets of grammatical rules that underlie the production of well-formed sentences, or else messages will not be intelligible. The description of such rules is a precondition for the study of all types of linguistic phenomena. But it is only the starting point in the sociolinguistic analysis of language behavior.

Grammatical rules define the bounds of the linguistically acceptable. For example, they enable us to identify 'How do you do?' 'How are you?' and 'Hi' as proper American English sentences and to reject others like 'How do you?' and 'How you are?' Yet speech is not constrained by grammatical rules alone. An individual's choice from among permissible alternates in a particular speech event may reveal his family background and his social intent, may identify him as a Southerner, a Northerner, an urbanite, a rustic, a member of the educated or uneducated classes, and may even indicate whether he wishes to appear friendly or distant, familiar or deferential, superior or inferior.

Just as intelligibility presupposes underlying grammatical rules, the communication of social information presupposes the existence of regular relationships between language usage and social structure. Before we can judge a speaker's social intent, we must know something about the norms defining the appropriateness of linguistically acceptable alternates for particular types of speakers; these norms vary among subgroups and among social settings. Wherever the relationships between language choice and rules of social appropriateness can be formalized, they allow us to group relevant linguistic forms into distinct dialects, styles, and occupational or other special parlances. The sociolinguistic study of speech communities deals with the linguistic similarities and differences among these speech varieties.

In linguistically homogeneous societies the verbal markers of social distinctions tend to be confined to structurally marginal features of phonology, syntax and lexicon. Elsewhere they may include both standard literary languages and grammatically divergent local dialects. In many multilingual societies the choice of one language over another has the same signification as the selection among lexical alternates in linguistically homogeneous societies. In such cases, two or more grammars may be required to cover the entire scope of linguistically acceptable expressions that serve to convey social meanings.

Regardless of the linguistic differences among them, the speech varieties employed within a speech community form a system because they are related to a shared set of social norms. Hence, they can be classified according to their usage, their origins, and the relationship between speech and social action that they reflect. They become indices of social patterns of interaction in the speech community.

Historical orientation in early studies

Systematic linguistic field work began in the middle of the nineteenth century. Prior to 1940 the best-known studies were concerned with dialects, special parlances, national languages, and linguistic acculturation and diffusion.

Dialectology

Among the first students of speech communities were the dialectologists, who charted the distribution of colloquial speech forms in societies dominated by German, French, English, Polish and other major standard literary tongues. Mapping relevant features of pronunciation, grammar, and lexicon in the form of *isoglosses*, they traced in detail the range and spread of historically documented changes in language habits. Isoglosses were grouped into bundles of two or more and then mapped; from the geographical shape of such isogloss bundles, it was possible to distinguish the *focal areas*, centers from which innovations radiate into the surrounding regions; *relic zones*, districts where forms previously known only from old texts were still current; and *transition zones*, areas of internal diversity marked by the coexistence of linguistic forms identified with competing centers of innovation.

Analysis along these lines clearly established the importance of social factors in language change. The distribution of rural speech patterns was found to be directly related to such factors as political boundaries during the preceding centuries, traditional market networks, the spread of important religious movements, etc. In this fashion dialectology became an important source of evidence for social history.

Special parlances, classical languages

Other scholars dealt with the languages of occupationally specialized minority groups, craft jargons, secret argots and the like. In some cases, such as the Romany of the gypsies and the Yiddish of Jews, these parlances derive from foreign importations which survive as linguistic islands surrounded by other tongues. Their speakers tend to be bilinguals, using their own idiom for in-group communication and the majority language for interaction with outsiders.

Linguistic distinctness may also result from seemingly intentional processes of distortion. One very common form of secret language, found in a variety of tribal and complex societies, achieves unintelligibility by a process of verbal play with majority speech, in which phonetic or grammatical elements are systematically reordered. The pig Latin of English-speaking schoolchildren, in which initial consonants are transferred to the end of the word and followed by 'ay', is a relatively simple example of this process. Thieves' argots, the slang of youth gangs, and the jargon of traveling performers and other occupational groups obtain similar results by assigning special meanings to common nouns, verbs and adjectives.

Despite their similarities, the classical administrative and liturgical languages – such as the Latin of medieval Europe, the Sanskrit of south Asia and the Arabic of the Near East – are not ordinarily grouped with special parlances because of the prestige of the cultural traditions associated with them. They are quite distinct from and often unrelated to popular speech, and the elaborate ritual and etiquette that surround their use can be learned only through many years of special training. Instruction is available only through private tutors and is limited to a privileged few who command the necessary social status or financial resources. As a result, knowledge of these languages in the traditional societies where they are used is limited to relatively small elites, who tend to maintain control of their linguistic skills in somewhat the same way that craft guilds strive for exclusive control of their craft skills.

The standard literary languages of modern nation-states, on the other hand, tend to be representative of majority speech. As a rule they originated in rising urban centers, as a result of the free interaction of speakers of a variety of local dialects, they became identified with new urban elites, and in time replaced older administrative languages. Codification of spelling and grammar by means of dictionaries and dissemination of this information through public school systems are characteristic of standard-language societies. Use of mass media and the prestige of their speakers tend to carry idioms far from their sources; such idioms eventually replace many pre-existing local dialects and special parlances.

Linguistic acculturation, language shift

Wherever two or more speech communities maintain prolonged contact within a broad field of communication, there are cross-currents of diffusion. The result is the formation of a *Sprachbund*, comprising a group of varieties which coexist in social space as dialects, distinct neighboring languages, or special parlances. Persistent borrowing over long periods creates within such groups similarities in linguistic structure, which tend to obscure pre-existing genetic distinctions; a commonly cited example is the south Asian subcontinent, where speakers of Indo–Aryan, Dravidian and Munda languages all show significant overlap in their linguistic habits.

It appears that single nouns, verbs and adjectives are most readily diffused, often in response to a variety of technological innovations and cultural or religious trends. Pronunciation and word order are also frequently affected. The level of phonological and grammatical pattern (i.e. the structural core of a language), however, is more resistant to change, and loanwords tend to be adapted to the patterns of the recipient language. But linguistic barriers to diffusion are never absolute, and in situations of extensive bilingualism – two or more languages being regularly used in the course of the daily routine – even the grammatical cores may be affected.

Cross-cultural influence reaches a maximum in the cases of pidgins and creoles, idioms combining elements of several distinct languages. These hybrids typically arise in colonial societies or in large trading centers where laborers torn out of their native language environments are forced to work in close cooperation with speakers of different tongues. Cross-cultural influence may also give rise to language shift, the abandonment of one native tongue in favor of another. This phenomenon most frequently occurs when two groups merge, as in tribal absorption, or when minority groups take on the culture of the surrounding majority.

Although the bulk of the research on speech communities that was conducted prior to 1940 is historically oriented, students of speech communities differ markedly from their colleagues who concentrate upon textual analysis. The latter tend to treat languages as independent wholes that branch off from uniform protolanguages in accordance with regular sound laws. The former, on the other hand, regard themselves primarily as students of behavior, interested in linguistic phenomena for their broader sociohistorical significance. By relating dialect boundaries to settlement history, to political and administrative boundaries, and to culture areas and by charting the itineraries of loanwords in relation to technical innovations or cultural movements, they established the primacy of social factors in language change, disproving earlier theories of environmental or biological determinism.

The study of language usage in social communities, furthermore, revealed little of the uniformity ordinarily ascribed to protolanguages and their descendants; many exceptions to the regularity of sound laws were found wherever speakers of genetically related languages were in regular contact. This led students of speech communities to challenge the 'family-tree theory', associated with the neogrammarians of nineteenth-century Europe, who were concerned primarily with the genetic reconstruction of language history. Instead, they favored a theory of diffusion which postulates the spread of linguistic change in intersecting 'waves' that emanate from different centers of innovation with an intensity proportionate to the prestige of their human carriers.

Thus, while geneticists regarded modern language distribution as the result of the segmentation of older entities into newer and smaller subgroups, diffusionists viewed the speech community as a dynamic field of action where phonetic change, borrowing, language mixture, and language shift all occur because of social forces, and where genetic origin is secondary to these forces. In recent years linguists have begun to see the two theories as complementary. The assumption of uniformity among protolanguages is regarded as an abstraction necessary to explain existing regularities of sound change and is considered extremely useful for the elucidation of long-term prehistoric relationships, especially since conflicting short-term diffusion currents tend to cancel each other. Speech-community studies, on the other hand, appear better adapted to the explanation of relatively recent changes.

Language behavior and social communication

The shift of emphasis from historical to synchronic problems during the last three decades has brought about some fundamental changes in our theories of language, resulting in the creation of a body of entirely new analytical techniques. Viewed in the light of these fresh insights, the earlier speech-community studies are subject to serious criticism on grounds of both linguistic and sociological methodology. For some time, therefore, linguists oriented toward formal analysis showed very little interest. More recent structural studies, however, show that this criticism does not affect the basic concept of the speech community as a field of action where the distribution of linguistic variants is a reflection of social facts. The relationship between such variants when they are classified in terms of usage rather than of their purely linguistic characteristics can be examined along two dimensions: the *dialectal* and the *superposed*.

Dialectal relationships are those in which differences set off the vernaculars of local groups (for example, the language of home and family) from those of other groups within the same, broader culture. Since this classification refers to usage rather than to inherent linguistic traits, relationships between minority languages and majority speech (e.g., between Welsh and English in Britain or French and English in Canada) and between distinct languages found in zones of intensive intertribal contact (e.g., in modern Africa) can also be considered dialectal, because they show characteristics similar to the relationship existing between dialects of the same language.

Whereas dialect variation relates to distinctions in geographical origin and social background, superposed variation refers to distinctions between different types of activities carried on within the same group. The special parlances described above form a linguistic extreme, but similar distinctions in usage are found in all speech communities. The language of formal speechmaking, religious ritual, or technical discussion, for example, is never the same as that employed in informal talk among friends, because each is a style fulfilling particular communicative needs. To some extent the linguistic markers of such activities are directly related to their different technical requirements. Scientific discussion, for instance, requires precisely defined terms and strict limitation on their usage. But in other cases, as in greetings, forms of address, or choosing between 'isn't' and 'ain't', the primary determinant is the social relationship between speakers rather than communicative necessity. Language choice in these cases is limited by social barriers; the existence of such barriers lends significance to the sociolinguistic study of superposed variation.

This distinction between dialectal and superposed varieties obviates the usual linguistic distinction between geographically and socially distributed varieties, since the evidence indicates that actual residence patterns are less important as determinants of distribution than social interaction patterns and usage. Thus, there seems to be little need to draw conceptual distinctions upon this basis.

Descriptions of dialectal and superposed variation relate primarily to social groups. Not all individuals within a speech community have equal control of the entire set of superposed variants current there. Control of communicative resources varies sharply with the individual's position within the social system. The more narrowly confined his sphere of activities, the more homogeneous the social environment within which he interacts, and the less his need for verbal facility. Thus, housewives, farmers and laborers, who rarely meet outsiders, often make do with only a narrow range of speech styles, while actors, public speakers, and businessmen command the greatest range of styles. The fact that such individual distinctions are found in multilingual as well as in linguistically homogeneous societies suggests that the common assertion which identifies bilingualism with poor scores in intelligence testing is in urgent need of re-examination, based, as it is, primarily on work with underprivileged groups. Recent work, in fact, indicates that the failure of some self-contained groups to inculcate facility in verbal manipulation is a major factor in failures in their children's performances in public school systems.

Social norms of language choice vary from situation to situation and from community to community. Regularities in attitudes to particular speech varieties, however, recur in a number of societies and deserve special comment here. Thieves' argots, gang jargons, and the like serve typically as group boundary maintaining mechanisms, whose linguistic characteristics are the result of informal group consensus and are subject to continual change in response to changing attitudes. Individuals are accepted as members of the group to the extent that their usage conforms to the practices of the day. Similar attitudes of exclusiveness prevail in the case of many tribal languages spoken in areas of culture contact where other superposed idioms serve as media of public communication. The tribal language here is somewhat akin to a secret ritual, in that it is private knowledge to be kept from outsiders, an attitude which often makes it difficult for casual investigators to collect reliable information about language distribution in such areas.

Because of the elaborate linguistic etiquette and stylistic conventions that surround them, classical, liturgical, and administrative languages function somewhat like secret languages. Mastery of the conventions may be more important in gaining social success than substantive knowledge of the information dispensed through these languages. But unlike the varieties mentioned above, norms of appropriateness are explicit in classical languages; this permits them to remain unchanged over many generations.

In contrast, the attitude to pidgins, trade languages and similar intergroup media of communication tends to be one of toleration. Here little attention is paid to linguistic markers of social appropriateness. It is the function of such languages to facilitate contact between groups without constituting their respective social cohesiveness; and, as a result, communication in these languages tends to be severely restricted to specific topics or types of interaction. They do not, as a rule, serve as vehicles for personal friendships.

We speak of *language loyalty* when a literary variety acquires prestige as a symbol of a particular nationality group or social movement. Language loyalty tends to unite diverse local groups and social classes, whose members may continue to speak their own vernaculars within the family circle. The literary idiom serves for reading and for public interaction and embodies the cultural tradition of a nation or a sector thereof. Individuals choose to employ it as a symbol of their allegiance to a broader set of political ideals than that embodied in the family or kin group.

Language loyalty may become a political issue in a modernizing society when hitherto socially isolated minority groups become mobilized. Their demands for closer participation in political affairs are often accompanied by demands for language reform or for the rewriting of the older, official code in their own literary idiom. Such demands often represent political and socioeconomic threats to the established elite, which may control the distribution of administrative positions through examination systems based upon the official code. The replacement of an older official code by another literary idiom in modernizing societies may thus represent the displacement of an established elite by a rising group.

The situation becomes still more complex when socioeconomic competition between several minority groups gives rise to several competing new literary standards, as in many parts of Asia and Africa, where language conflicts have led to civil disturbances and political instability. Although demands for language reform are usually verbalized in terms of communicative needs, it is interesting to observe that such demands do not necessarily reflect important linguistic differences between the idioms in question. Hindi and Urdu, the competing literary standards of north India, or Serbian and Croatian, in Yugoslavia, are grammatically almost identical. They differ in their writing systems, in their lexicons, and in minor aspects of syntax. Nevertheless, their proponents treat them as separate languages. The conflict in language loyalty may even affect mutual intelligibility, as when speakers' claims that they do not understand each other reflect primarily social attitudes rather than linguistic fact. In other cases serious linguistic differences may be disregarded when minority speakers pay language loyalty to a standard markedly different from their own vernacular. In many parts of Alsace-Lorraine, for example, speakers of German dialects seem to disregard linguistic fact and pay language loyalty to French rather than to German.

Varietal distribution

Superposed and dialectal varieties rarely coincide in their geographical extent. We find the greatest amount of linguistic diversity at the level of local, tribal, peasant, or lower-class urban populations. Tribal areas typically constitute a patchwork of distinct languages, while local speech distribution in many modern nations takes the form of a dialect chain in which the speech of each locality is similar to that of adjoining settlements and in which speech differences increase in proportion to geographical distance. Variety at the local level is bridged by the considerably broader spread of superposed varieties, serving as media of supralocal communication. The Latin of medieval Europe and the Arabic of the Near East form extreme examples of supralocal spread. Uniformity at the superposed level in their case, however, is achieved at the expense of large gaps in internal communication channels. Standard languages tend to be somewhat more restricted in geographical spread than classical languages, because of their relationship to local dialects. In contrast to a society in which classical languages are used as superposed varieties, however, a standard-language society possesses better developed channels of internal communication, partly because of its greater linguistic homogeneity and partly because of the internal language loyalty that it evokes.

In fact, wherever standard languages are well-established they act as the ultimate referent that determines the association of a given local dialect with one language or another. This may result in the anomalous situation in which two linguistically similar dialects spoken on different sides of a political boundary are regarded as belonging to different languages, not because of any inherent linguistic differences but because their speakers pay language loyalty to different standards. Language boundaries in such cases are defined partly by social and partly by linguistic criteria.

Verbal repertoires

The totality of dialectal and superposed variants regularly employed within a community make up the *verbal repertoire* of that community. Whereas the bounds of a language, as this term is ordinarily understood, may or may not coincide with that of a social group, verbal repertoires are always specific to particular populations. As an analytical concept the verbal repertoire allows us to establish direct relationships between its constituents and the socioeconomic complexity of the community.

We measure this relationship in terms of two concepts: *linguistic range* and *degree of compartmentalization*. Linguistic range refers to internal language distance between constituent varieties, that is, the total amount of purely linguistic differentiation that exists in a community, thus distinguishing among multilingual, multidialectal, and homogeneous communities. Compartmentalization refers to the sharpness with which varieties are set off from each other, either along the superposed or the dialectal dimension. We speak of compartmentalized repertoires, therefore, when several languages are spoken without their mixing, when dialects are set off from each other by sharp isogloss bundles, or when special parlances are sharply distinct from other forms of speech. We speak of fluid repertoires, on the other hand, when transitions between adjoining vernaculars are gradual or when one speech style merges into another in such a way that it is difficult to draw clear borderlines.

Initially, the linguistic range of a repertoire is a function of the languages and special parlances employed before contact. But given a certain period of contact, linguistic range becomes dependent upon the amount of internal interaction. The greater the frequency of internal interaction, the greater the tendency for innovations arising in one part of the speech community to diffuse throughout it. Thus, where the flow of communication is dominated by a single all-important center – for example, as Paris dominates central France – linguistic range is relatively small. Political fragmentation, on the other hand, is associated with diversity of languages or of dialects, as in southern Germany, long dominated by many small, semi-independent principalities.

Over-all frequency in interaction is not, however, the only

determinant of uniformity. In highly stratified societies speakers of minority languages or dialects typically live side by side, trading, exchanging services, and often maintaining regular social contact as employer and employee or master and servant. Yet despite this contact, they tend to preserve their own languages, suggesting the existence of social norms that set limits to freedom of intercommunication. Compartmentalization reflects such social norms. The exact nature of these sociolinguistic barriers is not yet clearly understood, although some recent literature suggests new avenues for investigation.

We find, for example, that separate languages maintain themselves most readily in closed tribal systems, in which kinship dominates all activities. Linguistically distinct special parlances, on the other hand, appear most fully developed in highly stratified societies, where the division of labor is maintained by rigidly defined barriers of ascribed status. When social change causes the breakdown of traditional social structures and the formation of new ties, as in urbanization and colonialization, linguistic barriers between varieties also break down. Rapidly changing societies typically show either gradual transition between speech styles or, if the community is bilingual, a range of intermediate varieties bridging the transitions between extremes.

11 C. A. Ferguson

Diglossia

C. A. Ferguson, 'Diglossia', *Word*, vol. 15, 1959, pp. 325–40.[1]

In many speech communities two or more varieties of the same language are used by some speakers under different conditions. Perhaps the most familiar example is the standard language and regional dialect as used, say, in Italian or Persian, where many speakers speak their local dialect at home or among family or friends of the same dialect area but use the standard language in communicating with speakers of other dialects or on public occasions. There are, however, quite different examples of the use of two varieties of a language in the same speech community. In Baghdad the Christian Arabs speak a 'Christian Arabic' dialect when talking among themselves but speak the general Baghdad dialect, 'Muslim Arabic', when talking in a mixed group. In recent years there has been a renewed interest in studying the development and characteristics of standardized languages (see especially Kloss, 1952, with its valuable introduction on standardization in general), and it is in following this line of interest that the present study seeks to examine carefully one particular kind of standardization where two varieties of a language exist side by side throughout the community, with each having a definite role to play. The term 'diglossia' is introduced here, modeled on the French *diglossie*, which has been applied to this situation, since there seems to be no word in regular use for

1. A preliminary version of this study, with the title 'Classical or colloquial, one standard or two', was prepared for presentation at the symposium on Urbanization and Standard Languages: Facts and Attitudes, held at the meeting of the American Anthropological Association in November 1958, in Washington, D.C. The preliminary version was read by a number of people and various modifications were made on the basis of comments by H. Blanc, J. Gumperz, B. Halpern, M. Perlmann, R. L. Ward and U. Weinreich.

this in English; other languages of Europe generally use the word for 'bilingualism' in this special sense as well. (The terms 'language', 'dialect', and 'variety' are used here without precise definition. It is hoped that they occur sufficiently in accordance with established usage to be unambiguous for the present purpose. The term 'superposed variety' is also used here without definition; it means that the variety in question is not the primary, 'native' variety for the speakers in question but may be learned in addition to this. Finally, no attempt is made in this paper to examine the analogous situation where two distinct (related or unrelated) languages are used side by side throughout a speech community, each with a clearly defined role.)

It is likely that this particular situation in speech communities is very widespread, although it is rarely mentioned, let alone satisfactorily described. A full explanation of it can be of considerable help in dealing with problems in linguistic description, in historical linguistics, and in language typology. The present study should be regarded as preliminary in that much more assembling of descriptive and historical data is required; its purpose is to characterize diglossia by picking out four speech communities and their languages (hereafter called the defining languages) which clearly belong in this category, and describing features shared by them which seem relevant to the classification. The defining languages selected are Arabic, Modern Greek, Swiss German, Haitian Creole. (See the references at the end of this Reading.)

Before proceeding to the description it must be pointed out that diglossia is not assumed to be a stage which occurs always and only at a certain point in some kind of evolution, e.g., in the standardization process. Diglossia may develop from various origins and eventuate in different language situations. Of the four defining languages, Arabic diglossia seems to reach as far back as our knowledge of Arabic goes, and the superposed 'Classical' language has remained relatively stable, while Greek diglossia has roots going back many centuries, but it became fully developed only at the beginning of the nineteenth century with the renaissance of Greek literature and the creation of a literary language based in large part on previous forms of literary Greek. Swiss German diglossia developed as a result of long religious and political isolation from the centers of German linguistic standardization, while Haitian Creole arose from a creolization of a pidgin French, with standard French later coming to play the role of the superposed variety. Some speculation on the possibilities of development will, however, be given at the end of the paper.

For convenience of reference the superposed variety in diglosias will be called the H ('high') variety or simply H, and the regional dialects will be called L ('low') varieties or, collectively, simply L. All the defining languages have names for H and L, and these are listed in the accompanying table.

Arabic

H is called	L is called
Classical (= H) *'al-fuṣḥā*	*'al-ᶜāmmiyyah*, *'ad-dārij*
Egyptian (= L) *'il-faṣīḥ, 'in-nahawi*	*'il-ᶜammıyya*

SW. German

Stand. German *Schriftsprache* (= H)	[*Schweizer*] *Dialekt*, *Schweizerdeutsch*
Swiss (= L) *Hoochtüütsch*	*Schwyzertüütsch*

H. Creole

French (= H) *français*	*créole*

Greek

H and L *katharévusa*	*dhimotikí*

It is instructive to note the problems involved in citing words of these languages in a consistent and accurate manner. First, should the words be listed in their H form or in their L form, or in both? Second, if words are cited in their L form, what kind of L should be chosen? In Greek and in Haitian Creole, it seems clear that the ordinary conversational language of the educated people of Athens and Port-au-Prince respectively should be selected. For Arabic and for Swiss German the choice must be arbitrary, and the ordinary conversational language of educated people of Cairo and of Zürich city will be used here. Third, what kind of spelling should be used to represent L? Since there is in no case a generally accepted orthography for L, some kind of phonemic or quasi-phonemic transcription would seem appropriate. The following choices were made. For Haitian Creole, the McConnell-

Laubach spelling was selected, since it is approximately phonemic and is typographically simple. For Greek, the transcription was adopted from the manual *Spoken Greek* (Kahane *et al.*, 1945), since this is intended to be phonemic; a transliteration of the Greek spelling seems less satisfactory not only because the spelling is variable but also because it is highly etymologizing in nature and quite unphonemic. For Swiss German, the spelling backed by Dieth (1938), which, though it fails to indicate all the phonemic contrasts and in some cases may indicate allophones, is fairly consistent and seems to be a sensible systematization, without serious modification, of the spelling conventions most generally used in writing Swiss German dialect material. Arabic, like Greek, uses a non-Roman alphabet, but transliteration is even less feasible than for Greek, partly again because of the variability of the spelling, but even more because in writing Egyptian colloquial Arabic many vowels are not indicated at all and others are often indicated ambiguously; the transcription chosen here sticks closely to the traditional systems of Semitists, being a modification for Egyptian of the scheme used by Al-Toma (1957).

The fourth problem is how to represent H. For Swiss German and Haitian Creole standard German and French orthography respectively can be used even though this hides certain resemblances between the sounds of H and L in both cases. For Greek either the usual spelling in Greek letters could be used or a transliteration, but since a knowledge of Modern Greek pronunciation is less widespread than a knowledge of German and French pronunciation, the masking effect of the orthography is more serious in the Greek case, and we use the phonemic transcription instead. Arabic is the most serious problem. The two most obvious choices are (1) a transliteration of Arabic spelling (with the unwritten vowels supplied by the transcriber) or (2) a phonemic transcription of the Arabic as it would be read by a speaker of Cairo Arabic. Solution (1) has been adopted, again in accordance with Al-Toma's procedure.

Function

One of the most important features of diglossia is the specialization of function for H and L. In one set of situations only H is appropriate and in another only L, with the two sets overlapping only very slightly. As an illustration, a sample listing of possible situations is given, with indication of the variety normally used:

	H	L
Sermon in church or mosque	x	
Instructions to servants, waiters, workmen, clerks		x
Personal letter	x	
Speech in parliament, political speech	x	
University lecture	x	
Conversation with family, friends, colleagues		x
News broadcast	x	
Radio 'soap opera'		x
Newspaper editorial, news story, caption on picture	x	
Caption on political cartoon		x
Poetry	x	
Folk literature		x

The importance of using the right variety in the right situation can hardly be overestimated. An outsider who learns to speak fluent, accurate L and then uses it in a formal speech is an object of ridicule. A member of the speech community who uses H in a purely conversational situation or in an informal activity like shopping is equally an object of ridicule. In all the defining languages it is typical behavior to have someone read aloud from a newspaper written in H and then proceed to discuss the contents in L. In all the defining languages it is typical behavior to listen to a formal speech in H and then discuss it, often with the speaker himself, in L.

(The situation in formal education is often more complicated than is indicated here. In the Arab world, for example, formal university lectures are given in H, but drills, explanation, and section meetings may be in large part conducted in L, especially in the natural sciences as opposed to the humanities. Although the teachers' use of L in secondary schools is forbidden by law in some Arab countries, often a considerable part of the teachers' time is taken up with explaining in L the meaning of material in H which has been presented in books or lectures.)

The last two situations on the list call for comment. In all the defining languages some poetry is composed in L, and a small handful of poets compose in both, but the status of the two kinds of poetry is very different, and for the speech community as a whole it is only the poetry in H that is felt to be 'real' poetry. (Modern Greek does not quite fit this description. Poetry in L is the major production and H verse is generally felt to be artificial.) On the other hand, in every one of the defining languages certain proverbs, politeness formulas, and the like are in H even when cited in ordinary conversation by illiterates. It has been estimated that as much as one-fifth of the proverbs in the active repertory of Arab villagers are in H (*Journal of the American Oriental Society*, 1955, vol. 75, pp. 124 ff.).

Prestige

In all the defining languages the speakers regard H as superior to L in a number of respects. Sometimes the feeling is so strong that H alone is regarded as real and L is reported 'not to exist'. Speakers of Arabic, for example, may say (in L) that so-and-so doesn't know Arabic. This normally means he doesn't know H, although he may be a fluent, effective speaker of L. If a non-speaker of Arabic asks an educated Arab for help in learning to speak Arabic the Arab will normally try to teach him H forms, insisting that these are the only ones to use. Very often, educated Arabs will maintain that they never use L at all, in spite of the fact that direct observation shows that they use it constantly in all ordinary conversation. Similarly, educated speakers of Haitian Creole frequently deny its existence, insisting that they always speak French. This attitude cannot be called a deliberate attempt to deceive the questioner, but seems almost a self-deception. When the speaker in question is replying in good faith, it is often possible to break through these attitudes by asking such questions as what kind of language he uses in speaking to his children, to servants, or to his mother. The very revealing reply is usually something like: 'Oh, but they wouldn't understand [the H form, whatever it is called].'

Even where the feeling of the reality and superiority of H is not so strong, there is usually a belief that H is somehow more beautiful, more logical, better able to express important thoughts, and the like. And this belief is held also by speakers whose command of H is quite limited. To those Americans who would like to evaluate speech in terms of effectiveness of communication it comes as a shock to discover that many speakers of a language involved in diglossia characteristically prefer to hear a political speech or an expository lecture or a recitation of poetry in H even though it may be less intelligible to them than it would be in L.

In some cases the superiority of H is connected with religion. In Greek the language of the New Testament is felt to be essentially the same as the *katharévusa*, and the appearance of a translation of the New Testament in *dhimotikí* was the occasion for serious rioting in Greece in 1903. Speakers of Haitian Creole are generally accustomed to a French version of the Bible, and even when the Church uses Creole for catechisms and the like, it resorts to a highly Gallicized spelling. For Arabic, H is the language of the Qur'an and as such is widely believed to constitute the actual words of God and even to be outside the limits of space and time, i.e. to have existed 'before' time began with the creation of the world.

Literary heritage

In every one of the defining languages there is a sizable body of written literature in H which is held in high esteem by the speech community, and contemporary literary production in H by members of the community is felt to be part of this otherwise existing literature. The body of literature may either have been produced long ago in the past history of the community or be in continuous production in another speech community in which H serves as the standard variety of the language. When the body of literature represents a long time span (as in Arabic or Greek) contemporary writers – and readers – tend to regard it as a legitimate practice to utilize words, phrases, or constructions which may have been current only at one period of the literary history and are not in widespread use at the present time. Thus it may be good journalistic usage in writing editorials, or good literary taste in composing poetry, to employ a complicated Classical Greek participial construction or a rare twelfth-century Arabic expression which it can be assumed the average educated reader will not understand without research on his part. One effect of such usage is appreciation on the part of some readers: 'So-and-so really knows his Greek [or Arabic]', or 'So-and-so's editorial today, or latest poem, is very good Greek [or Arabic].'

Acquisition

Among speakers of the four defining languages adults use L in speaking to children and children use L in speaking to one another. As a result, L is learned by children in what may be regarded as the 'normal' way of learning one's mother tongue. H may be heard by children from time to time, but the actual learning of H is chiefly accomplished by the means of formal education, whether this be traditional Qur'anic schools, modern government schools, or private tutors.

This difference in method of acquisition is very important. The speaker is at home in L to a degree he almost never achieves in H. The grammatical structure of L is learned without explicit discussion of grammatical concepts; the grammar of H is learned in terms of 'rules' and norms to be imitated.

It seems unlikely that any change toward full utilization of H could take place without a radical change in this pattern of acquisition. For example, those Arabs who ardently desire to have L replaced by H for all functions can hardly expect this to happen if they are unwilling to speak H to their children. (It has been very plausibly suggested that there are psychological implications following from this linguistic duality. This certainly deserves careful experimental investigation. On this point, see the highly controversial article which seems to me to contain some important kernels of truth along with much which cannot be supported – Shouby (1951).)

Standardization

In all the defining languages there is a strong tradition of grammatical study of the H form of the language. There are grammars, dictionaries, treatises on pronunciation, style, and so on. There is an established norm for pronunciation, grammar, and vocabulary which allows variation only within certain limits. The orthography is well established and has little variation. By contrast, descriptive and normative studies of the L form are either non-existent or relatively recent and slight in quantity. Often they have been carried out first or chiefly by scholars OUTSIDE the speech community and are written in other languages. There is no settled orthography and there is wide variation in pronunciation, grammar, and vocabulary.

In the case of relatively small speech communities with a single important center of communication (e.g., Greece, Haiti) a kind of standard L may arise which speakers of other dialects imitate and which tends to spread like any standard variety except that it remains limited to the functions for which L is appropriate.

In speech communities which have no single most important center of communication a number of regional L's may arise. In the Arabic speech community, for example, there is no standard L corresponding to educated Athenian *dhimotiki*, but regional standards exist in various areas. The Arabic of Cairo, for example, serves as a standard L for Egypt, and educated individuals from Upper Egypt must learn not only H but also, for conversational purposes, an approximation to Cairo L. In the Swiss German speech community there is no single standard, and even the term 'regional standard' seems inappropriate, but in several cases the L of a city or town has a strong effect on the surrounding rural L.

Stability

It might be supposed that diglossia is highly unstable, tending to change into a more stable language situation. This is not so. Diglossia typically persists at least several centuries, and evidence in some cases seems to show that it can last well over a thousand years. The communicative tensions which arise in the diglossia situation may be resolved by the use of relatively uncodified, unstable, intermediate forms of the language (Greek *mikti*, Arabic *al-lugah al-wustā*, Haitian *créole de salon*) and repeated borrowing of vocabulary items from H to L.

In Arabic, for example, a kind of spoken Arabic much used in certain semiformal or cross-dialectal situations has a highly classical vocabulary with few or no inflectional endings, with certain features of classical syntax, but with a fundamentally colloquial base in morphology and syntax, and a generous admixture of colloquial vocabulary. In Greek a kind of mixed language has become appropriate for a large part of the press.

The borrowing of lexical items from H to L is clearly analogous (or for the periods when actual diglossia was in effect in these languages, identical) with the learned borrowings from Latin to Romance languages or the Sanskrit *tatsamas* in Middle and New

Indo-Aryan. (The exact nature of this borrowing process deserves careful investigation, especially for the important 'filter effect' of the pronunciation and grammar of H occurring in those forms of middle language which often serve as the connecting link by which the loans are introduced into the 'pure' L.)

Grammar

One of the most striking differences between H and L in the defining languages is in the grammatical structure: H has grammatical categories not present in L and has an inflectional system of nouns and verbs which is much reduced or totally absent in L. For example, Classical Arabic has three cases in the noun, marked by endings; colloquial dialects have none. Standard German has four cases in the noun and two non-periphrastic indicative tenses in the verb; Swiss German has three cases in the noun and only one simple indicative tense. *Katharévusa* has four cases, *dhimotiki* three. French has gender and number in the noun, Creole has neither. Also, in every one of the defining languages there seem to be several striking differences of word order as well as a thorough-going set of differences in the use of introductory and connective particles. It is certainly safe to say that in diglossia *there are always extensive differences between the grammatical structures of H and L*. This is true not only for the four defining languages, but also for every other case of diglossia examined by the author.

For the defining languages it may be possible to make a further statement about grammatical differences. It is always risky to hazard generalizations about grammatical complexity, but it may be worthwhile to attempt to formulate a statement applicable to the four defining languages even if it should turn out to be invalid for other instances of diglossia (cf. Greenberg, 1954).

There is probably fairly wide agreement among linguists that the grammatical structure of language A is 'simpler' than that of B if, other things being equal,

1. the morphophonemics of A is simpler, i.e. morphemes have fewer alternants, alternation is more regular, automatic (e.g., Turkish -*lar*~-*ler* is simpler than the English plural markers);
2. there are fewer obligatory categories marked by morphemes

or concord (e.g., Persian with no gender distinctions in the pronoun is simpler than Egyptian Arabic with masculine-feminine distinction in the second and third persons singular);

3. paradigms are more symmetrical (e.g., a language with all declensions having the same number of case distinctions is simpler than one in which there is variation);

4. concord and rection are stricter (e.g., prepositions all take the same case rather than different cases).

If this understanding of grammatical simplicity is accepted, then we may note that in at least three of the defining languages, the grammatical structure of any given L variety is simpler than that of its corresponding H. This seems incontrovertibly true for Arabic, Greek, and Haitian Creole; a full analysis of standard German and Swiss German might show this not to be true in that diglossic situation in view of the extensive morphophonemics of Swiss.

Lexicon

Generally speaking, the bulk of the vocabulary of H and L is shared, of course with variations in form and with differences of use and meaning. It is hardly surprising, however, that H should include in its total lexicon technical terms and learned expressions which have no regular L equivalents, since the subjects involved are rarely if ever discussed in pure L. Also, it is not surprising that the L varieties should include in their total lexicons popular expressions and the names of very homely objects or objects of very localized distribution which have no regular H equivalents, since the subjects involved are rarely if ever discussed in pure H. But *a striking feature of diglossia is the existence of many paired items, one H one L, referring to fairly common concepts frequently used in both H and L, where the range of meaning of the two items is roughly the same, and the use of one or the other immediately stamps the utterance or written sequence as H or L.* For example, in Arabic the H word for 'see' is *ra'ā*, the L word is *šāf*. The word *ra'ā* never occurs in ordinary conversation and *šāf* is not used in normal written Arabic. If for some reason a remark in which *šāf* was used is quoted in the press, it is replaced by *ra'ā* in the written quotation. In Greek the H word for 'wine' is *inos*,

the L word is *krasí*. The menu will have *ínos* written on it, but
the diner will ask the waiter for *krasí*. The nearest American
English parallels are such cases as *illumination ~ light, purchase
~ buy*, or *children ~ kids*, but in these cases both words may be
written and both may be used in ordinary conversation: the gap
is not so great as for the corresponding doublets in diglossia.
Also, the formal-informal dimension in languages like English is
a continuum in which the boundary between the two items in
different pairs may not come at the same point, e.g., *illumination,
purchase*, and *children* are not fully parallel in their formal-
informal range of usage.

A dozen or so examples of lexical doublets from three of the
sample languages are given below. For each language two nouns,
a verb, and two particles are given.

Greek

H		L
íkos	house	spíti
ídhor	water	neró
éteke	gave birth	eyénise
alá	but	má

Arabic

ḥiðã'un	shoe	gazma
'anfun	nose	manaxír
ðahaba	went	rāḥ
mā	what	'ēh
'al'āna	now	dilwa'tí

Creole

homme, gens	person, people	moun (not connected with *monde*)
âne	donkey	bourik
donner	give	bay
beaucoup	much, a lot	âpil
maintenant	now	kou-n-yé-a

It would be possible to present such a list of doublets for
Swiss German (e.g., *nachdem ≅ no* 'after', *jemand ≅ öpper*
'someone', etc.), but this would give a false picture. In Swiss
German the phonological differences between H and L are very
great and the normal form of lexical pairing is regular cognation
(*klein ≅ chly* 'small', etc.).

C. A. Ferguson 243

Phonology

It may seem difficult to offer any generalization on the relationships between the phonology of H and L in diglossia in view of the diversity of data. H and L phonologies may be quite close, as in Greek; moderately different, as in Arabic or Haitian Creole; or strikingly divergent, as in Swiss German. Closer examination, however, shows two statements to be justified. (Perhaps these will turn out to be unnecessary when the preceding features are stated so precisely that the statements about phonology can be deduced directly from them.)

1. *The sound systems of H and L constitute a single phonological structure of which the L phonology is the basic system and the divergent features of H phonology are either a subsystem or a parasystem.* Given the mixed forms mentioned above and the corresponding difficulty of identifying a given word in a given utterance as being definitely H or definitely L, it seems necessary to assume that the speaker has a single inventory of distinctive oppositions for the whole H-L complex and that there is extensive interference in both directions in terms of the distribution of phonemes in specific lexical items. (For details on certain aspects of this phonological interference in Arabic, cf. Ferguson, 1957).

2. *If 'pure' H items have phonemes not found in 'pure' L items, L phonemes frequently substitute for these in oral use of H and regularly replace them in tatsamas.* For example, French has a high front rounded vowel phoneme /ü/; 'pure' Haitian Creole has no such phoneme. Educated speakers of Creole use this vowel in *tatsamas* such as *Luk* (/lük/ for the Gospel of St Luke), while they, like uneducated speakers, may sometimes use /i/ for it when speaking French. On the other hand /i/ is the regular vowel in such *tatsamas* in Creole as *linèt* 'glasses'.

In cases where H represents in large part an earlier stage of L, it is possible that a three-way correspondence will appear. For example, Syrian and Egyptian Arabic frequently use /s/ for /q/ in oral use of Classical Arabic, and have /s/ in *tatsamas*, but have /t/ in words regularly descended from earlier Arabic not borrowed from the Classical. (See Ferguson, 1957.)

Now that the characteristic features of diglossia have been outlined it is feasible to attempt a fuller definition. DIGLOSSIA *is a relatively stable language situation in which, in addition to the primary dialects of the language (which may include a standard or regional standards), there is a very divergent, highly codified (often grammatically more complex) superposed variety, the vehicle of a large and respected body of written literature, either of an earlier period or in another speech community, which is learned largely by formal education and is used for most written and formal spoken purposes but is not used by any sector of the community for ordinary conversation.*

With the characterization of diglossia completed we may turn to a brief consideration of three additional questions: How does diglossia differ from the familiar situation of a standard language with regional dialects? How widespread is the phenomenon of diglossia in space, time, and linguistic families? Under what circumstances does diglossia come into being and into what language situations is it likely to develop?

The precise role of the standard variety (or varieties) of a language *vis-à-vis* regional or social dialects differs from one speech community to another, and some instances of this relation may be close to diglossia or perhaps even better considered as diglossia. As characterized here, diglossia differs from the more widespread standard-with-dialects in that no segment of the speech community in diglossia regularly uses H as a medium of ordinary conversation, and any attempt to do so is felt to be either pedantic and artificial (Arabic, Greek) or else in some sense disloyal to the community (Swiss German, Creole). In the more usual standard-with-dialects situation the standard is often similar to the variety of a certain region or social group (e.g., Tehran Persian, Calcutta Bengali) which is used in ordinary conversation more or less naturally by members of the group and as a superposed variety by others.

Diglossia is apparently not limited to any geographical region or language family. (All clearly documented instances known to me are in literate communities, but it seems at least possible that a somewhat similar situation could exist in a non-literate community where a body of oral literature could play the same role as the body of written literature in the examples cited.) Three examples of diglossia from other times and places may be cited as illustrations of the utility of the concept. First, consider Tamil. As used by the millions of members of the Tamil speech community in India today, it fits the definition exactly. There is a literary Tamil as H used for writing and certain kinds of formal speaking and a standard colloquial as L (as well as local L dialects) used in ordinary conversation. There is a body of literature in H going back many centuries which is highly regarded by Tamil speakers today. H has prestige, L does not. H is always superposed, L is learned naturally, whether as primary or as a superposed standard colloquial. There are striking grammatical differences and some phonological differences between the two varieties. (There is apparently no good description available of the precise relations of the two varieties of Tamil; an account of some of the structural differences is given by Pillai (1960). Incidentally, it may be noted that Tamil diglossia seems to go back many centuries, since the language of early literature contrasts sharply with the language of early inscriptions, which probably reflect the spoken language of the time.) The situation is only slightly complicated by the presence of Sanskrit and English for certain functions of H; the same kind of complication exists in parts of the Arab world where French, English, or a liturgical language such as Syriac or Coptic has certain H-like functions.

Second, we may mention Latin and the emergent Romance languages during a period of some centuries in various parts of Europe. The vernacular was used in ordinary conversation but Latin for writing or certain kinds of formal speech. Latin was the language of the Church and its literature, Latin had the prestige, there were striking grammatical differences between the two varieties in each area, etc.

Third, Chinese should be cited because it probably represents diglossia on the largest scale of any attested instance. (An excellent, brief description of the complex Chinese situation is available in the introduction to Chao (1947, pp. 1–17).) The *weu-li* corresponds to H, while Mandarin colloquial is a standard L; there are also regional L varieties so different as to deserve the label 'separate languages' even more than the Arabic dialects, and at least as much as the emergent Romance languages in the Latin example. Chinese, however, like modern Greek, seems to be developing away from diglossia toward a standard-with-dialects in that the standard L or a mixed variety is coming to be used in writing for more and more purposes, i.e. it is becoming a true standard.

Diglossia is likely to come into being when the following three conditions hold in a given speech community: (1) There is a sizable body of literature in a language closely related to (or even identical with) the natural language of the community, and this literature embodies, whether as source (e.g., divine revelation) or reinforcement, some of the fundamental values of the community. (2) Literacy in the community is limited to a small elite. (3) A suitable period of time, of the order of several centuries, passes from the establishment of (1) and (2). It can probably be shown that this combination of circumstances has occurred hundreds of times in the past and has generally resulted in diglossia. Dozens of examples exist today, and it is likely that examples will occur in the future.

Diglossia seems to be accepted and not regarded as a 'problem' by the community in which it is in force, until certain trends appear in the community. These include trends toward (1) more widespread literacy (whether for economic, ideological or other reasons), (2) broader communication among different regional and social segments of the community (e.g., for economic, administrative, military, or ideological reasons), (3) desire for a full-fledged standard 'national' language as an attribute of autonomy or of sovereignty.

When these trends appear, leaders in the community begin to call for unification of the language, and for that matter, actual trends toward unification begin to take place. These individuals tend to support either the adoption of H or of one form of L as the standard, less often the adoption of a modified H or L, a 'mixed' variety of some kind. The arguments explicitly advanced seem remarkably the same from one instance of diglossia to another.

The proponents of H argue that H must be adopted because it connects the community with its glorious past or with the world community and because it is a naturally unifying factor as opposed to the divisive nature of the L dialects. In addition to these two fundamentally sound arguments there are usually pleas based on the beliefs of the community in the superiority of H: that it is more beautiful, more expressive, more logical, that it has divine sanction, or whatever their specific beliefs may be. When these latter arguments are examined objectively their validity is often quite limited, but their importance is still very great because they reflect widely held attitudes within the community.

The proponents of L argue that some variety of L must be adopted because it is closer to the real thinking and feeling of the people; it eases the educational problem since people have already acquired a basic knowledge of it in early childhood; and it is a more effective instrument of communication at all levels. In addition to these fundamentally sound arguments there is often great emphasis given to points of lesser importance such as the vividness of metaphor in the colloquial, the fact that other 'modern nations' write very much as they speak, and so on.

The proponents of both sides or even of the mixed language seem to show the conviction – although this may not be explicitly stated – that a standard language can simply be legislated into place in a community. Often the trends which will be decisive in the development of a standard language are already at work and have little to do with the argumentation of the spokesmen for the various viewpoints.

A brief and superficial glance at the outcome of diglossia in the past and a consideration of present trends suggests that there are only a few general kinds of development likely to take place. First, we must remind ourselves that the situation may remain stable for long periods of time. But if the trends mentioned above do appear and become strong, change may take place. Second, H can succeed in establishing itself as a standard only if it is already serving as a standard language in some other community and the diglossia community, for reasons linguistic and non-linguistic, tends to merge with the other community. Otherwise H fades away and becomes a learned or liturgical language studied only by scholars or specialists and not used actively in the community. Some form of L or a mixed variety becomes standard.

Third, if there is a single communication center in the whole speech community, or if there are several such centers all in one dialect area, the L variety of the center(s) will be the basis of the new standard, whether relatively pure L or considerably mixed with H. If there are several such centers in different dialect areas with no one center paramount, then it is likely that several L varieties will become standard as separate languages.

A tentative prognosis for the four defining languages over the next two centuries (i.e. to about AD 2150) may be hazarded:

SWISS GERMAN: Relative stability.

ARABIC: Slow development toward several standard languages, each based on an L variety with heavy admixture of H vocabulary. Three seem likely: Maghrebi (based on Rabat or Tunis?), Egyptian (based on Cairo), Eastern (based on Baghdad?); unexpected politico-economic developments might add Syrian (based on Damascus?), Sudanese (based on Omdurman-Khartoum), or others.

HAITIAN CREOLE: Slow development toward unified standard based on L of Port-au-Prince.

GREEK: Full development to unified standard based on L of Athens plus heavy admixture of H vocabulary.

This paper concludes with an appeal for further study of this phenomenon and related ones. Descriptive linguists in their understandable zeal to describe the internal structure of the language they are studying often fail to provide even the most elementary data about the socio-cultural setting in which the language functions. Also, descriptivists usually prefer detailed descriptions of 'pure' dialects or standard languages rather than the careful study of the mixed, intermediate forms often in wider use. Study of such matters as diglossia is of clear value in understanding processes of linguistic change and presents interesting challenges to some of the assumptions of synchronic linguistics. Outside linguistics proper it promises material of great interest to social scientists in general, especially if a general frame of reference can be worked out for analysis of the use of one or more varieties of language within a speech community. Perhaps the collection of data and more profound study will drastically modify the impressionistic remarks of this paper, but if this is so the paper will have had the virtue of stimulating investigation and thought.

References on the four defining languages

The judgements of this paper are based primarily on the author's personal experience, but documentation for the four defining languages is available, and the following references may be con-

sulted for further details. Most of the studies listed here take a
strong stand in favor of greater use of the more colloquial
variety since it is generally writers of this opinion who want to
describe the facts. This bias can, however, be ignored by the
reader who simply wants to discover the basic facts of the situation.

Modern Greek

HATZIDAKIS, G. N. (1905), *Die Sprachfrage in Griechenland*,
Chatzedaka, Athens.

KAHANE, H., KAHANE, R. and WARD, R. L. (1945), *Spoken Greek*,
Washington.

KRUMBACHER, K. (1902), *Das Problem der modernen griechischen
Schriftsprache*, Munich.

PERNOT, H. (1898), *Grammaire Grecque Moderne*, Paris, pp. vii–xxxi.

PSICHARI, J. (1928), 'Un Pays qui ne veut pas sa langue', *Mercure de
France*, 1 October, pp. 63–121. Also in Psichari, *Quelque travaux . . . .*,
Paris, 1930, vol. I, pp. 1283–1337.

STEINMETZ, A. (1936), 'Schrift und Volksprache in Griechenland',
Deutsche Akademie (Munich), *Mitteilungen*, pp. 370–379.

Swiss German

DIETH, E. (1938), *Schwyzertütsch Dialäkschrift*, Zurich.

GREYERZ, O. VON (1933), 'Vom Wert und Wesen unserer Mundart',
Sprache, Dichtung, Heimat, Berne, pp. 226–247.

KLOSS, H. (1952), *Die Entwicklung neuer germanischer Kultursprachen
von 1800 bis 1950*, Pohl, Munich.

SCHMID, K. (1936), 'Für unser Schweizerdeutsch', *Die Schweiz: ein
nationales Jahrbuch 1936*, Basel, pp. 65–79.

SENN, A. (1935), 'Das Verhältnis von Mundart und Schriftsprache in der
deutschen Schweiz', *Journal of English and Germanic Philology*, vol. 34,
pp. 42–58.

Arabic

AL-TOMA, S. J. (1957), 'The teaching of Classical Arabic to speakers of
the colloquial in Iraq: a study of the problem of linguistic duality',
Doctoral dissertation, Harvard University.

CHEJNE, A. (1958), 'The role of Arabic in present-day Arab society',
The Islamic Literature, vol. 10, no. 4, pp. 15–54.

LECERF, J. (1932), *Littérature Dialectale et renaissance arabe moderne*
(Damascus, 1932–3), pp. 1–14; *Majallat al-majmaʿal-ʿilmī al-ʿarabī*
(Dimashq), vol. 32, no 1 ʿAdad xāss bilmuʾtamar al-ʾawwal lilmajāmiʿ
al-lugawiyyah al-ʿilmiyyah al-ʿarabiyyah (Damascus, January 1957).

MARÇAIS, W. (1930–31), Three articles, *L'Enseignement Public*, vol. 97,
pp. 401–9; vol. 105, pp. 20–39, 120–33.

Haitian Creole

COMHAIRE-SYLVAIN, S. (1936), *Le Créole haitien*, Wetteren and Port-au-Prince.

HALL, R. A., Jr. (1953), *Haitian Creole*, Menasha, Wis.

MCCONNELL, H. O., and SWAN, E. (1945), *You Can Learn Creole*, Port-au-Prince.

Other references

CHAO, Y. R. (1947), *Cantonese Primer*, Harvard University Press.

FERGUSON, C. A. (1957), 'Two problems in Arabic phonology', *Word*, vol. 13, pp. 460–78.

GREENBERG, J. H. (1954), 'A quantitative approach to the morphological typology of language', in R. Spencer (ed.), *Method and Perspective in Anthropology*, University of Minnesota Press, pp. 192–220.

PILLAI, M. (1960), 'Tamil – literary and colloquial', in C. A. Ferguson and J. J. Gumperz (eds.), *Linguistic Diversity in South Asia*, Indiana University Research Center in Anthropology, Folklore and Linguistics: Publication 13, pp. 27–42.

SHOUBY, E. (1951), 'The influence of the Arabic language on the psychology of the Arabs', *Middle East Journal*, vol. 5, pp. 284–302.

12 R. Brown and A. Gilman

The Pronouns of Power and Solidarity

R. Brown and A. Gilman, 'The Pronouns of Power and Solidarity',
in T. A. Sebeok (ed.), *Style in Language*, MIT Press, 1960, pp. 253–76.

Most of us in speaking and writing English use only one pronoun
of address; we say 'you' to many persons and 'you' to one person. The pronoun 'thou' is reserved, nowadays, to prayer and
naïve poetry, but in the past it was the form of familiar address to
a single person. At that time 'you' was the singular of reverence
and of polite distance and, also, the invariable plural. In French,
German, Italian, Spanish and the other languages most nearly
related to English there are still active two singular pronouns of
address. The interesting thing about such pronouns is their close
association with two dimensions fundamental to the analysis of
all social life – the dimensions of power and solidarity. Semantic
and stylistic analysis of these forms takes us well into psychology
and sociology as well as into linguistics and the study of literature.

This paper is divided into five major sections.[1] The first three of
these are concerned with the semantics of the pronouns of
address. By semantics we mean covariation between the pronoun
used and the objective relationship existing between speaker and
addressee. The first section offers a general description of the
semantic evolution of the pronouns of address in certain European languages. The second section describes semantic differences existing today among the pronouns of French, German and
Italian. The third section proposes a connection between social
structure, group ideology, and the semantics of the pronoun. The
final two sections of the paper are concerned with expressive
style by which we mean covariation between the pronoun used

1. Our study was financed by a Grant-in-Aid-of-Research made by the
Ford Foundation to Brown, and the authors gratefully acknowledge this
assistance.

and characteristics of the person speaking. The first of these sections shows that a man's consistent pronoun style gives away his class status and his political views. The last section describes the ways in which a man may vary his pronoun style from time to time so as to express transient moods and attitudes. In this section it is also proposed that the major expressive meanings are derived from the major semantic rules.

In each section the evidence most important to the thesis of that section is described in detail. However, the various generalizations we shall offer have developed as an interdependent set from continuing study of our whole assemblage of facts, and so it may be well to indicate here the sort of motley assemblage this is. Among secondary sources the general language histories (Baugh, 1935; Brunot, 1937; Diez, 1876; Grimm, 1898; Jespersen, 1905; Meyer-Lübke, 1900) have been of little use because their central concern is always phonetic rather than semantic change. However, there are a small number of monographs and doctoral dissertations describing the detailed pronoun semantics for one or another language – sometimes throughout its history (Gedike, 1794; Grand, 1930; Johnston, 1904; Schliebitz, 1886), sometimes for only a century or so (Kennedy, 1915; Stidston, 1917), and sometimes for the works of a particular author (Byrne, 1936; Fay, 1920). As primary evidence for the usage of the past we have drawn on plays, on legal proceedings (Jardine, 1832–5), and on letters (Devereux, 1853; Harrison, 1935). We have also learned about contemporary usage from literature but, more importantly, from long conversations with native speakers of French, Italian, German and Spanish both here and in Europe. Our best information about the pronouns of today comes from a questionnaire concerning usage which is described in the second section of this paper. The questionnaire has thus far been answered by the following numbers of students from abroad who were visiting in Boston in 1957–8: 50 Frenchmen, 20 Germans, 11 Italians and two informants, each, from Spain, Argentina, Chile, Denmark, Norway, Sweden, Israel, South Africa, India, Switzerland, Holland, Austria and Yugoslavia.

We have far more information concerning English, French, Italian, Spanish and German than for any other languages. Informants and documents concerning the other Indo-European languages are not easily accessible to us. What we have to say is then largely founded on information about these five closely related languages. These first conclusions will eventually be tested by us against other Indo-European languages and, in a more generalized form, against unrelated languages.

The European development of two singular pronouns of address begins with the Latin *tu* and *vos*. In Italian they became *tu* and *voi* (with *Lei* eventually largely displacing *voi*); in French *tu* and *vous*; in Spanish *tu* and *vos* (later *usted*). In German the distinction began with *du* and *Ihr* but *Ihr* gave way to *er* and later to *Sie*. English speakers first used 'thou' and 'ye' and later replaced 'ye' with 'you'. As a convenience we propose to use the symbols *T* and *V* (from the Latin *tu* and *vos*) as generic designators for a familiar and a polite pronoun in any language.

The general semantic evolution of T and V

In the Latin of antiquity there was only *tu* in the singular. The plural *vos* as a form of address to one person was first directed to the emperor and there are several theories (Byrne, 1936; Châtelain, 1880) about how this may have come about. The use of the plural to the emperor began in the fourth century. By that time there were actually two emperors; the ruler of the eastern empire had his seat in Constantinople and the ruler of the west sat in Rome. Because of Diocletian's reforms the imperial office, although vested in two men, was administratively unified. Words addressed to one man were, by implication, addressed to both. The choice of *vos* as a form of address may have been in response to this implicit plurality. An emperor is also plural in another sense; he is the summation of his people and can speak as their representative. Royal persons sometimes say 'we' where an ordinary man would say 'I'. The Roman emperor sometimes spoke of himself as *nos*, and the reverential *vos* is the simple reciprocal of this.

The usage need not have been mediated by a prosaic association with actual plurality, for plurality is a very old and ubiquitous metaphor for power. Consider only the several senses of such English words as 'great' and 'grand'. The reverential *vos* could have been directly inspired by the power of an emperor.

Eventually the Latin plural was extended from the emperor to other power figures. However, this semantic pattern was not unequivocally established for many centuries. There was much inexplicable fluctuation between T and V in Old French, Spanish, Italian and Portuguese (Schliebitz, 1886), and in Middle English (Kennedy, 1915; Stidston, 1917). In verse, at least, the choice seems often to have depended on assonance, rhyme, or syllable count. However, some time between the twelfth and fourteenth centuries (Gedike, 1794; Grand, 1930; Kennedy, 1915; Schliebitz, 1886), varying with the language, a set of norms crystallized which we call the nonreciprocal power semantic.

The power semantic

One person may be said to have power over another in the degree that he is able to control the behavior of the other. Power is a relationship between at least two persons, and it is nonreciprocal in the sense that both cannot have power in the same area of behavior. The power semantic is similarly nonreciprocal; the superior says T and receives V.

There are many bases of power – physical strength, wealth, age, sex, institutionalized role in the church, the state, the army or within the family. The character of the power semantic can be made clear with a set of examples from various languages. In his letters, Pope Gregory I (590–604) used T to his subordinates in the ecclesiastical hierarchy and they invariably said V to him (Muller, 1914). In medieval Europe, generally, the nobility said T to the common people and received V; the master of a household said T to his slave, his servant, his squire, and received V. Within the family, of whatever social level, parents gave T to children and were given V. In Italy in the fifteenth century penitents said V to the priest and were told T (Grand, 1930). In Froissart (late fourteenth century) God says T to His angels and they say V; all celestial beings say T to man and receive V. In French of the twelfth and thirteenth century man says T to the animals (Schliebitz, 1886). In fifteenth century Italian literature Christians say T to Turks and Jews and receive V (Grand, 1930). In the plays of Corneille and Racine (Schliebitz, 1886) and Shakespeare (Byrne, 1936), the noble principals say T to their subordinates and are given V in return.

The V of reverence entered European speech as a form of

address to the principal power in the state and eventually generalized to the powers within that microcosm of the state – the nuclear family. In the history of language, then, parents are emperor figures. It is interesting to note in passing that Freud reversed this terminology and spoke of kings, as well as generals, employers and priests, as father figures. The propriety of Freud's designation for his psychological purposes derives from the fact that an individual learning a European language reverses the historical order of semantic generalization. The individual's first experience of subordination to power and of the reverential V comes in his relation to his parents. In later years similar asymmetrical power relations and similar norms of address develop between employer and employee, soldier and officer, subject and monarch. We can see how it might happen, as Freud believed, that the later social relationships would remind the individual of the familial prototype and would revive emotions and responses from childhood. In a man's personal history recipients of the nonreciprocal V are parent figures.

Since the nonreciprocal power semantic only prescribes usage between superior and inferior, it calls for a social structure in which there are unique power ranks for every individual. Medieval European societies were not so finely structured as that, and so the power semantic was never the only rule for the use of T and V. There were also norms of address for persons of roughly equivalent power, that is, for members of a common class. Between equals, pronominal address was reciprocal; an individual gave and received the same form. During the medieval period, and for varying times beyond, equals of the upper classes exchanged the mutual V and equals of the lower classes exchanged T.

The difference in class practice derives from the fact that the reverential V was always introduced into a society at the top. In the Roman Empire only the highest ranking persons had any occasion to address the emperor, and so at first only they made use of V in the singular. In its later history in other parts of Europe the reverential V was usually adopted by one court in imitation of another. The practice slowly disseminated downward in a society. In this way the use of V in the singular incidentally came to connote a speaker of high status. In later centuries Europeans became very conscious of the extensive use of V as a mark of elegance. In the drama of seventeenth century France the nobility and bourgeoisie almost always address one another as V. This is true even of husband and wife, of lovers, and of parent and child if the child is adult. Mme de Sévigné in her correspondence never uses T, not even to her daughter the Comtesse de Grignan (Schliebitz, 1886). Servants and peasantry, however, regularly used T among themselves.

For many centuries French, English, Italian, Spanish, and German pronoun usage followed the rule of nonreciprocal T–V between persons of unequal power and the rule of mutual V or T (according to social-class membership) between persons of roughly equivalent power. There was at first no rule differentiating address among equals but, very gradually, a distinction developed which is sometimes called the T of intimacy and the V of formality. We name this second dimension *solidarity*, and here is our guess as to how it developed.

The solidarity semantic

The original singular pronoun was T. The use of V in the singular developed as a form of address to a person of superior power. There are many personal attributes that convey power. The recipient of V may differ from the recipient of T in strength, age, wealth, birth, sex or profession. As two people move apart on these power-laden dimensions, one of them begins to say V. In general terms, the V form is linked with differences between persons. Not all differences between persons imply a difference of power. Men are born in different cities, belong to different families of the same status, may attend different but equally prominent schools, may practice different but equally respected professions. A rule for making distinctive use of T and V among equals can be formulated by generalizing the power semantic. Differences of power cause V to emerge in one direction of address; differences not concerned with power cause V to emerge in both directions.

The relations called *older than*, *parent of*, *employer of*, *richer than*, *stronger than*, and *nobler than* are all asymmetrical. If A is older than B, B is not older than A. The relation called 'more powerful than', which is abstracted from these more specific relations, is also conceived to be asymmetrical. The pronoun usage expressing this power relation is also asymmetrical or nonreciprocal, with the greater receiving V and the lesser T. Now we are concerned with a new set of relations which are symmetrical; for example, *attended the same school* or *have the same parents* or *practice the same profession*. If A has the same parents as B, B has the same parents as A. Solidarity is the name we give to the general relationship and solidarity is symmetrical. The corresponding norms of address are symmetrical or reciprocal with V becoming more probable as solidarity declines. The solidary T reaches a peak of probability in address between twin brothers or in a man's soliloquizing address to himself.

Not every personal attribute counts in determining whether two people are solidary enough to use the mutual T. Eye color does not ordinarily matter nor does shoe size. The similarities that matter seem to be those that make for like-mindedness or similar behavior dispositions. These will ordinarily be such things as political membership, family, religion, profession, sex, and birthplace. However, extreme distinctive values on almost any dimension may become significant. Height ought to make for solidarity among giants and midgets. The T of solidarity can be produced by frequency of contact as well as by objective similarities. However, frequent contact does not necessarily lead to the mutual T. It depends on whether contact results in the discovery or creation of the like-mindedness that seems to be the core of the solidarity semantic.

Solidarity comes into the European pronouns as a means of differentiating address among power equals. It introduces a second dimension into the semantic system on the level of power equivalents. So long as solidarity was confined to this level, the two-dimensional system was in equilibrium (see Figure 1a), and it seems to have remained here for a considerable time in all our languages. It is from the long reign of the two-dimensional semantic that T derives its common definition as the pronoun of either condescension or intimacy and V its definition as the pronoun of reverence or formality. These definitions are still current but usage has, in fact, gone somewhat beyond them.

The dimension of solidarity is potentially applicable to all persons addressed. Power superiors may be solidary (parents, elder siblings) or not solidary (officials whom one seldom sees). Power inferiors, similarly, may be as solidary as the old family retainer and as remote as the waiter in a strange restaurant. Extension of the solidarity dimension along the dotted lines of Figure 1b creates six categories of persons defined by their relations to a speaker. Rules of address are in conflict for persons in the upper left and lower right categories. For the upper left, power indicates *V* and solidarity *T*. For the lower right, power indicates *T* and solidarity *V*.

The abstract conflict described in Figure 1b is particularized in Figure 2a with a sample of the social dyads in which the conflict would be felt. In each case usage in one direction is unequivocal but, in the other direction, the two semantic forces are opposed. The first three dyads in Figure 2a involve conflict in address to inferiors who are not solidary (the lower right category of Figure 1b), and the second three dyads involve conflict in address to superiors who are solidary (the upper left category in Figure 1b).

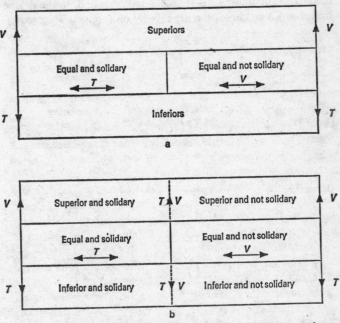

Figure 1 The two-dimensional semantic (a) in equilibrium and (b) under tension

Well into the nineteenth century the power semantic prevailed and waiters, common soldiers and employees were called *T* while parents, masters and elder brothers were called *V*. However, all our evidence consistently indicates that in the past century the solidarity semantic has gained supremacy. Dyads of the type shown in Figure 2a now reciprocate the pronoun of solidarity or the pronoun of nonsolidarity. The conflicted address has been resolved so as to match the unequivocal address. The abstract result is a simple one-dimensional system with the reciprocal *T* for the solidary and the reciprocal *V* for the nonsolidary.

It is the present practice to reinterpret power-laden attributes so as to turn them into symmetrical solidarity attributes. Relationships like *older than*, *father of*, *nobler than*, and *richer than* are now reinterpreted for purposes of *T* and *V* as relations of *the same age as*, *the same family as*, *the same kind of ancestry as*, and *the same income as*. In the degree that these relationships hold, the probability of a mutual *T* increases and, in the degree that they do not hold, the probability of a mutual *V* increases.

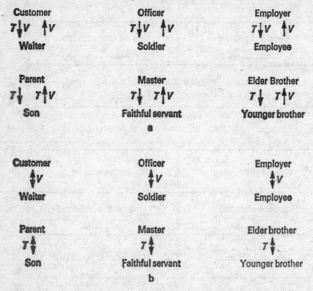

Figure 2 Social dyads involving (a) semantic conflict and (b) their resolution

There is an interesting residual of the power relation in the contemporary notion that the right to initiate the reciprocal T belongs to the member of the dyad having the better power-based claim to say T without reciprocation. The suggestion that solidarity be recognized comes more gracefully from the elder than from the younger, from the richer than from the poorer, from the employer than from the employee, from the noble than from the commoner, from the female than from the male.

In support of our claim that solidarity has largely won out over power we can offer a few quotations from language scholars. Littré (1882), writing of French usage, says: 'Notre courtoisie est même si grande, que nous ne dédaignons pas de donner du vous et du monsieur à l'homme de la condition la plus vile.' Grand (1930) wrote of the Italian V: 'On commence aussi à le donner aux personnes de service, à qui on disait tu autrefois.' We have found no authority who describes the general character of these many specific changes of usage: a shift from power to solidarity as the governing semantic principle.

The best evidence that the change has occurred is in our interviews and notes on contemporary literature and films and, most importantly, the questionnaire results. The six social dyads of Figure 2 were all represented in the questionnaire. In the past these would have been answered in accordance with asymmetrical power. Across all six of these dyads the French results yield only 11 per cent nonreciprocal power answers, the German 12 per cent, the Italian 27 per cent. In all other cases the usage is reciprocal, as indicated in Figure 2b. In all three of the languages, address between master and servant retains the greatest power loading. Some of the changes toward solidarity are very recent. Only since the Second World War, for instance, has the French Army adopted a regulation requiring officers to say V to enlisted men.

Finally, it is our opinion that a still newer direction of semantic shift can be discerned in the whole collection of languages studied. Once solidarity has been established as the single dimension distinguishing T from V the province of T proceeds to expand. The direction of change is increased in the number of relations defined as solidary enough to merit a mutual T and, in particular, to regard any sort of camaraderie resulting from a common task or a common fate as grounds for T. We have a favorite example of this new trend given us independently by several French informants. It seems that mountaineers above a certain critical altitude shift to the mutual *T*. We like to think that this is the point where their lives hang by a single thread. In general, the mutual *T* is advancing among fellow students, fellow workers, members of the same political group, persons who share a hobby or take a trip together. We believe this is the direction of current change because it summarizes what our informants tell us about the pronoun usage of the 'young people' as opposed to that of older people.

Contemporary differences among French, Italian and German

While *T* and *V* have passed through the same general semantic sequence in these three languages, there are today some differences of detailed usage which were revealed by the questionnaire data. Conversations with native speakers guided us in the writing of questionnaire items, but the conversations themselves did not teach us the characteristic semantic features of the three languages; these did not emerge until we made statistical comparison of answers to the standard items of the questionnaire.

The questionnaire is in English. It opens with a paragraph informing the subject that the items below all have reference to the use of the singular pronouns of address in his native language. There are 28 items in the full questionnaire, and they all have the form of the following example from the questionnaire for French students:

1.(a) Which pronoun would you use in speaking to your mother?

$$
\begin{aligned}
T \text{ (definitely)} &\quad ——\\
T \text{ (probably)} &\quad ——\\
\text{Possibly } T, \text{ possibly } V &\quad ——\\
V \text{ (probably)} &\quad ——\\
V \text{ (definitely)} &\quad ——
\end{aligned}
$$

1.(b) Which would she use in speaking to you?

$$
\begin{aligned}
T \text{ (definitely)} &\quad ——\\
T \text{ (probably)} &\quad ——\\
\text{Possibly } T, \text{ possibly } V &\quad ——\\
V \text{ (probably)} &\quad ——\\
V \text{ (definitely)} &\quad ——
\end{aligned}
$$

The questionnaire asks about usage between the subject and his mother, his father, his grandfather, his wife, a younger brother who is a child, a married elder brother, that brother's wife, a remote male cousin, and an elderly female servant whom he has known from childhood. It asks about usage between the subject and fellow students at the university at home, usage to a student from home visiting in America, and usage to someone with whom the subject had been at school some years previously. It asks about usage to a waiter in a restaurant, between clerks in an office, fellow soldiers in the army, between boss and employee, army private and general. In addition, there are some rather elaborate items which ask the subject to imagine himself in some carefully detailed social situation and then to say what pronoun he would use. A copy of the full questionnaire may be had on application to the authors.

The most accessible informants were students from abroad resident in Boston in the fall of 1957. Listings of such students were obtained from Harvard, Boston University, MIT, and the Office of the French Consul in New England. Although we have data from a small sample of female respondents, the present analysis is limited to the males. All the men in the sample have been in the United States for one year or less; they come from cities of over 300,000 inhabitants, and these cities are well scattered across the country in question. In addition, all members of the sample are from upper-middle-class, professional families. This homogeneity of class membership was enforced by the factors determining selection of students who go abroad. The occasional informant from a working-class family is deliberately excluded from these comparisons. The class from which we draw shows less regional variation in speech than does the working class and, especially, farmers. At the present time we have complete responses from 50 Frenchmen, 20 Germans and 11 Italians; many of these men also sent us letters describing their understanding of the pronouns and offering numerous valuable anecdotes of usage. The varying numbers of subjects belonging to the three nationalities result from the unequal representation of these nationalities among Boston students rather than from national characterological differences in willingness to answer a questionnaire. Almost every person on our lists agreed to serve as an informant.

In analyzing the results we assigned the numbers 0–4 to the five response alternatives to each question, beginning with 'Definitely V' as 0. A rough test was made of the significance of the differences among the three languages on each question. We dichotomized the replies to each question into : (a) all replies of either 'Definitely T' or 'Probably T'; (b) all replies of 'Definitely V' or 'Probably V' or 'Possibly V, possibly T'. Using the chi-squared test with Yates's correction for small frequencies we determined, for each comparison, the probability of obtaining by chance a difference as large or larger than that actually obtained. Even with such small samples, there were quite a few differences significantly unlikely to occur by chance ($P = .05$ or less). Germans were more prone than the French to say T to their grandfathers, to an elder brother's wife, and to an old family servant. The French were more prone than the Germans to say T to a male fellow student, to a student from home visiting in America, to a fellow clerk in an office, and to someone known previously as a fellow student. Italians were more prone than the French to say T to a female fellow student and also to an attractive girl to whom they had recently been introduced. Italians were more prone than the Germans to say T to the persons just described and, in addition, to a male fellow student and to a student from home visiting in America. On no question did either the French or the Germans show a significantly greater tendency to say T than did the Italians.

The many particular differences among the three languages are susceptible of a general characterization. Let us first contrast German and French. The German T is more reliably applied within the family than is the French T; in addition to the significantly higher T scores for grandfather and elder brother's wife there are smaller differences showing a higher score for the German T on father, mother, wife, married elder brother, and remote male cousin. The French T is not automatically applied to remote relatives, but it is more likely than the German pronoun to be used to express the camaraderie of fellow students, fellow clerks, fellow countrymen abroad, and fellow soldiers. In general it may be said that the solidarity coded by the German T is an ascribed solidarity of family relationships. The French T, in greater degree, codes an acquired solidarity, not founded on family relationship but developing out of some sort of shared fate. As for the Italian T, it very nearly equals the German in family solidarity and it surpasses the French in camaraderie. The camaraderie of the Italian male, incidentally, is extended to the Italian female; unlike the French or German student the Italian says T to the co-ed almost as readily as to the male fellow student.

There is a very abstract semantic rule governing T and V which is the same for French, German, and Italian and for many other languages we have studied. The rule is that usage is reciprocal, T becoming increasingly probable and V less probable as the number of solidarity-producing attributes shared by two people increases. The respect in which French, German, and Italian differ from one another is in the relative weight given to various attributes of persons which can serve to generate solidarity. For German, ascribed family membership is the important attribute; French and Italian give more weight to acquired characteristics.

Semantics, social structure and ideology

A historical study of the pronouns of address reveals a set of semantic and social psychological correspondence. The non-reciprocal power semantic is associated with a relatively static society in which power is distributed by birthright and is not subject to much redistribution. The power semantic was closely tied with the feudal and manorial systems. In Italy the reverential pronoun *Lei* which has largely displaced the older *voi* was originally an abbreviation for *la vostra Signoria* 'your lordship' and in Spanish *vuestra Merced* 'your grace' became the reverential *usted*. The static social structure was accompanied by the Church's teaching that each man had his properly appointed place and ought not to wish to rise above it. The reciprocal solidarity semantic has grown with social mobility and an equalitarian ideology. The towns and cities have led the way in the semantic change as they led the way in opening society to vertical movement. In addition to these rough historical correspondences we have made a collection of lesser items of evidence favoring the thesis.

In France the nonreciprocal power semantic was dominant

until the Revolution when the Committee for the Public Safety condemned the use of V as a feudal remnant and ordered a universal reciprocal T. On 31 October, 1793, Malbec made a Parliamentary speech against V: 'Nous distinguons trois personnes pour le singulier et trois pour le pluriel, et, au mépris de cette règle, l'esprit de fanatisme, d'orgueil et de féodalité, nous a fait contracter l'habitude de nous servir de la seconde personne du pluriel lorsque nous parlons à un seul' (quoted in Brunot, 1927). For a time revolutionary 'fraternité' transformed all address into the mutual *Citoyen* and the mutual *tu*. Robespierre even addressed the president of the Assembly as *tu*. In later years solidarity declined and the differences of power which always exist everywhere were expressed once more.

It must be asked why the equalitarian ideal was expressed in a universal T rather than a universal V or, as a third alternative, why there was not a shift of semantic from power to solidarity with both pronouns being retained. The answer lies with the ancient upper-class preference for the use of V. There was animus against the pronoun itself. The pronoun of the '*sans-culottes*' was T (Gedike, 1794), and so this had to be the pronoun of the Revolution.

Although the power semantic has largely gone out of pronoun use in France today native speakers are nevertheless aware of it. In part they are aware of it because it prevails in so much of the greatest French literature. Awareness of power as a potential factor in pronoun usage was revealed by our respondents' special attitude toward the saying of T to a waiter. Most of them felt that this would be shockingly bad taste in a way that other norm violations would not be, apparently because there is a kind of seignorial right to say T to a waiter, an actual power asymmetry, which the modern man's ideology requires him to deny. In French Africa, on the other hand, it is considered proper to recognize a caste difference between the African and the European, and the nonreciprocal address is used to express it. The European says T and requires V from the African. This is a galling custom to the African, and in 1957 Robert Lacoste, the French Minister residing in Algeria, urged his countrymen to eschew the practice.

In England, before the Norman Conquest, 'ye' was the second person plural and 'thou' the singular. 'You' was originally the accusative of 'ye', but in time it also became the nominative plural and ultimately ousted 'thou' as the usual singular. The first uses of 'ye' as a reverential singular occur in the thirteenth century (Kennedy, 1915), and seem to have been copied from the French nobility. The semantic progression corresponds roughly to the general stages described in the first section of this paper, except that the English seem always to have moved more freely from one form to another than did the continental Europeans (Jespersen, 1905).

In the seventeenth century 'thou' and 'you' became explicitly involved in social controversy. The Religious Society of Friends (or Quakers) was founded in the middle of this century by George Fox. One of the practices setting off this rebellious group from the larger society was the use of Plain Speech, and this entailed saying 'thou' to everyone. George Fox explained the practice in these words:

'Moreover, when the Lord sent me forth into the world, He forbade me to put off my hat to any, high or low; and I was required to Thee and Thou all men and women, without any respect to rich or poor, great or small' (quoted in Estrich and Sperber, 1946).

Fox wrote a fascinating pamphlet (Fox, 1660), arguing that T to one and V to many is the natural and logical form of address in all languages. Among others he cites Latin, Hebrew, Greek, Arabick, Syriack, Aethiopic, Egyptian, French, and Italian. Fox suggests that the Pope, in his vanity, introduced the corrupt and illogical practice of saying V to one person. Farnsworth, another early Friend, wrote a somewhat similar pamphlet (Farnsworth, 1655), in which he argued that the Scriptures show that God and Adam and God and Moses were not too proud to say and receive the singular T.

For the new convert to the Society of Friends the universal T was an especially difficult commandment. Thomas Ellwood has described (1714) the trouble that developed between himself and his father:

But whenever I had occasion to speak to my Father, though I had no Hat now to offend him; yet my language did as much: for I durst not say YOU to him, but THOU or THEE, as the Occasion required, and then would he be sure to fall on me with his Fists.

The Friends' reasons for using the mutual *T* were much the same as those of the French revolutionaries, but the Friends were always a minority and the larger society was antagonized by their violations of decorum.

Some Friends use 'thee' today; the nominative 'thou' has been dropped and 'thee' is used as both the nominative and (as formerly) the accusative. Interestingly many Friends also use 'you'. 'Thee' is likely to be reserved for Friends among themselves and 'you' said to outsiders. This seems to be a survival of the solidarity semantic. In English at large, of course, 'thou' is no longer used. The explanation of its disappearance is by no means certain; however, the forces at work seem to have included a popular reaction against the radicalism of Quakers and Levelers and also a general trend in English toward simplified verbal inflection.

In the world today there are numerous examples of the association proposed between ideology and pronoun semantics. In Yugoslavia, our informants tell us, there was, for a short time following the establishment of Communism, a universal mutual *T* of solidarity. Today revolutionary *esprit* has declined and *V* has returned for much the same set of circumstances as in Italy, France, or Spain. There is also some power asymmetry in Yugosalvia's 'Socialist manners'. A soldier says *V* and *Comrade General*, but the general addresses the soldier with *T* and surname.

It is interesting in our materials to contrast usage in the Afrikaans language of South Africa and in the Gujerati and Hindi languages of India with the rest of the collection. On the questionnaire, Afrikaans speakers made eight nonreciprocal power distinctions; especially notable are distinctions within the family and the distinctions between customer and waiter and between boss and clerk, since these are almost never power-coded in French, Italian, German, etc., although they once were. The Afrikaans pattern generally preserves the asymmetry of the dyads described in Figure 2, and that suggests a more static society and a less developed equalitarian ethic. The forms of address used between Afrikaans-speaking whites and the groups of 'coloreds' and 'blacks' are especially interesting. The Afrikaaner uses *T*, but the two lower castes use neither *T* nor *V*. The intermediate caste of 'coloreds' says *Meneer* to the white and the 'blacks' say *Baas*. It is as if these social distances transcend anything that can be found within the white group and so require their peculiar linguistic expressions.

The Gujerati and Hindi languages of India have about the same pronoun semantic, and it is heavily loaded with power. These languages have all the asymmetrical usage of Afrikaans and, in addition, use the nonreciprocal T and V between elder brother and younger brother and between husband and wife. This truly feudal pronominal pattern is consistent with the static Indian society. However, that society is now changing rapidly and, consistent with that change, the norms of pronoun usage are also changing. The progressive young Indian exchanges the mutual T with his wife.

In our account of the general semantic evolution of the pronouns, we have identified a stage in which the solidarity rule was limited to address between persons of equal power. This seemed to yield a two-dimensional system in equilibrium (see Figure 1a), and we have wondered why address did not permanently stabilize there. It is possible, of course, that human cognition favors the binary choice without contingencies and so found its way to the suppression of one dimension. However, this theory does not account for the fact that it was the rule of solidarity that triumphed. We believe, therefore, that the development of open societies with an equalitarian ideology acted against the non-reciprocal power semantic and in favor of solidarity. It is our suggestion that the larger social changes created a distaste for the face-to-face expression of differential power.

What of the many actions other than nonreciprocal T and V which express power asymmetry? A vassal not only says V but also bows, lifts his cap, touches his forelock, keeps silent, leaps to obey. There are a large number of expressions of subordination which are patterned isomorphically with T and V. Nor are the pronouns the only forms of nonreciprocal address. There are, in addition, proper names and titles, and many of these operate today on a nonreciprocal power pattern in America and in Europe, in open and equalitarian societies.

In the American family there are no discriminating pronouns, but there are nonreciprocal norms of address. A father says 'Jim' to his son but, unless he is extraordinarily 'advanced', he does not anticipate being called 'Jack' in reply. In the American South there are no pronouns to mark the caste separation of Negro and white, but there are nonreciprocal norms of address. The white man is accustomed to call the Negro by his first name, but he expects to be called 'Mr Legree'. In America and in Europe there are forms of nonreciprocal address for all the dyads of asymmetrical power; customer and waiter, teacher and student, father and son, employer and employee.

Differences of power exist in a democracy as in all societies. What is the difference between expressing power asymmetry in pronouns and expressing it by choice of title and proper name? It seems to be primarily a question of the degree of linguistic compulsion. In face-to-face address we can usually avoid the use of any name or title but not so easily the use of a pronoun. Even if the pronoun can be avoided, it will be implicit in the inflection of the verb. 'Dîtes quelque chose' clearly says *vous* to the French-man. A norm for the pronominal and verbal expression of power compels a continuing coding of power, whereas a norm for titles and names permits power to go uncoded in most discourse. Is there any reason why the pronominal coding should be more congenial to a static society than to an open society?

We have noticed that mode of address intrudes into conscious-ness as a problem at times of status change. Award of the doctoral degree, for instance, transforms a student into a colleague and, among American academics, the familiar first name is normal. The fledgling academic may find it difficult to call his former teachers by their first names. Although these teachers may be young and affable, they have had a very real power over him for several years and it will feel presumptuous to deny this all at once with a new mode of address. However, the 'tyranny of democratic manners' (Cronin, 1958) does not allow him to continue comfortably with the polite 'Professor X'. He would not like to be thought unduly conscious of status, unprepared for faculty rank, a born lickspittle. Happily, English allows him a respite. He can avoid any term of address, staying with the un-committed 'you', until he and his addressees have got used to the new state of things. This linguistic *rite de passage* has, for English speakers, a waiting room in which to screw up courage.

In a fluid society crises of address will occur more frequently than in a static society, and so the pronominal coding of power differences is more likely to be felt as onerous. Coding by title and name would be more tolerable because less compulsory. Where status is fixed by birth and does not change each man has enduring rights and obligations of address.

A strong equalitarian ideology of the sort dominant in America works to suppress every conventional expression of power asymmetry. If the worker becomes conscious of his unreciprocated polite address to the boss, he may feel that his human dignity requires him to change. However, we do not feel the full power of the ideology until we are in a situation that gives us some claim to receive deferential address. The American professor often feels foolish being given his title, he almost certainly will not claim it as a prerogative; he may take pride in being on a first-name basis with his students. Very 'palsy' parents may invite their children to call them by first name. The very President of the Republic invites us all to call him 'Ike'. Nevertheless, the differences of power are real and are experienced. Cronin has suggested in an amusing piece (Cronin, 1958) that subordination is expressed by Americans in a subtle, and generally unwitting, body language. 'The repertoire includes the boyish grin, the deprecatory cough, the unfinished sentence, the appreciative giggle, the drooping shoulders, the head-scratch and the bottom-waggle.'

Group style with the pronouns of address

The identification of style is relative to the identification of some constancy. When we have marked out the essentials of some action – it might be walking or speaking a language or driving a car – we can identify the residual variation as stylistic. Different styles are different ways of 'doing the same thing', and so their identification waits on some designation of the range of performances to be regarded as 'the same thing'.

Linguistic science finds enough that is constant in English and French and Latin to put all these and many more into one family – the Indo-European. It is possible with reference to this constancy to think of Italian and Spanish and English and the others as so many styles of Indo-European. They all have, for instance, two singular pronouns of address, but each language has an individual phonetic and semantic style in pronoun usage. We are ignoring phonetic style (through the use of the generic T and V), but in the second section of the paper we have described differences in the semantic styles of French, German and Italian.

Linguistic styles are potentially expressive when there is covariation between characteristics of language performance and characteristics of the performers. When styles are 'interpreted', language behavior is functionally expressive. On that abstract level where the constancy is Indo-European and the styles are French, German, English and Italian, interpretations of style must be statements about communities of speakers, statements of national character, social structure, or group ideology. In the last section we have hazarded a few propositions on this level.

It is usual, in discussion of linguistic style, to set constancy at the level of a language like French or English rather than at the level of a language family. In the languages we have studied there are variations in pronoun style that are associated with the social status of the speaker. We have seen that the use of V because of its entry at the top of a society and its diffusion downward was always interpreted as a mark of good breeding. It is interesting to find an organization of French journeymen in the generation after the Revolution adopting a set of rules of propriety cautioning members against going without tie or shoes at home on Sunday and also against the use of the mutual T among themselves (Perdiguier, 1914). Our informants assure us that V and T still function as indications of class membership. The Yugoslavians have a saying that a peasant would say T to a king. By contrast, a French nobleman who turned up in our net told us that he had said T to no one in the world except the old woman who was his nurse in childhood. He is prevented by the dominant democratic ideology from saying T to subordinates and by his own royalist ideology from saying it to equals.

In literature, pronoun style has often been used to expose the pretensions of social climbers and the would-be elegant. Persons aping the manners of the class above them usually do not get the imitation exactly right. They are likely to notice some point of difference between their own class and the next higher and then extend the difference too widely, as in the use of the 'elegant' broad [a] in 'can' and 'bad'. Molière gives us his '*précieuses ridicules*' saying *V* to servants whom a refined person would call *T*. In Ben Jonson's *Everyman in his Humour* and *Epicoene* such true gallants as Wellbred and Knowell usually say 'you' to one another but they make frequent expressive shifts between this form and 'thou', whereas such fops as John Daw and Amorous-La-Foole make unvarying use of 'you'.

Our sample of visiting French students was roughly homogeneous in social status as judged by the single criterion of paternal occupation. Therefore, we could not make any systematic study of differences in class style, but we thought it possible that, even within this select group, there might be interpretable differences of style. It was our guess that the tendency to make wide or narrow use of the solidary *T* would be related to general radicalism or conservatism of ideology. As a measure of this latter dimension we used Eysenck's Social Attitude Inventory (1957). This is a collection of statements to be accepted or rejected concerning a variety of matters – religion, economics, racial relations, sexual behavior, etc. Eysenck has validated the scale in England and in France on Socialist, Communist, Fascist, Conservative and Liberal party members. In general, to be radical on this scale is to favor change and to be conservative is to wish to maintain the status quo or turn back to some earlier condition. We undertook to relate scores on this inventory to an index of pronoun style.

As yet we have reported no evidence demonstrating that there exists such a thing as a personal style in pronoun usage in the sense of a tendency to make wide or narrow use of *T*. It may be that each item in the questionnaire, each sort of person addressed, is an independent personal norm not predictable from any other. A child learns what to say to each kind of person. What he learns in each case depends on the groups in which he has membership. Perhaps his usage is a bundle of unrelated habits.

Guttman (Stouffer, Guttman, *et al.*, 1950) has developed the technique of Scalogram Analysis for determining whether or not a collection of statements taps a common dimension. A perfect Guttman scale can be made of the statements: (a) I am at least 5′ tall; (b) I am at least 5′ 4″ tall; (c) I am at least 5′ 7″ tall; (d) I am at least 6′ 1″ tall; (e) I am at least 6′ 2″ tall. Endorsement of a more extreme statement will always be associated with endorsement of all less extreme statements. A person can be assigned a single score – a, b, c, d, or e – which represents the most extreme statement he has endorsed, and from this single score all his individual answers can be reproduced. If he scores c he has also endorsed a and b but not d or e. The general criterion for scalability is the reproducibility of individual responses from a single score, and this depends on the items being interrelated so that endorsement of one is reliably associated with endorsement or rejection of the others.

The Guttman method was developed during World War II for the measurement of social attitudes, and it has been widely used. Perfect reproducibility is not likely to be found for all the statements which an investigator guesses to be concerned with some single attitude. The usual thing is to accept a set of statements as scalable when they are 90 per cent reproducible and also satisfy certain other requirements; for example, there must be some statements that are not given a very one-sided response but are accepted and rejected with nearly equal frequency.

The responses to the pronoun questionnaire are not varying degrees of agreement (as in an attitude questionnaire) but are rather varying probabilities of saying T or V. There seems to be no reason why these bipolar responses cannot be treated like yes or no responses on an attitude scale. The difference is that the scale, if there is one, will be the semantic dimension governing the pronouns, and the scale score of each respondent will represent his personal semantic style.

It is customary to have 100 subjects for a Scalogram Analysis, but we could find only 50 French students. We tested all 28 items for scalability and found that a subset of them made a fairly good scale. It was necessary to combine response categories so as to dichotomize them in order to obtain an average reproducibility of 85 per cent. This coefficient was computed for the five intermediate items having the more-balanced marginal frequencies. A large number of items fell at or very near the two extremes. The solidarity or T-most end of the scale could be defined by father, mother, elder brother, young boys, wife or lover quite as well as by younger brother. The remote or V-most end could be defined by 'waiter' or 'top boss' as well as by 'army general'. The intervening positions, from the T-end to the V-end are:

the elderly female servant known since childhood, grandfather, a male fellow student, a female fellow student and an elder brother's wife.

For each item on the scale a *T* answer scores one point and a *V* answer no points. The individual total scores range from 1 to 7, which means the scale can differentiate only seven semantic styles. We divided the subjects into the resultant seven stylistically homogeneous groups and, for each group, determined the average scores on radicalism-conservatism. There was a set of almost perfectly consistent differences.

In Table 1 appear the mean radicalism scores for each pronoun style. The individual radicalism scores range between 2 and 13; the higher the score the more radical the person's ideology. The very striking result is that the group radicalism scores duplicate the order of the group pronoun scores with only a single reversal. The rank-difference correlation between the two sets of scores is .96, and even with only seven paired scores this is a very significant relationship.

There is enough consistency of address to justify speaking of a personal-pronoun style which involves a more or less wide use of the solidary *T*. Even among students of the same socioeconomic level there are differences of style, and these are potentially expressive of radicalism and conservatism in ideology. A Frenchman could, with some confidence, infer that a male university student who regularly said *T* to female fellow students would favor the nationalization of industry, free love, trial marriage, the abolition of capital punishment, and the weakening of nationalistic and religious loyalties.

What shall we make of the association between a wide use of *T* and a cluster of radical sentiments? There may be no 'sense' to it at all, that is, no logical connection between the linguistic practice and the attitudes, but simply a general tendency to go along with the newest thing. We know that left-wing attitudes are more likely to be found in the laboring class than in the professional classes. Perhaps those offspring of the professional class who sympathize with proletariat politics also, incidentally, pick up the working man's wide use of *T* without feeling that there is anything in the linguistic practice that is congruent with the ideology.

On the other hand perhaps there is something appropriate in

the association. The ideology is consistent in its disapproval of barriers between people: race, religion, nationality, property, marriage, even criminality. All these barriers have the effect of separating the solidary, the 'in-group', from the nonsolidary, the 'out-group'. The radical says the criminal is not far enough 'out' to be killed; he should be re-educated. He says that a nationality ought not to be so solidary that it prevents world organization from succeeding. Private property ought to be abolished, industry should be nationalized. There are to be no more out-groups and in-groups but rather one group, undifferentiated by nationality, religion, or pronoun of address. The fact that the pronoun which is being extended to all men alike is T, the mark of solidarity, the pronoun of the nuclear family, expresses the radical's intention to extend his sense of brotherhood. But we notice that

Table 1 Scores on the Pronoun Scale in Relation to Scores on the Radicalism Scale

Group pronoun score	Group mean radicalism score
1	5·50
2	6·66
3	6·82
4	7·83
5	6·83
6	8·83
7	9·75

the universal application of the pronoun eliminates the discrimination that gave it a meaning and that gives particular point to an old problem. Can the solidarity of the family be extended so widely? Is there enough libido to stretch so far? Will there perhaps be a thin solidarity the same everywhere but nowhere so strong as in the past?

The pronouns of address as expressions of transient attitudes

Behavior norms are practices consistent within a group. So long as the choice of a pronoun is recognized as normal for a group, its interpretation is simply the membership of the speaker in that group. However, the implications of group membership are often very important; social class, for instance, suggests a kind of family life, a level of education, a set of political views and much besides. These facts about a person belong to his character. They are enduring features which help to determine actions over many years. Consistent personal style in the use of the pronouns of address does not reveal enough to establish the speaker's unique character, but it can help to place him in one or another large category.

Sometimes the choice of a pronoun clearly violates a group norm and perhaps also the customary practice of the speaker. Then the meaning of the act will be sought in some attitude or emotion of the speaker. It is as if the interpreter reasoned that variations of address between the same two persons must be caused by variations in their attitudes toward one another. If two men of seventeenth century France properly exchange the V of upper-class equals and one of them gives the other T, he suggests that the other is his inferior since it is to his inferiors that a man says T. The general meaning of an unexpected pronoun choice is simply that the speaker, for the moment, views his relationship as one that calls for the pronoun used. This kind of variation in language behavior expresses a contemporaneous feeling or attitude. These variations are not consistent personal styles but departures from one's own custom and the customs of a group in response to a mood.

As there have been two great semantic dimensions governing T and V, so there have also been two principal kinds of expressive meaning. Breaking the norms of power generally has the meaning that a speaker regards an addressee as his inferior, superior, or equal, although by usual criteria, and according to the speaker's own customary usage, the addressee is not what the pronoun implies. Breaking the norms of solidarity generally means that the speaker temporarily thinks of the other as an outsider or as an intimate; it means that sympathy is extended or withdrawn.

The oldest uses of T and V to express attitudes seem everywhere to have been the T of contempt or anger and the V of admiration or respect. In his study of the French pronouns Schliebitz (1886) found the first examples of these expressive uses in literature of the twelfth and thirteenth centuries, which is about the time that the power semantic crystallized in France, and Grand (1930) has found the same thing for Italian. In saying *T*, where *V* is usual, the speaker treats the addressee like a servant or a child, and assumes the right to berate him. The most common use of the expressive *V*, in the early materials, is that of the master who is exceptionally pleased with the work of a servant and elevates him pronominally to match this esteem.

Racine, in his dramas, used the pronouns with perfect semantic consistency. His major figures exchange the *V* of upper-class equals. Lovers, brother and sister, husband and wife – none of them says *T* if he is of high rank, but each person of high rank has a subordinate confidante to whom he says *T* and from whom he receives *V*. It is a perfect nonreciprocal power semantic. This courtly pattern is broken only for the greatest scenes in each play. Racine reserved the expressive pronoun as some composers save the cymbals. In both *Andromaque* and *Phèdre* there are only two expressive departures from the norm, and they mark climaxes of feeling.

Jespersen (1905) believed that English 'thou' and 'ye' (or 'you') were more often shifted to express mood and tone than were the pronouns of the continental languages, and our comparisons strongly support this opinion. The 'thou' of contempt was so very familiar that a verbal form was created to name this expressive use. Shakespeare gives it to Sir Toby Belch (*Twelfth Night*) in the lines urging Andrew Aguecheek to send a challenge to the disguised Viola: 'Taunt him with the license of ink, if thou thou'st him some thrice, it shall not be amiss.' In life the verb turned up in Sir Edward Coke's attack on Raleigh at the latter's trial in 1603 (Jardine, 1832–5): 'All that he did, was at thy instigation, thou viper; for I thou thee, thou traitor.'

The *T* of contempt and anger is usually introduced between persons who normally exchange *V* but it can, of course, also be used by a subordinate to a superior. As the social distance is greater, the overthrow of the norm is more shocking and generally represents a greater extremity of passion. Sejanus, in Ben Jonson's play of that name, feels extreme contempt for the emperor Tiberius but wisely gives him the reverential *V* to his face. However, soliloquizing after the emperor has exited, Sejanus begins: 'Dull, heavy Caesar! Wouldst thou tell me ...' In

Jonson's *Volpone* Mosca invariably says 'you' to his master until the final scene when, as the two villains are about to be carted away, Mosca turns on Volpone with 'Bane to thy wolfish nature.'

Expressive effects of much greater subtlety than those we have described are common in Elizabethan and Jacobean drama. The exact interpretation of the speaker's attitude depends not only on the pronoun norm he upsets but also on his attendant words and actions and the total setting. Still simple enough to be unequivocal is the ironic or mocking 'you' said by Tamburlaine to the captive Turkish emperor Bajazeth. This exchange occurs in Act IV of Marlowe's play:

TAMBURLAINE: Here Turk, wilt thou have a clean trencher?
BAJAZETH: Ay, tyrant, and more meat.
TAMBURLAINE: Soft, Sir, you must be dietee; too much eating will make you surfeit.

'Thou' is to be expected from captor to captive and the norm is upset when Tamburlaine says 'you'. He cannot intend to express admiration or respect since he keeps the Turk captive and starves him. His intention is to mock the captive king with respectful address, implying a power that the king has lost.

The momentary shift of pronoun directly expresses a momentary shift of mood, but that interpretation does not exhaust its meaning. The fact that a man has a particular momentary attitude or emotion may imply a great deal about his characteristic disposition, his readiness for one kind of feeling rather than another. Not every attorney general, for instance, would have used the abusive 'thou' to Raleigh. The fact that Edward Coke did so suggests an arrogant and choleric temperament and, in fact, many made this assessment of him (Jardine, 1832–5). When Volpone spoke to Celia, a lady of Venice, he ought to have said 'you' but he began at once with 'thee'. This violation of decorum, together with the fact that he leaps from his sick bed to attempt rape of the lady, helps to establish Volpone's monstrous character. His abnormal form of address is consistent with the unnatural images in his speech. In any given situation we know the sort of people who would break the norms of address and the sort who would not. From the fact that a man does break the norms we infer his immediate feelings and, in addition, attribute to him the general character of people who would have such feelings and would give them that kind of expression.

With the establishment of the solidarity semantic a new set of expressive meanings became possible – feelings of sympathy and estrangement. In Shakespeare's plays there are expressive meanings that derive from the solidarity semantic as well as many dependent on power usage and many that rely on both connotations. The play *Two Gentlemen of Verona* is concerned with the Renaissance ideal of friendship and provides especially clear expressions of solidarity. Proteus and Valentine, the two Gentlemen, initially exchange 'thou', but when they touch on the subject of love, on which they disagree, their address changes to the 'you' of estrangement. Molière (Fay, 1920) has shown us that a man may even put himself at a distance as does George Dandin in the soliloquy beginning: 'George Dandin! George Dandin! Vous avez fait une sottise . . .'

In both French and English drama of the past, *T* and *V* were marvelously sensitive to feelings of approach and withdrawal. In terms of Freud's striking amoeba metaphor the pronouns signal the extension or retraction of libidinal pseudopodia. However, in French, German and Italian today this use seems to be very uncommon. Our informants told us that the *T*, once extended, is almost never taken back for the reason that it would mean the complete withdrawal of esteem. The only modern expressive shift we have found is a rather chilling one. Silverberg (1940) reports that in Germany in 1940 a prostitute and her client said *du* when they met and while they were together but when the libidinal tie (in the narrow sense) had been dissolved they resumed the mutual distant *Sie*.

We have suggested that the modern direction of change in pronoun usage expresses a will to extend the solidary ethic to everyone. The apparent decline of expressive shifts between *T* and *V* is more difficult to interpret. Perhaps it is because Europeans have seen that excluded persons or races or groups can become the target of extreme aggression from groups that are benevolent within themselves. Perhaps Europeans would like to convince themselves that the solidary ethic once extended will not be withdrawn, that there is security in the mutual *T*.

References

BAUGH, A. C. (1935), *A History of the English Language*, New York.

BRUNOT, F. (1927), *La pensée et la langue*, Paris.

BRUNOT, F. (1937), *Histoire de la langue française*, Paris.

BYRNE, SISTER ST G. (1936), 'Shakespeare's use of the pronoun of address', dissertation, Catholic University of America, Washington.

CHÂTELAIN, É. (1880), 'Du pluriel de respect en Latin', *Revue de philologie*, vol. 4, pp. 129–39.

CRONIN, M. (1958), 'The tyranny of democratic manners', *New Republic*, vol. 137, pp. 12–14.

DEVEREUX, W. B. (1853), *Lives and Letters of the Devereux, Earls of Essex, in the Reigns of Elizabeth, James I and Charles I, 1540–1646*, London.

DIEZ, F. (1876), *Grammaire des langues romanes*, Paris.

ELLWOOD, T. (1714), *The History of the Life of Thomas Ellwood*, London.

ESTRICH, R. M., and SPERBER, H. (1946), *Three Keys to Language*, New York.

EYSENCK, H. J. (1957), *Sense and Nonsense in Psychology*, Penguin.

FARNSWORTH, R. (1655), *The Pure Language of the Spirit of Truth ... or 'Thee' and 'Thou' in its Place. ...*, London.

FAY, P. B. (1920), 'The use of "tu" and "vous" in Molière', *University of California Publications in Modern Philology*, vol. 8, pp. 227–86.

FOX, G. (1660), *A Battle-Doore for Teachers and Professors to Learn Plural and Singular*, London.

GEDIKE, F. (1794), *Über Du und Sie in der deutschen Sprache*, Berlin.

GRAND, C. (1930), '*Tu, voi, lei': étude des pronoms allocutoires italiens*, Ingebohl.

GRIMM, J. (1898), *Deutsche Grammatik*, vol. 4, Gütersloh.

HARRISON, G. B. (ed.) (1935), *The Letters of Queen Elizabeth*, London.

JARDINE, D. (1832–5), *Criminal trials*, vols. 1–2, London.

JESPERSEN, O. (1905), *Growth and Structure of the English language*, Leipzig.

JOHNSTON, O. M. (1904), 'The use of "ella," "lei" and "la" as polite forms of address in Italian', *Modern Philology*, vol. 1, pp. 469–75.

KENNEDY, A. G. (1915), *The Pronoun of Address in English Literature of the Thirteenth Century*, Stanford University Press.

LITTRÉ, É. (1882), *Dictionnaire de la langue française*, vol. 4, Paris.

MEYER-LÜBKE, W. (1900), *Grammaire des langues romanes*, vol. 3, Paris.

MULLER, H. F. (1914), 'The uses of the plural of reverence in the letters of Pope Gregory I', *Romanic review*, vol. 5, pp. 68–89.

PERDIGUIER, A. (1914), *Mémoires d'un compagnon*, Moulins.

SCHLIEBITZ, V. (1886), *Die Person der Anrede in der französischen Sprache*, Breslau.

SILVERBERG, W. V. (1940), 'On the psychological significance of "Du" and "Sie"', *Psychoanalytic Quarterly*, vol. 9, pp. 509–25.

STIDSTON, R. O. (1917), *The Use of Ye in the Function of Thou: A Study of Grammar and Social Intercourse in Fourteenth-Century England*, Stanford University Press.

STOUFFER, S. A., GUTTMAN, L., *et al.* (1950), *Measurement and Prediction*, Princeton University Press.

13 W. Labov

The Study of Language in its Social Context

Excerpt from W. Labov, 'The study of language in its social context', *Studium Generale*, vol. 23, 1970, pp. 66–84.

Sociolinguistic structure

We may define a *sociolinguistic variable* as one which is correlated with some non-linguistic variable of the social context: of the speaker, the addressee, the audience, the setting, etc. Some linguistic features (which we will call *indicators*) show a regular distribution over socio-economic, ethnic, or age groups, but are used by each individual in more or less the same way in any context. If the social contexts concerned can be ordered in some kind of hierarchy (like socio-economic or age groups), these indicators can be said to be *stratified*. More highly developed sociolinguistic variables (which we will call *markers*) not only show social distribution over socio-economic, ethnic, or age groups, but are can be ordered along a single dimension according to the amount of attention paid to speech, so that we have *stylistic* as well as *social stratification*. Early studies such as those of Fischer (1958) or Kučera (1961) observed linguistic variables only one dimension at a time, but more recent studies (Labov, 1966; Wolfram, 1969; Anshen, 1969) look at the interrelation of both dimensions.

A stable sociolinguistic marker: (th)

One of the most general and simple sociolinguistic markers in English is (th): the phonetic form of the voiceless interdental fricative $/\theta/$ in *thing*, *thick*, etc. The prestige form is universally the fricative, while affricates and stops are stigmatized. The influence of other languages without this interdental fricative may reinforce the development of the stop form in various large cities of the United States, in Anglo-Irish and in NNE (Non-standard Negro English); but we also find this sociolinguistic variable in a great many other rural and urban areas in England and the United

States. It has apparently had roughly the same status for at least two centuries, and probably more.

There are a number of technical questions in the definition of this variable: the simplest approach is to consider only initial position. In the numerical index to be used here, a stop [t] is counted as 2 points, the affricate [tθ] as 1, and the prestige variant [θ] as 0. Invariant use of the stop form would yield an index score of (th) −200; of the prestige form, (th) −00. Figure 1 shows both stylistic and social stratification of (th) in New York City displayed on one diagram (Labov, 1966, p. 260).

The vertical axis is the (th) index, and the horizontal axis shows

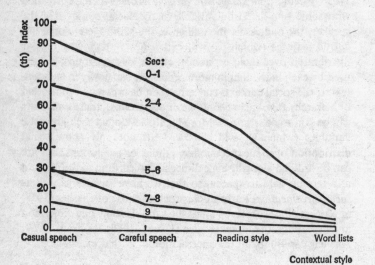

Socio-economic class

0–1   Lower class

2–4   Working class

5–6
7–8   Lower middle class

9   Upper middle class

Figure 1 Stylistic and social stratification of (th) in *thing, three,* etc. in New York City

contextual style, ranging from the most informal on the left to the most formal on the right. On the figure, the average (th) values for five different socio-economic groups are plotted, and scores for each group connected with straight lines. Figure 1 thus shows regular stratification of the (th) variable for each contextual style. This is merely one of many such sociolinguistic structures which might be displayed here; there are a number of common properties which Figure 1 exemplifies:

1. In every context, members of the speech community are differentiated by their use of (th).

2. Yet every group is behaving in the same way, as indicated by the parallel slope of style shifting for (th).

3. Since Figure 1 is not visible as a whole to members, facts (a) and (b) are not part of general knowledge. The portion of Figure 1 visible to any given individual is usually one vertical and one horizontal section: the range of style shifting used by his own group, and the stratified behavior of other groups in the few contexts where he interacts with them. He is not aware that others shift in the same way he does.

4. The same sociolinguistic variable is used to signal social and stylistic stratification. It may therefore be difficult to interpret any signal by itself – to distinguish, for example, a casual salesman from a careful pipefitter.[1]

5. Although it is impossible to predict for any one utterance which variant a speaker will use, the striking regularity of Figure 1 emerges from samples with as few as five individuals in one subgroup, and no more than five or ten utterances in a given style for each individual.

The pattern of Figure 1 shows us the exterior, sociolinguistic controls on the variable rule represented as **1**:

1. This is one of the most striking findings of sociolinguistic research, since essays about social usage, written from 'common-sense' knowledge, have tried to distinguish 'functional varieties' and 'cultural levels' as completely independent dimensions. But their interdependence is shown in this and every other careful empirical study to date. Though it may seem inconvenient to have one variable operate on both dimensions, it seems to be an inevitable result of the sociolinguistic processes involving attention to speech and perception of norms, as outlined below.

$$\begin{bmatrix} + \text{con} \\ - \text{vocs} \end{bmatrix} \rightarrow (\text{[} - \text{cont]}) \: / \begin{bmatrix} - \text{strid} \\ - \text{back} \\ + \text{cor} \end{bmatrix}^2 \qquad \textbf{1}$$

The variable input to this rule may be shown as a function of socio-economic class and style:

$$k_0 = f(SEC, \text{Style}) = a(SEC) + b(\text{Style}) + c \qquad \textbf{2}$$

These general traits hold for a number of sociolinguistic markers which have been studied in the research groups cited. The complete view of social stylistic stratification is not available in most of these studies: some provide data on relatively small sections of Figure 1 and its equivalents, while others cover a wider range. But all of this data can be interpreted in terms of the configuration shown in Figure 1 and fitted into this framework consistently.

The variable (th) is one of a pair which are remarkably similar and parallel. The other member is the voiced interdental fricative (dh) in *this*, *then*, etc., which has been charted in the general study of New York City (Labov, 1966) and in the Negro community (Labov *et al.*, 1968; Anshen, 1969).[3] A very similar stable sociolinguistic pattern appears for unstressed (ing) in *working*,

2. The notation used here differs from that of Chomsky and Halle (1968) only in the use of parentheses around the right hand member to indicate a variable rule. This parenthesis convention provides the automatic interpretation that $\varphi = 1 - k_0$, developed further in (2). The rule may be read as 'Consonants variably lose their continuant or fricative character if they are non-strident and articulated with the forward part of the tongue.' In this form, the rule applies to the voiced counterpart (dh) which shows the same structure, and to all environments. Variable constraints may appear to indicate the difference between (th) and (dh) (as $-\alpha$ tense in the environment shown here) or as variables attached to the preceding or following segments. Our discussion here concerns the variable input k_0, and such details are left unspecified.

3. The (dh) variable (in initial position) is more regular in the Negro community than (th). Final (th) is realized as [f] more often than as [t], though initially it is not realized as [f] in the Cockney pattern. It should be noted that (th) and (dh) are examples of inherent variation by the same criteria as used in section 2 [which has not been reprinted in this volume] in particular, we note the absence of hypercorrection, even though the phonetic forms overlap with /t/ and /d/ in some cases. See Wolfram (1969, pp. 100ff.) for a detailed analysis of the (th) variants.

nothing, etc. Almost universally, the (ɪn) variant is considered non-standard, and the sociolinguistic structure duplicates Figure 1 (Labov, 1966, p. 398). Confirming data appears in Fischer (1958) and Anshen (1969). Such stigmatized variables as negative concord and pronominal apposition have been studied by Shuy, Wolfram and Riley (1967), for Detroit. Ma and Herasimchuk examined style shifting of a number of Puerto Rican variables: final (S); (R), the neutralization of *r* and *l*; (R R), alternation of [r:] and [γ]; and (D), the deletion of intervocalic [d].

Figure 1 also has some features that are not shared by all sociolinguistic variables. One can observe a sharp break between the working-class groups and the middle-class groups – a pattern which I have termed 'sharp' stratification (see also Wolfram, 1969, p. 147). There is very little overlap between the working-class treatment of (th) and the middle-class values, while that is not the case for many other variables (see Figure 2 below). In a stable sociolinguistic marker, this may reflect discontinuities in the over-all pattern of socio-economic stratification in the society.

Men versus women

There is another aspect to the social stratification of (th) which is not shown on Figure 1. In careful speech, women use fewer stigmatized forms than men (Labov, 1966, p. 288), and are more sensitive than men to the prestige pattern. They show this in a sharper slope of style shifting, especially at the more formal end of the spectrum. This observation is confirmed innumerable times, in Fischer (1958), throughout Shuy and Fasold's work in Detroit, in Levine and Crockett, and in Anshen's study of Hillsboro. The pattern is particularly marked in lower middle-class women, who show the most extreme form of this behavior. There is some question as to whether lower-class women are also more sensitive to social of speech: the evidence is not clear here.

The hypercorrect pattern of the lower middle class

One of the most solidly established phenomena of sociolinguistic behavior is that the second-highest status group shows the most extreme style shifting, going beyond that of the highest status group in this respect. To see this most clearly, it is necessary to examine the sociolinguistic structure of a change in progress.

Figure 2 shows the pattern for final and pre-consonantal (r) in New York City (Labov, 1966, p. 240). This community has a basically r-less vernacular, but shortly after the end of World War II, r-pronunciation became the prestige norm (as to a lesser extent in other r-less areas of the United States). The vertical axis is the (r) index – the percentage of constricted [r] in words like ear, where, car, board, etc.[4] Higher scores reflect greater use of prestige form [r]. Note the sharp cross-over of the lower middle class group in the two most formal styles. This pattern recurs in several other variables from New York City. One of the most striking instances of quantitative convergence is supplied by Levine and Crockett's study (1966), as shown in Table 1.

Here data from a completely independent study with a more limited stylistic range shows the same cross-over phenomenon. The second highest status group – in this case, high school graduates – show a much greater shift towards the prestige norm in their more formal style. The significance of this pattern for the mechanism of linguistic change has been dealt with specifically in Labov

4. This variable does not include r following the mid-central vowel of her, heard, etc., which follows a different pattern with either a palatal up-glide or more constriction.

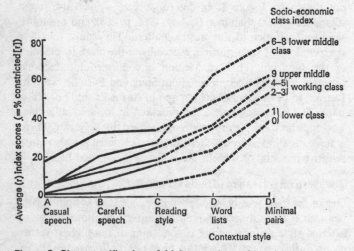

Figure 2 Class stratification of (r) in *guard, car, beer, beard*, etc. for native New York City adults

Table 1 R Scores by Sentence and Word-List and by Education and Sex in Hillsboro, North Carolina

	Sentence-list	Word-list	Net increase
Education			
Any college	52·7	58·9	6·2
High school graduate	54·6	65·6	11·0
Some high school	50·0	57·0	7·0
Grade school or none	52·6	57·3	4·7
Sex			
Male	52·3	57·4	5·1
Female	52·9	61·1	8·2

Source: Levine and Crockett, 1966, p. 223.

(1965). Here it will be helpful to see what formal simplification can be achieved for this complex pattern, abstractly:

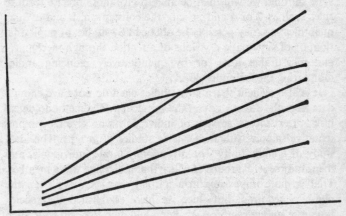

Figure 3

The slope of style shifting is very complex. The highest and lowest group have the shallowest slope. The interior groups follow behind the lead of the second highest group, which is the steepest. How can this be formalized? The rule for the vocalization of (r) in the white community has the general form:

$$[+ \text{cen}] \rightarrow ([- \text{cons}]) \, / \, [- \text{cons}] \, \underline{\quad\quad} \sim V^5.$$

The problem here is to write a formula for the basic constraint on the input variable k_0 comparable to the simple and straightforward **2**. The solution lies in an understanding of the significance of style shifting; it is governed by the recognition of an exterior standard of correctness. The strength of such behavior can be measured by an index of Linguistic Insecurity which gives us precisely the curvilinear pattern we need to describe the slope of style shifting in Figure 2, with the lower middle class at a maximum (Labov, 1966, p. 477). We can then write for **3**

$$k_0 = f(\text{Class, Style}) = a(SEC) + b(ILI)(\text{Style}) + c \qquad \textbf{4}$$

Problems of sociolinguistic structure

Perhaps the most immediate problem to be solved in the attack on sociolinguistic structure is the quantification of the dimension of style. If quantitative studies of attention can be related to style shifting, we will then be able to give more precise form to rules such as **2** or **4** and specify the constants a, b and c. Such quantification may possibly be obtained by studies of pupil dilation, or of systematic divisions of attention through mechanical and measurable tests, or by quantitatively reducing audio-monitoring through noise level.

It is also evident that many studies cited do not have enough data from the direct study of the vernacular. The methodological task is to combine surveys of individuals who give us a representative sample with longer-term studies of groups. The ideal study of a community would randomly locate individuals, and then study several groups of which that individual was a member. That is quite impossible in a normal social survey, given the numbers required, but since we have established that sociolinguistic studies require a smaller population to begin with, such a model is not beyond the realm of possibility.

A third problem lies in dealing with rules which show irregular lexical distribution. There is now good evidence that the course

5. This rule is the formal equivalent of 'A central consonant (r) variably loses its consonantal character after a vowel or glide if a vowel does not follow directly.' If a word boundary follows directly, and then a vowel, this rule is constrained so that [r] appears more often in *four o'clock*.

of linguistic change involves the temporary dissolution of word classes.[6] The most difficult problem here is that there are distributions across word classes which we would want to describe, but which are not likely to be a part of the knowledge of the native speaker. For example, only a certain proportion of English verbs with Latinate prefixes show a shift of stress when they appear as nouns like *convict* [V]: *cónvict* [N]; others retain end stress, like *consént* [V]: *consént* [N]. It can be shown that the proportion of words in any given sub-class is related to the length of the prefix, but this regularity is of no use to the native speaker since most words have a fixed accent. As another example, the tensing rule for short *a* in New York City does not normally operate in _C V environments, though there are a number of exceptions. The linguist is interested to discover that most of these exceptions have a sibilant as the medial consonant C. But in such cases, the native speaker again only needs to know in what class a given word falls. The proportion of the original word class which has been affected by the incoming rule is of no immediate interest to him if he has no choice in the pronunciation of any given item. It may be that we will enter rules into our grammar which are *not* a part of the 'knowledge' of native speakers. This particular metaphor may have lost its value at this point in our investigations.

A fourth major challenge is to enter more deeply into the study of higher level syntactic variables, such as extraposition, nominalization, placement of complementizers, negative raising, wh-attachment or relativization. The two chief stumbling blocks to investigating these features in their social context is the low frequency of occurrence of the critical sub-cases, and the lack of certainty in our abstract analyses. But some beginning has been

6. Although Figure 1 and 2 show word classes moving as a whole, we have encountered some rules which show a great deal of irregular lexical variation. The tensing of short /a/ in *bad*, *ask*, etc., now being investigated in New York City by Paul Cohen, shows such irregularity, while the raising rule which follows the tensing rule does not (Labov, 1966, pp. 51-2). It is the existence of a variable rule which allows the word class to be reconstituted when the change is completed, since it is defined as the class of lexical items which can vary between X and Y, as opposed to the classes which are always X or always Y. For some structural causes of such lexical variation, see Wang (1969).

made in our recent work in urban ghetto areas, and the challenges to work with more abstract matters cannot be ignored.

The fifth problem is to enlarge the scope of these studies beyond individual speech communities, and relate them to larger grammars of the English speech community as a whole. The work of C. J. Bailey is most challenging here: particularly his penetrating studies of phonological rules in Southern dialects (1969b), and his broader attempts to incorporate all English phonology into a single, pan-dialectal set of rules (1969a). Though these studies of Bailey are not based upon the study of language in context, one must eventually hope to provide reliable data to support work of this generality and this level of abstraction.

The relation of norms to behavior

So far, in our consideration of sociolinguistic structure, we have taken into account only what people say, and only incidentally what they think they *should* say. These are the 'secondary responses' to language that Bloomfield suggested that we might well observe (1944) as one part of popular lore. There is a very small vocabulary available to most people for talking about language: the same few terms recur over and over as we hear that the other people's pronunciation has a 'nasal twang', is 'sing-song', is 'harsh' or 'guttural', 'lazy' or 'sloppy'. Grammar is said to be 'mixed-up' or 'illogical'.

A small number of sociolinguistic markers rise to overt social consciousness, and become *stereotypes*. There may or may not be a fixed relation between such stereotypes and actual usage. The variables (ing) and (dh) are such stereotypes in the United States: someone may be said to 'drop his g's' or to be one of those 'dese, dem and dose guys'. Most communities have local stereotypes, such as 'Brooklynese' in New York City which focuses on 'thoity-thoid' for *thirty-third*; in Boston, the fronted broad *a* in 'cah' and 'pahk' receives a great deal of attention. Speakers of the isolated Cape Hatteras (North Carolina) dialect are known as 'hoi toiders' because of the backing and rounding of the nucleus in *high*, *tide*, etc.

Such social stereotypes yield a sketchy and unsystematic view of linguistic structure to say the least. In general, we can assert that overt *social correction* of speech is extremely irregular, focusing on the most frequent lexical items, while the actual course of linguistic evolution, which has produced the marked form of these variables, is highly systematic. This is the basic reason why the vernacular, in which minimum attention is paid to speech, gives us the most systematic view of linguistic structure. For example, the evolution of the New York City vernacular has led to the raising of the vowel in *off*, *lost*, *shore*, *more*, etc., until it has merged with the vowel of *sure* and *moor*. This high vowel has been stigmatized, and is now being corrected irregularly by middle-class speakers. But the same vowel, raised simultaneously in the nucleus of *boy*, *toy*, etc., is never corrected.[7]

But subjective reactions to speech are not confined to the few stereotypes that have risen to social consciousness. Unconscious social judgments about language can be measured by techniques such as Lambert's 'matched guise' test. One basic principle emerges: that *social attitudes towards language are extremely uniform throughout a speech community*.[8] Lambert's studies show, for example, that the negative attitude towards Canadian French is not only quite uniform in the English-speaking community, but almost as unanimously held among French speakers in Quebec (1967). In our study of unconscious subjective reactions to markers such as (r), we find the most extraordinary unanimity in speakers' reactions, despite the great variation in the use of [r] just described. There is a general axiom of sociolinguistic structure which can be stated as: *the correlate of regular stratification of a sociolinguistic variable in behavior is uniform agreement in subjective reactions towards that variable*. This may be illustrated by Figure 4, which compares behavior and subjective

7. We also find that the vowels of *my* and *mouth* are affected by the rotation of the long and ingliding vowels of *bad*, *bar*, *lost*. As *bar* moves to the back, *my* moves with it, and *mouth* moves in the opposite direction towards the front. But of all these systematically interrelated changes, only the raising of *bad* and *lost* shows style shifting and correction. Even for these cases, the correction is lexically irregular.

8. In fact, it seems plausible to define a speech community as a group of speakers who share a set of social attitudes towards language. In New York City, those raised out of town in their formative years show none of the regular pattern of subjective reactions characteristic of natives where a New York City variable such as the vowel of *lost* is concerned (Labov, 1966, p. 651).

reactions for (r) in New York City. Figure 4a shows the development of stratification of (r) in the vernacular for young adults. For those over 40, there is no particular connection between social class and the use of (r), but for those under 40, there is a striking difference between upper middle class and other groups. Figure 4b shows the normative correlate. For those over 40 responses to the subjective reaction test for (r) are close to the random level. But for those between 18 and 39, there is complete unanimity: 42 out of 42 subjects showed responses that unconsciously registered the prestige status of *r*-pronunciation.

As we re-examine the structures shown in Figures 1 and 2, it is

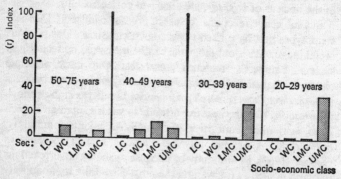

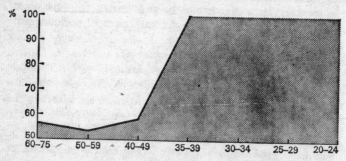

Figure 4 (a) Social stratification of (r) in *car, board*, etc. for four age levels in casual speech: New York City (Labov, 1966 p.344) (b) Per cent showing (r) — positive response on subjective reaction test by age level (two choice test): New York City (Labov 1966 p.435).

apparent that the uniform slope of style shifting also reflects the uniform attitudes held in the community. But for a stable socio-linguistic marker like (th), we can raise the question, what maintains this structure for such a long period of time? Why don't all people speak in the way that they obviously believe they should? The usual response is to cite laziness, lack of concern, or isolation from the prestige norm. But there is no foundation for the notion that stigmatized vernacular forms are easier to pronounce;[9] and there is strong evidence of concern with speech in large cities. Careful consideration of this difficult problem has led us to posit the existence of an opposing set of covert norms, which attribute positive values to the vernacular. In most formal situations in urban areas, such as an interview or a psycholinguistic test, these norms are extremely difficult to elicit. Middle-class values are so dominant in these contexts that most subjects cannot perceive any opposing values, no matter how strongly they may influence behavior in other situations. In our recent work in the Negro community, we have been able to uncover evidence of the existence of such opposing norms. Figure 5 shows responses to the first two items on our subjective reaction test, opposing a working-class speaker to a middle-class speaker on 'zero' sentences (which contain none of the variables to be tested). The upper line shows the percent of those who rated the middle-class speaker higher on the scale of 'job-suitability'. It begins very high with middle-class subjects and falls off slightly as we move to lower socio-economic groups. The lower line is the converse: this registers reactions to the 'fight' or 'toughness' scale: 'If the speaker was in a street fight, how likely would he be to come out on top?' There is a simple inverse relationship here: a stereotype that is probably reinforced by school teachers but also shows some recognition of social reality. But the third set of reactions to the 'friendship scale' shows that there is more involved. This

9. Some of the extreme developments of vernacular vowel shifts in New York City, Detroit or Chicago are tense vowels which seem to involve a great deal of muscular effort compared to the standard. Spectrographic analysis indicates that such vowels as short /a/ rising to the height of *here* are extremely fronted. An interesting correlate of such extreme movements is the pattern of subjective reaction tests which shows that those who use the highest percentage of stigmatized forms are quickest to stigmatize them in the speech of others.

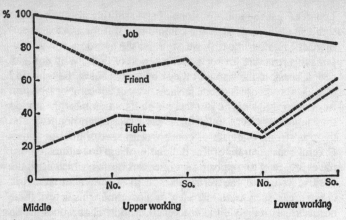

Figure 5 Per cent rating a middle-class speaker higher than a working-class speaker on three scales for five social groups (Labov *et al*, 1968, p.242)

scale is in response to the question 'If you knew the speaker for a long time, how likely would he be to become a good friend of yours?' For the three upper social groups, this follows the job scale closely; but for the lower working class, it switches abruptly, and follows the fight scale. The same phenomenon can be observed for a whole range of variables tested (Labov *et al.*, 1968, section 3.6).

We have therefore some empirical support in positing the opposition between two sets of values as the normative correlate of stable sociolinguistic markers such as (th) and (ing). In this type of study, we agree with Homans (1955) that the proper object of study should not be behavior alone, or norms alone, but rather the extent to which (and the rules by which) people deviate from the explicit norms which they hold. It is at this level of abstraction that we can best develop linguistic and sociolinguistic theory.

The role of social factors in linguistic evolution

Although this discussion is not primarily concerned with the problems of language change, I have already introduced some data which bears on this question. In speaking of the role of social factors influencing linguistic evolution, it is important not to overestimate the amount of contact or overlap between social values and the structure of language. Linguistic and social structure are by no means co-extensive. The great majority of linguistic rules are quite remote from any social value; they are part of the elaborate machinery which the speaker needs to translate his complex set of meanings or intentions into linear form.

Variables closer to surface structure frequently are the focus of social affect. In fact, social values are attributed to linguistic rules only when there is variation. Speakers do not readily accept the fact that two different expressions actually 'mean the same' and there is a strong tendency to attribute different meanings to them.[10] If a certain group of speakers uses a particular variant, then the social values attributed to that group will be transferred to that linguistic variant. Sturtevant (1947) has proposed a general model of linguistic change showing the opposition of two forms, each favored by a particular social group. When the issue is resolved, and one form becomes universal, the social value attached to it disappears.

We may think of social meaning as parasitic upon language. Given a uniform set of linguistic rules used to express certain meanings, language may be considered as a neutral instrument. But in the course of change, there are inevitably variable rules, and these areas of variability tend to travel through the system in a wave-like motion. The leading edge of a particular linguistic change is usually within a single group, and with successive generations the newer form moves out in wider circles to other groups. In New York City, the leading edge in the raising of short *a* is to be found among Italian working-class women, and the raising of open *o* in *off*, *lost*, etc., is most advanced among Jewish lower middle class women (Labov, 1966). Fasold's observations of the raising of short *a* in Detroit again show that lower middle class women play a leading role. Linguistic *indicators* which show social distribution but no style shifting represent

10. When New York City *cruller* (Dutch *kroeller*) was replaced by the standard term *doughnut*, the term *cruller* was variously assigned to other forms of pastry. Similarly the local *pot cheese* (Dutch *pot kees*) was replaced by *cottage cheese* and was differentiated to indicate a drier form. The oscillation of socially marked pronunciations of *vase* led one informant to say, 'These small ones are my [vezɪz] but these big ones are my [vazɪz].'

early stages of this process. *Markers* which show both stylistic and social stratification represent the development of social reaction to the change and the attribution of social value to the variants concerned. *Stereotypes*, which have risen to full social consciousness, may be based on older changes which may in fact have gone to completion; or they may actually represent stable oppositions of linguistic forms supported by two opposing sets of underlying social values.

Many of the individual sociolinguistic variables are members of a complex network of linguistic relations, and as change spreads slowly throughout this system (Labov, 1965), there is a gradual shift of social values. Generally speaking, it seems to take about thirty years for a change in one part of a system (as in a front vowel) to be generalized fully to a parallel member (like a back vowel). But social structures are seldom stable over such a period of time. For example, in Martha's Vineyard we see the gradual raising of the nucleus of the diphthong in *nice*, *right*, *side*, etc., among Yankee fishermen (Labov, 1963). This sound change was generalized to the corresponding diphthong in *out*, *proud*, etc. But in the interval, a large number of second and third generation Portuguese-Americans entered into the speech community, and for various reasons we find they favor the raising of the second vowel much more than the first, moving the whole process to higher levels. Thus succeeding generations re-interpret the on-going course of a linguistic change in terms of a changing social structure. It is the oscillation between the internal process of structural generalization, and interaction with the external social system, which provides the impetus for continuous linguistic evolution (Labov, 1965).

As far as the synchronic aspect of language structure is concerned, it would be an error to put too much emphasis on social factors. Generative grammar has made great progress in working out the invariant relations within this structure, even though it wholly neglects the social context of language. But it now seems clear that one cannot make any major advance towards understanding the mechanism of linguistic change without serious study of the social factors which motivate linguistic evolution.

Some invariant rules of discourse analysis

This presentation has so far concentrated almost entirely upon the variable rules of language: their use in providing decisive evidence on questions of linguistic structure, their place in socio-linguistic structure, and more briefly, with their role in the evolution of language. But a very great number of linguistic rules are not variable in the least: they are categorical rules which, given the proper input, always apply. More than any other field concerned with human behavior, linguistics has succeeded in isolating the invariant structures underlying the surface phenomena, and it is upon this achievement that we have been building in the work outlined above.[11] The formal representation of variable rules presented there depend upon, and interlock with, a number of invariant rules of grammar derived from studies of language quite apart from any social context.

There are some areas of linguistic analysis in which even the first steps towards the basic, invariant rules cannot be taken unless the social context of the speech event is considered. The most striking examples are in the analysis of discourse. The fundamental problem of discourse analysis is to show how one utterance follows another in a rational, rule-governed manner – in other words, how we understand coherent discourse. We rely upon our intuitions to distinguish coherent from incoherent discourse; for example, the following is plainly not governed by any rules that we can immediately recognize.

A: What is your name?
B: Well, let's say you might have thought you had
something from before, but you haven't got it any more.
A: I'm going to call you Dean.   5
(from Laffal, 1965, p. 85)

This is an excerpt from a conversation between a doctor and a schizophrenic patient. Our first data in dealing with such a passage

11. It is Lévi-Strauss who testifies most eloquently to the advantage of linguistics over other social sciences in its grasp of invariant relations (1963, pp. 31 ff.). The invariant rules we speak of here play the same role as the 'structural relations' which Lévi-Strauss admires in the work of Troubetzkoy and Jakobson. One hopes that anthropology will be able to absorb the advantages of that linguistic approach without its limitations.

will be our intuitive reactions to it, and the first challenge in discourse analysis is to account for our intuitions (as confirmed by the response of participants as in 5). The question is: how much and what kind of data do we need in order to form sound judgments and interpret sequences of utterances as the participants in the conversation do? The simplest case is that of elliptical responses, as in 6.

A: Are you going to work tomorrow?
B: Yes.   6

Here our normal knowledge of English syntax is sufficient to allow us to derive's B's utterance from *Yes, I am going to work tomorrow*. There is a simple rule of discourse of the following form:

If A utters a question of the form $Q-S_1$, and B responds
with an existential E (including *yes, no, probably, maybe*,
etc.), then B is heard as answering A with the statement $E-S_1$. 7

But now let us consider sequences of the following form:

A: She never helps at home.
B: Yes.   8

A: She told you what we are interested in.
B: Yes.   9

A: You live on 115th St.
B: No. I live on 116th.   10

We encounter many such examples in our analyses of therapeutic interviews and in every-day speech. Rule (7) obviously does not apply; there is no Q–S, in the A form. Is it true that any statement can be followed with a *yes* or *no*? The following sequences seem to indicate the opposite.

A: I don't like the way you said that.
B: *Yes.   11

A: I feel hot today.
B: *No.   12

It is not only that 11–12 do not require or tolerate a *yes* or *no* answer, but even more strikingly that statements like 7–10 seem to *demand* such a response. We find many cases where speakers will not let the conversation continue unless a *yes* or *no* answer is given to such statements. The rule which operates here is one of the simplest invariant rules of discourse. Given two parties in a conversation, A and B, we can distinguish as 'A-events' the things that A knows about but B does not; as 'B-events' the things which B knows but A does not; and as 'AB-events' knowledge which is shared equally by A and B. The rule then states:

If A makes a statement about a B-event, it is heard as a request for confirmation. **13**

Note that in **11–12**, A is making a statement about an A-event, but in **8–10** about a B-event. Anyone can immediately test this rule in an ordinary conversation and observe the force of its operation. This rule contains the social construct of 'shared knowledge' which is not normally part of a linguistic rule. This is merely one of many rules of interpretation which relate 'what is said' – questions, statements, imperatives – to 'what is done' – requests, refusals, assertions, denials, insults, challenges, retreats, and so on. There are no simple one-to-one relations between actions and utterances; rules of interpretation (and their nearly symmetrical rules of production) are extremely complex and relate several hierarchical levels of 'actions' to each other and to utterances. Sequencing rules do not operate between utterances, but between the notions performed with those utterances. In fact, there is usually no connection between successive utterances at all. The over-all pattern of discourse analysis may be sketched as:

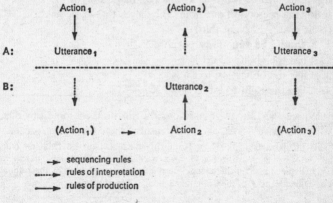

↦ sequencing rules
┅┅► rules of intepretation
──► rules of production

It may be helpful to consider a more difficult case, drawn from a therapeutic interview we have been investigating in some detail.[12]

A: Well, when do you plan to come home?
B: Oh why-y?   **14**

There is no syntactic connection between these two questions and no amount of abstract analysis will relate them correctly. One cannot interpret B as Q–S$_1$: 'Why do I plan to come home?' One might interpret B as addressed to an implicit underlying form, A: [I ask you] when do you ... B: Why [do you ask me. ...]? But this would be a wrong interpretation; without detailed knowledge of the speakers and the situation, one could not hope to arrive at the appropriate intuitive judgments to begin analyzing. We must be aware that A is a college student, and that B is her mother; that B has been away for four days helping a married daughter; that A and B both know that A wants B to come home; and that B has said many times in the past that A cannot take care of herself, which A denies. It is then clear that 14–A is a request for action, not for information: A is requesting that her mother come home.

There is a general rule for interpreting any utterance as a request for action (or command) which reads as follows:

If A requests B to perform an action X at a time T, A's utterance will be heard as a valid command only if the following pre-conditions hold: B believes that A believes (= it is an AB–event that)   **15**
1. X should be done for a purpose Y
2. B has the ability to do X
3. B has the obligation to do X
4. A has the right to tell B to do X.

Where the four pre-conditions do not hold in some obvious way, we have jokes or joking insults such as: 'Drop dead!' 'Go jump in the lake!' or 'Get this dissertation finished by the

12. From studies of therapeutic interviews being conducted by the author and David Fanshel of the Columbia School of Social Work.

time I get back from lunch!'[13] These preconditions appear in almost every rule of interpretation and production which concerns making or responding to commands. Note that the primitive terms of **15** include *rights* and *obligations* which are plainly social constructs. Given rule **15**, there is a rule of interpretation operating for B in responding to A's question in **14**.

If A makes a request for information of B about whether an action X has been performed, or at what time T X will be performed, and the four pre-conditions of **15** hold, then A will be heard as making an underlying form *B: do X*!   **16**

B's response 'Oh, why?' is then aimed not at the surface request for information, but rather at the pre-condition 1 of the more abstract request for action: 'Why are you asking me to come home?' By asking a question about pre-condition 1, B puts off A's request: since if any of the pre-conditions are not shared knowledge, the request is obviously not valid by rule **15**. A's next move in this discourse is to respond to B's request for information: she explains that the housework and her studies are altogether too much for her to do. Thus the content of A's response shows that she interprets B's question as we do here.

We now find intuitively that the original request of **14** is still in force, under the operation of a further invariant rule which states generally that

If A has made a request, and B responds with a request for information, A re-instates the original request by supplying that information.   **17**

Since the original request is put again, B must now respond a second time. This time B puts off the request by asking another question involving pre-condition 2 – by implying that Helen is the person who should have been asked, she indicates that she herself should not have been asked, implying that she (B) does not have the ability to comply with the requestion from A.

13. Harvey Sacks has pointed out that the first decision to be made in the interpretation of any utterance is whether it is serious or not (or we might say, the degree of seriousness involved). Appropriate reactions to jokes are limited, and almost independent of context, but if the utterance is serious more complex rules must be invoked. Rule **15** shows us one formal basis for this decision.

A: Well, things are getting just a little too much. [laugh] This is – it's just getting too hard . . .

B: Well, why don't you tell Helen that? **18**

It is obvious that the complexities of the situation do not end here. These illustrations of discourse rules should serve to show the form of such rules and the kind of primitive elements which they require. Although this exposition is based upon several years of analysis of therapeutic interviews and other speech events, it is not put forward with the same confidence as the solutions to the problems studied above. On the contrary, discourse analysis is at a much more primitive stage, analogous to the earliest developments in syntax and morphology. It is a matter of some interest that the most significant advances in this field have not been made by linguists, but by sociologists. The work of Sacks (1972) and Schegloff (1968) has located many fundamental questions concerning the selection of speakers and the identification of persons, and isolated a number of sequencing rules. Linguists have been handicapped in their approach to this field by their inability to utilize essential social constructs involving the roles of speaker and listener, obligations, power relationships, membership categories, and the like.

It should be evident that the approach to the study of language in its social context outlined in the previous sections of this paper, can easily accommodate the full range of elements which we need for discourse rules. The linguistic approach can contribute a number of concepts which are not well developed in anthropology or sociology. First there is the distinction between utterances and actions, and the hierarchical relations of actions whereby a question may be seen as a request for information, which is in turn interpreted as a request for action, which may appear on a higher level as a challenge. Further advancement of this field may depend upon the linguistic concept of an invariant rule, and the linguistic approach to the formalization of such rules.

Eventually, the exploration of discourse rules will reach a quantitative phase in which variable rules may be constructed and in which large bodies of data can be introduced to confirm or reject the tentative rules we have written. One area which plainly involves variable rules is in the degree of mitigation or aggravation which governs the selection of rules for making requests. We observe that in **14** the daughter *must* mitigate her request; to say to her mother 'Come home right now!' would be violating a strong social constraint, although a mother can easily say this to her daughter. The exact degree of mitigation, and the way in which the request is executed involve a number of variables: age, socio-economic class, relative status of speaker and listener, and the form of the preceding utterance. Such variable constraints will eventually appear in rules comparable to those written in the previous sections. But our present knowledge is too fragmentary to make such attempts fruitful.[14] Quantitative research implies that one knows what to count, and this knowledge is reached only through a long period of trial and approximation, and upon the basis of a solid body of theoretical constructs. By the time the analyst knows what to count, the problem is practically solved.

In recent years, there have been many attempts by social psychologists to characterize differences in the use of language by middle class and working class speakers (Bernstein, 1964; Lawton, 1968). There is little connection between the general statements made and the quantitative data offered on the use of language. It is said that middle class speakers show more verbal planning, more abstract arguments, more objective viewpoint, show more logical connections, and so on. But one does not uncover the logical complexity of a body of speech by counting the number of subordinate clauses. The cognitive style of a speaker has no fixed relation to the number of unusual adjectives or conjunctions that he uses. As the example given above shows, no useful purpose would be served by counting the number of questions that someone asks in an interview. The relation of argument and discourse to language is much more abstract than this, and such superficial indices can be quite deceptive. When we can say *what* is being done with a sentence, then we will be able to observe how often speakers do it [. . .]

14. The most thorough examination of a speech event which we have carried out so far is the analysis of ritual insults in the Negro community (Labov *et al.*, 1968 section 4.3; Labov, (1972). Although the discourse rules given there seem to be sound, we do not have the means of corroboration which are available in our studies of linguistic structure.

References

ANSHEN, F. (1969), 'Speech Variation among Negroes in a small southern community', unpublished New York University dissertation.

BAILEY, C.-J. N. (1969a), 'The integration of linguistic theory: internal reconstruction and the comparative method in descriptive linguistics, with an appendix of 107 pan-dialectal ordered rules', paper given before Conference on historical linguistics in the light of generative theory, Los Angeles.

BAILEY, C.-J. N. (1969b), 'Introduction to southern States phonetics', University of Hawaii working papers in linguistics, 4–5.

BERNSTEIN, B. (1964), 'Elaborated and restricted codes', in J. J. Gumperz and D. Hymes (eds.) *The Ethnography of Communication*, American Anthropologist, vol. 66, no. 6. Part 2, 1964, pp. 55–69.

BLOOMFIELD, L. (1944), 'Secondary and tertiary responses to language', *Language*, vol. 20, pp. 45–55.

CHOMSKY, N., and HALLE, M. (1968), *The Sound Pattern of English*, Harper and Row.

FISCHER, J. L. (1958), 'Social influence on the choice of a linguistic variant', *Word*, vol. 14, pp. 47–56.

HOMANS, G. C. (1955), *The Human Group*, Harcourt, Brace, Jovanovich.

KUČERA, H. (1961), *The Phonology of Czech*, Mouton.

LABOV, W. (1963), 'The social motivation of a sound change', *Word*, vol. 19, pp. 273–309.

LABOV, W. (1965), 'On the mechanism of linguistic change', Georgetown University monograph no. 18, *Language and Linguistics*, Washington D.C., Georgetown University.

LABOV, W. (1966), *The Social Stratification of English in New York City*, Washington D.C., Center for Applied Linguistics.

LABOV, W. (1972), 'Rules for ritual insults', in D. Sudnow (ed.), *Studies in Social Interaction*, Macmillan.

LABOV, W., COHEN, P., ROBINS, C., and LEWIS, J. (1968), *A study of the non-standard English of Negro and Puerto Rican speakers in New York City*, Final Report Cooperative Research Project 3288, vols 1 and 2, Washington D.C.: Office of Education.

LAFFAL, J. (1965), *Pathological and Normal Language*, Atherton Press.

LAMBERT, W. E. (1967), 'A social psychology of bilingualism', in V. Macnamara (ed.), *Problems of Bilingualism*, The Journal of Social Issues, vol. 23, pp. 91–109.

LAWTON, D. (1968), *Social Class, Language and Education*, London, Routledge and Kegan Paul.

LEVINE, L., and CROCKETT, H. J. Jr (1966), 'Speech variation in a Piedmont community: postvocalic r.', in S. Lieberson (ed.), 'Explorations in sociolinguistics', *Sociological Enquiry*, vol. 36, no. 2. Reprinted as Publication 44, International Journal of American Linguistics, 1966, pp. 91–109.

LÉVI-STRAUSS, C. (1963), *Structural Anthropology*, tr. C. Jacobson and B. Schoepf, Basic Books.

SACKS, H. (1972), 'An initial investigation into the usability of conversational data for doing sociology', in D. Sudnow (ed.), *Studies in Social Interaction*, Macmillan.

SCHEGLOFF, E. (1968), 'Sequencing in conversational openings', *Amer. Anthrop.*, vol. 70, pp. 1075–95.

SHUY, R., WOLFRAM, W., and RILEY, W. K. (1967), *A study of social dialects in Detroit*, Final Report, Project 6-1347, Washington D.C.: Office of Education.

STURTEVANT, E. (1947), *An Introduction to Linguistic Science*, Yale University Press.

WANG, W. S.-Y. (1969), 'Competing changes as a cause of residue', *Language*, vol. 45, pp. 9–25.

WOLFRAM, W. (1969), 'Linguistic correlates of social stratification in the speech of Detroit Negroes', Hartford Seminary Foundation Thesis.

Part Five
Language, Social Change and Social Conflict

Language is not only a good indicator of social change
(cf. Brown and Gilman's paper in Part Four), but also an
important cause of it. Language is a determining factor in two
of the most important moments in social and cultural
evolution: first, the origin of language coincides with that of
society, since a system of linguistic communication is a
necessary prerequisite for the existence of a human group;
second, written language may be considered the watershed in
the passage from primitive to intermediary societies (Parsons,
1966). The first selection in Part Five is dedicated to the
illustration of this latter point. Goody and Watt's paper starts
by sketching the characteristics of cultural transmission in
illiterate societies, where the lack of distinction between myth
and history due to the absence of written records fosters a
'homeostatic tendency' which disregards or modifies those
aspects of the past which are no longer functional for the
present. Then the authors discuss how the invention of writing
breaks down this cultural equilibrium, examining the case of
Greece, the country in which literacy first became widespread
among male citizens. The third part of the paper outlines the
cultural features of modern societies and relates them to the
impact of diffused literacy. Like every ideal-typical model,
Goody and Watt's paper is a conscious attempt to analyse a
very general problem (the contrast between two social and
cultural types) from a very particular viewpoint. In this sense,
it provides more a framework for further investigations[1] than
definitive answers, and its title, as Goody himself has
recognized (Goody, 1968, p. 4), would perhaps read more

1. Discussions on or generated by Goody and Watt's paper have been
collected in a volume edited by Goody (1968).

appropriately 'the implications' rather than 'the consequences' of literacy.

The second paper in Part Five explores the connections between language diversity and political conflicts. The identity of homogeneous language groups and nationalities is quite an old thesis, forcefully restated in the past century by German Romanticism and Idealism and very influential even today. In their article, Inglehart and Woodward study from a comparative point of view the conditions under which language cleavages are 'translated' into conflicts which may threaten the stability of the political community. They find that language differences become politically disruptive only when (a) social mobility is a normal expectation of most citizens and (b) it is blocked because of membership in a certain language group. These conclusions are particularly relevant for emerging countries affected by language differences, where 'literacy in the elite language is probably the most important cultural characteristic determining the shape of the stratification system' (Stinchcombe, 1968) and social mobilization creates diffuse expectations for social mobility.

References

GOODY, J. (ed.) (1968), *Literacy in Traditional Societies*, Cambridge University Press.

PARSONS, T. (1966), *Societies: Evolutionary and Comparative Perspectives*, Prentice-Hall.

STINCHCOMBE, A. (1968), 'The Structure of Stratification Systems', *International Encyclopedia of the Social Sciences*, Macmillan and Free Press, vol. 15, p. 327.

14 J. Goody and I. Watt

The Consequences of Literacy

Excerpts from J. Goody and I. Watt, 'The Consequences of Literacy',
Comparative Studies in Society and History, vol. 5, 1962–3, pp. 304–26,
332–45.

The accepted tripartite divisions of the formal study both of
mankind's past and present are to a considerable extent based on
man's development first of language and later of writing. Looked
at in the perspective of time, man's biological evolution shades
into prehistory when he becomes a language-using animal; add
writing, and history proper begins. Looked at in a temporal
perspective, man as animal is studied primarily by the zoologist,
man as talking animal primarily by the anthropologist, and man
as talking and writing animal primarily by the sociologist.

That the differentiation between these categories should be
founded on different modes of communication is clearly appropriate; it was language that enabled man to achieve a form of
social organization whose range and complexity was different
in kind from that of animals: whereas the social organization of
animals was mainly instinctive and genetically transmitted, that
of man was largely learned and transmitted verbally through the
cultural heritage. The basis for the last two distinctions, those
based on the development of writing, is equally clear: to the
extent that a significant quantity of written records are available
the prehistorian yields to the historian; and to the extent that
alphabetical writing and popular literacy imply new modes of
social organization and transmission, the anthropologist tends to
yield to the sociologist.

But why? And how? There is no agreement about this question, nor even about what the actual boundary lines between
non-literate and literate cultures are. At what point in the formalization of pictographs or other graphic signs can we talk of
'letters', of literacy? And what proportion of the society has to
write and read before the culture as a whole can be described as
literate?

These are some of the many reasons why the extent to which there is any distinction between the areas and methods peculiar to anthropology and sociology must be regarded as problematic; and the difficulty affects not only the boundaries of the two disciplines but also the nature of the intrinsic differences in their subject matter.[1] The recent trend has been for anthropologists to spread their net more widely and engage in the study of industrial societies side by side with their sociological colleagues. We can no longer accept the view that anthropologists have as their objective the study of primitive man, who is characterized by a 'primitive mind', while sociologists, on the other hand, concern themselves with civilized man, whose activities are guided by 'rational thought' and tested by 'logico-empirical procedures'. The reaction against such ethnocentric views, however, has now gone to the point of denying that the distinction between non-literate and literate society has any significant validity. This position seems contrary to our personal observation; and so it has seemed worthwhile to enquire whether there may not be, even from the most empirical and relativist standpoint, genuine illumination to be derived from a further consideration of some of the historical and analytic problems connected with the traditional dichotomy between non-literate and literate societies.

The cultural tradition in non-literate societies

For reasons which will become clear it seems best to begin with a generalized description of the ways in which the cultural heritage is transmitted in non-literate societies, and then to see how these ways are changed by the widespread adoption of an easy and effective means of written communication.

When one generation hands on its cultural heritage to the next, three fairly separate items are involved. First, the society passes on its material plant, including the natural resources available to its members. Secondly, it transmits standardized ways of acting. These customary ways of behaving are only partly communicated by verbal means; ways of cooking food, of growing

1. Some writers distinguish the field of social anthropology from that of sociology on the basis of its subject matter (i.e. the study of non-literate or non-European peoples), others on the basis of its techniques (e.g. that of participant observation). For a discussion of these points, see Nadel (1951).

crops, of handling children may be transmitted by direct imitation. But the most significant elements of any human culture are undoubtedly channelled through words, and reside in the particular range of meanings and attitudes which members of any society attach to their verbal symbols. These elements include not only what we habitually think of as customary behavior but also such items as ideas of space and time, generalized goals and aspirations, in short the *Weltanschauung* of every social group. In Durkheim's words, these categories of the understanding are 'priceless instruments of thought which the human groups have laboriously forged through the centuries and where they have accumulated the best of their intellectual capital' (Durkheim, 1915, p. 19). The relative continuity of these categories of understanding from one generation to another is primarily ensured by language, which is the most direct and comprehensive expression of the social experience of the group.

The transmission of the verbal elements of culture by oral means can be visualized as a long chain of interlocking conversations between members of the group. Thus all beliefs and values, all forms of knowledge, are communicated between individuals in face-to-face contact; and, as distinct from the material content of the cultural tradition, whether it be cave-paintings or hand-axes, they are stored only in human memory.

The intrinsic nature of oral communication has a considerable effect upon both the content and the transmission of the cultural repertoire. In the first place it makes for a directness of relationship between symbol and referent. There can be no reference to 'dictionary definitions', nor can words accumulate the successive layers of historically validated meanings which they acquire in a literate culture. Instead the meaning of each word is ratified in a succession of concrete situations, accompanied by vocal inflexions and physical gestures, all of which combine to particularize both its specific denotation and its accepted connotative usages. This process of direct semantic ratification, of course, operates cumulatively; and as a result the totality of symbol-referent relationships is more immediately experienced by the individual in an exclusively oral culture, and is thus more deeply socialized.

One way of illustrating this is to consider how the range of vocabulary in a non-literate society reflects this mode of semantic ratification. It has often been observed how the elaboration of the vocabulary of such a society reflects the particular interests of the people concerned. The inhabitants of the Pacific island of Lesu have not one, but a dozen or so, words for pigs (Powdermaker, 1933, p. 292; Henle, 1958, pp. 5–18) according to sex, color and where they come from – a prolixity which mirrors the importance of pigs in a domestic economy that otherwise includes few sources of protein. The corollary of this prolixity is that where common emphases and interests, whether material or otherwise, are not specifically involved, there is little verbal development. Malinowski reported that in the Trobriands the outer world was only named insofar as it yielded useful things, useful, that is, in the very broadest sense (Malinowski, 1936);[2] and there is much other testimony to support the view that there is an intimate functional adaptation of language in non-literate societies, which obtains not only for the relatively simple and concrete symbol-referents involved above, but also for the more generalized 'categories of understanding' and for the cultural tradition as a whole.

In an essay he wrote in collaboration with Mauss, 'De quelques formes primitives de classification' (1902–3, pp. 1–72; see also Czarnowski, 1925, pp. 339–359), Durkheim traces the interconnections between the ideas of space and the territorial distribution of the Australian aborigines, the Zuni of the Pueblo area and the Sioux of the Great Plains. This intermeshing of what he called the collective representations with the social morphology of a particular society is clearly another aspect of the same directness of relationship between symbol and referent. Just as the more concrete part of a vocabulary reflects the dominant interests of the society, so the more abstract categories are often closely linked to the accepted terminology for pragmatic pursuits. Among the LoDagaa of Northern Ghana, days are reckoned according to the incidence of neighboring markets; the very word for day and market is the same, and the 'weekly' cycle is a six-day revolution of the most important markets in the vicinity, a cycle which also defines the spatial range of everyday activities (Goody, 1950–52; Evans-Pritchard, 1940, chapter 3; Tait, 1961, pp. 17ff.).[3]

2. But see also the critical comments by Lévi-Strauss (1962).
3. For a general treatment of the subject, see Hallowell (1937, pp. 647–70).

The way in which these various institutions in an oral culture are kept in relatively close accommodation one to another surely bears directly on the question of the central difference between literate and non-literate societies. As we have remarked, the whole content of the social tradition, apart from the material inheritances, is held in memory. The social aspects of remembering have been emphasized by sociologists and psychologists, in particular by Maurice Halbwachs (1925, 1940–48, 1950).[4] What the individual remembers tends to be what is of critical importance in his experience of the main social relationships. In each generation, therefore, the individual memory will mediate the cultural heritage in such a way that its new constituents will adjust to the old by the process of interpretation that Bartlett calls 'rationalizing' or the 'effort after meaning'; and whatever parts of it have ceased to be of contemporary relevance are likely to be eliminated by the process of forgetting.

The social function of memory – and of forgetting – can thus be seen as the final stage of what may be called the homeostatic organization of the cultural tradition in non-literate society. The language is developed in intimate association with the experience of the community, and it is learned by the individual in face-to-face contact with the other members. What continues to be social relevance is stored in the memory while the rest is usually forgotten: and language – primarily vocabulary – is the effective medium of this crucial process of social digestion and elimination which may be regarded as analogous to the homeostatic organization of the human body by means of which it attempts to maintain its present condition of life.

In drawing attention to the importance of these assimilating mechanisms in non-literate societies, we are denying neither the occurrence of social change, nor yet the 'survivals' which it leaves in its wake. Nor do we overlook the existence of mnemonic devices in oral cultures which offer some resistance to the interpretative process. Formalized patterns of speech, recital under ritual conditions, the use of drums and other musical instruments, the employment of professional remembrancers – all such factors

4. See also Frederic C. Bartlett on the tendency of oral discourse to become an expression of ideas and attitudes of the group rather than the individual speaker (1932, pp. 265–7; 1923, pp. 42–3, 62–3, 256).

may shield at least part of the content of memory from the transmuting influence of the immediate pressures of the present. The Homeric epics, for instance, seem to have been written down during the first century of Greek literature between 750 and 650 BC; but 'they look to a departed era, and their substance is unmistakably old' (Finley, 1954).

With these qualifications, however, it seems correct to characterize the transmission of the cultural tradition in oral societies as homeostatic in view of the way in which its emphasis differs from that in literate societies. The description offered has, of course, been extremely abstract; but a few illustrative examples in one important area – that of how the tribal past is digested into the communal orientation of the present – may serve to make it clearer.

Like the Bedouin Arabs and the Hebrews of the Old Testament, the Tiv people of Nigeria give long genealogies of their forebears which in this case stretch some twelve generations in depth back to an eponymous founding ancestor (Bohannan, 1952, pp. 301–15; Peters, 1960, pp. 29–53; Wilson and Wilson, 1945, p. 27). Neither these genealogies, nor the Biblical lists of the descendants of Adam, were remembered purely as feats of memory. They served as mnemonics for systems of social relations. When on his deathbed Jacob delivered prophecies about the future of his twelve sons, he spoke of them as the twelve tribes or nations of Israel. It would seem from the account in Genesis that the genealogical tables here refer to contemporary groups rather than to dead individuals;[5] the tables presumably serve to regulate social relations among the twelve tribes of Israel in a manner similar to that which has been well analysed in Evans-Pritchard's work on the Nuer of the Southern Sudan (1940; Evans-Pritchard and Fortes, 1940) and in Fortes' account of the Tallensi of Northern Ghana (1945).

Early British administrators among the Tiv of Nigeria were aware of the great importance attached to these genealogies

5. Ch. 49; further evidence supporting this assumption is found in the etymology of the Hebrew term *Toledot*, which originally denoted 'genealogies', and assumed also the meaning of 'stories and accounts' about the origin of a nation. 'In this sense the term was also applied to the account of the creation of heaven and earth', (Gandz, 1935, p. 269).

which were continually discussed in court cases where the rights and duties of one man towards another were in dispute. Consequently they took the trouble to write down the long lists of names and preserve them for posterity, so that future administrators might refer to them in giving judgment. Forty years later, when the Bohannans carried out anthropological field work in the area, their successors were still using the same genealogies (Bohannan, 1952, p. 314). However, these written pedigrees now gave rise to many disagreements; the Tiv maintained that they were incorrect, while the officials regarded them as statements of fact, as records of what had actually happened, and could not agree that the unlettered indigenes could be better informed about the past than their own literate predecessors. What neither party realized was that in any society of this kind changes take place which require a constant readjustment in the genealogies if they are to continue to carry out their function as mnemonics of social relationships.

These changes are of several kinds: those arising from the turnover in personnel, from the process of 'birth and copulation and death'; those connected with the rearrangement of the constituent units of the society, with the migration of one group and the fission of another; and lastly those resulting from the effects of changes in the social system itself, whether generated from within or initiated from without. Each of these three processes (which we may refer to for convenience as the processes of generational, organizational and structural change) could lead to alterations of the kind to which the administration objected.

It is obvious that the process of generation leads in itself to a constant lengthening of the genealogy; on the other hand, the population to which it is linked may in fact be growing at quite a different rate, perhaps simply replacing itself. So despite its increasing length the genealogy may have to refer to just as many people at the present time as it did fifty, a hundred, or perhaps two hundred years ago. Consequently the added depth of lineages caused by new births needs to be accompanied by a process of genealogical shrinkage; the occurrence of this telescoping process, a common example of the general social phenomenon which J. A. Barnes has felicitously termed 'structural amnesia', has been attested in many societies, including all those mentioned above (Barnes, 1947, pp. 48–56; Fortes, 1944, p. 370; Evans-

Pritchard, 1940, pp. 199–200; Peters, 1960, p. 32; Cunnison, 1959, pp. 108–14).

Organizational changes lead to similar adjustments. The state of Gonja in Northern Ghana is divided into a number of divisional chiefdoms, certain of which are recognized as providing in turn the ruler of the whole nation. When asked to explain their system the Gonja recount how the founder of the state, Ndewura Jakpa, came down from the Niger Bend in search of gold, conquered the indigenous inhabitants of the area and enthroned himself as chief of the state and his sons as rulers of its territorial divisions. At his death the divisional chiefs succeeded to the paramountcy in turn. When the details of this story were first recorded at the turn of the present century, at the time the British were extending their control over the area, Jakpa was said to have begotten seven sons, this corresponding to the number of divisions whose heads were eligible for the supreme office by virtue of their descent from the founder of the particular chiefdom. But at the same time as the British had arrived, two of the seven divisions disappeared, one being deliberately incorporated in a neighboring division because its rulers had supported a Mandingo invader, Samori, and another because of some boundary changes introduced by the British administration. Sixty years later, when the myths of state were again recorded, Jakpa was credited with only five sons and no mention was made of the founders of the two divisions which had since disappeared from the political map.[6]

These two instances from the Tiv and Gonja emphasize that genealogies often serve the same function that Malinowski (1926, pp. 23, 43) claimed for myth; they act as 'charters' of present social institutions rather than as faithful historical records of times past. They can do this more consistently because they operate within an oral rather than a written tradition and thus tend to be automatically adjusted to existing social relations as they are passed by word of mouth from one member of the society to another. The social element in remembering results in the

6. Jack Goody, unpublished field notes, 1956–7; the heads of the divisions who could not succeed to the paramountcy also claimed descent from sons of the founding ancestor, Jakpa, but this was not an intrinsic part of the myth as usually told, and in any case their number remained constant during the period in question.

genealogies being transmuted in the course of being transmitted; and a similar process takes place with regard to other cultural elements as well, to myths, for example, and to sacred lore in general. Deities and other supernatural agencies which have served their purpose can be quietly dropped from the contemporary pantheon; and as the society changes, myths too are forgotten, attributed to other personages, or transformed in their meaning.

One of the most important results of this homeostatic tendency is that the individual has little perception of the past except in terms of the present; whereas the annals of a literate society cannot but enforce a more objective recognition of the distinction between what was and what is. Franz Boas wrote that for the Eskimo the world has always been as it is now (1904, p. 2).[7] It seems probable, at least, that the form in which non-literate societies conceive the world of the past is itself influenced by the process of transmission described. The Tiv have their genealogies, others their sacred tales about the origin of the world and the way in which man acquired his culture. But all their conceptualizations of the past cannot help being governed by the concerns of the present, merely because there is no body of chronologically ordered statements to which reference can be made. The Tiv do not recognize any contradiction between what they say now and what they said fifty years ago, since no enduring records exist for them to set beside their present views. Myth and history merge into one: the elements in the cultural heritage which cease to have a contemporary relevance tend to be soon forgotten or transformed; and as the individuals of each generation acquire their vocabulary, their genealogies, and their myths, they are unaware that various words, proper-names and stories have dropped out, or that others have changed their meanings or been replaced.

Kinds of writing and their social effects

The pastness of the past, then, depends upon a historical sensibility which can hardly begin to operate without permanent written records; and writing introduces similar changes in the

7. Lévi-Strauss treats the absence of historical knowledge as one of the distinctive features of *la pensée sauvage* in contrast to *la pensée domestiquée* (1962, p. 349).

transmission of other items of the cultural repertoire. But the extent of these changes varies with the nature and social distribution of the writing system; varies, that is, according to the system's intrinsic efficacy as a means of communication, and according to the social constraints placed upon it, that is, the degree to which use of the system is diffused through the society.

Early in prehistory, man began to express himself in graphic form; and his cave paintings, rock engravings and wood carvings are morphologically, and presumably sequentially, the forerunners of writing. By some process of simplification and stylization they appear to have led to the various kinds of pictographs found in simple societies (Gelb, 1952, pp. 24 ff.). While pictographs themselves are almost universal, their development into a self-sufficient system capable of extended discourse occurs only among the Plains Indians (Voegelin and Voegelin, 1961, pp. 84, 91).

Pictographs have obvious disadvantages as means of communication. For one thing a vast number of signs is needed to represent all the important objects in the culture. For another, since the signs are concrete, the simplest sentence requires an extremely elaborate series of signs: many stylized representations of wigwams, footprints, totemic animals and so on are required just to convey the information that a particular man left there a few days ago. Finally, however elaborately the system is developed, only a limited number of things can be said.

The end of the fourth millennium saw the early stages of the development of more complex forms of writing, which seem to be an essential factor in the rise of the urban cultures of the Orient. The majority of signs in these systems were simply pictures of the outside world, standardized representations of the object signified by a particular word; to these were added other devices for creating word signs or logograms, which permitted the expression of wider ranges of meaning. Thus in Egyptian hieroglyphics, the picture of a beetle was a code sign not only for that insect but also for a discontinuous and more abstract referent 'became' (Voegelin and Voegelin, 1961, pp. 75-6).

The basic invention used to supplement the logograms was the phonetic principle, which for the first time permitted the written expression of all the words of a language. For example, by the device of phonetic transfer the Sumerians could use the sign for *ti*, an arrow, to stand for *ti*, life, a concept not easy to express in pictographic form. In particular, the need to record personal names and foreign words encouraged the development of phonetic elements in writing.

But while these true writing systems all used phonetic devices for the construction of logograms (and have consequently been spoken of as word-syllabic systems of writing), they failed to carry through the application of the phonetic principle exclusively and systematically.[8] The achievement of a system completely based upon the representation of phonemes (the basic units of meaningful sound) was left to the Near Eastern syllabaries, which developed between 1500–1000 BC, and finally to the introduction of the alphabet proper in Greece. Meanwhile these incompletely phonetic systems were too clumsy and complicated to foster widespread literacy, if only because the number of signs was very large; at least six hundred would have to be learned even for the simplified cuneiform developed in Assyria, and about the same for Egyptian hieroglyphs (Diringer, 1948, pp. 48, 196; Gelb, 1952, p. 115). All these ancient civilizations, the Sumerian, Egyptian, Hittite and Chinese, were literate in one sense and their great advances in administration and technology were undoubtedly connected with the invention of a writing system; but when we think of the limitations of their systems of communication as compared with ours, the term 'protoliterate', or even 'oligoliterate', might be more descriptive in suggesting the restriction of literacy to a relatively small proportion of the total population.[9]

Any system of writing which makes the sign stand directly for

8. C. F. and F. M. Voegelin classify all these systems (Chinese, Egyptian, Hittite, Mayan and Sumerian-Akkadian) as 'alphabet included logographic systems': because they make use of phonetic devices, they include, under the heading 'self-sufficient alphabets', systems which have signs for consonant-vowel sequences (i.e. syllabaries), for independent consonants (IC), e.g. Phoenician, or for independent consonants plus independent vowels (IC + IV), e.g. Greek. In this paper we employ 'alphabet' in the narrower, more usual, sense of a phonemic system with independent signs for consonants and vowels (IC + IV).

9. 'Protoliterate' is often employed in a rather different sense, as when S. N. Kramer (1948, p. 161) uses the term to designate the Sumerian phase in Lower Mesopotamia when writing was first invented. There seems to be no generally accepted usage for societies where there is a fully developed but

the object must be extremely complex. It can extend its vocabulary by generalization or association of ideas, that is, by making the sign stand either for a more general class of objects, or for other referents connected with the original picture by an association of meanings which may be related to one another either in a continuous or in a discontinuous manner. Either process of semantic extension is to some extent arbitrary or esoteric; and as a result the interpretation of these signs is neither easy nor explicit. One might perhaps guess that the Chinese sign for a man carries the general meaning of maleness; it would be more difficult to see that a conventionalized picture of a man and a broom is the sign for a woman; it's a pleasing fancy, no doubt, but not one which communicates very readily until it has been learned as a new character, as a separate sign for a separate word, as a logogram. In Chinese writing a minimum of 3000 such characters have to be learned before one can be reasonably literate (Moorhouse, 1953, pp. 90, 163); and with a total repertoire of some 50,000 characters to be mastered, it normally takes about twenty years to reach full literate proficiency. China, therefore, stands as an extreme example of how, when a virtually non-phonetic system of writing becomes sufficiently developed to express a large number of meanings explicitly, only a small and specially trained professional group in the total society can master it, and partake of the literate culture.

Although systems of word signs are certainly easier to learn, many difficulties remain, even when these signs are supplemented by phonemic devices of a syllabic sort. Other features of the social system are no doubt responsible for the way that the writing systems developed as they did; but it is a striking fact that – for whatever ultimate causes – in Egypt and Mesopotamia, as in China, a literate elite of religious, administrative and commercial experts emerged and maintained itself as a centralized governing bureaucracy on rather similar lines. Their various social and in-

---

socially restricted phonetic writing system. Sterling Dow (1954, pp. 77–129) characterizes two stages of Minoan society: one of 'stunted literacy', where little use was made of writing at all (Linear A); and one of 'special literacy' where writing was used regularly but only for limited purposes (Linear B). Stuart Piggott refers to both these conditions under the name of 'conditional literacy' (1959, p. 104).

tellectual achievements were, of course, enormous; but as regards the participation of the society as a whole in the written culture, a wide gap existed between the esoteric literate culture and the exoteric oral one, a gap which the literate were interested in maintaining. Among the Sumerians and Akkadians writing was the pursuit of scribes and preserved as a 'mystery', a 'secret treasure'. Royalty were themselves illiterate; Ashurbanipal (668–626 BC) records that he was the first Babylonian king to master the 'clerkly skill' (Driver, 1954, pp. 62, 72). 'Put writing in your heart that you may protect yourself from hard labour of any kind', writes an Egyptian of the New Kingdom: 'The scribe is released from manual tasks; it is he who commands' (quoted in Gordon Childe, 1941, pp. 187–8; see also 1942, pp. 105, 118). Significantly, the classical age of Babylonian culture, beginning under Hammurabi in the late eighteenth century BC, appears to have coincided with a period when the reading and writing of Akkadian cuneiform was not confined to a small group, nor to one nation; it was then that nearly all the extant literature was written down, and that the active state of commerce and administration produced a vast quantity of public and private correspondence, of which much has survived.

These imperfectly phonetic methods of writing survived with little change for many centuries;[10] so too did the cultures of which they were part.[11] The existence of an elite group, which followed from the difficulty of the writing system, and whose continued influence depended on the maintenance of the present social order, must have been a powerfully conservative force, especially when it consisted of ritual specialists;[12] and so, it may be surmised, was the nature of the writing system itself. For pictographic and logographic systems are alike in their tendency to reify the

10. 'Egyptian hieroglyphic writing remained fundamentally unchanged for a period of three thousand years', according to David Diringer (1962, p. 48). He attributes the fact that it never lost its cumbrousness and elaboration to 'its unique sacredness' (p. 50).

11. Many authorities have commented upon the lack of development in Egypt after the initial achievements of the Old Kingdom: for a discussion (and a contrary view), see John A. Wilson (1949, pp. 115–116).

12. 'The world view of the Egyptians and Babylonians was conditioned by the teaching of sacred books; it thus constituted an orthodoxy, the maintenance of which was in the charge of colleges of priests' (Farrington, 1936, p. 37). See also Gordon Childe (1942, p. 121).

objects of the natural and social order; by so doing they register, record, make permanent the existing social and ideological picture. Such, for example, was the tendency of the most highly developed and longest-lived ancient writing system, that of Egypt, whose society has been described with picturesque exaggeration as 'a nation of fellahin ruled with a rod of iron by a Society of Antiquaries'.

This conservative or antiquarian bias can perhaps be best appreciated by contrasting it with fully phonetic writing; for phonetic writing, by imitating human discourse, is in fact symbolizing, not the objects of the social and natural order, but the very process of human interaction in speech: the verb is as easy to express as the noun; and the written vocabulary can be easily and unambiguously expanded. Phonetic systems are therefore adapted to expressing every nuance of individual thought, to recording personal reactions as well as items of major social importance. Non-phonetic writing, on the other hand, tends rather to record and reify only those items in the cultural repertoire which the literate specialists have selected for written expression; and it tends to express the collective attitude towards them.

The notion of representing a sound by a graphic symbol is itself so stupefying a leap of the imagination that what is remarkable is not so much that it happened relatively late in human history, but rather that it ever happened at all. For a long time, however, these phonetic inventions had a limited effect because they were only partially exploited; not only were logograms and pictograms retained, but a variety of phonograms were used to express the same sound. The full explicitness and economy of a phonetic writing system 'as easy as A B C' was therefore likely to arise only in less advanced societies on the fringes of Egypt or Mesopotamia, societies which were starting their writing system more or less from scratch, and which took over the idea of phonetic signs from adjoining countries, and used them exclusively to fit their own language.[13] These phonetic signs could, of

13. Gelb (1952, p. 196) maintains that all the main types of syllabary developed in just this way. Driver rejects the possibility that the Phoenician alphabet was invented on Egyptian soil, as it would have been 'stifled at birth' by the 'dead-weight of Egyptian tradition, already of hoary antiquity and in the hands of a powerful priesthood' (1954, p. 187).

course, be used to stand for any unit of speech, and thus developed either into syllabaries or into alphabets. In a few cases, such as Japanese, the particular nature of the language made it possible to construct a relatively simple and efficient syllabary; but as regards the great majority of languages the alphabet, with its signs for individual consonants and vowels, proved a much more economical and convenient instrument for representing sounds. For the syllabaries, while making writing easier, were still far from simple;[14] they were often combined with logograms and pictographs.[15] And whether by necessity or tradition or both, pre-alphabetic writing was still mainly restricted to elite groups. The Mycenean script disappeared completely after the twelfth century BC, a fact which was possible because of the very restricted uses of literacy and the close connection between writing and palace administration (Chadwick, 1958, p. 130; see also 1959, pp. 7–18). It is doubtful whether any such loss could have occurred in Greece after the introduction of a complete alphabetic script, probably in the eighth century BC.

The alphabet is almost certainly the supreme example of cultural diffusion[16]: all existing or recorded alphabets derive from Semitic syllabaries developed during the second millennium. Eventually there arose the enormous simplification of the Semitic writing system, with its mere twenty-two letters; and then only one further step remained: the Greek script, which is, of course, much closer than the Semitic to the Roman alphabet, took certain of the Semitic signs for consonants which the Greek language didn't need, and used them for vowels, which the Semitic syllabary did not represent (Diringer, 1948, pp. 214–18).[17] The directness of our inheritance from these two sources is suggested by the fact that our word 'alphabet' is the latinized form of the first two letters of the Greek alphabet, 'alpha', derived from the Semitic 'aleph', and 'beta', from the Semitic 'beth'.

The reason for the success of the alphabet, which David Diringer

14. 'Immensely complicated', Driver calls the pre-alphabetic forms of writing Semitic (1954, p. 67).

15. For Hittite, see Gurney (1952, pp. 120–21). For Mycenean, see Chadwick (1958).

16. As is exhaustively documented in Diringer (1948).

17. On the 'accidental' nature of this change see Voegelin and Voegelin (1961, pp. 63–4).

calls a 'democratic' script as opposed to the 'theocratic' scripts of Egypt, is itself based on the fact that, uniquely among writing systems, its graphic signs are representations of the most extreme and most universal example of cultural selection – the basic phonemic system. The number of sounds which the human breath stream can produce is vast; but nearly all languages are based on the formal recognition by the society of only forty or so of these sounds. The success of the alphabet (as well as some of its incidental difficulties) comes from the fact that its system of graphic representation takes advantage of this socially-conventionalized pattern of sound in all language systems; by symbolizing in letters these selected phonemic units the alphabet makes it possible to write easily and read unambiguously about anything which the society can talk about.

The historical picture of the cultural impact of the new alphabetic writing is not altogether clear. As regards the Semitic system, which was widely adopted elsewhere, the evidence suggests that – in part perhaps because of the intrinsic difficulties of the system, but mainly because of the established cultural features of the societies which adopted it – the social diffusion of writing was slow. There was, for one thing, a strong tendency for writing to be used as a help to memory rather than as an autonomous and independent mode of communication; and under such conditions its influence tended towards the consolidation of the existing cultural tradition. This certainly appears to be true of India and Palestine.[18] Gandz notes, for example, that Hebrew culture continued to be transmitted orally long after the Old Testament had begun to be written down. As he puts it, the introduction of writing:

did not at once change the habits of the people and displace the old method of oral tradition. We must always distinguish between the *first introduction* of writing and its *general diffusion*. It often takes several centuries, and sometimes even a millennium or more, until this invention becomes the common property of the people at large. In the beginning, the written book is not intended for practical use at all. It is a divine instrument, placed in the temple 'by the side of the ark of the

18. According to Ralph E. Turner (1941, vol. 1, pp. 346, 391), the Hebrews took over the Semitic system in the eleventh century BC, and the Indians a good deal later, probably in the eighth century BC.

covenant that it may be there for a witness' (Deuteronomy, xxxi, 26), and remains there as a holy relic. For the people at large, oral instruction still remained the only way of learning, and the memory – the only means of preservation. Writing was practiced, if at all, only as an additional support for the memory.

It was not, in fact, until some six centuries after the original Hebrew adoption of the Semitic writing system that, at the time of Ezra (c. 444 BC), an official 'generally recognized text' of the Torah was published, and the body of the religious tradition ceased to be 'practically . . . a sealed book' and became accessible to anyone who chose to study it (Gandz, 1935, pp. 253–4).

Even so, of course, as the frequent diatribes against the scribes in the Gospels remind us,[19] there remained a considerable gap between the literati and the laymen; the professionals who plied their trade in the market-place belonged to 'families of scribes', perhaps organized as guilds, within which the mystery was handed down from father to son.[20]

Anything like popular literacy, or the use of writing as an autonomous mode of communication by the majority of the members of society, is not found in the earliest societies which used the Semitic writing system; it was, rather, in the sixth and fifth centuries BC in the city states of Greece and Ionia that there first arose a society which as a whole could justly be characterized as literate. Many of the reasons why literacy became widespread in Greece, but not in other societies which had Semitic, or indeed any other, simple and explicit writing systems, necessarily lie outside the scope of this essay; yet considerable importance must surely be attributed to the intrinsic advantages of the Greek adaptation of the Semitic alphabet, an adaptation which made it the first comprehensively and exclusively phonetic system for transcribing human speech.[21] The system was easy, explicit and unambiguous – more so than the Semitic where the lack of vowels

19. e.g. Luke, xx; Matthew, xxxiii; in the seventh century BC, even kings and prophets employed scribes, Jeremiah, xxxvi, 4, 18.

20. Driver (1954, pp. 87–90), where he instances the case of one scribe who having no son 'taught his wisdom to his sister's son'.

21. 'If the alphabet is defined as a system of signs expressing single sounds of speech, then the first alphabet which can justifiably be so called is the Greek alphabet'. Gelb (1952, p. 166).

is responsible for many of the cruces in the Bible: for instance, since the consonant in the Hebrew words is the same, Elijah may have been fed by 'Ravens' or 'Arabs'.[22] Its great advantage over the syllabaries lay in the reduction of the number of signs and in the ability to specify consonant and vowel clusters. The system was easy to learn: Plato sets aside three years for the process in the *Laws*,[23] about the time taken in our schools today; and the much greater speed with which alphabetic writing can be learned is shown, not only by such reports as those of the International Institute of Intellectual Cooperation (1934)[24] but also by the increasing adoption of the Roman script, and even more widely of alphabetic systems of writing, throughout the world.

The extensive diffusion of the alphabet in Greece was also materially assisted by various social, economic and technological factors. In the first place the eighth century saw a great burst of economic activity following the revival of the eastern trade which had declined after the Mycenean collapse in the twelfth century (Starr, 1961, pp. 189–90, 349 ff.). Secondly, while the Greek society of the period had, of course, its various social strata, the political system was not strongly centralized; especially in the Ionic settlements there appears to have been a good deal of flexibility and in them we discern the beginnings of the Greek city state. Thirdly, the increased contact with the East brought material prosperity and technological advance. The wider use of iron, the advent of the true Iron Age, was perhaps one of the results (Starr, 1961, pp. 87–8, 357). More closely connected with literacy was the fact that trade with Egypt led to the importation of papyrus; and this made writing itself easier and less expensive, both for the individual writer and for the reader who wanted to buy books; papyrus was obviously much cheaper than parchment made from skins, more permanent than wax tablets, easier to handle than the stone or clay of Mesopotamia and Mycenae.

The chronology and extent of the diffusion of literacy in Greece remains a matter of debate. With the Mycenean collapse in the twelfth century, writing disappeared; the earliest Greek

22. I Kings xvii, 4–6; see Hastings (1898–1904, *s.v.* 'Elijah').

23. 810 a. From the ages 10 to 13.

24. For more recent developments and documentation, see Gray (1956, especially pp. 31–60).

inscriptions in the modified Semitic alphabet occur in the last two decades of the eighth century (Starr, 1961, p. 169). Recent authorities suggest the new script was adopted and transformed about the middle of the eighth century in Northern Syria (Jeffery, 1961, p. 21; Cook and Woodhead, 1959, pp. 175–8).[25] The extensive use of writing probably came only slowly in the seventh century, but when it eventually came it seems to have been used in a very wide range of activities, intellectual as well as economic, and by a wide range of people.[26]

It must be remembered, of course, that Greek writing throughout the classical period was still relatively difficult to decipher, as words were not regularly separated (Kenyon, 1951, p. 67); that the copying of manuscripts was a long and laborious process; and that silent reading as we know it was very rare until the advent of printing – in the ancient world books were used mainly for reading aloud, often by a slave. Nevertheless, from the sixth century onwards literacy seems to be increasingly presumed in the public life of Greece and Ionia. In Athens, for example, the first laws for the general public to read were set up by Solon in 593–4 BC; the institution of ostracism early in the fifth century assumes a literate citizen body – 6,000 citizens had to write the name of the person on their potsherds before he could be banished (Carcopino, 1935, pp. 72–110); there is abundant evidence in the fifth century of a system of schools teaching reading and writing (*Protagoras*, 325 d) and of a book-reading public – satirized already by Aristophanes in *The Frogs*;[27] while the final form of the Greek alphabet, which was established fairly late in the fifth century, was finally adopted for use in the official records of Athens by decree of the Archon Eucleides in 403 BC.

25. For North Syria, see Woolley (1953).

26. Chester Starr speaks of its use by 'a relatively large aristocratic class' (1961, p. 171) and Miss Jeffery notes that 'writing was never regarded as an esoteric craft in early Greece. Ordinary people could and did learn to write, for many of the earliest inscriptions which we possess are casual graffiti' (1961, p. 63).

27. 1. 1114; in 414 BC. See also Plato, *Apology*, 26 d, and the general survey of Kenyon (1951).

Alphabetic culture and Greek thought

The rise of Greek civilization, then, is the prime historical example of the transition to a really literate society. In all subsequent cases where a widespread introduction of an alphabetic script occurred, as in Rome, for example, other cultural features were inevitably imported from the loan country along with the writing system; Greece thus offers not only the first example of this change, but also the essential one for any attempt to isolate the cultural consequences of alphabetic literacy.

The fragmentary and ambiguous nature of our direct evidence about this historical transformation in Greek civilization means that any generalizations must be extremely tentative and hypothetical; but the fact that the essential basis both of the writing systems and of many characteristic cultural institutions of the Western tradition as a whole are derived from Greece, and that they both arose there simultaneously, would seem to justify the present attempt to outline the possible relationships between the writing system and those cultural innovations of early Greece which are common to all alphabetically-literate societies.

The early development of the distinctive features of Western thought is usually traced back to the radical innovations of the pre-Socratic philosophers of the sixth century BC. The essence of their intellectual revolution is seen as a change from mythical to logico-empirical modes of thought. Such, broadly speaking, is Werner Jaeger's view (1947); and Ernst Cassirer writes that 'the history of philosophy as a scientific discipline may be regarded as a single continuous struggle to effect a separation and liberation from myth' (1953, pp. 106–30, 281–3; 1955, vol. 2, p. xiii).

To this general picture there are two kinds of theoretical objection. First, that the crucial intellectual innovations – in Cassirer as in Werner Jaeger – are in the last analysis attributed to the special mental endowments of the Greek people; and insofar as such terms as 'the Greek Mind' or 'genius' are not simply descriptive, they are logically dependent upon extremely questionable theories of man's nature and culture. Secondly, such a version of the transformation from 'unphilosophical' to 'philosophical' thought assumes an absolute – and untenable – dichotomy between the 'mythical' thought of primitives and the 'logico-empirical' thought of civilized man.

The dichotomy, of course, is itself very similar to Lévy-Bruhl's earlier theory of the 'prelogical' mentality of primitive peoples, which has been widely criticized. Malinowski and many others have demonstrated the empirical elements in non-literate cultures (1925),[28] and Evans-Pritchard has carefully analysed the 'logical' nature of the belief systems of the Azande of the Sudan (1937);[29] while on the other hand the illogical and mythical nature of much Western thought and behavior is evident to anyone contemplating either our past or our present.

Nevertheless, although we must reject any dichotomy based upon the assumption of radical differences between the mental attributes of literate and non-literate peoples, and accept the view that previous formulations of the distinction were based on faulty premises and inadequate evidence, there may still exist general differences between literate and non-literate societies somewhat along the lines suggested by Lévy-Bruhl. One reason for their existence, for instance, may be what has been described above: the fact that writing establishes a different kind of relationship between the word and its referent, a relationship that is more general and more abstract, and less closely connected with the particularities of person, place and time, than obtains in oral communication. There is certainly a good deal to substantiate this distinction in what we know of early Greek thought. To take, for instance, the categories of Cassirer and Werner Jaeger, it is surely significant that it was only in the days of the first wide-spread alphabetic culture that the idea of 'logic' – of an immutable and impersonal mode of discourse – appears to have arisen; and it was also only then that the sense of the human past as an

28. For an appreciation of Lévy-Bruhl's positive achievement, see Evans-Pritchard (1934, pp. 1–36). In his later work, Lévy-Bruhl modified the rigidity of his earlier dichotomy.

29. See also Max Gluckman's essay, 'Social Beliefs and Individual Thinking in Primitive Society' (1949–50, pp. 73–98). From a rather different standpoint, Lévi-Strauss has analysed 'the logic of totemic classifications' (1962, p. 48 ff.) and speaks of two distinct modes of scientific thought; the first (or 'primitive') variety consists in 'the science of the concrete', the practical knowledge of the handy man (*bricoleur*), which is the technical counterpart of mythical thought (p. 26).

objective reality was formally developed, a process in which the distinction between 'myth' and 'history' took on decisive importance.

Myth and history

Non-literate peoples, of course, often make a distinction between the lighter folk-tale, the graver myth and the quasi-historical legend.[30] But not so insistently, and for an obvious reason. As long as the legendary and doctrinal aspects of the cultural tradition are mediated orally, they are kept in relative harmony with each other and with the present needs of society in two ways; through the unconscious operations of memory, and through the adjustment of the reciter's terms and attitudes to those of the audience before him. There is evidence, for example, that such adaptations and omissions occurred in the oral transmission of the Greek cultural tradition. But once the poems of Homer and Hesiod, which contained much of the earlier history, religion and cosmology of the Greeks had been written down, succeeding generations were faced with old distinctions in sharply aggravated form: how far was the information about their Gods and heroes literally true? how could its patent inconsistencies be explained? and how could the beliefs and attitudes implied be brought into lines with those of the present?

The disappearance of so many early Greek writings, and the difficulties of dating and composition in many that survive, make anything like a clear reconstruction impossible. Greek had of course been written, in a very limited way, during Mycenean times. At about 1200 BC writing disappeared and the alphabet was not developed until some four hundred years later. Most scholars agree that in the middle or late eighth century the Greeks adapted the purely consonantal system of Phoenicia, possibly at the trading port of al Mina (Poseidon?). Much of the early writing consisted of 'explanatory inscriptions on existing objects – dedications on offerings, personal names on property, epitaphs on tombs, names of figures in drawings' (Jeffery, 1961, p. 46). The Homeric poems were written down between 750 and 650 BC, and the seventh century saw first the recording of lyric verse and then (at the end) the emergence of the great Ionian school of

30. e.g. the Trobriands (Malinowski, 1926, pp. 33 ff.).

scientist philosophers.[31] Thus within a century or two of the writing down of the Homeric poems, many groups of writers and teachers appeared, first in Ionia and later in Greece, who took as their point of departure the belief that much of what Homer had apparently said was inconsistent and unsatisfactory in many respects. The logographers, who set themselves to record the genealogies, chronologies and cosmologies which had been handed down orally from the past, soon found that the task led them to use their critical and rational powers to create a new individual synthesis. In non-literate society, of course, there are usually some individuals whose interests lead them to collect, analyse and interpret the cultural tradition in a personal way; and the written records suggest that this process went considerably further among the literary elites of Egypt, Babylon and China, for example. But perhaps because in Greece reading and writing were less restricted to any particular priestly or administrative groups, there seems to have been a more thorough-going individual challenge to the orthodox cultural tradition in sixth-century Greece than occurred elsewhere. Hecataeus, for example, proclaimed at about the turn of the century, 'What I write is the account I believe to be true. For the stories the Greeks tell are many and in my opinion ridiculous' (Jacoby, 1923, vol. 1, fr. 1a), and offered his own rationalizations of the data on family traditions and lineages which he had collected. Already the mythological mode of using the past, the mode which, in Sorel's words (1941, p. 136), makes it 'a means of acting on the present', has begun to disappear.

That this trend of thought had much larger implications can be seen from the fact that the beginnings of religious and natural philosophy are connected with similar critical departures from the inherited traditions of the past; as W. B. Yeats wrote, with another tradition in mind, 'Science is the critique of myths, there would be no Darwin had there been no *Book* of Genesis' (quoted in Hone, 1942, p. 405 [author's italics]). Among the early pre-Socratics there is much evidence of the close connection between

31. 'It was in Ionia that the first completely rationalistic attempts to describe the nature of the world took place' (Kirk and Raven, 1957, p. 73). The work of the Milesian philosophers, Thales, Anaximander and Anaximenes, is described by the authors as 'clearly a development of the genetic or genealogical approach to nature exemplified by the Hesiodic *Theogony*' (p. 73).

new ideas and the criticism of the old. Thus Xenophanes of Colophon (*fl. c.* 540 BC) rejected the 'fables of men of old', and replaced the anthropomorphic gods of Homer and Hesiod who did 'everything that is disgraceful and blameworthy among men' with a supreme god, 'not at all like mortals in body and mind' (Diels, 1951, fr. 11, 23; see also Burnet, 1908, pp. 131, 140–41; Jaeger, 1947, pp. 42–7; Kirk and Raven, 1957, pp. 168 ff.); while Heraclitus of Ephesus (*fl. c.* 500 BC), the first great philosopher of the problems of knowledge, whose system is based on the unity of opposites expressed in the *logos* or structural plan of things, also ridiculed the anthropomorphism and idolatry of the Olympian religion (Diels, 1951, fr. 40, 42, 56, 57, 106; see also Cornford, 1952, pp. 112 ff.; Kirk and Raven, 1957, pp. 182 ff.).

The critical and sceptical process continued, and according to Cornford, 'a great part of the supreme god's biography had to be frankly rejected as false, or reinterpreted as allegory, or contemplated with reserve as mysterious myth too dark for human understanding' (Cornford, 1923, xv–xvi; see also Burnet, 1908, p. 1). On the one hand the poets continued to use the traditional legends for their poems and plays; on the other the prose writers attempted to wrestle with the problems with which the changes in the cultural tradition had faced them. Even the poets, however, had a different attitude to their material. Pindar, for example, used *mythos* in the sense of traditional stories, with the implication that they were not literally true; but claimed that his own poems had nothing in common with the fables of the past (first Olympian Ode). As for the prose writers, and indeed some of the poets, they had set out to replace myth with something else more consistent, with their sense of the *logos*, of the common and all-encompassing truth which reconciles apparent contradictions.

From the point of view of the transmission of the cultural tradition, the categories of understanding connected with the dimensions of time and space have a particular importance. As regards an objective description of space, Anaximander (b. 610 BC) and Hecataeus (*fl. c.* 510–490), making use of Babylonian and Egyptian techniques, drew the first maps of the world (see Warmington, 1934, pp. xiv, xxxviii). Then their crude beginnings were subject to a long process of criticism and correction – by Herodotus (*History*, 4, 36–40) and others; and from this emerged the more scientific cartography of Aristotle, Eratosthenes and their successors (Warmington, 1934, pp. xvii–xviii, xli ff.).

The development of history appears to have followed a rather similar course, although the actual details of the process are subject to much controversy. The traditional view gave priority to local histories which were followed by the more universal accounts of Herodotus and Thucydides. Dionysius of Halicarnasus writes of the predecessors of these historians who 'instead of coordinating their accounts with each other ... treated of individual peoples and cities separately. ... They all had the one same object, to bring to the general knowledge of the public the written records that they found preserved in temples or in secular buildings in the form in which they found them, neither adding nor taking away anything; among these records were to be found legends hallowed by the passage of time ...' (quoted in Pearson 1939, p. 3).

Jacoby however has insisted 'the whole idea is wrong that Greek historiography began with local history' (1949, p. 354). As far as Athens is concerned, history begins with the foreigner Herodotus who, not long after the middle of the fifth century, incorporated parts of the story of the town in his work because he wanted to explain the role it played in the great conflict between East and West, between Europe and Asia. The aim of Herodotus' *History* was to discover what the Greeks and Persians 'fought each other for' (I, 1; see also Finley, 1959, pp. 4 ff.); and his method was *historia* – personal inquiry or research into the most probable versions of events as they were to be found in various sources. His work rested on oral tradition and consequently his writings retained many mythological elements. So too did the work of the logographer, Hellanicus of Lesbos, who at the end of the fifth century wrote the first history of Attica from 683 to the end of the Peloponnesian war in 404. Hellanicus also tried to reconstruct the genealogies of the Homeric heroes, both backwards to the Gods and forwards to the Greece of his own time; and this inevitably involved chronology, the objective measurement of time. All he could do, however, was to rationalize and systematize largely legendary materials (Pearson, 1939, pp. 152–233, especially pp. 193, 232–3). The development of history as a documented and analytic account of the past and present of the society in permanent written form took an important step forward with Thucydides, who made a decisive distinction between myth and history, a distinction to which little attention is paid in non-literate society (see for instance Malinowski, 1922, pp. 290–333). Thucydides wanted to give a wholly reliable account of the wars between Athens and Sparta; and this meant that unverified assumptions about the past had to be excluded. So Thucydides rejected, for example, the chronology that Hellanicus had worked out for the prehistory of Athens, and confined himself very largely to his own notes of the events and speeches he related, or to the information he sought out from eye-witnesses and other reliable sources (*History*, I, 20–22, 97).[32]

And so, not long after the widespread diffusion of writing throughout the Greek world, and the recording of the previously oral cultural tradition, there arose an attitude to the past very different from that common in non-literate societies. Instead of the unobtrusive adaptation of past tradition to present needs, a great many individuals found in the written records, where much of their traditional cultural repertoire had been given permanent form, so many inconsistencies in the beliefs and categories of understanding handed down to them that they were impelled to a much more conscious, comparative and critical, attitude to the accepted world picture, and notably to the notions of God, the universe and the past. Many individual solutions to these problems were themselves written down, and these versions formed the basis for further investigations.[33]

32. For a picture of note-taking (*hypomnemata*) among Athenians, see *Theaetetus*, 142 c–143 c.

33. Felix Jacoby notes that 'fixation in writing, once achieved, primarily had a preserving effect upon the oral tradition, because it put an end to the involuntary shiftings of the *mnemai* (remembrances), and drew limits to the arbitrary creation of new *logoi* (stories)' (1949, p. 217). He points out that this created difficulties for the early literate recorders of the past which the previous oral *mnemones* or professional 'remembrancers' did not have to face: whatever his own personal view of the matter, 'no true Atthidographer could remove Kekrops from his position as the first Attic king.... Nobody could take away from Solon the legislation which founded *in nuce* the first Attic constitution of historical times.' Such things could no longer be silently forgotten, as in an oral tradition.

The general conclusion of Jacoby's polemic against Wilamowitz's hypothesis of a 'pre-literary chronicle' is that 'historical consciousness ... is not older than historical literature' (p. 201).

In non-literate society, it was suggested, the cultural tradition functions as a series of interlocking face-to-face conversations in which the very conditions of transmission operate to favor consistency between past and present, and to make criticism – the articulation of inconsistency – less likely to occur; and if it does, the inconsistency makes a less permanent impact, and is more easily adjusted or forgotten. While scepticism may be present in such societies, it takes a personal, non-cumulative form; it does not lead to a deliberate rejection and reinterpretation of social dogma so much as to a semi-automatic readjustment of belief.[34]

In literate society, these interlocking conversations go on; but they are no longer man's only dialogue; and insofar as writing provides an alternative source for the transmission of cultural orientations it favors awareness of inconsistency. One aspect of this is a sense of change and of cultural lag; another is the notion that the cultural inheritance as a whole is composed of two very different kinds of material; fiction, error and superstition on the one hand; and on the other, elements of truth which can provide the basis for some more reliable and coherent explanation of the gods, the human past and the physical world. [...]

Literate culture: some general considerations

It is hardly possible, in this brief survey, to determine what importance must be attributed to the alphabet as the cause or as the necessary condition of the seminal intellectual innovations that occurred in the Greek world during the centuries that followed the diffusion of writing; nor, indeed, does the nature of the evidence give much ground for believing that the problem can ever be fully resolved. The present argument must, therefore, confine itself to suggesting that some crucial features of Western culture came into being in Greece soon after the existence, for the first time, of a rich urban society in which a substantial portion of the population was able to read and write; and that, consequently, the overwhelming debt of the whole of contemporary civilization

34. As writers on the indigenous political systems of Africa have insisted, changes generally take the form of rebellion rather than revolution; subjects reject the King, but not the kingship. See Evans-Pritchard (1948, pp. 35 ff.); Gluckman (1952).

to classical Greece must be regarded as in some measure the result, not so much of the Greek genius, as of the intrinsic differences between non-literate (or proto-literate) and literate societies; the latter being mainly represented by those societies using the Greek alphabet and its derivatives. If this is so, it may help us to take our contrast between the transmission of the cultural heritage in non-literate and alphabetically-literate societies a little further.

To begin with, the case of alphabetic reading and writing was probably an important consideration in the development of political democracy in Greece: in the fifth century a majority of the free citizens could apparently read the laws, and take an active part in elections and legislation. Democracy as we know it, then, is from the beginning associated with widespread literacy; and so to a large extent is the notion of the world of knowledge as transcending political units: in the Hellenic world diverse people and countries were given a common administrative system and a unifying cultural heritage through the written word. Greece is therefore considerably closer to being a model for the world-wide intellectual tradition of the contemporary literate world than those earlier civilizations of the Orient which each had its own localized traditions of knowledge: as Oswald Spengler put it, '*Writing is the grand symbol of the Far*' (1934, vol. 2, p. 150).

Yet although the idea of intellectual, and to some extent, political, universalism is historically and substantively linked with literate culture, we too easily forget that this brings with it other features which have quite different implications, and which go some way to explain why the long-cherished and theoretically feasible dream of an 'educated democracy' and a truly egalitarian society has never been realized in practice. One of the basic premises of liberal reform over the last century and a half has been that of James Mill, as it is described in the *Autobiography* of his son, John Stuart Mill:

So complete was my father's reliance on the influence of reason over the minds of mankind, whenever it is allowed to reach them, that he felt as if all would be gained if the whole population were taught to read, if all sorts of opinions were allowed to be addressed to them by word and in writing, and if, by means of the suffrage they could nominate a legislature to give effect to the opinions they adopted (1924, p. 74).

All these things have been accomplished since the days of the Mills, but nevertheless 'all' has not been 'gained'; and some of the causes of this may be found in the intrinsic effects of literacy on the transmission of the cultural heritage, effects which can be seen most clearly by contrasting them with their analogues in non-literate society.

The writing down of some of the main elements in the cultural tradition in Greece, we say, brought about an awareness of two things: of the past as different from the present; and of the inherent inconsistencies in the picture of life as it was inherited by the individual from the cultural tradition in its recorded form. These two effects of widespread alphabetic writing, it may be surmised, have continued and multiplied themselves ever since, and at an increasing pace since the development of printing. 'The printers,' Jefferson remarked, 'can never leave us in a state of perfect rest and union of opinion,'[35] and as book follows book and newspaper newspaper, the notion of rational agreement and democratic coherence among men has receded further and further away, while Plato's attacks on the venal purveyors of knowledge in the market place have gained increased relevance.

But the inconsistency of the totality of written expression is perhaps less striking than its enormous bulk and its vast historical depth. Both of these have always seemed insuperable obstacles to those seeking to reconstruct society on a more unified and disciplined model: we find the objection in the book-burners of all periods; and it appears in many more respectable thinkers. In Jonathan Swift, for example, whose perfectly rational Houyhnhnms 'have no letters', and whose knowledge, 'consequently ... is all traditional' (1726, part 4, ch. 9, p. 296). These oral traditions were of a scale, Swift tells us, that enabled 'the historical

35. Quoted in Innis (1951, p. 24). Harold Innis was much occupied with the larger effects of modes of communication, as appears also in his *Empire and Communications* (1950). This direction of investigation has been taken up by the University of Toronto review *Explorations;* and the present authors are also indebted to the as yet unpublished work of Professor E. A. Havelock on the alphabetic revolution in Greece. Among the many previous writers who have been concerned with the Greek aspect of the problem, Nietzsche (1909, p. 247) and José Ortega y Gasset (1959, pp. 1–17) may be mentioned. Among those who have treated the differences between oral and literate modes of communication in general, Reisman (1956, pp. 22–28) and Park (1938, pp. 187–205) are especially relevant here.

part' to be 'easily preserved without burdening their memories'. Not so with the literate tradition, for, lacking the resources of unconscious adaptation and omission which exist in the oral transmission, the cultural repertoire can only grow; there are more words than anybody knows the meaning of – some 142,000 vocabulary entries in a college dictionary like the *Webster's New World*. This unlimited proliferation also characterizes the written tradition in general; the mere size of the literate repertoire means that the proportion of the whole which any one individual knows must be infinitesimal in comparison with what obtains in oral culture. Literate society, merely by having no system of elimination, no 'structural amnesia', prevents the individual from participating fully in the total cultural tradition to anything like the extent possible in non-literate society.

One way of looking at this lack of any literate equivalent to the homeostatic organization of the cultural tradition in non-literate society is to see literate society as inevitably committed to an ever-increasing series of culture lags. The content of the cultural tradition grows continually, and in so far as it affects any particular individual he becomes a palimpsest composed of layers of beliefs and attitudes belonging to different stages in historical time. So too, eventually, does society at large, since there is a tendency for each social group to be particularly influenced by systems of ideas belonging to different periods in the nation's development; both to the individual, and to the groups constituting society, the past may mean very different things.

From the standpoint of the individual intellectual, of the literate specialist, the vista of endless choices and discoveries offered by so extensive a past can be a source of great stimulation and interest; but when we consider the social effects of such an orientation, it becomes apparent that the situation fosters the alienation that has characterized so many writers and philosophers of the West since the last century. It was surely, for example, this lack of social amnesia in alphabetic cultures which led Nietzsche to describe 'we moderns' as 'wandering encyclopaedias', unable to live and act in the present and obsessed by a 'historical sense', that injures and finally destroys the living thing, be it a man or a people or a system of culture' (1909, pp. 9, 33). Even if we dismiss Nietzsche's views as extreme, it is still evident that the literate individual has in practice so large a field of personal selection from the total cultural repertoire that the odds are strongly against his experiencing the cultural tradition as any sort of patterned whole.

From the point of view of society at large, the enormous complexity and variety of the cultural repertoire obviously creates problems of an unprecedented order of magnitude. It means, for example, that since Western literate societies are characterized by these always increasing layers of cultural tradition, they are incessantly exposed to a more complex version of the kind of culture-conflict that has been held to produce *anomie* in oral societies when they come into contact with European civilization, changes which, for example, have been illustrated with a wealth of absorbing detail by Robert Redfield in his studies of Central America (1934; 1941; 1950; 1953, pp. 73, 108; see also Worsley, 1957).[36]

Another important consequence of alphabetic culture relates to social stratification. In the proto-literate cultures with their relatively difficult non-alphabetic systems of writing, there existed a strong barrier between the writers and the non-writers; but although the 'democratic' scripts made it possible to break down this particular barrier, they led eventually to a vast proliferation of more or less tangible distinctions based on what people had read. Achievement in handling the tools of reading and writing is obviously one of the most important axes of social differentiation in modern societies; and this differentiation extends on to more minute differences between professional specializations so that even members of the same socio-economic groups of literate specialists may hold little intellectual ground in common.

Nor, of course, are these variations in the degree of participation in the literate tradition, together with their effects on social structure, the only causes of tension. For, even within a literate culture, the oral tradition – the transmission of values and attitudes in face-to-face contact – nevertheless remains the primary mode of cultural orientation, and, to varying degrees, it is out of step with the various literate traditions. In some respects, perhaps, this is fortunate. The tendency of the modern mass-communications industries, for example, to promote ideals of conspicuous consumption which cannot be realized by more than

36. For the concept of *anomie*, see Durkheim (1897, Book 2, ch. 5).

a limited proportion of society, might well have much more radical consequences but for the fact that each individual exposed to such pressures is also a member of one or more primary groups whose oral converse is probably much more realistic and conservative in its ideological tendency; the mass media are not the only, and they are probably not even the main, social influences on the contemporary cultural tradition as a whole.

Primary group values are probably even further removed from those of the 'high' literate culture, except in the case of the literate specialists. This introduces another kind of culture conflict, and one which is of cardinal significance for Western civilization. If, for example, we return to the reasons for the relative failure of universal compulsory education to bring about the intellectual, social and political results that James Mill expected, we may well lay a major part of the blame on the gap between the public literate tradition of the school, and the very different and indeed often directly contradictory private oral traditions of the pupil's family and peer group. The high degree of differentiation in exposure to the literate tradition sets up a basic division which cannot exist in non-literate society: the division between the various shades of literacy and illiteracy. This conflict, of course, is most dramatically focussed in the school, the key institution of society. As Margaret Mead has pointed out:

Primitive education was a process by which continuity was maintained between parents and children. . . . Modern education includes a heavy emphasis upon the function of education to create discontinuities – to turn the child . . . of the illiterate into the literate (1943, p. 637).

A similar and probably even more acute stress develops in many cases between the school and the peer group; and quite apart from the difficulties arising from the substantive differences between the two orientations, there seem to be factors in the very nature of literate methods which make them ill-suited to bridge the gap between the street-corner society and the blackboard jungle.

First, because although the alphabet, printing, and universal free education have combined to make the literate culture freely available to all on a scale never previously approached, the literate mode of communication is such that it does not impose itself as forcefully or as uniformly as is the case with the oral transmission of the cultural tradition. In non-literate society every social situation cannot but bring the individual into contact with the group's patterns of thought, feeling and action: the choice is between the cultural tradition – or solitude. In a literate society, however, and quite apart from the difficulties arising from the scale and complexity of the 'high' literate tradition, the mere fact that reading and writing are normally solitary activities means that in so far as the dominant cultural tradition is a literate one, it is very easy to avoid; as Bertha Phillpotts wrote in her study of Icelandic literature:

Printing so obviously makes knowledge accessible to all that we are inclined to forget that it also makes knowledge very easy to avoid. . . . A shepherd in an Icelandic homestead, on the other hand, could not avoid spending his evenings in listening to the kind of literature which interested the farmer. The result was a degree of really national culture such as no nation of today has been able to achieve (1931, pp. 162–3).

The literate culture, then, is much more easily avoided than the oral one; and even when it is not avoided its actual effects may be relatively shallow. Not only because, as Plato argued, the effects of reading are intrinsically less deep and permanent than those of oral converse; but also because the abstractness of the syllogism and of the Aristotelian categorizations of knowledge do not correspond very directly with common experience. The abstractness of the syllogism, for example, of its very nature disregards the individual's social experience and immediate personal context; and the compartmentalization of knowledge similarly restricts the kind of connections which the individual can establish and ratify with the natural and social world. The essential way of thinking of the specialist in literate culture is fundamentally at odds with that of daily life and common experience; and the conflict is embodied in the long tradition of jokes about absent-minded professors.

It is, of course, true that contemporary education does not present problems exactly in the forms of Aristotelian logic and taxonomy; but all our literate modes of thought have been profoundly influenced by them. In this, perhaps, we can see a major difference, not only with the transmission of the cultural heritage of oral societies, but with those of proto-literate ones. Thus Marcel Granet relates the nature of the Chinese writing system to the 'concreteness' of Chinese thought, and his picture of its primary concentration on social action and traditional norms suggests that the cultural effect of the writing system was in the direction of intensifying the sort of homeostatic conservation found in non-literate cultures; it was indeed conceptualized in the Confucian *tao-'tung*, or 'orthodox transmission of the way'. In this connection it may be noted that the Chinese attitude to formal logic, and to the categorization of knowledge in general, is an articulate expression of what happens in an oral culture (Granet, 1934, especially pp. vii–xi, 8–55; see also Hu Shih, 1922). Mencius, for example, speaks for the non-literate approach in general when he comments: 'Why I dislike holding to one point is that it injures the *tao*. It takes up one point and disregards a hundred others' (quoted in Richards, 1932, p. 35).

The social tension between the oral and literate orientations in Western society is, of course, complemented by an intellectual one. In recent times the Enlightenment's attack on myth as irrational superstition has often been replaced by a regressive yearning for some modern equivalent of the unifying function of myth: 'have not,' W. B. Yeats asked, 'all races had their first unity from a mythology that marries them to rock and hill?' (1955, p. 194).

In his nostalgia for the world of myths Plato has had a long line of successors. The Rousseauist cult of the Noble Savage, for instance, paid unwitting tribute to the strength of the homogeneity of oral culture, to the yearning admiration of the educated for the peasant's simple but cohesive view of life, the timelessness of his living in the present, the unanalytic spontaneity that comes with an attitude to the world that is one of absorbed and uncritical participation, a participation in which the contradictions between history and legend, for example, or between experience and imagination, are not felt as problems. Such, for example, is the literary tradition of the European peasant from Cervantes' Sancho Panza to Tolstoy's Platon Karataev. Both are illiterate; both are rich in proverbial lore; both are untroubled by intellectual consistency; and both represent many of the values which, it was suggested above, are characteristic of oral culture. In these two works, *Don Quixote* and *War and Peace*, which might well be considered two of the supreme achievements of modern Western literature, an explicit contrast is made between the oral and literate elements of the cultural tradition. Don Quixote himself goes mad by reading books; while, opposed to the peasant Karataev, stands the figure of Pierre, an urban cosmopolitan, and a great reader. Tolstoy writes of Karataev that – in this like Mencius or like Malinowski's Trobrianders – he

did not, and could not, understand the meaning of words apart from their context. Every word and every action of his was the manifestation of an activity unknown to him, which was his life. But his life, as he regarded it, had no meaning as a separate thing. It had a meaning only as part of a whole of which he was always conscious.

Tolstoy, of course, idealizes; but conversely, even in his idealization he suggests one major emphasis of literate culture and one which we immediately associate with the Greeks – the stress upon the individual; Karataev does not regard 'his life . . . as a separate thing'. There are, of course, marked differences in the life-histories of individual members of non-literate societies: the story of Crashing Thunder differs from that of other Winnebago (Radin, 1926; 1927), that of Baba of Karo from other Hausa women (Smith, 1954), and these differences are often given public recognition by ascribing to individuals a personal tutelary or guardian spirit. But on the whole there is less individualization of personal experience in oral cultures, which tend, in Durkheim's phrase, to be characterized by 'mechanical solidarity' (1933, p. 130) – by the ties between like persons, rather than by a more complicated set of complementary relationships between individuals in a variety of roles. Like Durkheim, many sociologists would relate this greater individualization of personal experience in literate societies to the effects of a more extensive division of labor. There is no single explanation; but the techniques of reading and writing are undoubtedly of very great importance. There is, first of all, the formal distinction which alphabetic culture has emphasized between the divine, the natural and the human orders; secondly, there is the social differentiation to which the institutions of literate culture give rise; third, there is the effect of professional intellectual specialization on an unprecedented scale: lastly, there is the immense variety of choice offered by the whole corpus of recorded literature; and from these four factors there ensues, in any individual case, the highly complex totality deriving from the selection of these literate orientations and from the series of primary groups in which the individual has also been involved.

As for personal awareness of this individualization, other factors doubtless contributed, but writing itself (especially in its simpler, more cursive forms) was of great importance. For writing, by objectifying words, and by making them and their meaning available for much more prolonged and intensive scrutiny than is possible orally, encourages private thought; the diary or the confession enables the individual to objectify his own experience, and gives him some check upon the transmutations of memory under the influences of subsequent events. And then, if the diary is later published, a wider audience can have concrete experience of the differences that exist in the histories of their fellow men from a record of a life which has been partially insulated from the assimilative process of oral transmission.

The diary is, of course, an extreme case; but Plato's dialogues themselves are evidence of the general tendency of writing to increase the awareness of individual differences in behavior, and in the personality which lies behind them;[37] while the novel, which participates in the autobiographical and confessional direction of such writers as St Augustine, Pepys and Rousseau, and purports to portray the inner as well as the outer life of individuals in the real world, has replaced the collective representations of myth and epic.

From the point of view of the general contrast between oral and alphabetically literate culture, then, there is a certain identity between the spirit of the Platonic dialogues and of the novel:[38] both kinds of writing express what is a characteristic intellectual effort of literate culture, and present the process whereby the

37. In the *Theaetetus*, for example, emphasis is placed on the inner dialogue of the soul in which it perceives ethical ideas 'by comparing within herself things past and present with the future' (186 b).

38. Jaeger (1944, vol. 2, 18), speaks of the dialogues and the memoirs by many members of the circle of Socrates as 'new literary forms invented by the Socratic circle... to re-create the incomparable personality of the master'.

individual makes his own more or less conscious, more or less personal selection, rejection and accommodation, among the conflicting ideas and attitudes in his culture. This general kinship between Plato and the characteristic art form of literate culture, the novel, suggests a further contrast between oral and literate societies: in contrast to the homeostatic transmission of the cultural tradition among non-literate peoples, literate society leaves more to its members; less homogeneous in its cultural tradition, it gives more free play to the individual, and particularly to the intellectual, the literate specialist himself; it does so by sacrificing a single, ready-made orientation to life. And, insofar as an individual participates in the literate, as distinct from the oral, culture, such coherence as a person achieves is very largely the result of his personal selection, adjustment and elimination of items from a highly differentiated cultural repertoire; he is, of course, influenced by all the various social pressures, but they are so numerous that the pattern finally comes out as an individual one.

Much could be added by way of development and qualification on this point, as on much else that has been said above. The contrast could be extended, for example, by bringing it up to date and considering later developments in communication, from the invention of printing and of the power press, to that of radio, cinema and television. All these latter, it may be surmised, derive much of their effectiveness as agencies of social orientation from the fact that their media do not have the abstract and solitary quality of reading and writing, but on the contrary share something of the nature and impact of the direct personal interaction which obtains in oral cultures. It may even be that these new modes of communicating sight and sound without any limit of time or place will lead to a new kind of culture: less inward and individualistic than literate culture, probably, and sharing some of the relative homogeneity, though not the mutuality, of oral society.

To speculate further on such lines would be to go far beyond the purposes of this essay; and it only remains to consider briefly the consequences of the general course of the argument for the problem as it was posed at the outset in terms of the distinction between the disciplines primarily (though not exclusively) concerned in the analysis of non-literate and literate societies, that is, anthropology and sociology.

One aspect of the contrast drawn between non-literate and alphabetic culture would seem to help explain one of the main modern trends in the development of anthropology; for part of the progress which anthropology has made beyond the ethnocentrism of the nineteenth century surely derives from a growing awareness of the implications of one of the matters discussed above: an awareness, that is, of the extent to which, in the culture of oral societies, non-Aristotelian models[39] are implicit in the language, the reasoning and the kinds of connection established between the various spheres of knowledge. The problem has been approached in many ways; particularly illuminating, perhaps, in Dorothy D. Lee's contrast between the 'lineal' codifications of reality in Western culture, and the 'non-lineal' codifications of the Trobriand Islanders; and there, incidentally, although Aristotle is not mentioned, his characteristically analytic, teleological and relational thinking is recognizable in the governing attitudes that Dorothy Lee presents as the typical literate mode of thought in contrast to that of the Trobrianders (1959, pp. 105–20; see also 1938, pp. 82–102). Benjamin Lee Whorf makes a similar point in his contrast of Hopi with SAE (standard average European). He sees the 'mechanistic way of thinking' of Europeans as closely related to the syntax of the languages they speak, 'rigidified and intensified by Aristotle and the latter's medieval and modern followers' (1941a). The segmentation of nature is functionally related to grammar; Newtonian space, time and matter, for example, are directly derived from SAE culture and language (1941b). He goes on to argue that 'our objectified view of time is ... favorable to historicity and to everything connected with the keeping of records, while the Hopi view is unfavorable thereto.' And to this fact he links the presence of:

1. Records, diaries, bookkeeping, accounting, mathematics stimulated by accounting.

39. Just as it has been argued that a proper understanding of Homer depends upon a 'non-Aristotelian literary criticism' which is appropriate to oral literature: Notopoulos (1949, pp. 1, 6).

2. Interest in exact sequences, dating, calendars, chronology, clocks, time wages, time graphs, time as used in physics.

3. Annals, histories, the historical attitude, interest in the past, archaeology, attitudes of introjection towards past periods, e.g. classicism, romanticism (1941b).

Many of these features are precisely those which we have mentioned as characteristic of societies with easy and widespread systems of writing. But while Whorf and other anthropological linguists have noted these differences between European institutions and categories on the one hand and those of societies like the Trobriands and the Hopi on the other, they have tended to relate these variations to the languages themselves, giving little weight to the influence of the mode of communication as such, to the intrinsic social consequences of literacy.[40]

On the other hand, what has been said about literacy and the consequent developments of Greek thought leading to the logical methods and to the categories of Aristotle may seem to attribute to one individual, and to the civilization to which he belonged, a kind of absolute claim to intellectual validity to which neither the philosopher, the anthropologist, nor the historian of ancient civilization, is likely to assent. The currency of such diffuse assumptions in general long ago moved John Locke to an unwonted burst of wintry humour: 'God has not been so sparing to men to make them barely two-legged creatures, and left it to Aristotle to make them rational' (1690, *Essay Concerning Human Understanding*, bk. IV, ch. 17, p. 84). Nevertheless Locke's own treatment of the 'forms of argumentation' and of 'the division of the sciences' is itself recognizably within the tradition that derives from Aristotle and his time; and so, in some important ways, is

40. For example in his paper 'A linguistic consideration of thinking in primitive communities' (1956, pp. 65–86), Whorf discusses Lévy-Bruhl's account of the thinking of primitive man as characterized by *participation mystique*, and suggests that the differences are related to the structure of language. No mention is made of the role of writing and he seems to see language itself as the independent variable, although in his later paper on 'Habitual thought', he does make a passing reference to writing, as well as to the *interdependence* of language and culture (p. 153). Lévi-Strauss, who is much concerned with the linguistic aspects of the problem, makes no mention of the role of literacy in his analysis of the differences between *la pensée sauvage* and *la pensée domestiquée*, but again the actual process of domestication is peripheral to his study (1962).

the literate culture, not only of the West, but of the civilized world today. There is obviously some more or less absolute efficacy in the organization of human knowledge which appears in the thoughtways of the first substantially literate culture, although its definition (which could hardly be more difficult) is well beyond the scope of this paper. Max Weber saw as the essential differentiating factor of Western civilization the 'formal rationality' of its institutions; and this, in turn, he regarded as a more fully developed and more exclusively practised version of the ordinary human tendency to act reasonably – to behave with 'substantive rationality'. For Weber 'formal rationality' was merely an institutionalized form of this general tendency working through 'rationally established norms, by enactment, decrees, and regulations' (Gerth and Wright Mills, 1946, pp. 298–9; see also Weber, 1947, pp. 184–6) rather than through personal, religious, traditional or charismatic allegiances. Weber's differentiation in some respects parallels the differentiation made above between oral and alphabetic culture and in various places he anticipates part of the argument advanced in this paper.[41]

The present study then, is an attempt to approach a very general problem from one particular point of view. In that perspective it suggests one reason for what has been widely remarked upon in the comparison between anthropology and sociology: the relative incompleteness of sociological analyses as compared with those of anthropology, and the tendency for anthropologists studying European societies to limit their observations to village communities or family groups. For, quite apart from differences of scale and complexity of social structure, there are two other dimensions of analysis which can in practice be largely disregarded by the anthropologist but not by the student of literate societies.

First the reifying of the past in written record means that sociology must inevitably be the more deeply concerned with history. The kinds of practical and theoretical issues involved

41. Especially in the 'Author's Introduction' to *The Protestant Ethic* (1930, pp. 13–31), where Weber gives a rapid but comprehensive survey of the problem of 'what combination of circumstances' made some aspects of Western civilization 'lie in a line of development having *universal* significance and value'. See also his lecture 'Science as a Vocation' (Gerth and Wright Mills, 1946, especially pp. 138–43).

here are numerous, for the great importance of the historical dimension, and its very different kind of impact on various social groups, obviously poses acute methodological problems. At the most general level, the analytic model of the sociologist must take into account the fact that from one point of view his data include materials accumulated from earlier cultures and periods, and that the existence of these records greatly increases the possible alternative ways of thinking and behaving for the members of the society he is studying, as well as influencing their action in other ways. This added complexity means that certain aspects of the past continue to be relevant (or at least potentially so) for the contemporary scene; and it also means that when functional theoretical models are used, the interconnections can hardly be as direct or immediate as those the anthropologist might expect in non-literate societies.

Secondly, the sociologist must in any case recognize that since in alphabetic society much of the homeostatic function of the oral tradition works at the inward and individual rather than at the overt and public level, sociological descriptions, which inevitably deal primarily with collective life, are considerably less complete than those of anthropology, and consequently provide a less certain guide to understanding the behavior of the particular individuals of whom the society is composed.

Summary

Recent anthropology has rightly rejected the categorical distinctions between the thinking of 'primitive' and 'civilized' peoples, between 'mythopoeic' and 'logico-empirical' modes of thought. But the reaction has been pushed too far: diffuse relativism and sentimental egalitarianism combine to turn a blind eye on some of the most basic problems of human history. Where the intellectual differences in the cultural traditions of complex and simple societies are given adequate recognition, the explanations offered are unsatisfactory. In the case of Western civilization, for example, the origins are sought in the nature of the Greek genius, in the grammatical structure of the Indo-European languages, or, somewhat more plausibly, in the technological advances of the Bronze Age and the associated developments in the division of labor.

In our view, however, insufficient attention has been paid to the fact that the urban revolution of the Ancient Near East produced one invention, the invention of writing, which changed the whole structure of the cultural tradition. Potentially, human intercourse was now no longer restricted to the impermanency of oral converse. But since the first methods of writing employed were difficult to master, their effects were relatively limited, and it was only when the simplicity and flexibility of later alphabetic writing made widespread literacy possible that for the first time there began to take concrete shape in the Greek world of the seventh century BC a society that was essentially literate and that soon established many of the institutions that became characteristic of all later literate societies.

The development of an easy system of writing (easy both in terms of the materials employed and the signs used) was more than a mere pre-condition of the Greek achievement; it influenced its whole nature and development in fundamental ways. In oral societies the cultural tradition is transmitted almost entirely by face-to-face communication; and changes in its content are accompanied by the homeostatic process of forgetting or transforming those parts of the tradition that cease to be either necessary or relevant. Literate societies, on the other hand, cannot discard, absorb, or transmute the past in the same way. Instead, their members are faced with permanently recorded versions of the past and its beliefs; and because the past is thus set apart from the present, historical enquiry becomes possible. This in turn encourages scepticism; and scepticism, not only about the legendary past, but about received ideas about the universe as a whole. From here the next step is to see how to build up and to test alternative explanations: and out of this there arose the kind of logical, specialized, and cumulative intellectual tradition of sixth-century Ionia. The kinds of analysis involved in the syllogism, and in the other forms of logical procedure, are clearly dependent upon writing, indeed upon a form of writing sufficiently simple and cursive to make possible widespread and habitual recourse both to the recording of verbal statements and then to the dissecting of them. It is probable that it is only the analytic process that writing itself entails, the written formalization of sounds and syntax, which makes possible the habitual separating out into formally distinct units of the various cultural elements whose indivisible wholeness is the essential basis of the 'mystical participation' which Lévy-Bruhl regards as characteristic of the thinking of non-literate peoples.

One of the problems which neither Lévy-Bruhl nor any other advocate of a radical dichotomy between 'primitive' and 'civilized' thought has been able to resolve is the persistence of 'non-logical thinking' in modern literate societies. But, of course, we must reckon with the fact that in our civilization, writing is clearly an addition, not an alternative, to oral transmission. Even in our *Buch und Lesen* culture, childrearing and a multitude of other forms of activity both within and outside the family depend upon speech; and the relationship between the written and the oral traditions must be regarded as a major problem in Western cultures.

A consideration of the consequences of literacy in these terms, then, throws some light not only upon the nature of the Greek achievement but also upon the intellectual differences between simple and complex societies. There are, of course, many other consequences we have not discussed – for instance, the role of writing in the running of centralized states and other bureaucratic organizations; our aim has only been to discuss in very general terms some of the more significant historical and functional consequences of literacy.[42]

42. The authors are much indebted to John Beattie, Glyn Daniel, Lloyd Fallers, Moses Finley, Joseph Fontenrose, Harry Hoijer, the late Alfred Kroeber, Simon Pembroke and Nur Yalman for reading and commenting upon earlier versions of this paper. They are also grateful to the Center for Advanced Studies in the Behavioral Sciences, California, for the opportunity of working together on the manuscript in Spring, 1960.

References

BARNES, J. A. (1947), 'The collection of genealogies', *Rhodes-Livingstone Journal: Human Problems in British Central Africa*, vol. 5.

BARTLETT, F. C. (1923), *Psychology and Primitive Culture*, Cambridge University Press.

BARTLETT, F. C. (1932), *Remembering*, Cambridge University Press.

BOAS, F. (1904), 'The folklore of the Eskimo', *Journal of American Folklore*, vol. 64.

BOHANNAN, L. (1952), 'A genealogical charter', *Africa*, vol. 22.

BURNET, J. (1908), *Early Greek Philosophy*, 2nd edn, London.

CARCOPINO, J. (1935), *L'Ostracisme athénien*, Paris.

CASSIRER, E. (1953), *An Essay on Man*, New York.

CASSIRER, E. (1955), *The Philosophy of Symbolic Forms*, Yale University Press.

CHADWICK, J. (1958), *The Decipherment of Linear B*, Cambridge University Press.

CHADWICK, J. (1959), 'A Prehistoric Bureaucracy', *Diogenes*, vol. 26.

COOK, R. M., and WOODHEAD, A. G. (1959), 'The diffusion of the Greek alphabet', *American Journal of Archaeology*, vol. 63.

CORNFORD, F. M. (1923), *Greek Religious Thought from Homer to the Age of Alexander*, London.

CORNFORD, F. M. (1952), *Principium Sapientiae: The Origins of Greek Philosophical Thought*, Cambridge University Press.

CUNNISON, I. G. (1959), *The Luapula Peoples of Northern Rhodesia*, Manchester University Press.

CZARNOWSKI, S. (1925), 'Le morcellement de l'étendue et sa limitation dans la religion et la magie', *Actes du congrès international d'histoire des religions*, Paris, vol. 1.

DIELS, H. (1951), *Die Fragmente der Vorsokratiker*, Berlin.

DIRINGER, D. (1948), *The Alphabet: A Key to the History of Mankind*, New York.

DIRINGER, D. (1962), *Writing*, London.

DOW, S. (1954), 'Minoan writing', *American Journal of Archaeology*, vol. 58.

DRIVER, G. R. (1954), *Semitic Writing*, London, rev. edn.

DURKHEIM, E. (1897), *Le Suicide*, Paris.

DURKHEIM, E. (1915), *The Elementary Forms of Religious Life*, trans. J. W. Swain, London.

DURKHEIM, E. (1933), *The Division of Labor in Society*, trans. G. Simpson, New York.

DURKHEIM, E., and MAUSS, M. (1902-3), 'De quelques formes primitives de classification', *L'Année Sociologique*, vol. 7.

EVANS-PRITCHARD, E. E. (1934), 'Lévi-Bruhl's theory of primitive mentality', *Bulletin of the Faculty of Arts, University of Egypt*, vol. 2.

EVANS-PRITCHARD, E. E. (1937), *Witchcraft, Oracles and Magic among the Azande*, Clarendon Press.

EVANS-PRITCHARD, E. E. (1940), *The Nuer*, Oxford University Press.

EVANS-PRITCHARD, E. E. (1948), *The Divine Kingship of the Shilluk of the Nilotic Sudan*, The Frazer Lecture, Cambridge.

EVANS-PRITCHARD, E. E., and FORTES, M. (1940), *African Political Systems*, London.

FARRINGTON, B. (1936), *Science in Antiquity*, London.

FINLEY, M. I. (1954), *The World of Odysseus*, New York.

FINLEY, M. I. (ed.) (1959), *The Greek Historians*, New York.

FORTES, M. (1944), 'The significance of descent in Tale social structure', *Africa*, vol. 14.

FORTES, M. (1945), *The Dynamics of Clanship among the Tallensi*, London.

GANDZ, S. (1935), 'Oral tradition in the Bible', in S. W. Baron and
A. Marx (eds.), *Jewish Studies in Memory of George A. Kohut*, New York.
GELB, I. J. (1952), *A Study of Writing*, Chicago.
GERTH, H. H., and WRIGHT MILLS, C. (eds. and trans.) (1946),
From Max Weber: Essays in Sociology, New York.
GLUCKMAN, M. (1949–50), 'Social beliefs and individual thinking
in primitive society', *Memoirs and Proceedings of the Manchester
Literary and Philosophical Society*, vol. 91.
GLUCKMAN, M. (1952), 'Rituals of rebellion in South-East Africa',
The Frazer Lecture, Cambridge.
GOODY, J. (1950–52), Unpublished field notes.
GORDON CHILDE, V. (1941), *Man Makes Himself*, London.
GORDON CHILDE, V. (1942), *What Happened in History*, London.
GRANET, M. (1934), *La Pensée Chinoise*, Paris.
GRAY, W. S. (1956), *The Teaching of Reading and Writing: An
International Survey*, *UNESCO Monographs on Fundamental
Education*, vol. 10.
GURNEY, O. R. (1952), *The Hittites*, London.
HALBWACHS, M. (1925), *Les Cadres sociaux de la mémoire*, Paris.
HALBWACHS, M. (1940–48), 'Mémoire et société', *L'Année Sociologique*,
3rd series, vol. 1.
HALBWACHS, M. (1950), *La Mémoire collective*, Paris.
HALLOWELL, A. L. (1937), 'Temporal orientations in Western
civilization and in preliterate society', *American Anthropologist*, vol. 39.
HASTINGS, J. (ed.) (1898–1904), *A Dictionary of the Bible*, New York.
HENLE, P. (ed.) (1958), *Language, Thought and Culture*, Ann Arbor.
HONE, J. (1942), *W. B. Yeats*, London.
HU SHIH (1922), *The Development of the Logical Method in Ancient
China*, Shanghai.
INNIS, H. (1951), 'Minerva's owl', *The Bias of Communication*, Toronto
University Press.
INTERNATIONAL INSTITUTE OF INTELLECTUAL COOPERATION
(1934), *L'Adoption universelle des caractères latins*, Paris.
JACOBY, F. (1923), *Die Fragmente der Griechischen Historiker*, Berlin.
JACOBY, F. (1949), *Atthis*, Clarendon Press.
JAEGER, W. (1944), *Paideia*, Clarendon Press.
JAEGER, W. (1947), *The Theology of the Early Greek Philosophers*,
Clarendon Press.
JEFFERY, L. H. (1961), *The Local Scripts of Archaic Greece*, Oxford
University Press.
KENYON, F. G. (1951), *Books and Readers in Ancient Greece and Rome*,
2nd edn, Oxford.
KIRK, G. S., and RAVEN, J. E. (1957), *The Presocratic Philosophers*,
Cambridge University Press.
KRAMER, S. N. (1948), 'New light on the early history of the Ancient
Near East', *American Journal of Archaeology*, vol. 52.
LEE, D. D. (1938), 'Conceptual implications of an Indian language',
Philosophy of Science, vol. 5.

LEE, D. D. (1959), 'Codifications of Reality: Lineal and Non-lineal, *Freedom and Culture*, Englewood Cliffs.

LÉVI-STRAUSS, C. (1962), *La Pensée Sauvage*, Paris.

LOCKE, J. (1960), *Essay Concerning Human Understanding*.

MALINOWSKI, B. (1922), *Argonauts of the Western Pacific*, London.

MALINOWSKI, B. (1925), 'Magic, science and religion', in J. Needham (ed.), *Science, Religion and Reality*, New York.

MALINOWSKI, B. (1926), *Myth in Primitive Psychology*, London.

MALINOWSKI, B. (1936), 'The problem of meaning in primitive languages', in C. K. Ogden and I. A. Richards (eds.), *The Meaning of Meaning*, London.

MEAD, M. (1943), 'Our educational emphases in primitive perspective', *Amer. J. Soc.*, vol. 48.

MILL, J. S. (1873), *Autobiography of John Stuart Mill*, J. J. Cross (ed.), New York, 1924.

MOORHOUSE, A. C. (1953), *The Triumph of the Alphabet*, New York.

NADEL, S. F. (1951), *The Foundations of Social Anthropology*, London.

NIETZSCHE, F. (1900), 'The use and abuse of history', in *Thoughts out of Season*, trans. A. Collins, Edinburgh University Press.

NIETZSCHE, F. (1909), *Beyond Good and Evil*, Edinburgh University Press.

NOTOPOULOS, J. A. (1949), 'Parataxis in Homer: a new approach to Homeric literary criticism', *Transactions of the Amer. Philological Assoc.*, vol. 80.

ORTEGAY GASSET, J. (1959), 'The difficulty of reading', *Diogenes*, vol. 28.

PARK, R. (1938), 'Reflections on communication and culture', *Amer. J. Soc.*, vol. 44.

PEARSON, L. (1939), *Early Ionian Historians*, Oxford.

PETERS, E. (1960), 'The proliferation of segments in the lineage of the Bedouin of Cyrenaica', *J. Roy. Anthrop. Inst.*, vol. 90.

PHILLPOTTS, B. (1931), *Edda and Saga*, London.

PIGGOTT, S. (1959), 'Conditional Literacy', *Approach to Archaeology*, London.

POWDERMAKER, H. (1933), *Life in Lesu*, New York.

RADIN, P. (1926), *Crashing Thunder: the Autobiography of an American Indian*, New York.

RADIN, P. (1927), *Primitive Man as Philosopher*, New York.

REDFIELD, R. (1934), *Chan Kom, a Maya Village*, Washington, D.C.

REDFIELD, R. (1941), *The Folk Culture of Yucatan*, Chicago.

REDFIELD, R. (1950), *A Village That Chose Progress: Chan Kom Revisited*, Chicago.

REDFIELD, R. (1953), *The Primitive World and Its Transformations*, Ithaca.

REISMAN, D. (1956), 'The oral and the written traditions', *Explorations*, vol. 6.

RICHARDS, I. A. (1932), *Mencius on the Mind*, London.

SMITH, M. F. (1954), *Baba of Karo, a Woman of the Muslim Hausa*, London.

SOREL, J. (1941), *Reflections on Violence*, trans. T. E. Hulme, New York.

SPENGLER, O. (1934), *The Decline of the West*, trans. C. F. Atkinson, New York.

STARR, C. G. (1961), *The Origins of Greek Civilization*, New York.

SWIFT, J. (1726), *Gulliver's Travels*, ed. A. E. Case (1938), New York.

TAIT, D. (1961), *The Konkomba of Northern Ghana*, London.

TURNER, R. E. (1941), *The Great Cultural Traditions*, New York.

VOEGELIN, C. F. and VOEGELIN, F. M. (1961), 'Typological classification of systems with included, excluded and self-sufficient alphabets', *Anthropological Linguistics*, vol. 3.

WARMINGTON, E. H. (1934), *Greek Geography*, London.

WEBER, M. (1930), *The Protestant Ethic* (trans. T. Parsons), London.

WEBER, M. (1947), *The Theory of Social and Economic Organizations* (trans. A. M. Henderson and T. Parsons), New York.

WHORF, B. L. (1941a), 'Languages and logic', *Technological Review*, vol. 43, reprinted in Whorf, B. L. (1956).

WHORF, B. L. (1941b), 'The relation of habitual thought and behavior', in L. Spier (ed.), *Language, Culture and Personality, Essays in Memory of Edward Sapir*, Menasha, Wis., reprinted in Whorf, B. L. (1956).

WHORF, B. L. (1956), *Language, Thought and Reality*, Selected Writings of B. L. Whorf, New York.

WILSON, G. and WILSON, M. (1945), *The Analysis of Social Change*, Cambridge.

WILSON, J. A. (1949), 'Egypt', in H. Frankfort *et al.* (eds.), *Before Philosophy*, London.

WOOLLEY, L. (1953), *A Forgotten Kingdom*, London.

WORSLEY, P. (1957), *The Trumpet Shall Sound*, London.

YEATS, W. B. (1955), *Autobiographies*, London.

15 R. F. Inglehart and M. Woodward

Language Conflicts and Political Community[1]

Excerpts from R. F. Inglehart and M. Woodward, 'Language conflicts and political community', *Comparative Studies in Society and History*, vol. 10, 1967, pp. 27–40, 45.

Must a viable nation be made up largely of one language group? If this is true, then there are almost insuperable difficulties in the way of establishing a European political community. Recent events in India, Canada, Belgium, Nigeria and several other areas give one cause to think that there may be some basis for drawing that conclusion.

In the Western world of the mid-nineteenth century, language became accepted as the most important single defining characteristic of nationality. Fichte summed up a widely influential attitude when he asserted: 'Wherever a separate language is found, there is also a separate nation which has the right to manage its affairs ... and to rule itself' (Roy, 1962, p. 158). In the twentieth century this notion has had continued prominence. The peacemakers of Versailles tended to define national boundaries on the basis of language zone (with appropriate exceptions in favor of the victor powers), and showed an unprecented respect for the rights of linguistic minorities. This general attitude was also reflected in the subsequent transfers of population.[2] Mussolini seemed to feel that his claim to the south Tyrol would be valid only if the region were populated by Italian-speaking people, and urged Italians to migrate there (Dauzat, 1953, pp. 108 ff.). Hitler later invoked the same principle against the Western allies when, in the 1930s, he claimed the right of all

1. The authors are indebted to David Appel, Raymond Grew, Duncan MacRae, Jr, Richard Park and David Segal for critical comments on an earlier draft of this paper.

2. Poles immigrated in large numbers into the Polish corridor and Germans left the same region; in 1923, the Turkish minority of Thrace and the Greeks of Western Asia Minor were exchanged. For other examples see Dauzat (1953, pp. 108 ff.).

German-speaking peoples – of Austria, the Sudetenland, Alsace and Poland – to be united; and important elements of public opinion in the West found it difficult to deny his claim, at least in the first two instances. Even today, De Gaulle appears to be highly sceptical of the possibility that any nation could be constructed as a federation of the various West European language groups.[3]

An examination of this question in comparative and historical perspective suggests that political separatism is not inherent in the existence of linguistic pluralism, as the foregoing position implies. On the contrary, the centrifugal force which it exerts can be strong or weak, and is largely dependent on two related situaional factors:

1. The level of economic and political development attained by the country in question.

2. The degree to which social mobility is blocked because of membership in a given language group. This second factor is related to the first, in that it appears to be particularly critical in societies undergoing the transitional stages of early industrialization.

A political community may be viewed as a group of people living together under a common regime, with a common set of authorities to make important decisions for the group as a whole.[4] To the extent that the regime is 'legitimate', we would further specify that the people have internalized a common set of rules. Given the predominantly achievement-oriented norms which seem to be a necessary concomitant of industrial society, these rules must apply equally to the entire population – or precisely those criteria (e.g., language) which are a basis for blocking individual social mobility, can become the basis for cleavage which threatens the disintegration of the political community.

Among post-tribal multilingual populations where the masses are illiterate, generally unaware of national events, and have low

3. See, for example, his sarcastic reference to stateless people speaking 'some kind of integrated Esperanto or Volapük'. Statement of 15 May, 1962, cited in Macridis (1966).

4. This definition is derived from the work of David Easton (1965).

expectations of social and economic mobility, the problem is largely irrelevant – even if such populations have a linguistically-distinct elite group. In contrast, when the general population of a society is going through the early stages of social mobilization,[5] language group conflicts seem particularly likely to occur; they may develop animosities which take on a life of their own and persist beyond the situation which gave rise to them.[6] The degree to which this happens may be significantly affected by the type of policy which the government adopts during the transitional period.

The likelihood that linguistic division will lead to political conflict is particularly great when the language cleavages are linked with the presence of a dominant group which blocks the social mobility of members of a subordinate group, partly, at least, on the basis of language factors. Where a dominant group holds the positions of power at the head of the major bureaucracies in a modern society, and gives preference in recruitment to those who speak the dominant language, any submerged group has the options of assimilation, non-mobility or group-resistance. If an individual is overwhelmed numerically or psychologically by the dominant language, if his group is proportionately too small to maintain a self-contained community within the society, assimilation usually occurs. In contrast, if one is part of a numerous or geographically-concentrated minority group, assimilation is more difficult and is more likely to seem unreasonable. If the group is numerous and mobilized, political resistance is likely.

A special case of the linkage between social mobility and linguistic pluralism among transitional populations may exist when ambitious members of minority groups see the opportunity to make careers for themselves by fanning a large potential group into consciousness of its separate identity. Language is well suited to become the basis of such a cleavage, even if awareness of group identity is at first low. Such men presumably calculate that they can rise higher at the head of a large but relatively leaderless minority group than as an assimilated member of the majority society.

5. For a discussion of 'social mobilization' as we will use the term, see Lerner (1959) and Deutsch (1953).
6. The Belgian case seems to reflect this tendency.

In the United States, the pattern was predominantly one of assimilation. Non-English-speaking immigrant groups spoke many languages and were fairly well dispersed among the English-speaking populations. Even in the case of concentrated ethnic ghettos, usually confined to large Eastern cities, assimilation to the English-speaking group seemed to be an obvious route for eventual social mobility, one which was encouraged and facilitated by the American public school system. But in many other countries, assimilation was slow and painful, and in some cases has not occurred to this day.

In Canada, for example, the French-speaking groups have been a compact mass until the last few decades, with most of their contacts limited to other French Canadians. The distinctness of the two 'races' was institutionalized by the British North America Act of 1867 which set up a federal system of government.[7] Unilingualism has been the rule ever since in the Canadian national government, in the armed forces and in the overwhelming majority of businesses: one had to know English to advance beyond the menial level. The differences between the French and the British populations were multiplied by the fact that until relatively recently, the former were largely an agrarian people, so that linguistic differences were complicated by the antagonism of farm versus commercial interests. The situation was further aggravated by the fact that the French Canadians placed less emphasis on education than the Canadian population in general; not until the Second World War did a secondary education become a normal expectation for them. As a consequence of their lack of formal education, and social and geographical isolation in Quebec, their level of mastery of English have never approached linguistic assimilation: nearly 75 per cent of the ethnically French population of Quebec speaks French only. Yet the business activity of the province is almost entirely in the hands of the English-speaking minority (see Royal Commission on Bilingualism and Biculturalism, 1965, pp. 73-83). Describing a series of public meetings held in Quebec, an investigating commission reported:

7. The union of the two Canadas was attempted in 1840 with very little success. The French clung more firmly than ever to their language, religion and outlook on life, and suspected that the British – having conquered and forcibly ruled them – were trying to destroy their identity.

R. Inglehart and M. Woodward 361

The reiterated contrast between 'master' and 'servant' always conjured up an image of a collective personage – 'the English'. . . . Basically it seemed to us that the French Canadians who attended our meetings mainly wanted to put on record their indignation at their 'economic weakness' in a province where they are in a majority (p. 78).

By the 1950s, French Canada had developed a leadership class capable of effective political organization, and separatist activity became important. A demand for equal dignity, a resentment at the superior attitude often adopted by the dominant English minority has been associated with the competition for economic positions. Religious differences also have contributed to the problem to some extent, tending to reinforce the line of linguistic cleavage, but they seem to have been a delining factor. While the Church may well have contributed in the past to the perpetuation of the French as a distinct and compact group, one cannot argue that the French are now rebelling primarily as Catholics against Protestants. They rebel almost in *spite* of being Catholics, with separatist leaders generally being among the least church-oriented of the French Canadian population (see Amyot, 1966; Malheux, 1958, pp. 341–62; Trudeau, 1955, pp. 297–314). Another contributing factor to the discord in Canada may be the ambition of a small French elite group whose careers are dependent upon leading their people against the English.

The situation in Belgium parallels that of Canada, with additional complications. In 1815 the socio-economic elite of Belgium had become largely French-speaking, partly as a result of twenty years of French rule, and the Dutch language there 'was in a bad way'.[8] At this juncture, the area was handed over to William I of Orange as part of the Kingdom of The Netherlands. The king was a Dutch-speaking Calvinist, and Dutch was made the official language in all except the Walloon districts of Belgium. Within fifteen years, however, the Catholic Belgians – both Flemish and Walloon – rebelled against their union with Holland and gained independence. The new Belgian state launched into a violent reaction against the late Dutch regime – now Dutch (or Flemish) was banned from administration, from the law courts, from the

8. Geyl (1958, p. 216). At that time, a variety of dialects of Dutch were spoken in Northern Belgium, some of them mutually incomprehensible. The dialects were known as Flemish.

army, universities and secondary schools, causing a tremendous hardship for the Dutch speakers included within the new state. The nineteenth century was thus a period of profound humiliation for Flanders, and every aspect of public life, including business, tended to be dominated by the French. Only in the twentieth century was Dutch again made a medium of higher education; key demands made recently by the Flemings (who constitute a majority of the population) have been for equal status for their language in government and military service. Membership in the Dutch-speaking group has a persisting connotation of lower social status.[9] Though the Flemings are now economically resurgent, past discrimination and animosity persist as a tradition influencing the present.

The situation there contrasts strongly with that in Holland. At the time of the revolution in 1830, in the Low Countries, religious cleavages took precedence over linguistic boundaries – as they did in the India of 1946. Holland contrived to have her boundary drawn so as to include certain areas populated by Dutch-speaking Catholics, while still leaving herself with a comfortable majority of Protestants. The Catholics of Holland were subjected to much the same sort of discrimination as was inflicted on the Flemings of Belgium ('The Catholics were still regarded as not quite what a true Dutch citizen or patriot should be' (Geyl, 1958, p. 213)). Yet today relations between the major religious denominations of Holland are relatively cordial. The contrast between Dutch tranquillity and Belgian strife seem to be based on the relatively strong relationship which persisted between language and social mobility, as compared with the relatively mild economic discrimination based on religion. We must acknowledge the presence of a difference in reinforcing factors, however: the Flemish Belgians tend to be practising Catholics to a greater extent than do the Walloons; deliberate efforts were made by the Germans to divide Belgium in World Wars I and II; and the monarchical question and different rates of economic progress in the two regions of Belgium have added complications

9. Flemish families in the Brussels region still have a tendency to learn French and 'pass' as Walloons. See 'Debat in Belgische Kamer Over Taalgemeenschappen', *Nieuwe Rotterdamse Courant*, 27 January 1966. Over a period of many years, this has contributed to making Brussels – once part of the Flemish region – a largely French-speaking city.

not present in Holland. But the linkage of linguistic cleavage with differences in social status and preferential treatment by the government have been central to the conflict.

In Europe where religion was traditionally a source of much contention and even warfare, a change has taken place: today a stable political cooperation exists between Protestants and Catholics in the Netherlands and West Germany and the Catholic Churches of Italy and France seem to be moving toward depoliticization. Language seems more important than religion as a basis of political cleavage in modern societies: but this is true only in so far as it becomes linked with differences in social mobility. In India, on the other hand, religion has remained a predominant basis of cleavage, as was manifested in the partition of Bengal and the Punjab in 1947 along religious rather than linguistic lines. Among Hindus, linguistic cleavages have frequently been complicated by caste conflicts as well (Roy, 1962, p. 121).

With autonomy from Britain and the secession of Pakistan, however, the foreign-native conflict largely disappeared from India, religious conflicts were partly transferred from the internal to the international sphere, and linguistic cleavages have emerged as an increasingly important basis of conflict. In some ways this conflict bears a resemblance to the separatist movements in Belgium and Canada: it seems closely related to the demands of emerging parochial elements for a share of the government jobs in competition with a cosmopolitan elite. In the absence of extensive opportunities for employment in business and industry, government jobs have been the chief avenues of upward social mobility. The elite which had administered India under the British was generally bilingual, speaking English in addition to a regional language. The less educated masses, on the other hand, could communicate only in one of the regional languages. They were, and are, effectively excluded from office except in so far as the locus of power has been shifted to regional centers, and the medium of communication shifted from English to regional languages. Since government jobs are a chief source of social mobility, this exclusion came to be an important problem. Widespread riots made a series of reorganizations necessary, beginning with the creation of a Telegu-speaking Andhra state in

1953, and continuing (most recently) with the agreement to set up a separate Punjabi-Sikh state in 1966. The partition of 1953 was typical of the pattern: Telegu aspirations for separate statehood were especially strong because of the dominance in the Madras government of the generally more highly-educated Tamils, who had a considerably higher rate of command of English. Indian federalism seems to be a rather uneasy compromise between two forces: the need for central coordination by a national government, which necessarily communicates largely in English, against centrifugal demands to turn a maximum amount of activity over to regional linguistic states.

Let us note another interesting aspect of India's language controversies: the use of English as an official language has continued despite powerful opposition; at first glance, this might seem astonishing considering the fact that it was the language of colonial dominance, and in view of the small percentage of Indians who speak it. What has been even more adamantly opposed is the adoption of Hindi as the sole national language, for this would tend to give the Hindi-speaking group preferential access to political office. Attempts to abolish the use of English and replace it with Hindi have been shelved repeatedly, in the face of bitter opposition from non-Hindi groups. The attempt to make Hindi the official language is seen as the work of Hindi imperialism: Hindi-speaking Indians from the north tend to dominate the national government. Feelings of resentment against this are, no doubt, aggravated by the fact that the coastal areas had previously been the most advanced parts of the sub-continent. These regions are largely non-Hindi and their inhabitants experienced the disagreeable sensation of being passed up by the inhabitants of the interior. To a limited extent, another factor may be an attitude of racial superiority on the part of the fairer-skinned and generally higher-caste Hindi-speaking northerners. But the feeling that establishment of Hindi as the sole national language would block social mobility of the non-Hindis remains a key concern for the non-parochial minority. As expressed by a southern politician: 'Be just, Hindustanis, that you may be true to your democracy and not merely exploit it by seeking to make what you possess by birth the sole passport to full Indian civilization and all its honors' (Rajagopalachari, 1957, p. 45).

Where languages are of officially equal status and social mobility is not blocked by a dominant elite made up of one language group, upwardly motivated individuals can seek to rise as individuals. Where social mobility is blocked by the existence of one preferred language among several, language differences seem to be politically divisive: the individual must unite with others of his language for political action to raise the group as a whole, as in Belgium and Canada. On the other hand, where all major languages are on an equal official footing, as in Switzerland, the presence of several language groups may not necessarily be divisive. Similarly, although it is far less widespread than Hindi, English is less divisive as an official language in India because all groups there are more or less equally handicapped by it. Belgium, Canada and India have one factor in common: the conflicts have been aggravated by a situation in which social mobility tends to be blocked by the presence of a dominant language group. In other ways, as we have emphasized, they are less similar: in the Indian sub-continent religious conflicts are considerably more important than in either Belgium or Canada.

Only when social mobility is a normal expectation will it be an important variable in defining the boundaries of political conflict. For the large traditional sector of Indian society at the time of independence, such expectations were, no doubt, very weak. The dominant values for most individuals were defined by the Hindu tradition. This has been changing rapidly in India, giving rise to a stratum which demands equal opportunity for social mobility. Although the Hindu culture may represent an extreme case in the degree to which it de-emphasized individual social mobility, there seems to be a general tendency for industrial societies to place a higher value on achievement, as contrasted with ascriptive status. The history of the Low Countries reinforces the suggestion that progressive stages of socio-economic development may give rise to changing bases of political cleavage.

One of the most important cases of language conflict in modern times has been the Austro-Hungarian Monarchy. In terms of social development it seems to occupy a position between that of India and the two Western countries. Starting from a stable system based on an agrarian, Christian, Latin-speaking elite, it was eventually shattered by the mobilization of new elements, partly because those elements found their social mobility blocked by the existence of a dominant and alien language.

There was a time in the eighteenth century when Maria Theresa seemed capable of welding the diverse and multilingual segments of the Austrian state into one cohesive mass. Magyar appeared to be dying out at the elite level, and the Hungarian nobles were flocking to the court, marrying German princesses, and apparently ready to cooperate with the Habsburgs. Or at least so it seemed until Joseph II attempted to establish German as the universal language of empire (along with other sweeping reforms). Revolts broke out across the land. Resentment against the policies of the Austrians combined with the emphasis of intellectuals such as Herder on languages and folk culture to encourage linguistic separatism within the empire. The example of mass participation in politics set by the French Revolution led to aspirations for a political voice among progressively broader classes of the empire's population. Napoleon's creation of separate states for favored minorities[10] made the idea look like a concrete possibility. Given the educational facilities of the time, mass participation necessarily implied linguistic separatism: unlike the ruling elite, the aspiring middle classes of the ethnic minorities generally did not have instruction in the cosmopolitan language.

In the first quarter of the nineteenth century, practically every ethnic group in the empire showed signs of emerging from parochialism and demanding the restoration of real or imagined traditional privileges, laws and languages. The Magyars were the first on the scene, the most intransigent in their demands, and the most successful. Academies, newspapers, clubs and societies were founded, all demanding the exclusive use of Magyar within their kingdom; and political leaders led by Lajos Kossuth tirelessly stirred up the anger and pride of the people. In 1839, the Diet declared Magyar the official language of government and clergy, and in 1843 made it the exclusive language of the schools. Hungary revolted against Austria in 1848, and although brutally crushed, its people grew increasingly restive under the control of

10. Within Austria, the most outstanding example was his creation of Illyria. See Wendel (1921) and Kohn (1965, pp. 47 ff.).

Vienna. When the humiliating defeat by Prussia in the war of 1866 forced the Habsburgs to make a drastic change in the government, the Magyars were on hand to push through their demands (see Seton Watson, 1908, pp. 38 ff.; Jaszi, 1961).

By the terms of the *Ausgleich* of 1867 the empire was divided into two parts and re-labeled the Austro-Hungarian Monarchy, each half having its own government, laws and courts, with only a vague and rather amorphous super-structure over the whole. Seton Watson argued that the real motive behind the Dual System was a league between the two strongest races – the German and Magyar – who divided the monarchy between them and granted autonomy to the next two strongest races – the Poles and the Croats – who were to be their accomplices in holding down the remaining eight (Seton Watson, 1908, p. 137). Although a series of laws granted equality to all the different nationality groups and respected their languages, these laws were applied only partially in Austria and not at all in Hungary.

Language restrictions had the effect of stifling the ambitions and slowing the economic development of the subject races. In the respective halves of the monarchy the state gave preferential treatment to Hungarians and Germans. In Hungary, government was effectively closed to all but Magyars,[11] and Magyar alone was spoken in her courts. 'It is no exaggeration,' commented Seton Watson in 1908, 'to say that the non-Magyar peasant stands like an ox before the courts of his native lands ...' (pp. 150–55). Of the state elementary schools, as of 1904–5, 91 per cent were Magyar, although 48 per cent of the population consisted of other nationality groups. There was not one Slovak or Ruthenian secondary school in existence at the time. Yet due to the scarcity of teachers who knew Magyar, the most important effect of 'Magyarization' was not that Slovak, Croatian or Rumanian children were forced to learn the language, but rather, that an increasing percentage of them received no education at all: from 1900 to 1906 the percentage of children not attending school rose

11. While nationality was not supposed to be an obstacle to the holding of office, in 11 counties where Rumanians and 7 counties where Slovaks formed a majority of 66 to 96 per cent, no Rumanians or Slovaks were appointed High Sheriff for the succeeding generation. In 1891, in areas where 60 per cent of the population was Rumanian, only 5·8 per cent of the officials were of that nationality.

from 18 to 24 per cent (Seton Watson, 1908; Jaszi, 1961, pp. 279 ff., 304 ff.). Thus, one important result of 'Magyarization' was to cut off the principal prerequisites for social mobility.

The Croat case illustrates once again how social mobility, when blocked by language barriers contributed to the dissolution of the Empire. For 700 years, the Croats had enjoyed relative autonomy. In the 1840s sharp contention arose over the proposal to replace Latin with Magyar as the official instrument of administration. Croatian was not even considered as a possibility, and the only Croats involved were the upper classes – the only ones apt to know Latin. The Magyars crushed the opposition by a number of laws enforcing their own language, and overnight the conflict intensified. 'The wide implications of this Magyar law and the valiant Croat opposition to it made the language conflict the chief promoting factor, if not the ultimate cause, of Croatian anti-Magyar policy in the pre-March era' (Kann, 1950, vol. 1, p. 239). Just as important, practically the entire Croatian population began to develop, in reaction to the Hungarian policy, a sense of group awareness:

the introduction of the national language widened the range of group interests concerned with Croatian state affairs from carriers of Latin culture – the nobles and the clergy – to the representatives of bourgeois culture – trade, commerce and a growing professional class (Kann, 1950, vol. 1, p. 241).

This was a pattern to be repeated, with various modifications, from one end of the empire to the other.

In the Austrian half of the monarchy, no group was more vociferous in their language demands than the Czechs. From the 1870s on, the language question was the 'main issue of official Czech policy', 'the permanent, unhealed wound of the national struggle' (Kann, 1950, vol. 1, p. 199). A climax of sorts was reached in 1897 when several decrees were issued by Minister Badeni in Bohemia requiring all judges in Czech lands to conduct trials in the language of the accused, and requiring all civil servants to be bilingual. Since it was far more common for a Czech to know German than the reverse, the two laws would have established a body of Czech judges and civil servants. In this case it was the Germans who felt oppressed and who resorted to riots to have the laws repealed. German waiters refused to serve Czech customers, Germans obstructed parliament and refused to pay taxes. Badeni was forced to resign and the hated decrees were repealed, which in turn inflamed Czech extremists led by Karel Kramář, who demanded a Pan-Slav state (see May, 1960, pp. 325 ff.).

It is clear that language was not the sole divisive element at work within the Austro-Hungarian Monarchy. As Masaryk commented in 1907, 'The national question is not only the language question. It is at the same time an economic and social question . . .' (quoted Kann, 1950, vol. 1, p. 211). Yet as issues grew more complex and the factions jostling for power more numerous, language tended to become a symbol that summed up other conflicts. In the early phases of social mobilization and economic modernization, linguistic nationalism was seized upon by reactionary elements (such as the feudal nobility) as a means by which they might isolate themselves from cosmopolitan influences. At the same time it was seen by a variety of upwardly aspiring groups, particularly the new middle class, as a potential vehicle for smashing through the existing lines of stratification.[12] In general, the minority groups found themselves in a position where social mobility was blocked unless they were willing to learn the dominant language, particularly in the Hungarian half of the monarchy. Probably the most notorious example of the use of language to block the mobility of minority groups is the Railway Servants Act of 1907. It arbitrarily decreed that all railway workers not conversant in Magyar be fired from their jobs.[13]

There is at least one other case to be discussed in our typology of motivating forces behind language-group conflicts: the occasions in which language conflicts are encouraged by political

12. Each economic class of the minority linguistic groups turned to language as a rallying symbol against the central government, even though the basic interests of some of these classes (such as peasants versus nobles) were diametrically opposed. For a discussion of this point see Jaszi, (1961, pp. 284–6).

13. Language conflicts remain a potential problem in the former Austrian lands. In March 1967, President Tito of Yugoslavia 'angrily warned' Croatians and Serbs to stop stirring up linguistic disputes. See the *New York Times*, 27 March 1967, p. 1.

leaders to promote their special interests. Such a case can be found in the Catalan language conflict in Spain.[14]

Since the unification of Spain, the Catalans have been an industrious and relatively prosperous people, frequently discontented with their union with the economically less progressive Castilians. Feelings that they were being exploited by the rest of Spain led to revolts in 1640 and again in 1705. By the nineteenth century their principal grievance was that the low-tariff policy of the central government in Madrid was hurting their industry. In the 1890s their resentment widened to include anger over the prospective loss of Cuba, for at that time Catalans more or less dominated American trade. Language had very little to do with these basic, economic grievances, and in fact, the Catalan language had been on the verge of dying out completely. In 1860 it was spoken only in the most remote and obscure villages (Brenan, 1962, pp. 26–8), while Castilian was taking hold in cities like Barcelona. The revival of the language was originally the work of a small group of intellectuals and poets, but after the defeat of the conservative forces in the Carlist War of 1876, the Church turned to the support of Catalanism. Businessmen who had grievances against Madrid joined them in a party, the *Lliga Regionalista*, led by Francisco Cambo. Catalan nationalism flourished greatly at the turn of the century, to the dismay of the central government, and became increasingly troublesome in its demands. A climax was reached about 1917 when the Catalan industrialists united with the Socialists and other left-wing parties in open revolt against the government, demanding, among other things, a freely elected legislature. A strike was called and in the ensuing violence the industrialists took fright. They retreated completely to form an alliance with the army and the central government. Economically, they were rumored to have made a secret pact with Madrid: a pact by which Castile would become the economic tributary of Catalonia, while Catalonia remained the political tributary of Castile. So timid had the industrialists become that they even supported Diego Primo de

14. Out of 28·6 million people in 1950, there were 5 million Catalans – a force to be reckoned with. An equally discontented group are the Basques, but as of 1950 they only numbered a half million people (Dauzat, 1953, p. 155).

Rivera as dictator in 1923. He responded by terminating Catalan privileges, including the use of their language in the schools. When the conservative Catalan leaders sold out to their principal enemies, the issue of Catalanism did not die: instead it was taken up by elements from the opposite political and social spectrum. The radical extremist Colonel Macia formed a new party, the Esquerra.[15] Its motives were political and not economic, radical instead of clerical or conservative, yet it effectively represented Catalan nationalism throughout the 1920s and 30s. It was even successful. The vote of the Catalan leftists was one of the main reasons for the fall of the monarchy and the advent of the Republic, and the Esquerra was rewarded by a large measure of autonomy, with Catalan declared the official language (Brenan, 1962, pp. 29–34, 63–7, 83; see also Thomas, 1963, p. 29).[16]

One can see the issue of Catalanism, in which the free use of the language is an important part, taken up and discarded by political leaders of extremely varied interests as it suited their needs. Franco declared open war on the language and on Catalan nationalism, with the result that today the leftists are still its primary defenders. Ironically, the Church has now joined forces with the left, and has caused considerable trouble by demanding the right to use Catalan in services.

The case of Catalonia is, in a sense, an exception to our general rule: it could hardly be described as an instance of an economically oppressed group opposing the use of an alien language which was blocking their upward mobility. In part, it seems to be an example of the role of ambitious political leaders turning to language as a device to inflame the masses against the central government. As such it was not an isolated phenomenon, but one which was repeated in various other European countries. One of the most obvious indications that languages, oftentimes, were not intrinsically a cause for conflict is that a good many of them were actually dying out a hundred years ago. In the eighteenth century Magyar was on the decline, and in the nineteenth, both Catalan

15. In the Basque country conservative nationalism also failed, but the people were too religious and concerned with tradition to turn to the left. Instead, extremists urged Basques to learn English or French instead of Spanish. See Carr (1966, p. 556).

16. The bibliography on Catalanism is quite extensive. One of the most useful works is Punal (1958, especially vols. 6 and 7).

and Gaelic seemed on the point of disappearing (Dauzat, 1953, **p. 177**).[17] Yet in each case, within a generation Magyar, Catalan and Gaelic suddenly gained new vigor and became a cause for revolting against an alien government. Slovak is another example of this pattern. By 1890 it was hailed as the mother tongue and its use claimed as the inalienable right of the Slovak people; yet a generation before it had lacked even a basic grammar or a modern vocabulary (Seton Watson, 1908, p. 38). In each case the dying embers of an antiquated, archaic or primitive speech were consciously fanned up by intellectuals and political leaders at least partly to provide an audience and a constituency.

Yet whatever the role of Catalan leaders with ulterior motives for emphasizing the distinctiveness of their language, in a more general sense the Catalan case can be considered to support our main point. For the fact remains that the Catalans felt they were being oppressed and economically exploited as a group. This case, like that of the Swedes of Finland (and, briefly, the Germans of Bohemia) illustrates the converse of a language minority whose social mobility is blocked by lack of access to the cosmopolitan language: the case of a minority with a *favored* position which is threatened by pressures toward predominance by the majority. In both cases, however, the threatened individuals must react as a group: its members are ñot free to seek social mobility as individuals (the normal course, in the absence of pressures to act collectively) but are either blocked or threatened in their social status *as a group*.

Another force can motivate social conflicts which may well polarize along linguistic lines. We refer to the situation in which individuals seek ego support by identifying with a powerful *Volk* or nation state, asserting its superiority over other peoples. This phenomenon may have contributed to many of the conflicts discussed above; it seems, however, especially likely to be associated with the transitional period of social mobilization, when large numbers of people are in the process of being uprooted from a traditional social order without yet being integrated into a modern society. With the attainment of a high level of economic development (what W. W. Rostow terms a 'high mass consump-

17. In 1800, 4 million Irishmen spoke Gaelic, yet by 1921 there were only 300,000.

tion society') the appeal of an asserted superiority over other peoples in the abstract seems to lose ground to the pursuit of more immediate, more concrete and personal symbols of status such as television sets, automobiles, private homes, vacation abroad, etc. Perhaps for this reason, De Gaulle's consuming interest in playing a glorious and dominant role on the international stage seems not to be shared by the French population at large – they are more interested in the fruits of prosperity (Leites, 1965). Public opinion in the Common Market countries in general has shown an increasing tendency to support the dilution of national sovereignty on behalf of a European Community (see Inglehart, 1967; cf. Rabier, 1966):[18] it has come to be associated with unprecedented prosperity. It may be significant in this connection that the imagery of 'national honor' has largely fallen into disuse among the statesmen of economically developed nations.

In conclusion, we would advance the generalization that there is a curvilinear relationship between political/economic development and the divisive effect of linguistic pluralism.

1. At a low level of development, the masses of the population are are normally inert and irrelevant to the national politics of an extensive[19] political community. Whereas it is relatively easy to provide a small ruling elite with education in a cosmopolitan language[20] and to assimilate them into a stable allegiance to the regime, to do this on behalf of the general public requires an elaborate apparatus for public education, and a highly developed communications network. Consequently,

2. At a transitional stage – where the masses are 'mobilized', but not yet assimilated – the divisive force exerted by multiple language groups will be greatest.

18. Support for European nation building is most pronounced among those groups which have attained the greatest measure of prosperity.
19. By 'extensive', we refer to a policy which goes beyond the scale of a city-state or tribe: where political activity can no longer be based on face to face communication.
20. Latin, Mandarin, French, German or English, as the case may be in states with a multiplicity of parochial vernaculars.

3. At a high level of political/economic development (e.g., contemporary Western Europe) exchanges of persons among language areas are numerous, mass media (e.g. Eurovision) minimize the remoteness of foreign groups and, above all, most upwardly mobile individuals have the opportunity to become fluent in one or more foreign languages. [...]

We would argue that blockage of social mobility has been the chief motivating force behind language group conflicts, especially in transitional countries. It is of little use for predicting the limits of political community among non-mobilized populations, or in societies which are not oriented toward achievement of individual social mobility. There are ways in which the conflict can be neutralized:

1. Cases in which the politically mobilized strata master a cosmopolitan language; or wherever one finds widespread bilingualism. Symmetrical bilingualism is desirable, but not necessary, and would require a highly developed educational system.

2. Cases where equality exists or is granted to major language groups.

Both types of neutralization can be seen operating in Europe today. In contrast to the Belgian and Canadian cases, where action was deferred until violence had erupted, the statesmen of 'Europe' have shown considerable sensitivity to the potential language problem from the start. The European institutions give a scrupulous formal equality to the four principal languages, staffing their bureaucracies with representatives of each group, making all documents and facilities available in the four official languages. Modern communications technology also lends a hand; proceedings are held with simultaneous translations in all four languages. Today with widespread public education and increasingly achievement-oriented technocratic societies, there are few groups in Western Europe which need feel that they as a group are being exploited and restricted. Bilingualism will probably become increasingly valuable within the European Community, but the highly developed educational systems of these countries place language preparation within the reach of most upwardly mobile individuals. The increasing tendency toward bilingualism is impressive: a six-nation survey indicates that in 1962, a *majority* of adult Dutch and Belgians claimed to understand one or more foreign languages; a quarter of adult Germans and a third of the adult French reported that they could understand a foreign tongue (cited in *Sondages*, 1963, no. 1, p. 41). A tendency toward asymmetrical bilingualism exists and will probably increase, but it does not present one language as being the language of the 'Establishment'. The German-speakers have been the most numerous and wealthiest single group in the Community without in any sense dominating it. An intelligent awareness of the tensions which would result if one language were given preference may prevent language from becoming a serious basis of cleavage.

References

AMYOT, P. R. (1966), 'Factors leading to integrative or non-integrative attitudes towards Canada among French Canadians of Quebec', unpublished Ph.D. thesis, Northwestern University.

BRENAN, G. (1962), *The Spanish Labyrinth*, Cambridge University Press.

CARR, R. (1966), *Spain, 1808–1939*, Oxford University Press.

DAUZAT, A. (1953), *L'Europe linguistique*, Paris.

DEUTSCH, K. W. (1953), *Nationalism and Social Communication*, New York.

EASTON, D. (1965), *A Systems Analysis of Political Life*, New York.

GEYL, P. (1958), *Debates with Historians*, World Publishing Co.

INGLEHART, R. (1967), 'An end to European integration?', *American Political Science Review*, March.

JASZI, O. (1961), *The Dissolution of the Habsburg Monarchy*, Chicago University Press.

KANN, R. (1950), *The Multinational Empire*, New York.

KOHN, H. (1965), *Nationalism: Its Meaning and History*, Princeton University Press.

LEITES, N. (1965), *The 'Europe' of the French*, Rand Research memorandum, Santa Monica.

LERNER, D. (1959), *The Passing of Traditional Society*, Free Press of Glencoe.

MACRIDIS, R. C. (1966), *De Gaulle; Implacable Ally*, New York.

MALHEUX, A. (1958), 'Democracy and the French Canadian', in G. Douglas (ed.), *Quebec Today*, Toronto University Press.

MAY, A. (1960), *The Habsburg Monarchy*, Harvard University Press.

PUNAL, J. C. (1958), *Historia politica de Catalonia*, Barcelona.

RABIER, J.-R. (1966), *L'Opinion publique et L'Europe*, Brussels.

RAJAGOPALACHARI, C. (1957), *Our Democracy*, Madras.

ROY, N. C. (1962), *Federalism and Linguistic States*, Calcutta.

Royal Commission on Bilingualism and Biculturalism (1965), *Preliminary Report*, Quebec.

Seton Watson, R. W. (1908), *Racial Problems in Hungary*, London.

Thomas, H. (1963), *The Spanish Civil War*, New York.

Trudeau, P. E. (1955), 'Some obstacles to democracy in Quebec', *Canadian Journal of Economics and Political Science*, vol. 24.

Wendel, H. (1921), *Aus dem südslavischen Risorgimento*, Gotha.

Further Reading

Part One
Approaches to Sociolinguistics

(i) *Classics of linguistics and sociology*

E. Durkheim and M. Mauss, *Primitive Classification*, University of Chicago Press, 1963 (originally published 1901/2)

G. H. Mead, *Mind, Self and Society*, University of Chicago Press, 1967 (originally published 1934)

A. Meillet, *Linguistique historique et linguistique générale*, La Société linguistique de Paris, 1921

E. Sapir, *Language*, Harcourt, Brace, 1921

E. Sapir, *Culture, Language, and Personality*, ed. D. G. Mandelbaum, University of California Press, 1957

F. de Saussure, *Course in General Linguistics*, McGraw-Hill, 1966 (originally published 1916)

B. Whorf, *Language, Thought and Reality*, Wiley, 1956

(ii) *Collected papers*

B. Bernstein, *Class, Codes and Control*, 3 vols., Routledge, 1971–5

S. Ervin-Tripp, *Language Acquisition and Language Choice*, Stanford University Press, 1973

C. Ferguson, *Language Structure and Language Use*, Stanford University Press, 1971

J. Fishman, *Language in Sociocultural Change*, Stanford University Press, 1972

P. Friedrich, *Language, Context and the Imagination*, Stanford University Press, 1979

M. Halliday, *Language as Social Semiotics*, Arnold, 1978

D. Hymes, *Foundations in Sociolinguistics: an Ethnographic Approach*, University of Pennsylvania Press, 1974

W. Labov, *Sociolinguistic Patterns*, University of Pennsylvania Press, 1972

W. Lambert, *Language, Psychology and Culture*, Stanford University Press, 1972

(iii) *Readers*

H. P. Dreitzel (ed.), *Recent Sociology no. 2: Patterns of Communicative Behaviour*, Macmillan, 1970

J. Fishman (ed.), *Readings in the Sociology of Language*, Mouton, 1968

J. Fishman (ed.), *Advances in the Sociology of Language*, Mouton, 1971

J. Gumperz and D. Hymes (ed.), *The Ethnography of Communication*, The American Anthropological Association, 1964

J. Gumperz and D. Hymes (eds.), *Directions in Sociolinguistics: the Ethnography of Communication*, Holt, Rinehart & Winston, 1972

D. Hymes (ed.), *Language in Culture and Society*, Harper & Row, 1964

S. Lieberson (ed.), *Explorations in Sociolinguistics*, special issue of *Sociological Inquiry*, vol. 36, no. 2, 1966

J. B. Pride and J. Holmes (eds.), *Sociolinguistics*, Penguin, 1972

(iv) Textbooks

N. Dittmar, *Sociolinguistics*, Arnold, 1976

A. D. Edwards, *Language in Culture and Class*, Heinemann, 1976

J. Fishman, *The Sociology of Language*, Newbury House, 1972

R. A. Hudson, *Sociolinguistics*, Cambridge University Press, 1980

W. P. Robinson, *Language and Social Behaviour*, Penguin, 1972

P. Trudgill, *Sociolinguistics*, Penguin, 1974

Part Two
Speech and Situated Action

J. L. Austin, *How To Do Things With Words*, Oxford University Press, 1965

A. Cicourel, *Cognitive Sociology*, Penguin, 1973

J. Cook-Gumperz and J. Gumperz, *Papers on Language and Context*, Working paper no. 46, Language Behavior Research Center, University of California, Berkeley, 1976

M. Coulthard, *An Introduction to Discourse Analysis*, Longman, 1977

H. Garfinkel, *Studies in Ethnomethodology*, Prentice-Hall, 1967

E. Goffman, *Frame Analysis*, Harper & Row, 1974

E. Goffman, *Forms of Talk*, Philadelphia, University of Pennsylvania Press, 1980

J. Gumperz and D. Hymes (eds.), *Directions in Sociolinguistics: the ethnography of communication*, Holt, Rinehart & Winston, 1972

W. Labov and D. Fanshel, *Therapeutic Discourse: Psychotherapy as Conversation*, Columbia University Press, 1979

T. Myers (ed.), *The Development of Conversation and Discourse*, Edinburgh University Press, 1979

J. Searle, *Speech Acts*, Cambridge University Press, 1969

J. Schenkein (ed.), *Studies in the Organization of Conversational Interaction*, Academic Press, 1978

J. Sinclair and R. Coulthard, *Towards an Analysis of Discourse: the English Used by Teachers and Pupils*, Oxford University Press, 1975

D. Sudnow (ed.), *Studies in Social Interaction*, Free Press, 1971

Part Three
Language, Socialization and Subcultures

B. Bernstein, *Class, Codes and Control*, 3 vols., Routledge, 1971–5

C. Cazden, V. John, and D. Hymes (eds.), *Functions of Language in the Classroom*, Teachers College Press, 1972

A. Cicourel *et al.*, *Language Use and School Performance*, Academic Press, 1974

J. Cook-Gumperz, *Social Control and Socialization: a Study of Class Differences In The Language of Maternal Control*, Routledge, 1973

J. R. Edwards, *Language and Disadvantage*, Arnold, 1979

F. Williams (ed.), *Language and Poverty*, Markham, 1970

Part Four
Language and Social Structures

P. Friedrich, *Language, Context and the Imagination*, Stanford University Press, 1979

J. Gumperz, *Language in Social Groups*, Stanford University Press, 1971

W. Labov, *The Social Stratification of English in New York City*, Center for Applied Linguistics, 1966

W. Labov, *Sociolinguistics Patterns*, University of Pennsylvania Press, 1972

W. Labov, *Language in the Inner City*, University of Pennsylvania Press, 1973

R. Lakoff, *Language and Woman's Place*, Harper & Row, 1975

W. Lambert, *Language, Psychology and Culture*, Stanford University Press, 1972

J. McNamara (ed.), *Problems of Bilingualism*, special issue of *Journal of Social Issues*, vol. 23, no. 2, 1967

B. Thorne and N. Henley (eds.), *Language and Sex*, Newbury House, 1975

P. Trudgill, *The Social Differentiation of English in Norwich*, Cambridge University Press, 1974

U. Weinreich, *Languages in Contact*, Mouton, 1966

Part Five
Language, Social Change and Social Conflict

E. Allardt, 'Implications of the ethnic revival in modern industrialized society: a comparative study of linguistic minorities in Western Europe', *Commentationes scientiarum socialium*, no. 12, Helsinki, Societas Scientiarum Finnica, 1979

J. Das Gupta, *Language Conflicts and National Development*, University of California Press, 1970

J. Fishman (ed.), *Language Loyalty in the United States*, Mouton, 1966

J. Fishman *et al.* (eds.), *Language Problems of Developing Nations*, Wiley, 1968

H. Giles (ed.), *Language, Ethnicity and Intergroup Relations*, Academic Press, 1979

J. Goody (ed.), *Literacy in Traditional Societies*, Cambridge University Press, 1968

J. Goody, *The Domestication of the Savage Mind*, Cambridge University Press, 1977

R. Haugen, *Language Conflict and Language Planning: the Case of Modern Norwegian*, Harvard University Press, 1966

S. Lieberson, *Language and Ethnic Relations in Canada*, Wiley, 1970

Acknowledgements

Permission to reproduce the Readings in this volume is acknowledged to the following sources:

1 American Anthropological Association and Dell Hymes
2 Basic Books Inc. and Joshua A. Fishman
3 American Anthropological Association and Erving Goffman
4 *Southwestern Journal of Anthropology* and Keith H. Basso
5 American Anthropological Association and Charles O. Frake
6 Free Press and Emanuel Schegloff
7 George Allen & Unwin Ltd and Cornell University Press
8 Institute of Contemporary Arts
9 Georgetown University and William Labov
10 Free Press and John J. Gumperz
11 *Word*
12 MIT Press, T. A. Sebeok, Roger Brown and Albert Gilman
13 Springer Verlag and William Labov
14 Cambridge University Press, Jack R. Goody and Ian Watt
15 Cambridge University Press